Our Hearts Are Changed

The First Principles and Ordinances Series
Volume One – Faith

Philip M. Hudson

Copyright 2019 by Philip M. Hudson.

Published 2019.

Printed in the United States of America.

All rights reserved.

No portion of this book may be reproduced, stored in a retrieval system, or transmitted in any form or by any means – electronic, mechanical, photocopy, recording, scanning, or other – except for brief quotations in critical reviews or articles, without the prior written permission of the author.

ISBN 978-1-50647-02-6

Library of Congress Control Number 2019905887

Illustrations – Google Images.

This book may be ordered from online bookstores.

Publishing Services by BookCrafters
Parker, Colorado.
www.bookcrafters.net

Table of Contents

Acknowledgements..1
Preface...5
Introduction..9

Chapter One: The testimony of faith...15
Chapter Two: The seeds of faith..19
Chapter Three: The faith to trust...33
Chapter Four: The reach of faith...39
Chapter Five: The faith to build temples unto God..45
Chapter Six: The germination of faith..67
Chapter Seven: The foundation of faith..71
Chapter Eight: The faith to change our hearts..77
Chapter Nine: The faith to be Born Again..87
Chapter Ten: The faith to make connections..95
Chapter Eleven: The knowledge of faith...109

Chapter Twelve: The fabric of faith..117
Chapter Thirteen: The faith to act...125
Chapter Fourteen: The power of faith...135
Chapter Fifteen: The faith to choose the harder right.......................................151

Chapter Sixteen: The faith to live abundantly..169
Chapter Seventeen: The faith to call down pennies from heaven..........................177
Chapter Eighteen: Put a thmile on your faith...181
Chapter Nineteen: The focus of faith..199
Chapter Twenty: The faith to believe...211
Chapter Twenty One: The humility of faith..227
Chapter Twenty Two: The faith to become as little children................................231
Chapter Twenty Three: The be-happy attitudes of faith.......................................243
Chapter Twenty Four: The faith to properly prepare...249
Chapter Twenty Five: The moral discipline of faith...253
Chapter Twenty Six: The obedience of faith..257
Chapter Twenty Seven: The courage of faith...263
Chapter Twenty Eight: The faith to profess His name...273
Chapter Twenty Nine: The wisdom of faith...281
Chapter Thirty: The endurance of faith...285
Chapter Thirty One: The faith to go the second mile..289
Chapter Thirty Two: The faith to touch His garment..299
Chapter Thirty Three: The nobility of faith..303
Chapter Thirty Four: The faith to see all the way to heaven...............................307
Chapter Thirty Five: The divine center of faith...317
Chapter Thirty Six: The faith to be perfect in Christ...331
Chapter Thirty Seven: The faith to know the mind of God....................................363
Chapter Thirty Eight: The faith to keep our feet on the ground..........................371
Chapter Thirty Nine: The faith to stay spiritually fit...381

About The Author..389
By The Author...391
What More Can I Say?...396

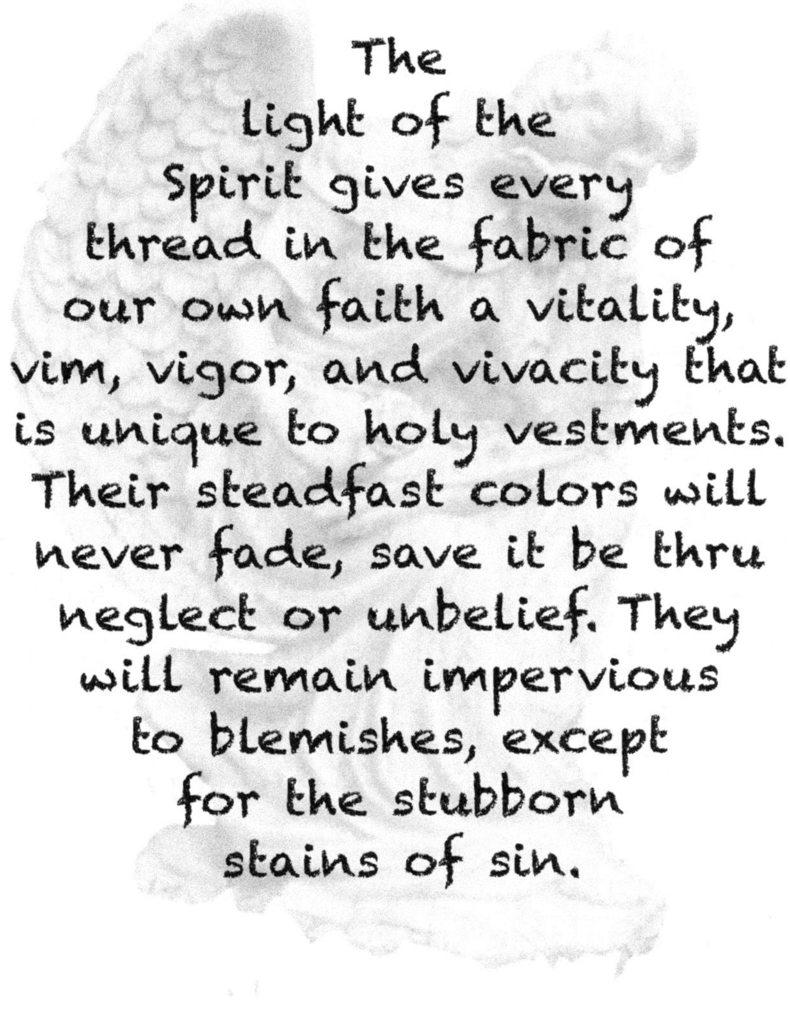

The
light of the
Spirit gives every
thread in the fabric of
our own faith a vitality,
vim, vigor, and vivacity that
is unique to holy vestments.
Their steadfast colors will
never fade, save it be thru
neglect or unbelief. They
will remain impervious
to blemishes, except
for the stubborn
stains of sin.

Those with
the faith to choose
the harder right are like
"brave Horatius, the Captain
of the Gate," who declared: "To
each of us upon this earth, death
cometh soon or late. And how can
we die better, than facing fearful
odds, for the ashes of our fathers
and the temples of our gods?"
(Thomas Macaulay).

Acknowledgements

In this volume, I have attributed quotations to original authors whenever possible, as well as when I have editorialized their ideas. In many cases, however, my language will naturally reflect the teachings of leaders and members of The Church of Jesus Christ of Latter-day Saints.

The list of those who have contributed to this book is endless. As I have organized my own thoughts, I have realized how heavily I have borrowed from the towering examples of those who, over the years, have been my mystical mentors, my sensible chaperones, my spiritual guides, my surrogate saviors, my compassionate critics, and everything in between.

They are my avatars, manifestations of deity in bodily forms, my na'vi, the visionaries, who communicate with God on a level to which I can only aspire, and

my tsaddik, whom I esteem as intuitive interpreters of biblical law and scripture. They are my divine teachers incarnate. They have offered listening ears, extended open arms. lifted my spirits, shown me the way, emboldened me with words of encouragement, cheered me on with wise counsel, stretched my mind, reinforced my faith, strengthened my testimony, vitalized my conversion, helped me to discover my wings, given immaterial support, provided of their means, taught me humility, been there to steady me, soothed my troubled soul, stepped in to nurture me, led me to fountains of living water, wet my parched lips with inspired counsel, and bound up my wounds.

Every family member, teacher, student, classmate, business associate, mentor, friend, priesthood brother, relief society sister, ordinance worker, and temple patron with whom I have come in contact has influenced me. Every author, poet, journalist, essayist, thespian, satirist, and lyricist, has moved me in some positive way. They have taught me to find the silk purse in every sow's ear and the silver lining in every cloud. When I have been given a lemon, they have shown me where to find the recipe for lemonade.

With their positive influence, I have learned to keep tempests in teapots where they belong, and to put them in perspective. I have tried to retain the joyful anticipation of the optimistic little boy, who, when faced with the daunting task of shoveling up an enormous pile of manure in a horse stall near his home, enthusiastically set about his task with the exclamation: "There's got to be a pony in there, somewhere!"

Well did the poet teach: "No man is an island, entire of itself. Every man is a piece of the continent, a part of the main. If a clod be washed away by the sea, Europe is the less, as well as if a promontory were, as well as if a manor of thy friends or of thine own were. Any man's death diminishes me, because I am involved in mankind, and therefore never send to know for whom the bell tolls. It tolls for thee." (John Donne).

When I think of the influence of a multitude of angels thinly disguised as my family, friends, and peers, I remember the words of Sir Isaac Newton, who, when

pressed to reveal the great secret behind his accomplishments, simply replied: "I stood on the shoulders of giants." Of course, at the end of the day, I alone am responsible for the contents of this volume. But I hope my interpretation of principles and doctrine will cultivate your interest to dig deeper into the themes woven into this tapestry, by turning to the scriptures and seeking inspiration from the Spirit. My only goal is to help you to expand your insights into the telestial mile markers, the terrestrial truths, and the celestial guidelines that accompany each of us during our quest for enlightenment.

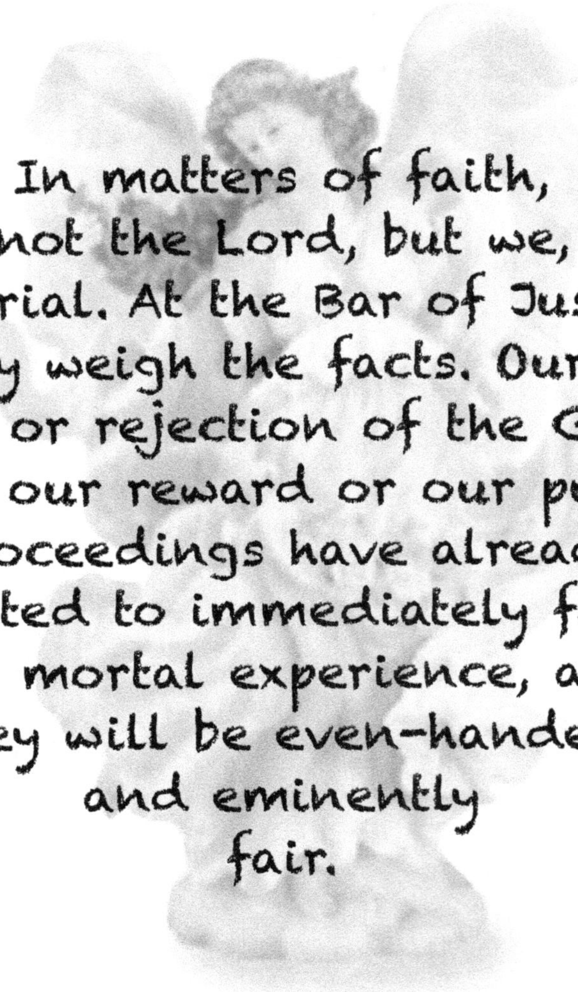

In matters of faith,
it is not the Lord, but we, who
are on trial. At the Bar of Justice, He
will simply weigh the facts. Our previous
acceptance or rejection of the Gospel will
determine our reward or our punishment.
Trial proceedings have already been
docketed to immediately follow
our mortal experience, and
they will be even-handed
and eminently
fair.

Preface

I love to learn by reading the scriptures, and I often think of St. Hilary, who, in the third century, wrote: "Scripture consists not in what we read, but in what we understand." In each of the chapters in this volume, I have consistently tried to find a scriptural foundation and a spiritual confirmation as I put my pen to paper. For me, it has been exciting to find that the ideas swirling around inside my head can generally be anchored to, and find relevance in, the scriptures, because holy writ gives me a sense of coherence and stability. On a much smaller scale, I feel as Albert Einstein must have, when the mathematical equivalents to scriptural understanding crystallized, and he said of the experience: "A storm broke loose in my mind."

I believe the Spirit has the generative power to energize, vitalize, and quicken our axons and dendrites to craft a neural environment that stimulates creative thought. Those who have experienced the illumination of the Spirit know what Einstein meant

when he said: "A splendid light dawned on me." So, the challenge for each of us is to enlist the aid of the Holy Ghost to assist in our understanding, with whatever tools we utilize to process the world around us.

Every time I proofed a chapter (and I did this many times) I found myself scribbling additional notes in the margins, and thinking to myself: "Why didn't I see that before." That is precisely what I hope will be the experience of those who read this volume; that in the process, they will be instructed by the Spirit to be led in directions that will prove to be of personal value.

I hope that as you read this volume, you will be uniquely impacted and that you will be touched differently each time you re-visit it. When I am long-gone, perhaps the considerable thought that went into its production will generate a palpable bond between us that will span the years separating us, and the gulf that then divides us will be bridged by our shared energies to establish the foundation for an eventual joyous reunion.

One of the reasons why I may seem to others to be obsessed with writing is that I enjoy the rush when I find wisdom and great treasures of knowledge, and even hidden treasures. I experience an understanding of doctrinal themes that are to me as pearls that I could not have discerned after only a cursory glance. I hope that, within these pages, you will find scattered seeds that generate within you a similar quest for greater understanding.

I had the opportunity to visit the Holy Land many years ago. We stopped, too briefly, at the ruins of Qumran. There, the Dead Sea Covenanters had lived, and in their scriptorium, I was able to pause and reflect upon their Eleventh Hymn that had been preserved on scrolls hidden in caves high above their community. In part, it reads: "Behold, for mine own part I have reached the intervision, and through the spirit thou has placed within me, come to know Thee, my God." In a similar fashion, Moses wrote: "But now mine own eyes have beheld God; but not my natural, but my spiritual eyes, for ... his glory was upon me; and I beheld his face." (Moses 1:11).

I am continually reminded of Nephi's counsel to press forward with complete dedication and steadfastness, or confidence with a firm determination in Christ, having a perfect brightness of hope, or perfect faith, and charity, or a love of

God and of all men. If we do this, feasting upon the word of Christ, or receiving strength and nourishment as we ponder the principles and doctrines of the Gospel, and as we endure to the end in righteousness, we shall have eternal life, which is the greatest of God's gifts. (See 2 Nephi 31:20). It is with love, then, that I extend to you the invitation to enjoy this volume. Take it at face value, and use its messages as a springboard to your own personal levels of discovery, as you are taught by the Spirit to move in the direction of your dreams.

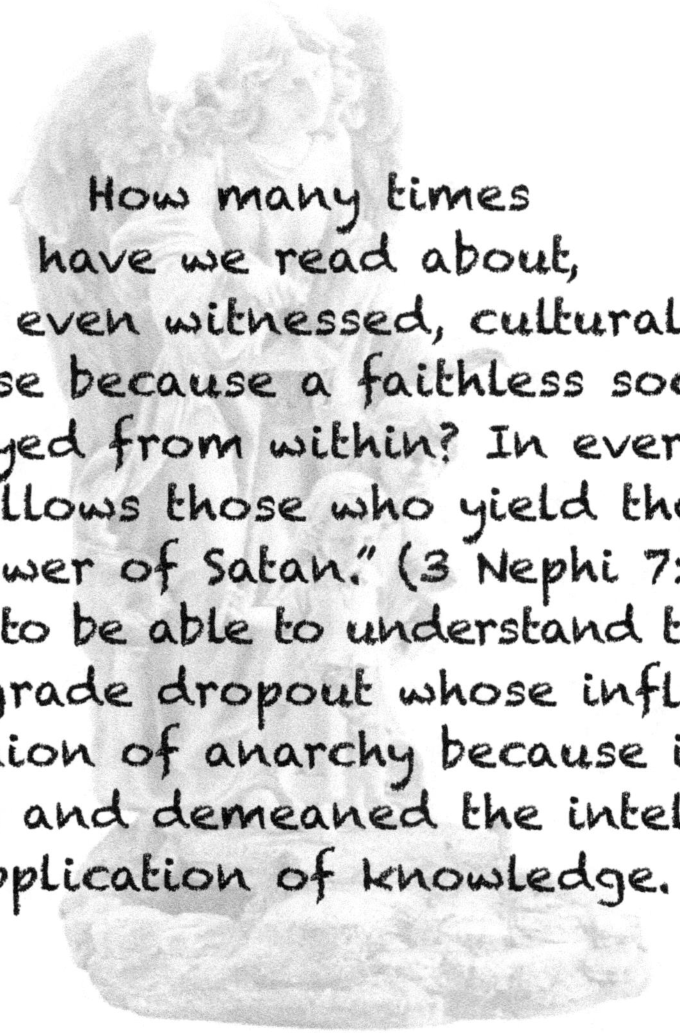

How many times
have we read about,
or even witnessed, cultural
collapse because a faithless society
has decayed from within? In every case,
iniquity follows those who yield themselves
"unto the power of Satan." (3 Nephi 7:5). People
do not seem to be able to understand that Lucifer
was a first-grade dropout whose influence was
the companion of anarchy because it denied
the faith and demeaned the intelligent
application of knowledge.

Introduction

If they are fortunate, novice quilters quickly learn a bit of wisdom from the Amish, who make some of the finest quilts in the world. On purpose, the Amish build mistakes into their designs, because they believe that any attempt on their part to produce a flawless creation would be a mockery to God, Who alone is perfect. The humility of the Amish makes me think of my own weak attempts to put the thoughts expressed in this volume to paper. In His infinite wisdom, God knows very well that I do not need to consciously plan on lacing my efforts with errors. That will come quite naturally, without the need for me to intentionally contribute to my short-comings.

Perhaps this volume will do little more than help to define quirks in my personality. Each of us is different, and many things, including our family and friends, the circumstances in which we find ourselves, the quality of our education, and our own personalities, inspire and mold our oral and written expressions. I would like to think

that all of these influences have been encouraging, affirmative, and constructive. Most of the chapters within this volume weave and wobble their way to a conclusion, although finality has not been my goal. As a thinker, writer and teacher who values careful scholarship, I would rather leave the door ajar for the reader, to allow shafts of the light of understanding to creep in as the dawning of recognition awakens interest in particular subject areas. I would hope that within the pages of this volume there is enough latitude to allow for divergent opinions and independent ideas, not to mention constructive criticism. I hope each chapter poses more questions than it answers. If, as I laid down my thoughts, utilizing just under one hundred and ten thousand words, I misstated myself a few times, or flat-out got it wrong, I ask the patient indulgence and gentle correction of the reader.

I find that no matter how often I have re-read a chapter that is under construction, I continue to come up with different ways of expressing myself. The ink on the page may barely have dried before I am busy at work on a significant revision. There is no way to complete the process, and I have given up trying to do so. So this printed volume is a work in progress. I think of it as a living and breathing entity because, even in its imperfection, it is my hope that it has the generative power to stimulate intellectual, philosophical, imaginative, and spiritual thought processes. If this volume has any real value, it would be to provoke inquiry in the minds of all who ponder its themes.

The chapters are somewhat random in their subject matter and sequentially they follow no particular pattern. If any seem undecipherable, I invite you to recall Albert Einstein's observation: "That which is impenetrable to us really exists. Veneration for this force beyond anything that we can comprehend is my religion." My own faith is less esoteric, and has blessed me with an understanding of some of the very things that one of the greatest minds of the Twentieth Century found "subtle, intangible, and inexplicable." I hope that because of my faith-based heritage, this volume does more than scratch the surface of spiritual inquiry; I have tried to extend its reach beyond mathematical equations to plumb the depth and measure the breadth of the foundation principle of faith.

The subject matter of the chapters was conceived in the white-hot crucible of thought that is common to all of us, but that never becomes ordinary. It excites me to think that we have at our beck and call 10 to 20 billion cerebral cortical neurons, each with 60 to 100 dendrites and axons making 60 to 240 trillion interconnections. Recent estimates suggest that our brains can store around one petabyte of information (four quadrillion bytes – more than the entire Internet). So, this volume could have been a lot worse. I have tried very hard to be mindful of the attention span of my target readership.

I've tried really hard to arouse my creative expression, by reading myself full, thinking myself straight, praying myself hot, and letting myself go! When I do this, I nurture nature and let it caper.

Just as a chef de cuisine might throw a number of ingredients into a "slow cooker" and let them simmer for hours on the stove, some of the chapters only found shape and substance over time as they were nurtured in the subconscious recesses of my mind. The reduction sauce that provided flavor in other chapters was the product of the distillation of weeks, months, and even years of contemplation. And yet, now and then, a fresh thought would quickly sizzle into existence as if the idea had been thrown into a cauldron of boiling oil.

At times, a storm did break loose in my mind, but more often than not, my experiences were more like the whispers of a gentle breeze. I do not pretend to have provided much in the way of meaning to even my little corner of the cosmos, but I have enjoyed the mental and spiritual exercise in my attempts to do so.

When, in just 24 days, George Frideric Handel created the 259 pages of musical score that comprise "The Messiah," the notes came to him so quickly that he could barely keep up, as he furiously scratched out the oratorio on whatever paper was handy. After he had written the "Hallelujah Chorus" in a fervor of divine inspiration, he exclaimed that he had "seen all heaven before him." At the end of the manuscript,

in acknowledgement of his own puny efforts, he wrote the letters "SDG" that stood for "Soli Deo Gloria" or "To God alone the glory."

On a much smaller scale, we have all had similar experiences with light and knowledge, and we have been permitted, at times, to catch a glimpse of the flurry of activity that takes place just beyond the parted veil. Revelatory experiences that have been both nurturing and stimulating have, therefore, found their way into the grammar of this volume.

Too often, though, I realize how easily my thoughts and expressions can be "carefully disguised with hypocrisy and glittering words," as Einstein put it. Although I do fancy myself a wordsmith, I have tried to avoid pedestrian expressions, idle language, and lazy scholarship. I do not pretend to be an authority on the doctrine of faith, and if the factual tone within the chapters is sometimes disengaging, the truth is that I typically experienced a deep personal involvement in my interpretation of the principles that illuminate their meaning.

There are those among us who can write out pi (π) to tens of thousands of digits. In 2005, in China, Chao Lu memorized π to 67,890 digits, which was a world record. I cannot come close to that, 3.14 being the extent of my knowledge of this irrational number, but I have been blessed with an imperfect ability to grasp concepts and expand them to proportions that seem to me to be at once both timely and timeless. When you open this volume, I hope you will read it with as much enjoyment as I have experienced while creating it.

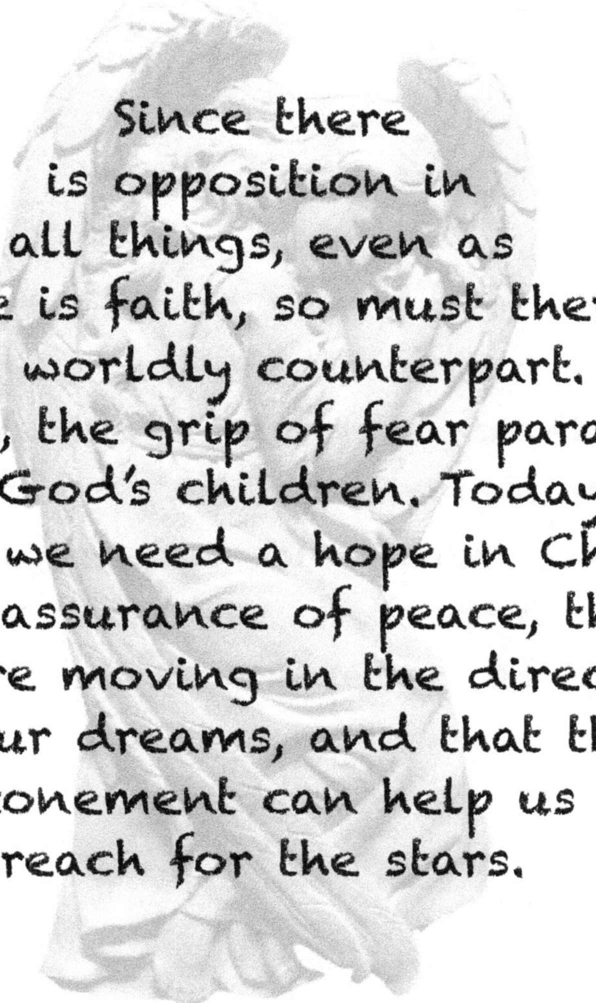

Since there
is opposition in
all things, even as
there is faith, so must there
be its worldly counterpart. In
our day, the grip of fear paralyzes
many of God's children. Today, more
than ever, we need a hope in Christ. We
need the assurance of peace, that our
lives are moving in the direction
of our dreams, and that the
Atonement can help us
reach for the stars.

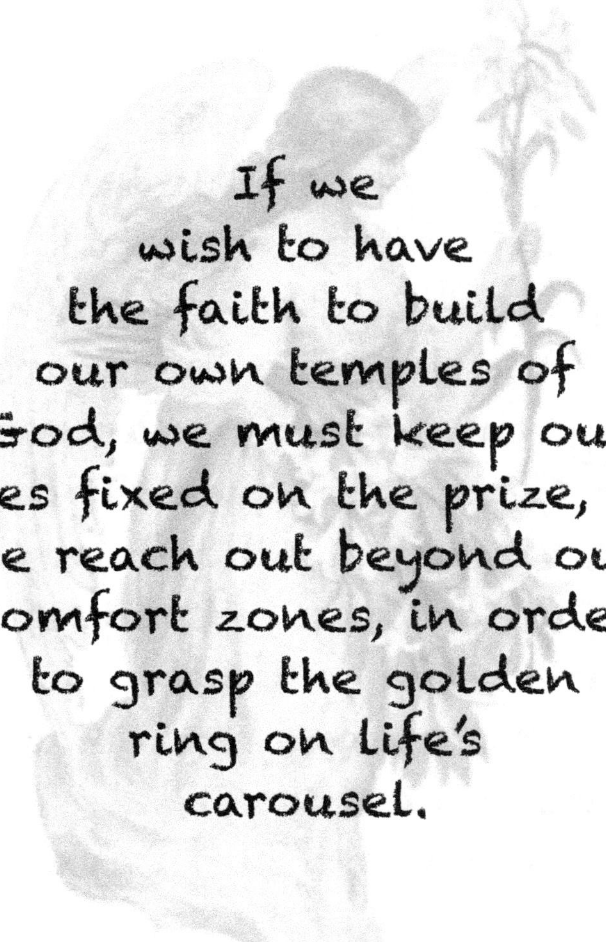

If we
wish to have
the faith to build
our own temples of
God, we must keep our
eyes fixed on the prize, as
we reach out beyond our
comfort zones, in order
to grasp the golden
ring on life's
carousel.

Chapter One
The testimony of faith.

"We, having the same spirit of faith, according as it is written, I believed, and therefore have I spoken; we also believe, and therefore speak." (2 Corinthians 4:13).

We believe in Christ. We belong to The Church of Jesus Christ of Latter-day Saints. The Book of Mormon is Another Testament of Jesus Christ. We are Saints of the Most High God!

We testify of His ante-mortal existence and of His foreordination to be the Redeemer of the world. The scriptures speak of His relationship with the Father, and of His divine investiture of authority. His appearances to His servants throughout history were many. In particular, The Book of Mormon explains His condescension in taking upon Himself a mortal body. Thus, we can better understand His temptations, as well as the power, might, dominion, and authority that typified His earthly ministry.

At His baptism, He demonstrated by example the way for us to follow. In His ministry,

He taught with simplicity the truths of the Gospel. In the Garden of Gethsemane, He revealed His strength and compassion. The crucifixion, then, was only an apostrophe, and His death but a pause, allowing us to re-focus our attention on His resurrection and ascension into heaven.

When He comes again, it will be in the clouds, accompanied by The Church of the Firstborn. His Second Coming will usher in His millennial reign. For a thousand years, His Gospel will penetrate every soul and burn brightly in every bosom.

He is our Advocate with the Father and is the Bread of Life. He is the Cornerstone of our creation, and the foundation beneath our existence. He is the Creator of worlds without number and the Deliverer of the Everlasting Covenant.

He is Emmanuel, for truly, God is with us. He is perfect in every detail and was the Firstborn of the Spirit Children of our Father. He is the Good Shepherd and the Judge of both the quick and the dead. As Lord, King, and Jehovah, He has all power to act as our Mediator and Messenger of the Covenant.

The Lamb of God, He is the Messiah, the Anointed One, and our Redeemer. He is our Rock and our Savior, the Only Begotten Son of God in the flesh. He is the Son of Man of Holiness, and our Second Comforter. Surely, as we develop the testimony of faith, goodness and mercy will follow us all the days of our lives, and we will dwell in the house of the Lord for ever. (See Psalms 23:6).

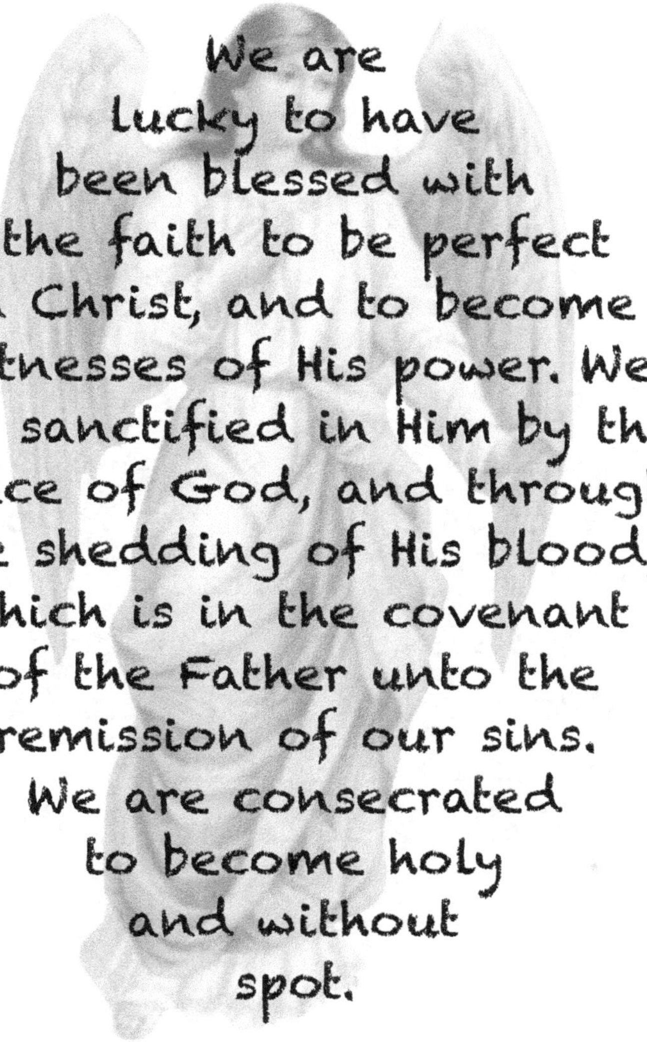

We are
lucky to have
been blessed with
the faith to be perfect
in Christ, and to become
witnesses of His power. We
are sanctified in Him by the
grace of God, and through
the shedding of His blood,
which is in the covenant
of the Father unto the
remission of our sins.
We are consecrated
to become holy
and without
spot.

We have
faith that
there is enough
room and enough
time in the eternities
for each of us develop
the capacity to see beyond
the limited horizon of our
vision all the way to the
Atonement that reaches
out to the best of us,
the worst of us, and
to everyone in
between.

Chapter Two
The seeds of faith.

"The kingdom of heaven is likened unto a man
which sowed good seed in his field."
(Matthew 13:24).

Many members of the Church turn to Alma's discourse, that is recorded in The Book of Mormon Alma Chapter 32, for understanding concerning the principle of faith. It seems appropriate to address his perspective on the subject, in this, the second chapter of volume one in the "First Principles and Ordinances Series."

Those who read Alma 32 must remember that he was speaking to members of the Church who had a poor understanding of basic Gospel principles; to a people who had been living in a state of apostasy; and to a people who had previously been taught only false doctrine. Therefore, Alma did not explain all there is to understand about the first principle of the Gospel, because his spiritually immature audience was capable of processing the details of only the initial steps that must be taken

to develop faith. It is important for members of the Church, who have a firm foundation in Gospel doctrine, to keep this in mind when reading Alma's oft-quoted discourse on faith.

Alma was on solid ground when he invited the Zoramites to test the truths of the Gospel. The Apostle James also challenged: "If any of you lack wisdom, let him ask of God, that giveth to all men liberally, and upbraideth not; and it shall be given him." (James 1:5). Joseph Smith put this promise to the test with spectacular results. (See J.S.H. 1:17). So have countless others who have prayed with the desire to know of the divine authenticity of the latter-day restoration of Gospel doctrine, principles, ordinances, and covenants.

Alma first taught the people in their synagogues. (V. 1-2). Evidence of the depth of the apostasy of the Zoramites is revealed by the characterization of their places of assembly as "synagogues" and not as "churches." The Book of Mormon invariably uses the term "synagogue," that is a Greek word, to designate early Jewish assemblies, and "church," from the Greek "ecclesia," to differentiate such assemblies after they had become Christian. It is hard to think of more appropriate terms, bearing in mind that this is a translation, and the purpose of the words is not to convey what the Nephites called their communities, but only to illustrate how they intended that we picture them in our own minds.

The wealthy Zoramites, who likely wore "fine twined linen," (1 Nephi 13:7), had scorned their poorer brethren "because of the coarseness of their apparel." (V. 2). The temporally disadvantaged Zoramites were "poor as to the things of the world, (but) also they were poor in heart." (V. 3). In other words, their straightened circumstances fostered humility, and in turn, teachability. They came to Alma expressing a common concern of those who seek the truth but do not know how or where to find it: "We have no place to worship our God," they lamented, "and behold, what shall we do?" (V. 5). They did not understand their true relationship to their Heavenly Father, but thought that they could only worship Him within the walls of their synagogues.

Alma was overjoyed that the poor Zoramites had come to him, for he "beheld that their afflictions had truly humbled them, and that they were in a preparation to hear the word." (V. 6). Immediately, he seized upon the opportunity, by clarifying two basic principles that they had grossly misunderstood. First, he explained that they could worship God wherever they might be, and secondly that every day is a day of worship. (V. 10-11).

Alma realized that the Zoramites had been blessed because circumstances had compelled them to be humble. He knew that with proper Gospel instruction, their humility would lead them through faith and repentance, to mercy and forgiveness via the ordinances of the Gospel, and finally to salvation by the grace of God. (See v. 13). "Because of the word," the guiding light of correct principles would instill within them even greater humility and meekness. (V. 14). Alma understood that, as the seeds of faith were planted in fertile soil, gentleness, mildness, and modesty would be harvested. (V. 15).

He wanted the Zoramites to enjoy the blessings that are related to enduring to the end in the light of the Gospel. Although endurance is often cast in a negative light, as in "enduring pain" or "enduring persecution," Alma knew by his own experience that it can ultimately be positive and pleasant. It does, however, carry a performance cost. If we wish to have physical endurance, for example, we must pay the price. Rigorously maintaining a good diet, and observing both mental and physical discipline are essential ingredients to achieve new heights that would otherwise have been beyond our reach.

With sound bodies, we can choose from a wider variety of options, and our opportunities to do so seem to be boundless. Walk all day without fatigue? Participate in consecutive endowment sessions? Ski in the mountains? Hike to a lake for a day of fishing? Tirelessly minister to the needs of less-fortunate ward members? Play three sets of tennis, or a round of golf? Given the natural limitations of age and our individual temporal circumstances, when we possess physical endurance there are

many worthwhile and uplifting activities from which we may choose.

Nor does spiritual fitness, or endurance, come without effort. A testimony of the Gospel and its exalting principles is a gift that must be earned. We read such things as: "Behold, you have not understood; you have supposed that I would give it unto you, when you took no thought save it was to ask me. But, behold, I say unto you, that you must study it out in your mind." (D&C 9:7-8). Lorenzo Snow concurred. "It is impossible to advance in the principles of truth," he declared, "to increase in heavenly knowledge, except we exercise our reasoning faculties and exert ourselves." (J.D., 18:371). Agency is not free, but is purchased at a substantial cost.

If we desire a testimony of family home evening, we must understand and apply the particular laws of the Gospel that are associated with that principle. "For all who will have a blessing at my hands shall abide the law which was appointed for that blessing, and the conditions thereof." (D&C 132:5, see also D&C 130:20-21). If we want to know that The Book of Mormon is the word of God, we must read with a desire to receive a spiritual witness. (See Moroni 10:4). If we want to know that obedience to the Gospel Plan is the path to happiness, we need to try the virtue of the word of God. (See Alma 31:5).

God has promised us "knowledge by ... the unspeakable gift of the Holy Ghost." (D&C 121:26, see also D&C 1:38). When knowledge and Spirit work in tandem to stir our souls, we become the lucky recipients of testimony. Our knowledge of the truth of a principle is internalized, but only after we have had experience dealing with it. Then, no one can rob us of our testimony. It can only be forfeit by embracing lifestyle behaviors that cause the confirming Spirit of Truth to withdraw. (See John 15:26).

The scriptures teach with clarity and finality: "All saints who remember to keep and do these sayings, walking in obedience to the commandments, shall receive health in their navel and marrow to their bones; and shall find wisdom and great treasures of knowledge, even hidden treasures; and shall run and not be weary,

and shall walk and not faint. And I, the Lord, give unto them a promise, that the destroying angel shall pass them by, as the children of Israel, and not slay them." (D&C 89:18-21).

During Alma's ministry among the poor Zoramites, his recent exhausting confrontation with Korihor must have weighed heavily on his mind. Perhaps he was thinking of that anti-Christ when he warned the Zoramites: "There are many who do say: If thou wilt show unto us a sign from heaven, then we shall know of a surety; then we shall believe." (V. 17). Alma wanted to instruct the Zoramites about the principle of saving faith without being reduced to giving them a sign in order to satisfy the need of faithless naysayers for theological titillation. Therefore, he was meticulous to carefully establish a foundation for the teaching moments that would follow. In his discourse, he figuratively sowed the seeds of faith.

Every discussion of faith must distinguish it from its caricatures. It is not naiveté or gullibility, nor is it wishful thinking. It is more than confidence and greater than optimism. Faith and positive thinking go hand in hand, but faith is far more than an attitude. Alma knew that receiving heavenly signs would not generate faith, even within softened Zoramite hearts. In fact, he told the Zoramites that they should not seek after signs, because faith precedes the miracle.

He explained that during the genesis of faith, it is necessary to take a few steps into the darkness, and then the spiritual strong searchlight of truth will illuminate the way. Only after the trial of our faith will it be confirmed by experience and will the Spirit validate God as its Author and Finisher. (See Hebrews 12:2). This is why Alma carefully taught the Zoramites: "If a man knoweth a thing he hath no cause to believe (or to actively exercise faith), for he knoweth it." (V. 18).

If a sign were to be given before our transformation through faith, we might have a sure knowledge of the principle, but it would have been received without our undisciplined and unprepared minds having aforetime made the necessary expenditure of faith. This was Korihor's fatal flaw. He demanded a sign from heaven without having

beforehand demonstrated the appropriate and necessary exercise of faith.

Under proper circumstances, however, as we gain spiritual maturity "by doing our duty, faith increases until it becomes perfect knowledge." (Heber J. Grant, C.R.,

4/1934). This is a key principle relating to the doctrine of faith. Certainly, God Himself is full of faith, and yet He is omniscient. There is nothing that He does not know. As Joseph Smith taught, it was by faith that "the worlds were framed, (and) all things in heaven, on the earth, or under the earth. (These) exist by reason of faith as it existed in (the mind of the Gods). Had it not been for this principle of faith, the worlds would never have been framed, neither would man have been formed of the dust. It is this principle by which Jehovah works, and through which he exercises power over all temporal as well as eternal things." ("Lectures on Faith," #1).

For our part, as imperfect mortals who are similar to the poor Zoramites, struggling to believe what we do not see, the reward of our maturing faith is to see what we believe. Some things just have to be believed to be seen, as our faith is perfected.

Heavenly Father has not left us destitute, and He has not abandoned us to tap our way through the lone and dreary world, as do the blind leading the blind. (See Matthew 5:14 & 2 Nephi 2). "Faith in Christ is not a leap in the dark. It is, instead, trust in what the spirit learned eons ago; and religious recognition is just that, a re-cognition, a re-knowing, the sum of existence. If we thwart or suppress that instinctive response, we are accountable, and to a degree, we condemn ourselves. We knew Christ before this life, we know Him here, and we will know Him hereafter. His sheep do indeed know His voice." (Truman Madsen). The impact that truth has on our minds and our spirits becomes our ultimate test of faith.

Thus, Alma taught: "How much more cursed is he that knoweth the will of God and doeth it not, than he that only believeth, or only hath cause to believe, and falleth into transgression?" (V. 18). Belief embodies a mental assent to the truth or actuality of a precept, principle, or doctrine, without the moral element of

responsibility that we call faith. (See v. 21). To those to whom much is given, however, much is expected. The gift of faith demands action. Therefore, when we exercise our moral agency, even if we perform good works, without faith it falls short. It "is dead, being alone." (James 2:17).

"Without faith, we are free, and that can be a pleasant feeling, at first. There are no questions of conscience and no constraints, except those of custom, convention, and the law, and these are flexible enough for most purposes. It is only later that the terror comes. We are free in chaos, in an unexplainable world, and in a desert from which there is no retreat but inward, toward our hollow core." (Morris West, "The Devil's Advocate"). Agency is catalyzed by faith to drive us to purposeful and positive performance that confirms the principles of The Plan of Salvation.

Therefore, Alma told the Zoramites: "Now of this thing ye must judge. Behold, I say unto you, that it is on the one hand even as it is on the other; and it shall be unto every man according to his work." (V. 20). He was asking the Zoramites to cast aside their fears that they might take a tremendous step as they stood at a crossroads. (See Joshua 24:15). As Robert Frost wrote: "I shall be telling this with a sigh somewhere ages and ages hence: Two roads diverged in a wood, and I took the one less traveled by, and that has made all the difference." ("The Road Not Taken").

Alma hoped the Zoramites would develop faith unto salvation, knowing full well that Heavenly Father does not expect us to exercise faith in things for which there is insufficient evidence. As his sermon unfolded, Alma gave the Zoramites a formula for the development of justifiable faith that would be the key to their liberation from enslavement to apostate religious dogma. Alma knew by his own experience that in matters of faith it is we, and not the Lord, who are on trial. The responsibility to make the next critical move would rest upon the shoulders of the Zoramites. At the Bar of Justice, the evidence will be presented, and our previous conformity with or rejection of eternal law will determine our reward or punishment. Our innate tendency to generate faith, with the impetus coming from the Light of Christ, makes the trials of mortality eminently fair. In fact, the deck is stacked in our favor.

Because they had neither a doctrinal nor an experiential foundation in the application

of Gospel principles, the Zoramites were told: "Faith is not to have a perfect knowledge of things; therefore, if ye have faith ye hope for things which are not seen, which are true." (V. 21, see Hebrews 11:1). This is correct in the ultimate sense, and must be accepted as a given, as long as we concede one important point. It is precisely this: Alma illustrated in his discourse to the Zoramites that faith is unnecessary if its object is demonstrable to our physical senses.

You see, in Alma's usage, verse 21 might more clearly read: "Faith is not to have a perfect knowledge of things that can be gained through our own experiences." Remember that Korihor's demand for a sign had been the condition for his faith, since he trusted only his physical senses. That rational approach is the enemy of faith. Thus, secular humanism and other similar ideologies that extoll the virtues of the intellect and demand physical proof destroy faith and are devilish doctrines, subtle though they may be. They are abominable to God because they divert us from a Plan whose successful execution hinges upon nourishing the seeds of faith in a higher power.

Because truth is at the very foundation of saving faith, Heavenly Father will not lead us to have faith in that which is false; for example, in professional faith healers. In these cases, Satan, who has limited power over life and death, is responsible for the healing. (See Job 2:6). Nevertheless, God may sanction the healing of those evincing pure and simple faith, misguided though it may be. Hence, we are familiar with examples of those whose faith has rewarded them with healing, without the authority of the priesthood that is commonly deemed to be necessary in order to call upon the powers of heaven.

Faith may lead us to believe the truth "in the first place," that we might obtain mercy. (V. 23). Faith is more than intellectual assent, however. Because the influence of faith extends as far as our deeds, works become an important companion to vital, active faith. (See James 2:17, & Matthew 5:16). Faith without works, as a matter of fact, lacks life-generating and life-sustaining power. Faith is impotent when it does not lead to purposeful performance by the penitent. It is the sizzle without the steak. Real faith

involves a vital, personal self-commitment to a practical belief. But at the end of the day, our good works lack the efficacy for salvation. What makes us good is faith in Jesus Christ, and faith in Christ activates God's grace in our behalf.

After the aside in verses 22-25, Alma returned to his subject in verse 26: "Now, as I said concerning faith, that it was not a perfect knowledge" in its infancy, "even so it is with my words. Ye cannot know of their surety at first, unto perfection, any more than faith is," at first, "a perfect knowledge." (V. 26). Therefore, in verses 27-43, Alma proposed an experiment to generate incipient faith. He asked the Zoramites to "awake and arouse (their) faculties, even to an experiment upon (his) words." (V. 27). The experiment involved desire, planting a seed, nourishing it, and harvesting fruit. (See verses 27, 28, 37-41, & 42-43).

The Zoramites were asked to "exercise a particle of faith" even if they wee able to muster no more than the "desire to believe." (V. 27). The principle that they were asked to believe was that the Son of God would come and atone for the sins of the world. (See Alma 33-35). Alma was counting on the fact that "truth as well as untruth may be recognized by their effects. Rendering obedience to its principles of action tests the claims of the Gospel. Practicing our religion is the most direct method of gaining a testimony of the truth." (John Widtsoe). In an insightful invitation to two of His disciples, the Savior said: "Come and see" for yourself, whether my message "be of God, or whether I speak of myself." (John 1:39 & 7:17).

Comparing the word to a seed, Alma similarly asked the Zoramites to "give place," or study, pray and commit themselves to a specific plan of action. He knew that if they would do so, they would feel the word enlarge their souls and enlighten their understanding. (V. 28). As Brigham Young said: "Every Gospel principle carries within it a witness that it is true." (J.D., 9:149). It is within the economy of the Gospel principle of faith that "we often catch a spark from the awakened memories of the immortal soul, which lights up our whole being as with the glory of our former home." (Joseph F. Smith, "Gospel Doctrine," p. 14).

In the Last Days, the missionaries often ask those to whom they have introduced

the Gospel to engage in the experiment suggested by Alma and reiterated by Moroni. (See Moroni 10:4). They ask that they determine for themselves the validity of the message of the Restoration and of the divine authenticity of The Book of Mormon. They do so with confidence, because the Restored Gospel is one of the great realities of our time, and what makes it so is that a growing body of disciples who call themselves "Saints" believe it. They testify that its one and only merit is that it is founded on truth. Without that merit, it is all that non-believers say it is. With it, it is all that believers say it is. (See Hugh Nibley, "Of All Things," p. 93). It is the key element of faith that makes all the difference when the test of truth is applied to any of the principles of the Gospel.

However, it is important to reiterate the very narrow sense in which Alma proposed the experiment to the Zoramites. After its completion, their knowledge of that specific principle would be perfect, and the faith that had been required to accept it would have been profitably expended, and would thereafter become "dormant." (V. 34, see v. 21).

Because the successful completion of the experiment proposed by Alma invariably results in the budding testimony of a Gospel principle, his invitation to the poor Zoramites has universal applicability. In every possible scenario, testimony includes three essential elements. First, is the introduction to and recognition of an eternal principle. Second, is the correct understanding of the Lord's counsel concerning the principle, and third, is personal experience with the principle, which is the fruits of faith. (See Galatians 5:22). The Zoramites had been asked to experiment only upon the words of Alma, whose objective was that they simply inaugurate a connection with the principle of faith. He recognized that they would first have to build upon a desire to believe, and next establish a groundwork of knowledge that would thereafter provide the solid foundation upon which their newfound faith could flourish.

As he explained: "Neither must ye lay aside your faith, for ye have only exercised your faith to plant the seed that ye might try the experiment to know if the seed

was good." (V. 36). As the seed was nurtured, it would "grow up, and bring forth fruit." (V. 37). In other words, additional knowledge would be added to their expanding foundation of faith. The poor Zoramites did not realize it, but Alma was asking them to embrace the doctrine of the kingdom that they might understand the mysteries of God as they were taught by the Spirit. The challenge was clothed in simple terms that they could easily understand. (See D&C 88:77). As Paul would later teach the Corinthian Saints: "And I, brethren, could not speak unto you as unto spiritual, but as unto carnal, even as unto babes in Christ. I have fed you with milk, and not with meat: for hitherto ye were not able to bear it, neither yet now are ye able." (1 Corinthians 3:1-2).

If the seed were neglected, Alma cautioned: "Behold, it will not get any root; and when the heat of the sun cometh and scorcheth it, because it hath no root, it withers away." (V. 38). This, he explained to the Zoramites, is "because your ground is barren, and ye will not nourish the tree." (V. 39). There is no revelation where there is no student, and as long as we persist in asking the wrong questions, we will be at eternal odds with faith. Our rational minds will never find a way to bridge the gap between the secular and the divine. "As humanity continues to struggle with death, despair, hopelessness, fear, and anxiety, the scriptures speak a far more relevant message to society than any rational explanation." ("Newsweek" Magazine, 11/1980).

"If you will not nourish the word," cautioned Alma, you must not think that the experiment failed. We "can never pluck of the fruit of the tree of life" without accepting the fact that perspiration must precede inspiration. (V. 40). If we choose mediocrity over the nobility of faith, if we abandon all we know to be true to worldly enticements, if we surrender our will-power to won't-power, if we succumb to selfish pleasures, if we are bedazzled by the honors of men more than by the illuminating truths of the Gospel, if we are willfully disobedient, or if we will not nourish the seeds of faith, our priorities are out of order, we lose power, and the experiment will fail.

As long as we remain in this state of rebellion against the Spirit, the fruit of the tree of

life will remain just beyond our reach, even if we occasionally have outstretched arms. If we do not raise our eyes to search eternal horizons, the world before us will appear as a barren desert, devoid of refreshing oases, the welcome shade of trees, and an abundance of well-watered gardens. If we will not nourish the word, we cannot, in turn, be sustained by living water.

"But if ye will nourish the word," explained Alma, "it shall take root; and behold it shall be a tree springing up unto everlasting life," reminiscent of the tree in Lehi's dream that represented the love of God and its ultimate expression of celestial glory. (V. 41, see 1 Nephi 8:10-12). Alma cautioned the Zoramites that it would take diligence and patience to "reap (the) rewards of (their) faith." (V. 42-43). We call these efforts "enduring to the end in righteousness," in a process whereby the seeds of faith are multiplied unto us. (See 2 Peter 1:1-2).

This message from Alma to the poor Zoramites is as relevant today as it was two thousand years ago, because our world is distracted by the same temporal problems and is in the same spiritual predicament. In materialistic western societies that reflect the conditions found so long ago among the more affluent Zoramites, the challenges are even greater, but that is a story for another chapter in this book.

The world seems to be in a quandary from which there is no escape. So many in our day "tend to fill space, as if what they have, what they are, is not enough. Seeking privileged circumstances, they strangle themselves with what they can buy, things whose opacity obstructs their ability to see what is really there." (Gretel Erlich, "Under Wyoming's Skies," The Atlantic Monthly, 5/1985).

Alma's counsel to the poor Zoramites demonstrates what we can do to avoid the pitfalls associated with seeking "for things (that we cannot) understand." (Jacob 4:14). As he taught, the Spirit whispered to him: These poor Zoramites "have need that one teach (them) which be the first principles of the oracles of God, (for they are) such as have need of milk and not of strong meat." (Hebrews 5:12). In in every

age, the tender shoots of young testimony spring up and are carefully nurtured in accordance with Alma's inspired formula, without the ecclesiastical embroidery that too often needlessly complicates the simple sewing, and sowing, of Gospel messages.

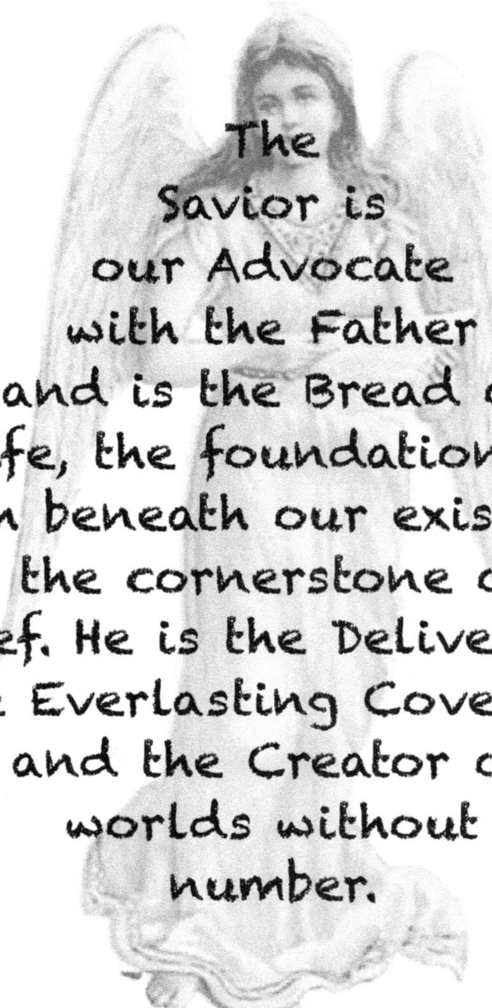

The Savior is our Advocate with the Father and is the Bread of Life, the foundation of faith beneath our existence, and the cornerstone of our belief. He is the Deliverer of the Everlasting Covenant and the Creator of worlds without number.

Chapter Three
The faith to trust.

"Once the game is over, the King and the pawn go back in the same box."
(Italian Proverb).

There will be those who come to the Judgment Bar believing that there were many equally acceptable paths leading to the Kingdom of God. They will argue that it mattered little whether they were Methodist, Quaker, or Lutheran. They will reason that evincing a simple faith in Christ was the determining factor relating to their qualification for salvation.

But the Savior cautioned: "Many will say to me in that day: Lord, Lord, have we not prophesied in thy name, and in thy name have cast out devils, and in thy name done many wonderful works?" (3 Nephi 14:22). At the Bar of Justice, He will declare: "I never knew you." (Matthew 7:23). Or, as the Joseph Smith Translation renders this

verse: "Ye never knew me." (J.S.T. Matthew 7:23). What a contrast this will be to those who are as Job, who had the faith to trust in the Lord, and of whom He said: "There is none like him in the earth, a perfect and an upright man, one that feareth God, and escheweth evil." (Job 1:8).

We are on the path leading to eternal life when we move forward with inspired direction and with dedicated purpose. In other words, the Lord links discipleship to spiritual consistency. It is not enough to have been baptized and to have received the Holy Ghost. We must not camp out on grassy fields adjacent to the strait and narrow way, allow ourselves to be lulled to sleep while zoned out on autopilot, or comfortably settle in to a vegetative state that makes no demands upon our creative capabilities. We must have the faith to trust in the Lord as we continue to take halting steps into the unknown, even before the spiritual strong searchlight of faith illuminates the way. "Therefore, who heareth these sayings ... and doeth them," may be likened "unto a wise man, who built his house upon a rock." (3 Nephi 14:24).

Brigham Young declared: "I never count the cost of anything. I just find out what the Lord wants me to do, and I do it." This is precisely what Joseph Smith did, when he found a quiet place near his home where he could ask God which church was right. When his simple faith to trust was acknowledged, he pressed on in the Light of Christ, and was rewarded with an illumination of Gospel principles that bathed him in a cascade of inspiration and revelation.

In the springtime of the year 1820, he was not yet a member of The Church of Jesus Christ, nor did he have a clear understanding of the nature of God. Nevertheless, he recognized that he lacked wisdom, and so he determined to ask of God, in faith, nothing wavering. (See James 1:5-6). His humble prayer was answered with spectacular results. Since that time, the same drama has been replayed millions of times, as the Holy Ghost has visited those who have faithfully trusted in the promise of Moroni, that they might receive a witness of the truth. (See Moroni 10:4).

The Savior has high expectations of those who have joined the community of Christ.

(See Ephesians 2:19). "For of him unto whom much is given, much is required; and he who sins against the greater light shall receive the greater condemnation." (D&C 82:3).

At the same time, those who never had the opportunity to embrace the Gospel will be judged according to their more limited understanding of the doctrines and principles of God's Plan. Therefore, when they approach the bar of Justice, they will necessarily vary in their accountability to law. Therein lies the hidden power of the Gospel to ultimately bless our lives, whatever our individual circumstances might be and whatever cards we have been dealt in life.

The Plan makes note of the privileged frames of reference. Provisions have been set in place to address our unique needs, that all might eventually be brought to the full stature of Christ. (See Moses 1:39). There is enough room and there is enough time in the eternities for each of us develop the capacity to see beyond the limited horizon of our vision, as the magnificent Atonement reaches out to the best of us, the worst of us, and to everyone in between. It extends to those who endured tumultuous periods of apostasy, who lived through expansive times of restoration, and who enjoyed the thunderous roll of revelation that has typified the dispensations of the Gospel. It extends to those who knew no law, to those who understood and obeyed the law, as well as to those who transgressed the law. The incomprehensible resurrection itself, we are told, is sown in corruption, but is raised in incorruption. (See 1 Corinthians 15:42). All we can say is that those who hope to become holy and without spot, must have the faith to trust in the Lord's promises.

With a clear understanding of scope of The Plan of Salvation, Paul wrote to the Ephesian Saints: "I bow my knees unto the Father of our Lord Jesus Christ, of whom the whole family in heaven and earth is named, that he would grant you, according to the riches of his glory, to be strengthened with might by his Spirit in the inner man; that Christ may dwell in your hearts by faith that ye, being rooted and grounded in love, may be able to comprehend with all saints what is the breadth, and length, and height; and to know the love of Christ, which passeth knowledge,

that ye might be filled with all the fulness of God." (Ephesians 3:14-19).

He knew his limitations, and recognized his inadequacies and imperfections, but he understood that he needed to roll up his sleeves and get to work in the ministry;

in his own words "for the perfecting of the saints" and "for the edifying of the body of Christ: 'till we all come in the unity of the faith, and of the knowledge of the Son of God, unto a perfect man, unto the measure of the stature of the fulness of Christ." (Ephesians 4:11-13). That day will come to those who have the faith to trust in the promises of the Father. (See D&C 108:5).

In the eternities, those who knew no law will be sufficiently instructed, that they might "have part in the first resurrection; and it shall be tolerable for them." (D&C 45:54). This is because of the infinite breadth, depth, and height of the Atonement, for "His blood atoneth for the sins of (all) those who have fallen by the transgression of Adam, who have died not knowing the will of God concerning them, or who have ignorantly sinned." (Mosiah 3:11). "For how knoweth a man the master he has not served, and who is a stranger unto him, and is far from the thoughts and intents of his heart?" (Mosiah 5:13).

Life begins as "a sheet of paper white, where each of us may write a line or two, and then comes night. Greatly begin. If thou hast time but for a line, make that sublime. Not failure, but low aim is crime." (James Russell Lowell). When Bruce R. McConkie was asked: "How can we reach the Celestial Kingdom?" his simple seven word answer was: "Set your course, and move along it." He might just as easily have uttered these seven words: "Have faith to trust in the Lord." The Restored Gospel provides the way to do just that, as the Church builds upon the rock of revelation. May we ever remember Brigham Youngs' counsel to keep our dish right side up, so that when the shower of porridge does come, we can catch our dish full. (See D.B.Y., p. 310).

The legal tender of trusting faith is the currency we will need to purchase the Golden Ticket for our passage Home.

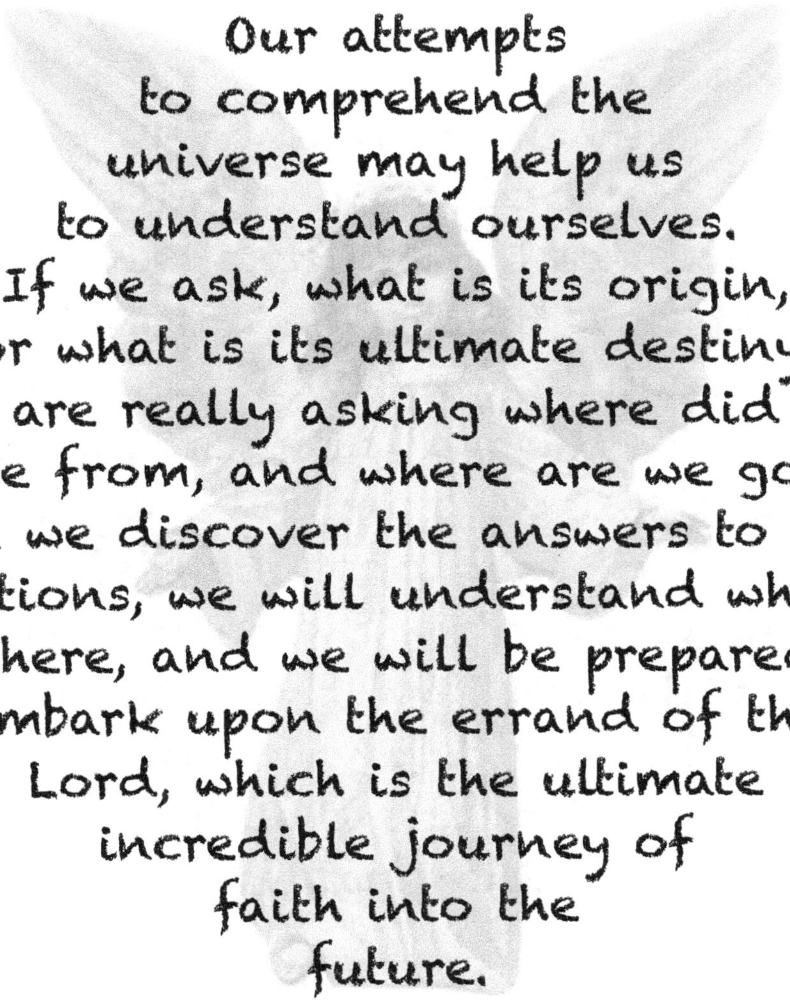

Our attempts
to comprehend the
universe may help us
to understand ourselves.
If we ask, what is its origin,
or what is its ultimate destiny,
we are really asking where did we
come from, and where are we going.
When we discover the answers to these
questions, we will understand why we
are here, and we will be prepared to
embark upon the errand of the
Lord, which is the ultimate
incredible journey of
faith into the
future.

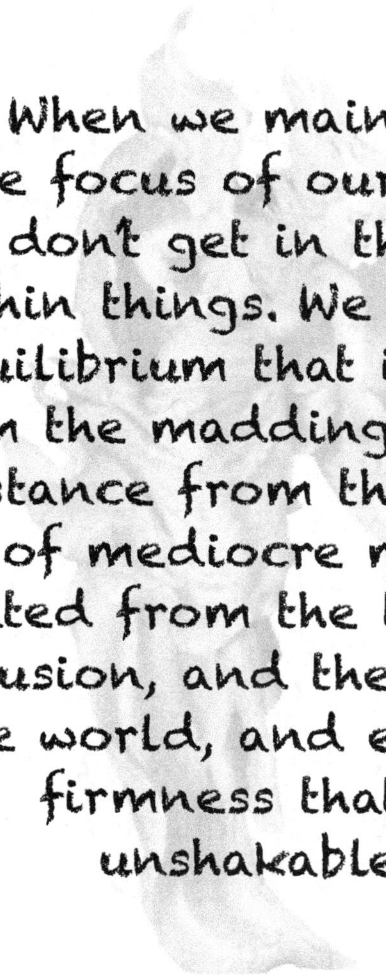

When we maintain
the focus of our faith,
we don't get in the thick
of thin things. We cultivate
an equilibrium that is centered
far from the madding crowd, at a
safe distance from the ego-filled
minds of mediocre men. We are
insulated from the tumult, the
confusion, and the cares of
the world, and enjoy a
firmness that is
unshakable.

Chapter Four
The reach of faith.

"No prophecy of the scripture is of
any private interpretation."
(2 Peter 1:20).

Just how far does the reach of faith extend within a church that extols the virtues of personal revelation?

"Many Latter-day Saints, from the Presidents of the Church and members of the Quorum of the Twelve to individual members who may write books or articles, have expressed their own opinions on doctrinal matters. Nevertheless, until such opinions are presented to the Church in General Conference and sustained by vote of the conference, they are neither binding nor the official doctrine of the Church. Critics of LDS doctrine seldom recognize this vital distinction. Rather, if any Latter-day Saint, especially one of the presiding brethren, ever said a thing,

these critics take it to represent "Mormonism," regardless of whether any other Latter-day Saint ever said it or believed it. Often, the Latter-day Saints themselves are guilty of this same error and search through the Journal of Discourses as if it were some sort of Mormon Talmud, looking for 'new' doctrines not found in the standard works and not taught in the Church today." (Stephen Robinson, "Are Mormons Christian?" p. 15).

Henry B. Eyring said: "We must be cautious and careful not to go beyond teaching true doctrine." This requires that we be sensitive to the whisperings of the Holy Ghost, Whose confirmation is invited as we eschew speculation or personal interpretation. One of the surest ways to avoid even getting near false doctrine is to choose to be simple in our teaching. Safety is gained by that simplicity, and little is lost." (C.R., 4/2009).

Jeffrey Holland addressed a similar concern in a General Conference address: "The scriptures are not the ultimate source of knowledge for Latter-day Saints," he said. "The living God is the ultimate source, and His teaching comes as vibrant revelation. This doctrine is central to the message of the Restoration. God is engaged in our lives, and continues to speak His word and reveal His truth. This basic belief by faithful Latter-day Saints demands that we maintain a set of religious writings regarded as authentic and definitive, as an open canon." (C.R., 4/2008).

Dallin Oaks said much the same thing about scripture: "For us, the ultimate source of knowledge (is) revelation. Because of our belief in continuing revelation, we Latter-day Saints maintain that the canon (the authoritative body) of scriptures is open, (and) continuing revelation is crucial." ("Ensign," 1/1995).

Both Elders Holland and Oaks mentioned an "open canon" in the sense that we believe that God may freely amend, or add to, the existing body of scripture, through His prophet. B.H. Roberts explained: "The Church has confined the sources of doctrine by which it is willing to be bound before the world to the things that God has revealed and which the Church has officially accepted, and those alone. These

include the Bible, the Book of Mormon, the Doctrine and Covenants, (and) the Pearl of Great Price. These have been repeatedly accepted and endorsed by the Church in General Conference assembled, and are the only sources of absolute appeal for our doctrine." (Sermon delivered in Salt Lake Tabernacle, 7/10/1921, reported in "Deseret News," 7/23/1921).

This has been the pattern and the practice of the Church since its organization. It is in General Conference of the Church that the membership votes on proposed new revelation. After its ratification, it is added to the existing canon. For example, this is how Official Declaration 2 and Section 138 were added to the Doctrine & Covenants in 1978, and in 1981, respectively.

We also believe in an open canon in the sense that God is free to clarify for our understanding His existing doctrine. This is a bit more complicated, because it is our belief that revelation is either public (coming through prophets, seers, and revelators) or private, (coming to students of the scriptures who invite the promptings of the Holy Ghost), and that illumination is tailored to our individual spiritual capacity. Hugh Nibley astutely observed: "Men fool themselves when they think for a moment that they can read the scripture without ever adding something to the text, or omitting something from it." In the words of St. Hilary, "Scripture consists not in what one reads, but in what one understands." "Consequently, in the reading of scripture, we must always have an interpreter" which is the Holy Ghost. ("The World and the Prophets," 3:202).

Dallin Oaks taught: "Latter-day Saints know that learned or authoritative commentaries can help us with scriptural interpretation, but we maintain that they must be used with caution. Commentaries are not a substitute for the scriptures any more than a good cookbook is a substitute for food. When I refer to "commentaries," I mean everything that interprets scripture, from the comprehensive book-length commentary to the brief interpretation embodied in a lesson or an article, such as this one."

"One trouble with commentaries," he continued, "is that their authors sometimes focus on only one meaning, to the exclusion of others. As a result, if not used with great care, commentaries may illuminate the author's chosen and correct meaning but close our eyes and restrict our horizons to other possible meanings.

Sometimes those other less obvious meanings can be the ones most valuable and useful to us as we seek to obtain answers to our own questions. This is why the teaching of the Holy Ghost is a better guide to scriptural interpretation than even the best commentary." ("Ensign," 1/1995, p. 7).

If we depend only upon our own reasoning, or upon the scholarship or reasoning of others, including the manuals of instruction provided by the Curriculum Department of the Church, we will never obtain the understanding that comes through personal inspiration and revelation. Even worse, if we "harden our hearts" in any degree to the influence of the Spirit, we will receive "the lesser portion of the word, until (we) know nothing concerning his mysteries" that are the saving principles of the Gospel. (Alma 12:11).

There was quiet prophetic wisdom in the counsel of Spencer W. Kimball, who told the members of the Church that he was "convinced that each of us, at some time in our lives, must discover the scriptures for ourselves." ("Ensign," 9/1976, p. 5). This process invites personal revelation, as we extend the reach of our faith.

Our faith
puts the day to
day elements of The
Plan in perspective, that
we might more clearly be
able to distinguish the grey
-toned obstacles that lie in
our path. These barriers to our
progression will then stand out
in sharp contrast against the
polychromatic backdrop of
the design that God has
created for each
of us.

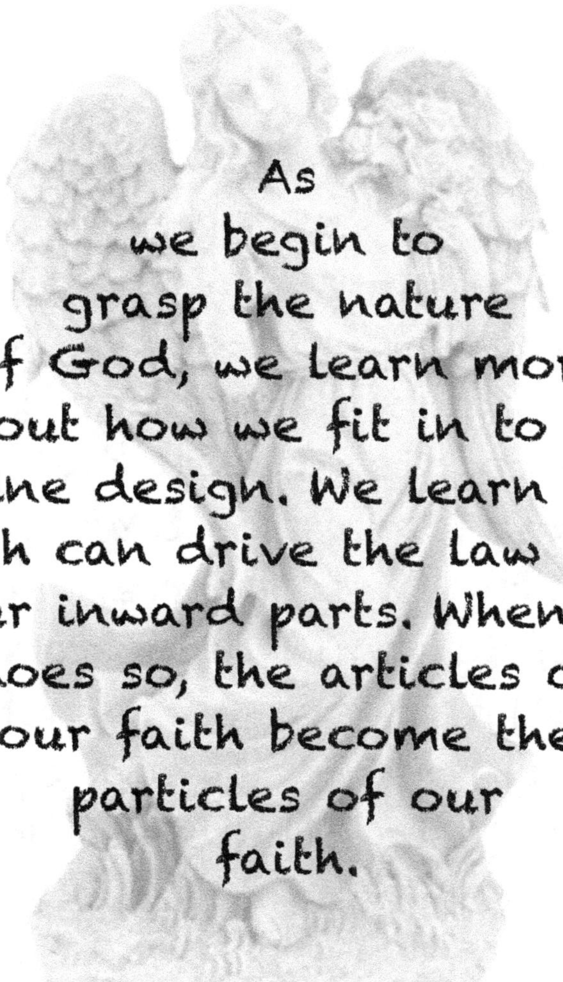

As
we begin to
grasp the nature
of God, we learn more
about how we fit in to His
divine design. We learn how
faith can drive the law into
our inward parts. When it
does so, the articles of
our faith become the
particles of our
faith.

Chapter Five
The faith to build temples unto God.

"Know ye not that ye are the temple of God,
and that the Spirit of God dwelleth in you?"
(1 Corinthians 3:16, see D&C 93:35).

C.S. Lewis suggested that we should imagine ourselves as living houses. "God comes in to rebuild the house. At first, perhaps, you can understand what He is doing. He is getting the drains right and stopping the leaks in the roof and so on. You knew that those jobs needed doing, and so you are not surprised. But presently, He starts knocking the house about in a way that hurts abominably and does not seem to make any sense. What on earth is He up to? The explanation is that He is building quite a different house from the one you thought of - throwing out a new wing here, putting on an extra floor there, running up towers, and making courtyards. You thought you were being made into a decent little cottage: but He is building a palace." ("Mere Christianity"). One might say He is building a temple of God, as the Apostle Paul suggested.

Our Heavenly Father is the quintessential "real estate" investor. He is a Master at taking run-down and worn out resources and transforming them into 5-star all-inclusive properties with a 100% approval as risk-weighted assets. He does this at basically no cost, save an expenditure of the currency of faith. He empowers us to build our own individually crafted temples that, under ideal conditions, are dedicated to His glory. He inspires us, as His subcontractors, with the faith to put our trust in His perfect design. Thus, He becomes the Architect of our destiny, the Author of a Plan that is clothed in principles that independently testify that He "doth not walk in crooked paths, neither doth he turn to the right hand nor to the left, neither doth he vary from that which he hath said, therefore, his paths are straight, and his course is one eternal round." (D&C 3:2).

To bring to pass His work and glory, He has carefully purchased a vast array of real estate holdings throughout the world, and has dedicated them for the building of His temples. (See Moses 1:39). He has a balanced investment portfolio that is always expanding and is constantly increasing in value. It is essentially self-perpetuating within a universe that becomes "a machine for the making of Gods." (Henri Bergson, "Two Sources of Morality and Religion," 1932).

We get a sense of how significantly He is involved in our lives when we consider the relationship capital that He has invested to finance the construction of His temples. These "tools of the trade" are founded in faith, and may be considered against the backdrop of an obscure carpenter shop, in an inconsequential Middle-Eastern back-water village. It was in that setting that Jesus was mentored by Joseph, the Carpenter of Nazareth, who had skilled hands, a caring heart, and a sensitive spirit. The Savior learned to use the tools of Joseph's trade to craft many of the household items that made life in ancient Israel more tolerable. But more importantly, Joseph taught Jesus simple lessons that we can incorporate into our own lives, as we vitalize by faith an assortment of metaphysical tools with which we may build holy temples of God. (See D&C 93:35, Mosiah 2:37, & Alma 7:21).

First, Jesus learned to "measure twice and cut once." With the scarcity of wood in

ancient Israel, He couldn't afford to make costly mistakes. Joseph's example taught the boy that He must know exactly what He was doing and why He was doing it, to proceed carefully, delegate conscientiously, accept responsibility with sobriety, earn trust with diligence, delight in appreciation, and joyfully experience gratitude.

By measuring twice and cutting once, Jesus learned the important life-lesson that persistent priesthood preparation and proper prior planning prevent the propensity for poverty-stricken perceptivity, poorly perceived and pusillanimous performance and the peripheral procurement of only pedestrian proficiency.

Secondly, Jesus learned to "use the right tool for the job," just as we must, if we wish to have the faith to boldly envision ourselves as gods in embryo, and to humbly consecrate our bodies as temples that are dedicated to the glory of God. In His youth, Jesus learned when and how to use chisels, drills, hammers, nails, pegs, glue, and clamps. He learned how much pressure to apply with His adze, in order to shape both soft and hard wood, and how to deal with the bark pockets, bird pecks, burls, knots, rot, shakes, spalting, stains, and other imperfections that He would encounter in the materials with which He was working. He also learned to trust His instincts, and to rely upon the relationship tools of appreciation, benevolence, comfort, concern, empathy, encouragement, forgiveness, friendship, gentleness, humility, kindness, patience, persuasion, sincerity, tolerance, and understanding.

Thirdly, Jesus learned that by taking care of the tools of His trade, they would take care of Him. He learned how to use these tools without abusing them or damaging them, how to coax the best out of them, and how to maintain them so that he could utilize them to contribute to the temporal needs of His growing family. He also learned how to use the spiritual tools of conviction, devotion, fasting, holiness, meditation, prayer, purity, reverence, scripture study, self-control, wisdom, and worship. In short, He learned to use His head and his hands under the watchful eye of Joseph, but He also learned to use His heart in a process of self-discovery, as He plumbed the depths of His capacity for compassion and gauged the scope of His unconditional love.

As His carpentry skills developed, a confidence born of the Spirit spilled over into every other aspect of His life, for those who knew Him testified that "He spake not as other men, neither could He be taught; for He needed not that any man should teach Him." (J.S.T. Matthew 3:25). He mastered the innovative and original utilization of tools relating to priesthood keys, that confirmed what had earlier been spoken through His prophet Isaiah: "My thoughts are not your thoughts, neither are your ways my ways." (Isaiah 55:8). In the process, He nurtured in the armory of His own thoughts the success strategies of strength and peace, and the devices to build bastions of joy. These tools helped Him to become the shaper of condition, the master of environment, the architect of destiny, and the Author of Salvation. (See Hebrews 5:9). He fine-tuned the abilities of adaptive and positive behavior that we must all master if we wish to have the faith to allow our Heavenly Father to transform our earthly tabernacles into holy temples.

The Son of the Carpenter of Nazareth also utilized simple tools that relate to provident living. He knew that "when health is absent, then wisdom cannot reveal itself, culture cannot become manifest, strength cannot fight, and intelligence cannot be applied." (Heraclitus - Philosopher of the Golden Age of Greece). Truly, had the prophet Isaiah declared: "They that wait upon the Lord shall renew their strength, they shall mount up with wings as eagles, they shall run, and not be weary, and they shall walk, and not faint." (Isaiah 40:31). Jesus utilized the tools that nurture the dependent relationship between obedience to the commandments and physical and spiritual well-being, as we must all do, if we wish to have the faith to follow a divine design during the construction of our temples of God.

Jesus uses simple telestial tools with which we are all familiar, to adorn His celestial agenda with seemingly trivial temporal trappings that, nevertheless, resonate with symbolism. He uses the color white as the symbol of purity. We are familiar with white bandages that bind up our wounds, with flags of submission that are white, and with wedding dresses that feature long white trains. Our venerable elders have flowing white manes. When a wound has been cleaned with hydrogen peroxide, the flesh turns white. Because of the Atonement, our sins shall be as white as snow. (See

Isaiah 1:18). The linens used in the burial of the dead are white. The light at the end of the tunnel is a dazzling white. Puffy white clouds that stand out against blue skies herald spring days that are filled with fields of beautiful white daisies. It may be no coincidence that our eyes are calibrated to behold the Milky Way, as

a blaze of white light smeared across the background of the night sky. Healthy teeth are white, and a bright, white smile is the universal language that is our best form of communication. The Lone Ranger and all the good cowboys of yesteryear wore white hats. When Satan tries to disguise his deceptions, he perverts white, which is the symbol of purity, by tricking us with the falsehood of "little white lies."

The Son of the Carpenter of Nazareth did not hesitate to take "that for which all virtue is sold, and almost every vice – almighty gold" and use it as a symbolic tool. (Ben Jonson, "Epistle to Elizabeth, Countess of Rutland"). While the desire for gold can certainly corrupt, the bright, shiny metal that cannot be corroded symbolizes the purity that turns our thoughts to the inestimable worth of the Celestial Kingdom. Gold that has been heated in the crucible of the refiner's fire turns a dazzling white, and when the earth is renewed to achieve its paradisiacal glory, the streets of its cities will be paved with "pure gold, as it were transparent glass." (Revelation 21:21, see Luke 23:43, 2 Corinthians 12:4, Revelation 2:7, 2 Nephi 9:13, Alma 40:12, 4 Nephi 1:14, Moroni 10:34, D&C 77:2, & Article of Faith 10).

The Son of the Carpenter of Nazareth had at His disposal enough tools and to spare to build the incomparable Emerald City of Oz. We pat ourselves on the back when, with telestial tools, we create palatial surroundings fit for kings, but these are poor temporal trappings that provide nothing more than second-class accommodations in lodgings illuminated by a single bare bulb suspended from the ceiling by a frayed cord. Contrast that bleak existence with the experience of entering the prototype of heaven itself, the celestial room in the House of the Lord.

As breathtaking as that chamber is, and as much as it might orient our thoughts to eternity, it was still built with corruptible tools such as hammers, nails, saws, levels, and tape measures. This product of the best efforts of telestial craftsman, the

celestial room, is only a type or a shadow of the heavenly home that beckons to us from afar. This is why, during our sojourn on the earth, we are invited to build our own temples with tools of a more enduring substance: faith and charity, repentance and forgiveness, covenants and obedience, contrition and humility, ordinances and priesthood, and mercy and atonement. It is no coincidence that the covenants we are invited to make in the temple are designed to help us to utilize these imperishable tools in order to transform our earthly tabernacles into holy temples of God. Our promises made with God empower us to move beyond the here-and-now into an otherworldly hereafter that can only be appreciated when we have been spiritually quickened by an endowment of priesthood power.

That benefaction teaches us how to use the spiritual tools provided by the Son of the Carpenter of Nazareth. It has the power to influence our destiny, so that our growth and development may be of generation, and not just of maturation. In the ordinances of the temple, we are born again through a mystical and preternatural transformation that utilizes tools that can scarcely be described. (See 2 Corinthians 5:17). The spiritual dismantling of our earthly clay is traumatic, inasmuch as it is generally accomplished with the figurative equivalents of sledgehammers and crowbars, and the occasional small explosive. The lingering debris kicked up into the air, however, has the unmistakable sparkle of stardust, and through the glitter we discern how the secular can be transformed into the sacred. (See 1 Corinthians 15:42).

The run-down shanty in which we had been living, that has previously been described by C.S. Lewis, is slowly transformed by a celestial craftsman who utilizes Gospel principles that help us visualize the tabernacle that was created to be the eternal dwelling place of our spirits. We realize that Heavenly Father is using tools that run on the inexhaustible power of the priesthood, that have the horsepower of heaven, that draw upon an infinite supply of energy from rechargeable spiritual batteries, and that have been designed to create an environment and an experience for us that will be so much more than just an overnight stay in accommodations that were designed for budget-minded travelers.

The course of our transformation into holy temples of God may involve costly change-orders, but the Savior's objective is to remodel us into spiritual figures that are the embodiment of our "perfect frame." (Alma 40:23). An accounting of cost overruns will be meticulously kept by angels in heaven, but it will be measured only in terms of contrition, and will be swallowed up in humility that relies upon our capacity for repentance, and the blessing of forgiveness through the infinite Atonement of Jesus Christ.

During the construction of our temples, He will gauge our charity by putting the tape measure around our hearts, and not our heads. He will use blueprints that call for the use of tools upon which a monetary value cannot be placed, and that do not rely upon intellectual capacity. His workplace safety standards will far exceed those established by OSHA. The premium for Workman's Compensation Insurance will be affordable to all, paid for with the tool of repentance, and the policy into which is written His sacrifice will have a zero deductible. The Atonement will provide the illimitable benefit of forgiveness with an annuity whose term stretches into the eternities.

During the process, not a hair of our heads will be lost. (See Luke 21:18). Our struggle to establish the faith to build temples of God, to achieve the spiritual equivalent of cardiovascular fitness, will be measured in soul-sweat and the joy of honest labor. Somehow, we will be able to call upon our bodies to produce the spiritual equivalent of more red blood cells. Their greater oxygen carrying capacity will enable us to go the second mile, to receive the tool of independence that neutralizes our insensitivity to our destiny. As we follow the Savior's program of spiritually aerobic fitness, we will run and not be weary, and walk and not faint. We will organize building blocks that become the tangible particles of our faith, and in the process, temples of God will be created, cell by cell, tissue by tissue, organ by organ, and system by system. As our capabilities expand, the transformation will bind the energy of heaven, not to hemoglobin, but to the other-worldly tools of oaths and covenants, and the life-generating promise of ordinances, leading to the confirmation of our faith.

To facilitate our progression, the Son of the Carpenter of Nazareth uses a tool known as The Word of Wisdom. Its principles are as weapons that have been provided to the Saints to combat the particularly persuasive and well-entrenched influences of institutional wickedness in our society. This tool has been given "in consequence of the evil and designs which do and will exist in the hearts of conspiring men in the Last Days." (D&C 89:4). It levels the playing field and neutralizes the opposition that is so necessary to the satisfaction of our mortal experience. The Word of Wisdom enhances our enjoyment of moral agency and allows its exercise to rule without abatement.

The truth be told, we are given some wiggle room relating to our obedience to the law of health, even as we follow pointed and specific instructions that identify the pathway to happiness. But this is the only way that free will may be preserved, "that every man may act in doctrine and principle pertaining to futurity, according to the moral agency which (has been) given unto him, that every man may be accountable for his own sins in the day of judgment." (D&C 101:78).

We should be quite pleased with ourselves, that we are able to use sophisticated tools of the trade that provide Twenty-first Century health care. The 1950s saw medical advances that enabled surgeons to perform open-heart surgical procedures that had been heretofore unthinkable. And yet, coronary artery disease remains one of our daunting challenges. Physicians prescribe a cornucopia of chemo-therapeutics like blood thinners, high blood pressure medications, and statin drugs, but these stop-gap measures are largely ineffective tools that only skirt the real issue, which is the need for a change of heart. As we construct our temples of God, inferior substitutes for the best materials cannot be tolerated.

The world gropes for diagnosis, even as the Gospel of Jesus Christ provides a virtual war chest of therapies for cold, stony, and hard hearts. The Atonement is the tool of choice for reconciliation, of which the Son of the Carpenter of Nazareth has said: "If they harden not their hearts, and stiffen not their necks against me, they shall be converted, and I will heal them." (D&C 112:13).

Over time, cholesterol deposits may build up in our arteries that choke the life-blood from our hearts. Arteriosclerosis can threaten our physical lives. However, when we use Gospel carpentry tools as the antidotes to the spiritual stagnation that clogs the pathways to our eternal well-being, we become pliable clay in the hands of the

Master Potter. The virtue of the massive collection of remedies, collectively known as The Plan of Salvation, is its incredible power to touch our hearts, to change our nature, to soften us, and to humble us. As its principles mold us to become as little children, we become new creatures in Christ, so that when we look in the mirror, we see holy temples. We are blessed with the faith to be perfect in Christ, and to validate His power. We are sanctified in Him by the grace of God, through the shedding of His blood, which is in the covenant of the Father unto the remission of our sins. We are consecrated to become holy and without spot. (See Moroni 10:33).

Many of us work hard to avoid physical obesity, but no matter what our body-type may be, we have an untapped resource in the Savior. If we allow Him to join us in our daily workout routines, He will be our personal trainer. He has many accreditations, but His greatest endorsement is His celestial certification. It was with no small fanfare that His Father introduced Him with the words: "This is my beloved Son; hear him." (Mark 9:7). The Savior encourages us to avoid the sugar-coated temptations that contribute to spiritual flabbiness. We have learned by sad experience that the sticky sweets of sin might taste good, but they pile on the empty calories of corruption. It is very difficult to shed the weight of worldliness.

Indulgence in telestial treats damages the pathways through which faith is developed. Excess distorts our self-esteem, and interferes with our awareness of personal responsibility. Extravagance twists our perception of accountability, and makes it more difficult for us to deal with delayed gratification. Fortunately, the Savior has provided us with the tools we need to combat our persistent obsession with self-absorption. These include not only faith, but also divine nature, individual worth, knowledge, choice and accountability, good works, integrity, and virtue. (See: Young Women Values).

Those who utilize these tools have the faith to stand with Joshua, who long ago demanded of Israel: "Choose ye this day whom ye will serve. ...But as for me and my house, we will serve the Lord." (Joshua 24:15). In other words, for each of us there is a line that has been drawn in the sand. We have been invited to put on our hard hats and cross over that line into the construction zone of Zion, where the Savior actively oversees the work of the creation of our temples of God.

"Aha!" said the cartoon philosopher Pogo, who might have been talking about the reckless, self-centered, and self-destructive behavioral lifestyle tools of those who decline the invitation to join the household of faith. "Here we have someone paying for the sin of excess. The hobnailed boots of indiscretion's marathon dancer tap a rowdy two-step across the terracotta of his consciousness. Gluttony was his master. Reason was cast into the rumble seat of his libidinous juggernaut." With a siren song, the adversary leads the unwary to destruction, where the piper must be paid.

Indulgence in the self-defeating behaviors that neglect the tools of fasting and prayer, the Sabbath day, and tithing, comes at a heavy cost. For every physical regulation relating to our environment, the Son of the Carpenter of Nazareth has provided tools that are their spiritual counterparts. But, at the end of the day, to Him, a tool is a tool; He sees no distinction between the physical and spiritual sides of our nature, and He expects us to reconcile the two, that both might be given equivalent devotion, and that both might be nurtured with equal attention. (See D&C 29:34, & 2 Nephi 2:11).

As we learn to use the tools of the trade to transform our tabernacles of clay into holy temples that have been consecrated to God, we will find "wisdom and great treasures of knowledge." (D&C 89:19). These riches include mighty faith, inexhaustible reserves of spiritual power, invincible testimony, and a reverential appreciation of the artistry, creativity, and imagination of our Heavenly Father. These gifts subtly augment the effort we expend during the undertaking. They permit us to catch a glimpse of how Daniel must have felt in the worldly court of Darius, when he received the tools of "knowledge and skill in all learning and

wisdom," and "understanding in all visions and dreams." (Daniel 1:17).

We live in the midst of Spiritual Babylon, and recoil as we encounter a sprawling wasteland of worldliness that reeks of the rotting stench of sin. But we must not allow our faith to be contaminated by the raw sewage that is unleashed by Satan's servants, who are often thinly disguised as sanitation workers. The tools of the Savior's trade allow us, as celestial-bound souls, to free ourselves from that mire, and to cleanse ourselves in the redeeming blood of the Savior, that we might stand firmly on Gospel sod. Obedience to the principles of The Plan separates us from those who precariously hop about, attempting to balance on the flotsam and jetsam that bob about on the sea of life. Our faith to build temples of God protects us from the fate of those who are "tossed to and fro, and carried about with every wind of doctrine, by the sleight of men, and cunning craftiness." (Ephesians 4:14).

If we wish to have the faith to build temples of God, we must keep our eyes fixed on the prize, and reach out beyond our comfort zone, that we might grasp the golden ring on the carousel of life, because "vice is a monster of such frightful mien, as to be hated needs but to be seen; Yet seen too oft, familiar with her face, we first endure, then pity, then embrace." (Alexander Pope).

In the physical world, we have learned that if we do not ingest enough iron, we will become anemic. The Savior employs metaphysical mechanisms to bind equivalent trace elements to the blood that is coursing through our veins. These protect us from the pitiable condition of spiritual anemia, wherein it is easier to embrace wickedness simply because our natural defense mechanisms have been compromised. If pregnant women are deficient in folic acid, their babies will be at risk of serious spinal cord anomalies. Just so, if we do not consistently include in our diet the folic acid of faith as we build our temples of God, we will suffer spiritual spina bifida. As we subject ourselves to spiritual anencephalia, we will become double-minded. We will be "unstable in all our ways. (See James 1:8). For all practical purposes, a major portion of our brain, that would have otherwise meticulously harmonized all aspects of our physical nature with our spiritual development, will be missing.

We will be unable to lay one brick on the top of another. Our holy temples will remain uncompleted, and stand as a stark testament to our indecisiveness.
If the octane rating of the fuel that fires our faith to build our temples of God is too low, we may be able to just barely get by, but only for a time. As we limp

along with our engines misfiring badly, our fear will ultimately overpower our faith. As anxiety solidifies its icy grip, the fortress of our faith will falter, until it unceremoniously tumbles to the ground. To counter that frightening scenario, the Son of the Carpenter of Nazareth has a patent on the fuel additive of mercy, that is designed to provide needed horsepower to give us a push to the finish line. Think of how He was able to catalyze the performance of Paul, who provided us with an inspiring endorsement that has withstood the test of time: "I have fought a good fight, I have finished my course, I have kept the faith." (2 Timothy 4:7).

In the 1970s, a medical procedure was perfected to remove impurities from the bodies of those suffering from kidney disease. Today, many individuals go to dialysis centers to have contaminants removed from their blood, because their kidneys cannot accomplish the task on their own. The natural man is the spiritual equivalent of those who are in acute renal failure. He "is an enemy to God, and has been from the Fall of Adam, and will be, forever and ever, unless he yields to the enticings of the Holy Spirit … and becometh as a child, submissive, meek, humble, patient, full of love, willing to submit to all things which the Lord seeth fit to inflict upon him, even as a child doth submit to his father." (Mosiah 3:19). We all recognize the natural man as that stubborn individual who will not use the tools that have been providentially provided for him. He strikes out on his own, fashions works of his own hands, and worships false gods of wood and stone. He desperately clings to them in a misguided effort that offers only a caricature of that which could have been his most valuable personal possession; even a temple of God.

The Sacrament has been provided as a tool that removes impurities from our hearts, so that we might generate the faith to build holy accommodations in which our spirits might dwell. "Though your sins be as scarlet," counseled Isaiah, "they shall be

as white as snow; though they be red like crimson, they shall be as wool." (Isaiah 1:18). The Sacrament effectively treats not only bad blood, but also gall, hostility, and rancor. Ward meeting houses become urgent care centers for wounded souls. They provide a haven where the poor in spirit may seek relief, and where they may rest from their labors for a season. The ordinance provides them with transfusions of the spiritual element to keep them going, at least until in a week's time it becomes necessary to repeat the process. When we frequent the Gospel blood-bank at our Sacrament services, we are not only recipients but also donors We are both beneficiaries and benefactors. In that holy setting, we preach, teach, expound, and exhort others, even as we partake of the Sacrament ourselves, in a solemn ritual of renewal. We learn to appreciate the power of the Atonement from the perspective of both the penitent and the priest.

Just as the liver removes toxins from our bodies, in the ordinance of the Sacrament we experience the culmination of a week-long process of renewal. We use the tool of repentance to remove the stain and canker of sin from our souls. Reconciliation through the Atonement "detoxifies" us from the cares and the conditioning influences of the world, and from the unrelenting process of homogenization that occurs as we are assaulted, and sometimes worn down, by the vicissitudes of life.

Epinephrine secreted by the adrenal glands helps us to deal with every-day stress. But those with the faith to build temples of God use the tool of prayer to deal with the anxiety that seems to be a built-in element of mortality. The pituitary has been called the master gland because it secretes hormones that regulate many of the vital functions of our bodies, including our moods. As we draw closer to the Son of the Carpenter of Nazareth, however, we find its spiritual equivalent in the Holy Ghost, Who comforts us and help us to maintain the equilibrium we need in order to stand tall as we muster the faith to persevere in the sometimes painful, and always arduous, process of temple construction.

We give little thought to our autonomic nervous systems that regulate the day-to-day physical activities of our bodies. Likewise, the Light of Christ nurtures our

spirits, but most of us give it equally little attention. But as we study matters out in our own minds preparatory to receiving answers to our prayers, rather than remaining passively apathetic regarding the direction in which our lives are headed, we become actively involved in the two-way mechanism of inquiry. We dust off the tool of agency, and actually use it as it was envisioned. We move beyond the rusted tools of control, coercion, and compulsion, and the broken tools of intimidation and external influence. We engage the bright and shiny precision instruments of friendly persuasion and independence of action. We expand our capabilities, as we exercise the gifts, resources, and reserves providentially provided by the perfect Plan of Salvation.

President Kimball promised: "If there be eyes to see, there will be visions to inspire. If there be ears to hear, there will be revelations to experience. If there be hearts which can understand, know this: that the exalting truths of Christ's Gospel will no longer be hidden and mysterious, and all earnest seekers may know God." (C.R., 10/1966). As we become participants in His ambitious program of temple building, we realize that it includes all of His children, for "He denieth none that come unto him, black and white, bond and free, male and female; and he remembereth the heathen; and all are alike unto God, both Jew and Gentile." (2 Nephi 26:33).

Each of our tabernacles of clay utilizes the 5 physical senses of sight, hearing, smell, taste, and touch. But each of us has a spiritual sixth sense that binds us to eternity, and as we become sensitive to its whisperings, we are rendered holy. The Spirit is like a "Leatherman;" it is the original multi-tool. Lorenzo Snow recalled the cascade of feelings that poured forth following his own baptism as "a tangible immersion in the heavenly principle or element, the Holy Ghost; and even more real and physical in its effects upon every part of (his) system than the immersion by water; dispelling forever, so long as reason and memory last, all possibility of doubt or fear in relation to the fact handed down to us historically, that the Babe of Bethlehem is truly the Son of God." ("Biography and Family Record of Lorenzo Snow," p. 7-9).

Our spiritual sixth sense is a tool that allows us to see beyond the limited horizon

of our sight, to be touched by a vision of the virtue of the word of God. This enables us to savor revealed truth with a discriminating taste that discerns the distinctive flavor of eternal worlds. Our spiritual sixth sense helps us to smell the sweet fragrance of celestial gardens and to hear its harmonic melodies, not just with our noses and our ears, but also with our hearts, as well as with our joints and sinews.

When we walk in the light of life and go out of our way to grasp the principles of truth, we brim over with charity as we find luxurious accommodations in the household of faith. We let virtue garnish our thoughts unceasingly. We cultivate a comfortable, contented, and confident companionship with the Spirit, and the doctrine of the priesthood washes over us as the dews from heaven. We celebrate the way, we exult in the light, and we reverence The Plan as a talisman of truth. Exalting faith has the capacity to become the fundamental element of a tapestry whose intricate design will reveal itself, in all its glory, as an expression of our being. When we attain the full stature of our spirits because our nature has finally conformed to the harmony of heaven, our perfect frames will burst free of the shackles of our mortal clay, as vibrant coats of many colors. Without compulsion or coercion, we will be clothed in the fabric of faith, that we might feel against our skin the safety and security of vestments that protect our holy temples of God. (See D&C 121:45-46).

To keep us in the right way, however, the Son of the Carpenter of Nazareth uses the tool of discomfort. Those who are busily engaged in the construction of their temples view chastisement as their friend, and not as their foe. They understand the practical purposes of pain receptors, and realize that physical discomfort has tangible benefits. For example, diabetics are at a tremendous sensory disadvantage and entertain a real risk of injury because the damaged peripheral nerve endings in their extremities cannot register pain. We need to be able to feel and deal with the growing pains of physical and emotional distress in order to develop empathy for the Savior and His sacrifice. He uses our wounds as portals to allow light to enter our tabernacles of clay, that we might better comprehend the Atonement.

The Son of the Carpenter of Nazareth uses perspiration as a tool to teach us about fortitude. We all experience "soul sweat," but if we can't stand the heat, we are admonished to get out of the kitchen! "I would thou wert hot or cold," said the Savior. (Revelation 3:14). The application of heat is an essential element in the process of purification. It ramps up our metabolism, gets our juices flowing, and reminds us to speedily repent so that we can resume construction as we exercise our faith to build temples of God. In a powerful description of the refiner's fire with which we must all become familiar, Isaiah wrote: "Then flew one of the seraphims unto me, having a live coal in his hand, which he had taken with the tongs from off the altar. And he laid it upon my mouth, and said, Lo, this hath touched thy lips; and thine iniquity is taken away, and thy sin purged." (Isaiah 6:6-7).

The Son of the Carpenter of Nazareth also judiciously uses the tool of friendly persuasion. The word "beseech" is used in the scriptures 118 times, and 65 times in the New Testament alone. When working with homeowners who didn't have a clear vision of what accessories they wanted, or needed, to transform their houses into homes, Joseph had to be an armchair psychologist as well as a carpenter. He had a lot more experience than his neighbors when it came to crafting fine furnishings, and his suggestions were based not only on their perceived needs, but also on what would actually be the best fit for them, given their circumstances. Joseph was a good example to Jesus, Who was being groomed to become a motivational speaker without equal. History confirms that He developed enough charisma to change the world, one Galilean at a time, utilizing the tools He had learned to employ in Joseph's shop.

With the daunting challenge laid on our doorstep to follow in His footsteps, we soberly remember that the Son of the Carpenter of Nazareth uses the tool of fatigue. Joseph had deadlines to meet, and customers who had unreasonable expectations, but his work ethic kept him in his shop no matter what, until their demands had been addressed and their orders successfully completed. We never read in the scriptures about their dissatisfaction, or about careless or shoddy workmanship on his part. Joseph never succumbed to expediency, or used inferior materials to cut costs. He never got a negative review on Angie's List. Jesus learned from Joseph what

it feels like to experience the rush of endorphins when we have pushed ourselves to perfection, which often means that we persevere to the point that we feel that we have no more to give. It is at that moment of utter exhaustion that we must yield to powers that are greater than ourselves, if we are to survive.

In his abridgment of the Large Plates of Nephi, Mormon observed that the people prospered when "they did fast and pray oft, and did wax stronger and stronger in their humility, and firmer and firmer in the faith of Christ, unto the filling their souls with joy and consolation, yea, even to the purifying and the sanctification of their hearts, which sanctification cometh because of their yielding their hearts unto God." (Helaman 3:35).

Just when we think we have done enough, and that we can rest on our laurels, we read the Savior's admonition: "Whosoever shall compel thee to go a mile, go with him twain." (Matthew 5:41). We realize that He took His temporal and spiritual responsibilities to another level. The tool of fatigue can teach us a lot about ourselves, and about who we really are, especially when the angels in heaven are holding their breath in hopeful anticipation, everything is on the line, and all eternity hangs in the balance.

Then, like the proverbial footprints in the sand, when we have utterly exhausted our own resources, when there is no-one else to whom we may turn, the Savior will step in and carry our burdens for us. As the weight is lifted from our shoulders, we realize that He is in a league all His own, and that He has descended below any sacrifice we could ever make. (See D&C 122:8). Born into humble circumstances without a silver spoon in His mouth, His empathy and His compassion speak volumes to those who would hope to engage the faith to build temples of God.

The Son of the Carpenter of Nazareth uses the tool of testimony. All of us have been faced with times when withdrawals from our spiritual bank accounts have needed to be made. If we are fortunate, we have beforehand faithfully and consistently made deposits, in order to be prepared for these inevitable moments of need. We are blessed with a cushion of confidence and with a cornucopia of comfort that flow

from our own courage and commitment, as well as from the condescension and compassion of our Creator. The powerful financial tool of testimony provides overdraft protection as we invest in the theater of life. Testimony stands as a guardian, as a personal asset manager, to make sure we are not writing checks along the way that cannot later be cashed by our creditors, when our debts become due. As we persevere in the faith to build temples unto God, our spiritual credit rating score will soar to a perfect 850.

The Lord's people have always been identified by their zeal toward the building of temples. At the conclusion of General Conference in April, 1998, President Gordon B. Hinckley memorably announced the construction by the Church of its 100th temple. He said: "This will make a total of 47 new temples in addition to the 51 now in operation. I think we had better add 2 more to make it an even 100 by the end of this century."

Interestingly, in D&C 88, received in December 1832 and January 1833, the Lord commanded the Saints to organize themselves, and to prepare every needful thing; to establish a house of prayer, of fasting, of faith, of learning, of glory, of order, and of God. When we read this scripture, most of us visualize the House of the Lord, which is today a prominent architectural feature and spiritual symbol of the Church. But, in light of 1 Corinthians 3:16 cited at the beginning of this chapter, these passages may equally apply to our own efforts to generate the faith to build temples of God that are composed, not of brick and mortar, of our own flesh, bones, and sinews.

Think of this scripture that ostensibly speaks of the physical temple, but that might have another hidden metaphysical layer of meaning: "If (either the temple or the body) be defiled, I will not come into it, and my glory shall not be there; for I will not come into unholy temples." (D&C 97:17). Other scripture speaks of the rituals we perform with our physical bodies for the glory and honor of God. These "are ordained by the ordinance of my holy house, which my people are always commanded to build unto my holy name." (D&C 124:39). Do we not consecrate ourselves, our time, our talents, and everything with which the Lord has blessed us, or with which He

may bless us, to the building of the kingdom? We figuratively prostrate ourselves upon the altar of faith, and yield our hearts to Him "Who hath also sealed us, and given the earnest of the Spirit in our hearts." (2 Corinthians 1:22). We are at-one with our Creator when we are in His image and likeness; when the tabernacles of our spirits are holy and without spot. (See Moroni 10:33).

When, in General Conference, we hear the announcement of new temples in far-off lands like American Samoa, Cambodia, Nigeria, Peru, Portugal, South Africa, and Tonga, to name just a few, we envision their locations on prominent hills or in beautiful garden settings. But should we not also think of the Saints living in those lands who have made their construction possible because of their faith to conduct their lives in accordance with His holy will, and because of their dedication to pattern their lives after the example of the Son of God? Surely, when we no longer see our obedience as inconvenient, then will God reveal His power.

These faithful Saints receive no economic stipend or annuity associated with participation in The Plan of Salvation, but they are provided with the tools of the trade, that by the sweat of their brow they might earn enough money to secure their own accommodations, pay their bills on time, and occasionally indulge themselves with some of the finer things of life. And always before them stands the prototypical example of the temple, after which they are invited to pattern their lives.

No matter what our temporal circumstances might be, The Plan anticipates that eventually we'll return Home to live with our heavenly Parents under one roof in celestial accommodations, as we did at first. One day, we may show up at Their doorstep with nothing but the clothes on our backs and our testimonies in our hearts. Our faith to build temples of God notwithstanding, we may find ourselves in the same condition as the Navy combat pilot who barely made it back to his ship. As the story goes, this World War II aviator had left the security of his aircraft carrier to undertake a dangerous mission over hostile waters. True to the predictions of his superior officers, he endured bad weather, flack from enemy anti-aircraft fire, and he engaged in lethal dogfights with adversaries whose sole purpose was to kill him.

His craft was hit numerous times by machine gun fire that riddled his fuselage, and by shrapnel that tore away parts of his wings. His Plexiglas canopy was shattered, and he could hardly see through blood-splattered goggles to navigate back to his vessel and shipmates.

In the midst of a developing typhoon, as he approached the lurching deck of the carrier, his controls were nearly useless, his descent was too steep, and his roll, pitch, and yaw were all wrong. He was frantically waved off by the crewman on deck who was guiding him in, but he figured he had only one chance, and he would take it. With a sickening thump, as he pancaked his aircraft on the deck, its fuel tank burst into flame, and the tail hook failed to engage the cables that jerked him to a halt. He careened into the safety net at the far end of the flight deck, and what was left of his plane crumpled into twisted metal.

A rescue crew in asbestos suits rushed to his aid, smothered the wreckage in fire-retardant foam, clamored up to the cockpit, unsnapped his safety harness, grabbed him by the shoulders, yanked him out of the plane, and dragged him to safety. Doctors and nurses attended to his wounds even before he arrived at sickbay. Due to their skill and attention, as well as to his unconquerable spirit, he made a remarkable and full recovery. For his heroism and gallantry during action, he was awarded the Distinguished Flying Cross, and given thirty days' leave for rest and recuperation. This may presage how many of us will return from our mortal missions to the presence of our Father. God-speed to us all. (Paraphrased from an address given by Boyd K. Packer).

To be sure, one day we will leave the combat zone of mortality, and awaken in eternity, caressed by satin sheets, and serenaded by the sound of angels sweetly singing songs of redeeming love. We'll surely hear our Father's voice, as well, reassuring us that our trials and tribulations broadened our experience and were for our good. (See D&C 122:7). We will all be together again, busily re-engaged in the family business, utilizing the tools of the trade that have become familiar to us all, that have stood the test of time, and that transformed our lives by energizing the faith to build eternally enduring holy temples that testify of the glory of God.

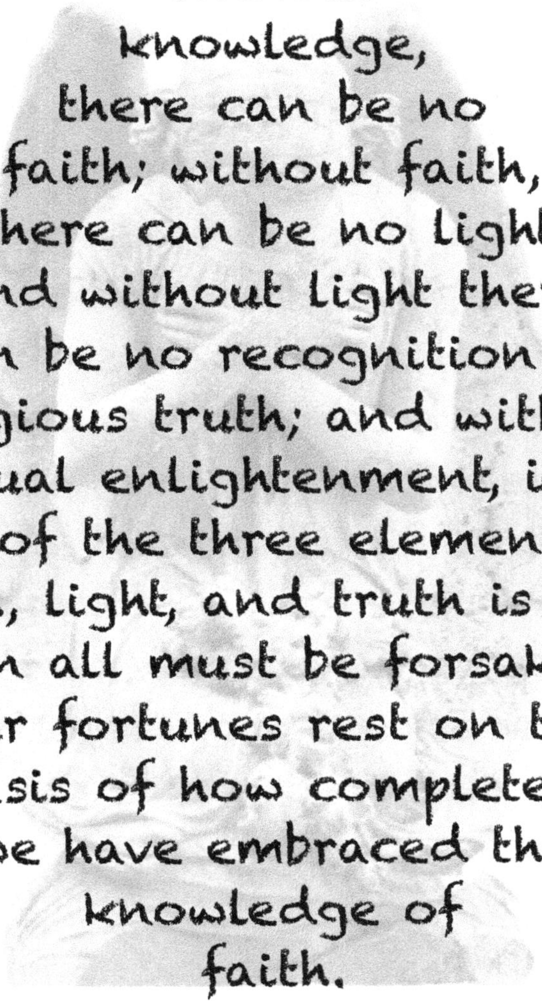

Without knowledge, there can be no faith; without faith, there can be no light, and without light there can be no recognition of religious truth; and without spiritual enlightenment, if just one of the three elements of faith, light, and truth is lost, then all must be forsaken. Our fortunes rest on the basis of how completely we have embraced the knowledge of faith.

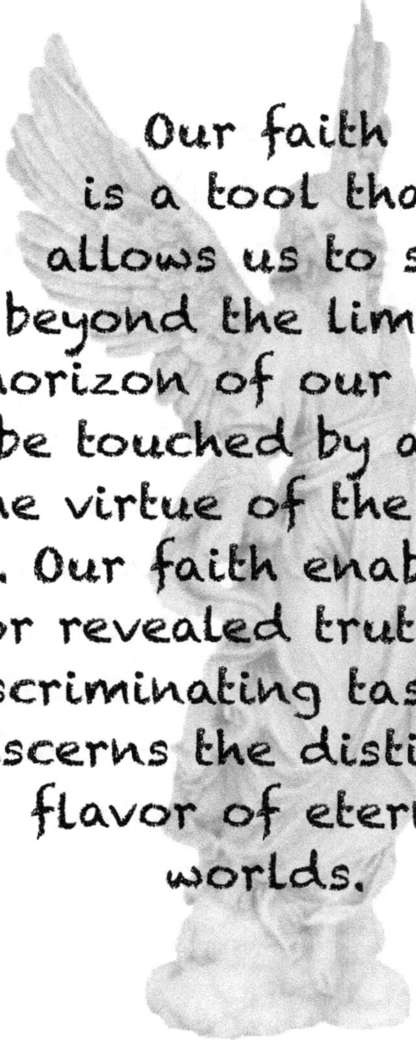

Our faith
is a tool that
allows us to see
beyond the limited
horizon of our sight,
to be touched by a vision
of the virtue of the word of
God. Our faith enables us to
savor revealed truth with a
discriminating taste that
discerns the distinctive
flavor of eternal
worlds.

Chapter Six
The germination of faith.

"Verily I say unto you, If ye have faith as a grain of mustard
seed, ye shall say unto this mountain, Remove hence
to yonder place; and it shall remove; and
nothing shall be impossible unto you."
(Matthew 17:20).

Garden seeds are good illustrations of our potential for salvation. At first glance, they may appear to be "lifeless," but all they typically need to sprout is sunlight, fertile soil, and water. If we want to germinate the god in embryo within us, we similarly need: 1) the light of the Gospel, 2) the loam of faith within which grows testimony, and 3) the living water that leads to conversion.

Gospel doctrine is quickened by ordinances that bring "life and immortality to light." (2 Timothy 1:10). Fertile soil recalls the symbolism utilized by Ezekiel, who spoke in a parable about a great vine that, in the Last Days that would be "planted in a good soil by great waters, that it might bring forth branches, and that it might

67

bear fruit." (Ezekiel 17:8). Living water is reminiscent of the gift offered by the Savior to the Samaritan woman by the well. (See John 4:7-14).

Without these essential elements, Gospel seeds cannot properly germinate. The example of kernels of grain discovered in an Egyptian Pharaoh's tomb helps to illustrate why this is so. Today, we know that most seeds will remain viable for only a few years, and anything over 50 to 100 years is quite remarkable. The reason is, of course, that during this time the seed is using up its food supply, albeit very slowly.

In Nineteenth Century Egypt, however, a mummy was discovered that had in its grasp a small bag of wheat. When the kernels were brought back to England, the 1843 edition of "The Gardeners' Chronicle" gushed: "Some of its grains have been sown, and they vegetated! What remains is to be sold in packets of 10 grains each at £1 per packet." That's $86.00 in today's currency. One bushel of wheat contains around a million kernels. At $8.60 per grain, $8.6 million would not have been a bad haul. I'm sure the Victorian entrepreneurs were disappointed that the mummy was only holding one bag, and not a bushel, of wheat! In any event, the public was infatuated with the notion that "mummy wheat," grain discovered in the tombs of kings, would spring to life after thousands of years.

From the start, however, botanists dismissed the claims of "The Gardeners' Chronicle" as romantic nonsense. Yet, the belief in the astonishing powers of ancient seeds persists. For 175 years, the media has reported regularly about the amazing regenerative powers of "mummy wheat" - grain that is up to 6000 years old - that is periodically discovered in desert tombs.

But, alas, just as the kernels of wheat from the Valley of Kings were destined to whither and die without the sustaining influence of light, water, and fertile soil, so our divine potential cannot germinate without the influences of the Gospel, active faith, and the teachings and example of Jesus Christ.

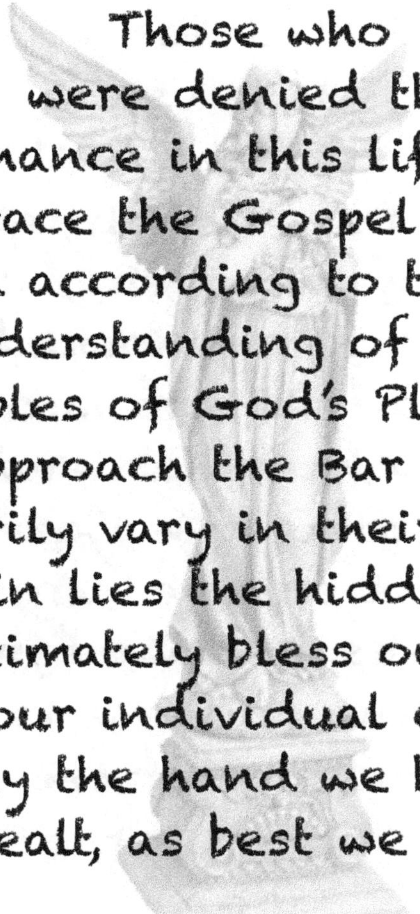

Those who
were denied the
chance in this life to
embrace the Gospel will be
judged according to their more
limited understanding of the doctrines
and principles of God's Plan. Therefore,
when they approach the Bar of Justice, they
will necessarily vary in their accountability
to law. Therein lies the hidden power of the
Gospel to ultimately bless our lives, without
regard to our individual circumstances
We play the hand we have been
dealt, as best we can.

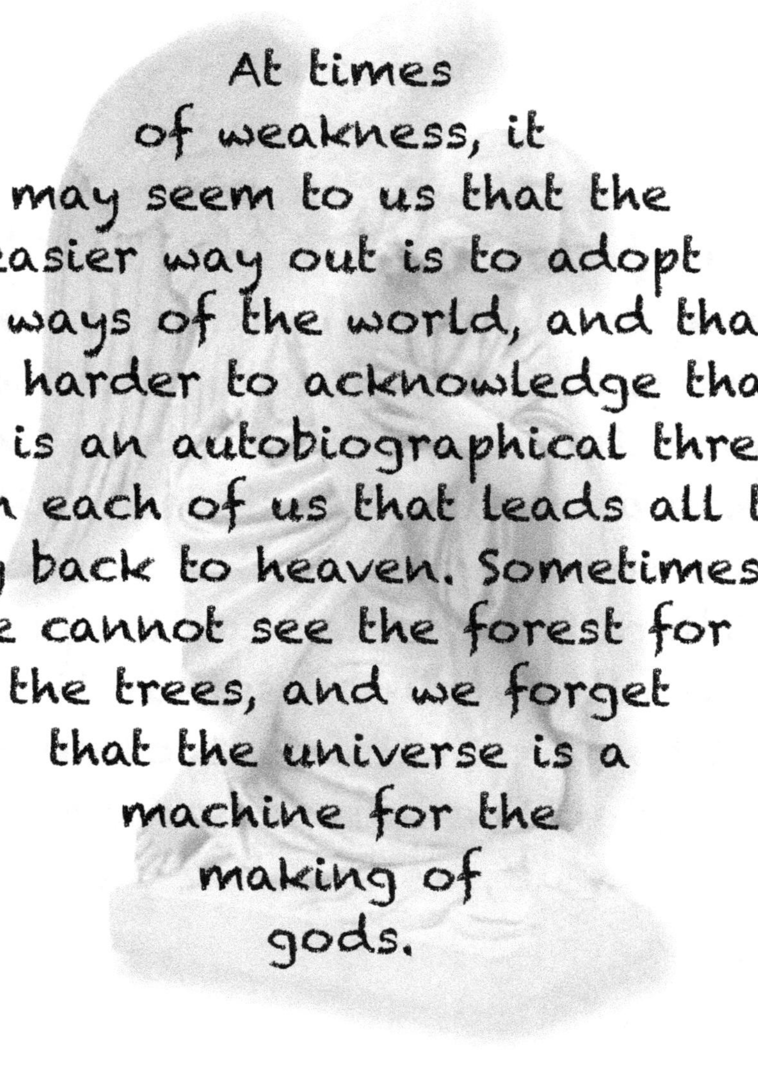

At times
of weakness, it
may seem to us that the
easier way out is to adopt
the ways of the world, and that
it is harder to acknowledge that
there is an autobiographical thread
within each of us that leads all the
way back to heaven. Sometimes,
we cannot see the forest for
the trees, and we forget
that the universe is a
machine for the
making of
gods.

Chapter Seven
The foundation of faith.

"And now I, Moroni, write
a few of the words of my father
Mormon, which he spake concerning
faith, hope, and charity."
(Moroni 7:1).

God bestows his Spirit upon us that we might exercise foundation faith in His Son Jesus Christ. With this gift, we may become His sons and daughters by seeking after everything that is virtuous, lovely, or of good report, or praiseworthy. As we do so, our Advocate before the Father exercises His power through the Atonement to be the means of our salvation and exaltation.

He builds our faith in many ways. Angels, who are His servants, are often commissioned

to the work. "And the office of their ministry is to call men unto repentance, and to fulfil and to do the work of the covenants of the Father, which he hath made unto the children of men, to prepare the way among the children of men, by declaring the word of Christ unto the chosen vessels of the Lord, that they may bear testimony of him." (Moroni 7:31).

The Lord told Joseph Smith: "To some it is given by the Holy Ghost to know that Jesus Christ is the Son of God, and that he was crucified for the sins of the world. To others, it is given to believe on their words, that they also might have eternal life if they continue faithful." (D&C 46:13-14). And by doing so, the Lord God prepareth the way that the residue of men may have faith in Christ, that the Holy Ghost may have place in their hearts." (Moroni 7:32).

The Twelve Apostles and other General Authorities of the Church bear their witness of the truth, that faith might increase in the hearts of all those who hear them. Hence, the following sampling, as I have listened over the years to the General Authorities of the Church: "I know Him. I testify that He is real. I testify as a witness." (Elder Enzio Busche). "I know that God lives, for as in the words of my predecessor, John Taylor, I have seen Him." (President Spencer W. Kimball). "I know of the divinity of the Lord Jesus Christ, for it has been revealed to me in a most interesting, complete, and beautiful way. And so, I leave you with that special witness which is mine to bear, for I have witnessed it with my own eyes, and heard it with my own ears." (L. Tom Perry). "In a coming day I shall feel the nail marks in his hands and in his feet and shall wet his feet with my tears. But I shall not know any better then than I know now that he is God's Almighty Son, that he is our Savior and Redeemer, and that salvation comes in and through his atoning blood and in no other way." (Bruce R. McConkie).

As the white-hot spark of faith, struck off the Divine Anvil of God, ignites our flame of resolve, we develop the "power to do whatsoever thing is expedient" or right to do under the circumstances. (Moroni 7:33). That thing is to "repent and be baptized ... in the name of Jesus Christ for the remission of sins, and ...

receive the Holy Ghost." (Acts 2:38). This is "the fruits of faith," which is to be saved in the Celestial Kingdom of God. (See Galatians 5:22). It is the very reason for the ministry of Jesus Christ and His servants among the children of men.

Christ will continue His ministry and work miracles as "long as time shall last, or the earth shall stand," or there shall be any of Heavenly Father's sons and daughters upon the face thereof to be saved. (Moroni 7:36). But when we are mesmerized by magic, spell-bound by sorcery, or wooed by witchcraft, or when we are caught up in conceptual cul-de-sacs, transfixed by telestial trivia, or preoccupied with the worship of idols of wood and stone, we lack the foundation of faith. Then, Satan gains the advantage, and the capacity of the Spirit to influence us wanes.

When the gifts of the Spirit are absent, "then has faith ceased also; and awful is the state of man, for they are as though there had been no redemption made." (Moroni 7:38). If we have procrastinated the day of our repentance, or have waited to develop saving faith until we have become spiritually blinded to the Light of Christ, we become subjected to the spirit of the devil. When he captures our hearts, they are mutated to become stony and cold, and we lose the capacity to distinguish good from evil and light from darkness. If we trade the sunshine that is generated by the foundation of faith for the wintry weather of worldliness, the Spirit of the Lord will withdraw to warmer climes, allowing Satan's icy breath to be sucked into the vortex.

This is the state of the wicked, from which there may be no recovery. For those who refuse to repent, it will be as if there had been no redemption made. Mormon hoped that we would rise to the occasion, when he wrote: "My beloved brethren, I judge better things of you, for I judge that ye have faith in Christ because of your meekness." (Moroni 7:39). He was like Tevya, in The Fiddler on The Roof, who told his daughters: "In Anatevka, God knows who you are, and what you may become."

Mormon's believed that his people were capable of choosing the better part, as long as they retained a hope in Christ. For "how is it," he asked, "that ye can attain unto faith, save ye shall have hope?" (Moroni 7:40). Later, Moroni would echo the same

optimistic sentiment, declaring: "Wherefore, there must be faith; and if there must be faith, there must also be hope." (Moroni 10:20).
Because there is opposition in all things, even as there is faith, so must there be its worldly counterpart. In our day, the grip of fear paralyzes many of God's children.

Today, more than ever, we need a hope in Christ. We need the assurance of peace, that our lives are headed in the right direction, and that the Atonement is real. As Mormon said, hope is born of faith. "Behold, I say unto you that ye shall have hope through the Atonement of Christ and the power of his resurrection, to be raised up unto life eternal, and this because of your faith in him according to the promise." (Moroni 7:41).

Our hope is not misguided trust in a wildly improbable promise, nor is it a high stakes gamble on a statistical long-shot. It is the inevitable result of well-founded faith, when we are meek and lowly of heart, and are in control of our desires and emotions; when our appetites and behavior lie within the bounds established by the Lord.

The supreme characteristic of faithful disciples is charity, that is built upon the foundation of faith and hope. Mormon taught that if we are "meek and lowly in heart, and confess by the power of the Holy Ghost that Jesus is the Christ," with a sure hope born of faith, we "must needs have charity." (Moroni 7:44).

"Charity suffereth long." It teaches us to view the challenges of life from God's perspective. It "is kind," or characterized by sensitivity toward others, and it is empathic, "and envieth not." It is less concerned with telestial trinkets and more focused on celestial sureties, "and is not puffed up," but is humble, and "seeketh not her own." It is selfless, and "is not easily provoked," but reflects poise under provocation, and "thinketh no evil." It has no secret agenda to follow, "and rejoiceth not in iniquity," but is repulsed by sin. It "rejoiceth in the truth," is spiritually quickened by the resonant realities of well-founded faith, and "beareth all things," and "believeth all things," because it is naturally drawn to truth and to light. Charity "hopeth all things, endureth all things," and is continually open to that

which is good. (Moroni 7:45).

If we lack these qualities, we cannot progress, either in time or in eternity. "If (we) have not charity, (we) are nothing, for charity never faileth. Wherefore, (we must) cleave unto charity, which is the greatest of all (the spiritual gifts), for all things must fail (without it)." (Moroni 7:46). "Charity is the pure love of Christ, and it endureth forever, and whoso is found possessed of it at the last day, it shall be well with him." (Moroni 7:47). Charity motivates us to Christian service, which prepares us to feel comfortable in the presence of God. It is bestowed upon the faithful by His grace. Charity is the catalyst that speeds up the reaction between faith and hope, that our foundation might be "firm and steadfast, and immovable," as it is cast in the concrete of true conversion. (1 Nephi 2:10).

"Wherefore," urged Mormon, with the foundation of faith, we must "pray unto the Father with all the energy of heart, that (we) may be filled with this love, which he hath bestowed upon all who are true followers of his Son, Jesus Christ; that (we) may become the sons of God; that when he shall appear we shall be like him, for we shall see him as he is; that we may have this hope; that we may be purified even as he is pure." (Moroni 7:48).

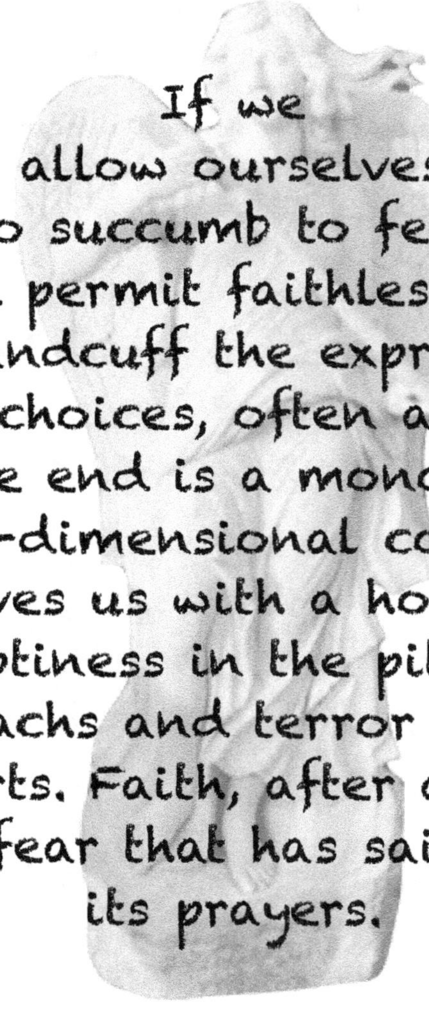

If we
allow ourselves
to succumb to fear,
and permit faithlessness
to handcuff the expression
of our choices, often all that is
left in the end is a monochromatic
and one-dimensional compromise
that leaves us with a hollow core
of emptiness in the pit of our
stomachs and terror in our
hearts. Faith, after all, is
fear that has said
its prayers.

Chapter Eight
The faith to change our hearts.

"And now, because of the covenant which ye have made ye shall
be called the children of Christ, his sons, and his daughters;
for behold, this day he hath spiritually begotten you; for
ye say that your hearts are changed through faith on
his name; therefore, ye are born of him."
(Mosiah 5:7).

For whatever reason, it is the heart, and not the head, that is the repository of feeling. We have all felt the anguish of heartache, whose pain is quantitatively and qualitatively different from a migraine headache. At special moments in our lives, our hearts leap for joy, but curiously, we never describe these experiences as if our heads were exploding with happiness. Our hearts race with excitement, even as our heads spin with dizziness. A particularly handsome young man may be described as a heart-throb, but rarely as a head-case. Conversely, when a guy has a crush on

a girl, it is his heart, and not his head, that feels the pressure. Kindred spirits are closer to our hearts than to our heads.

Instinct draws a baby close to its mother's nurturing breast, and little ones are comforted by the steady beat of momma's heart. The weak and timid, who are faint of heart, respond to the sweet influence of the Spirit better than to the analytical power of the rational mind. When we are broken-hearted, we are receptive to the teachable things of the kingdom, which is a far cry from the terrifying confusion of a mind that is out of synch with reality, or that tragically lacks clarity because of a dim wit. A racing heart may be calmed by a strong will, but when a storm breaks loose in the head there may be no easy remedy for the ensuing nervous exhaustion or mental breakdown that follows. When Heavenly Father measures our charity, He puts the tape around our hearts, and not our heads.

Those who listen to their hearts are caring, compassionate, considerate, empathetic, intuitive, and sensitive. When it is only our heads that influence us, we are too often callous; we are cold, harsh, pitiless, unfeeling, and even heartless. When we begin to lose our minds, others may first charitably characterize us as eccentric, and only later harshly describe us as demented. But when our hearts have been worn out in service, our weariness is related to joy. When we think of saints, we recall the capacity of their hearts, but when we think of sinners, we often remember only the numerical value of their brain power.

A pounding or racing heart may be the first sign of unbridled excitement. But unregulated stimulation of the brain is more commonly manifested as a grand mal seizure accompanied by foaming at the mouth. Endurance athletes may have enlarged hearts due to repetitive workouts involving vigorous aerobic exercise, while over-stressed business executives may have heads that are dangerously enlarged due to misguided perceptions of self-worth, and that are puffed up in pride.

It is far better to have a troubled heart that leads us to repentance and reformed behavior, than it is to have a disturbed mind that can only be managed with anti-

psychotic medication in a lock-down ward. Those with wounded or broken hearts may heal slowly, but their prognosis is far better than those whose brain injuries leave them in a persistent vegetative state. Although our hearts may burst with the pride of accomplishment, well-deserved achievement is easier to deal with than is the big head of one who is all wrapped up in himself. Those of us who have had our hearts stolen may be lucky enough to find our way back to happiness, but those who have lost their minds through physical or emotional trauma, disease, inappropriate use of chemo-therapeutics, or manipulation by others, are left with the irreversibility of a hollow core of existence from which there may be no easy avenue of escape.

When we are light-hearted, we don't have a care in the world; but when we are light-headed, we feel only dizziness and disorientation. With heart-felt sorrow, we experience empathy and compassion that defy definition and cannot be explained by the rational mind. Some emotions easily touch our hearts in ways that could never penetrate the rough exterior of our thick skulls. If our hearts are like flint, it is because they have become calcified through neglectful inattention and disuse. However, sometimes people are heartless simply because they are brainless.

We may have a forgiving heart that is pliable and elastic, but if we are soft in the head, it is because our minds have turned to mush because our hippocampus is no longer cranking out fresh neurons. A pounding heart may presage the excitement that accompanies new opportunities, but a throbbing headache is often the first symptom of poorly managed stress. A caring heart implies nurture, but a heart that is as cold as a lump of coal supposes neglect. A warm embrace draws people together, and in close proximity, hearts can be knit together in love. A sorrowful heart can also be a strong heart when it is sustained by the Spirit.

We must never be like the man of whom it was said: "If I ever need a heart transplant, I hope I get his. He obviously never used it." John Huntsman Sr. kept this sign on his desk: "No exercise is better for the human heart than reaching down and lifting another up."

Our hearts contract, on average, 80 times per minute, 4,800 times per hour, and 115,200 times per day. Over the course of a year, they beat over 42 million times. In 70 years, that's almost 3 billion beats. An adult heart pumps up to 2,000 gallons of blood daily, about 730,000 gallons per year, or over 51,000,000 gallons in 70 years, through around 100,000 miles of vessels in a circulatory system that brings nourishment to the 37.2 trillion cells that make up our bodies.

The ancients, who knew little about the anatomy or physiology of the circulatory system, nevertheless mentioned the heart almost 1,500 times in the scriptures. Many, if not all, of the prophets have used the heart as a metaphor for the seat of our deepest emotions. For example, Joseph Smith described his revelatory experience when reading in the New Testament's Book of James: "Never did any passage of scripture come with more power to the heart of man than this did at this time to mine," he wrote. "It seemed to enter with great force into every feeling of my heart." (Joseph Smith History 1:12).

The book of Proverbs is a rich source of references to the heart, as in: "Apply thine heart to understanding." (Proverbs 2:2). Or: "Let thine heart keep my commandments." (Proverbs 3:1). Or: "Trust in the Lord with all thine heart." (Proverbs 3:5). Or: "Write (the law) upon the table of thine heart." (Proverbs 7:3). Or: "Be ye of an understanding heart." (Proverbs 8:5). Or: "A sound heart is the life of the flesh." (Proverbs 14:30). Or: "A merry heart maketh a cheerful countenance: but by sorrow of the heart, the spirit is broken." (Proverbs 15:13).

Or: "The heart of him that hath understanding seeketh knowledge." (Proverbs 15:14). Or: "The light of the eyes rejoiceth the heart." (Proverbs 15:30). Or: "The heart of the wise teacheth his mouth, and addeth learning to his lips." (Proverbs 16:23). Or: "A merry heart doeth good like a medicine." (Proverbs 17:22). Or: "Apply thine heart unto instruction." (Proverbs 23:12). The Saints of all ages have understood the feelings of the people of Zarahemla, who exclaimed to their prophet Benjamin: "We believe all the words which thou hast spoken unto us; and also, we know of their surety and truth, because of the Spirit of the Lord Omnipotent, which has wrought

a mighty change in us, or in our hearts, that we have no more disposition to do evil, but to do good continually." (Mosiah 5:2).

Alma asked his brethren of the Church: "Have ye spiritually been born of God?

Have ye received his image in your countenances? Have ye experienced this mighty change in your hearts?" (Alma 5:14). Then, by extension, he reached out across the ages to ask each of us: "And now behold, I say unto you, my brethren, if ye have experienced a change of heart, and if ye have felt to sing the song of redeeming love, I would ask, can ye feel so now?" (Alma 5:26).

Sometimes, in the physical world, our hearts begin to falter. They may skip a beat or two. We may suffer from arrhythmia (an abnormal heart rhythm), tachycardia (an abnormally rapid heart rate), or bradycardia (an abnormally slow heart rate). We may experience angina (chest pain that is related to insufficient oxygenated blood reaching the heart muscle). When we experience any of the symptoms of heart disease, we are quick to initiate protocols designed to restore normal function. We make dietary changes, join a gym to engage in regular exercise, habitually take the stairs instead of the elevator, and modify other patterns of behavior. We read everything we can about the subject, and follow the counsel of experts in the fields of medicine, physical therapy, and biofeedback. We seek inspiration from lifestyle coaches and self-help gurus. We learn to monitor our cardiovascular health, and we establish benchmarks to more easily gauge our progress toward the achievement of our heart-healthy goals. To reach a sustainable level of fitness, we eschew lifestyle choices that would compromise our gains.

Although we have been told to "lift up (our) hearts and be glad," (D&C 29:5), scripture teaches us that in the Last Days, it is the heart that will bear the brunt of the consequences of wickedness. Amid signs in the sun, in the moon, in the stars, and upon the earth, all things shall be in commotion, and men's hearts will fail them for fear. (See Luke 21:24-26 & D&C 88:91).

These scriptures, and others, suggest that opposition presupposes both physical

and spiritual assaults on the integrity of our hearts. On the one hand, significant cardiovascular disease may require medicine such as digitalis to strengthen a weakened heart. A pacemaker may be necessary to restore proper rhythm. In extreme cases, cardiomyopathy may necessitate a heart transplant in order to prolong life.

Those who have had a physical heart transplant find it necessary to take a cocktail consisting of immuno-suppressant medication, according to a strict regimen, for the rest of their lives. The same prescriptions must be taken, in specific doses, at the same time every day. The routine must be followed without variation, in order to minimize the risk of failure of the surgical procedure. All doctor's appointments must be kept, every recommended laboratory test must be performed with exactness, medication side effects must be carefully monitored, and drug interactions and the signs and symptoms of organ rejection must be recognized and addressed.

Those who have forsaken the world and have faithfully embraced the lifestyle of Saints experience nothing short of a spiritual heart transplant. The same anti-rejection protocols must be followed after we have spiritually been given new hearts and have been born again. As the prophet Ezekiel declared: "A new heart also will I give you, and a new spirit will I put within you: and I will take away the stony heart out of your flesh." (Ezekiel 36:26).

But if we are not vigilant, our new hearts will surely fail us. We need to take immuno-suppressant medication in the form of prayer, service, and temple attendance. We need to follow a strict regimen of regular spiritually aerobic church activity. We need to be diligent with the therapy provided by the ordinances of the Gospel, including the bread and water that is offered on a weekly basis during our ward Sacrament services.

We must be diligent to maintain a schedule of regular accountability interviews with our spiritual physicians, and, in particular, to welcome the house calls that take the

form of visits from our priesthood leaders and other who minister to our needs. We must be diligent in our repentance, and learn to self-monitor the spiritual promptings that comfort us when Heavenly Father has forgiven our sins.

If we sense that our organ transplant has begun to fail, or if we feel that it is being rejected because of the subtle effects of carnality, sensuality, or devilish lifestyle choices, we must know to Whom we may turn for triage, and for guidance and direction, so that these destructive influences might be decisively eliminated. We must know how to call upon higher powers to restore our spiritual heart-health, that we might once again feel to sing the song of redeeming love without experiencing a shortness of breath when we come to the most challenging refrains.

We must strengthen our heart transplants by putting our shoulders to the wheel and pushing along at a steady pace without overdoing it. Cycling through the scriptures in Sunday School class may seem repetitive, but it is one of God's favorite spin classes. It is no more pedestrian than is a spectacular sunset, no more dreary than a rainbow after a storm, and no more uninteresting than a flight of migratory geese passing overhead on a cold autumn evening. It may seem daunting to come, and follow the Savior, as we wend our way through our devotions, but doing so establishes habit patterns that can propel us over the summit of even the most challenging passes that loom as obstacles to our progression.

In fact, sooner or later, there is for each of us who has had a spiritual heart transplant a moment in the sun, when the light of understanding illuminates our mind and confirms the divine potential of the new organ beating steadily in our chest. As the morning breaks over the eastern sky and heralds another day, once again the self-evident truth is confirmed: We have been born again and our hearts are changed through faith on His name.

The challenge before us has been met. As we have given ourselves completely to the Lord, we have been blessed with the faith to change our hearts, with gladness. (See Acts 14:17).

Our new hearts infuse us with the spiritual element that sustains our forward momentum, as we venture into the unexplored reaches of eternity. Our new hearts do not just expose us to an entirely new paradigm; they sustain our very lives. With all diligence, and with faithfulness, the principles, and doctrines, and ordinances, and covenants of the Gospel keep our hearts vital and healthy, with a spiritual reassurance that it is from their steady beat that the fundamental issues of life will continue to flow, as in a revelatory stream. (See Proverbs 4:23).

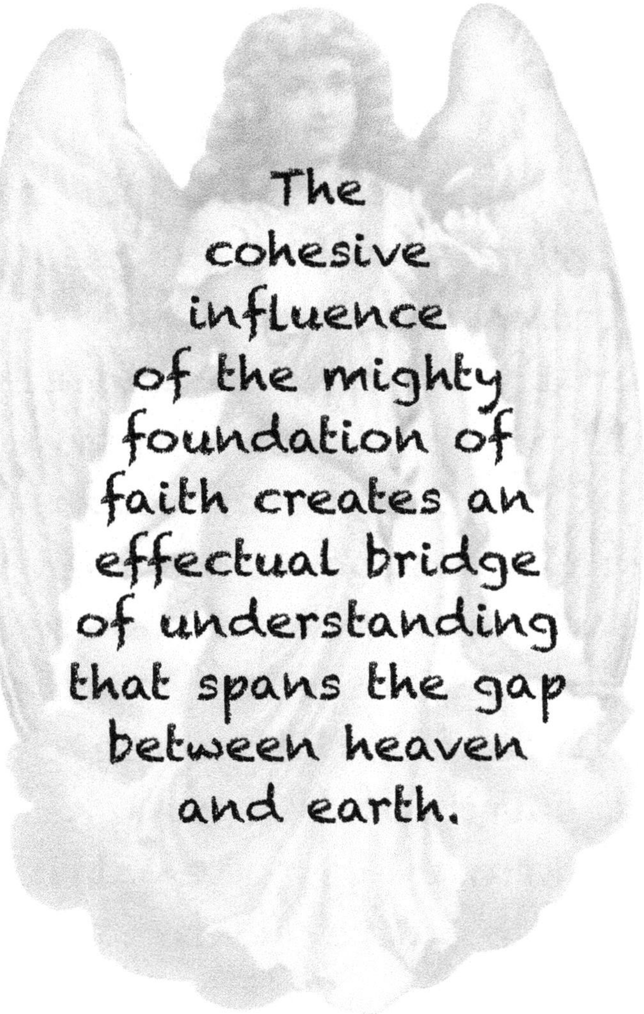

The
cohesive
influence
of the mighty
foundation of
faith creates an
effectual bridge
of understanding
that spans the gap
between heaven
and earth.

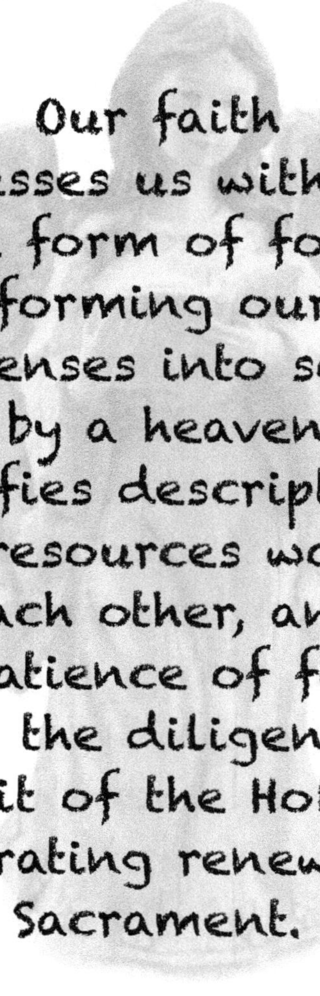

Our faith
blesses us with a
pure form of focus,
transforming our five
natural senses into something
wonderful by a heaven-sent sixth
sense that defies description. Physical
and spiritual resources work in tandem
to compound each other, and to condition
us through the patience of faith, the miracle
of repentance, the diligence of baptism,
the sweet spirit of the Holy Ghost, and
an exhilarating renewal in the
Sacrament.

Chapter Nine
The Faith to be Born Again.

"Now I say unto you that ye must repent and be born again; for the Spirit saith if ye are not born again ye cannot inherit the kingdom of heaven; therefore, come and be baptized unto repentance, that ye may be washed from your sins, that ye may have faith on the Lamb of God, who taketh away the sins of the world, who is mighty to save and to cleanse from all unrighteousness."
(Alma 7:14).

To receive eternal life, we must be "born again" as we are transformed to become "new creatures in Christ," with a determination to follow Him, wherever that journey might take us. (See Mosiah 27:26 & 2 Corinthians 5:17). But without His sustaining influence of divine nourishment, it is inevitable that we would, sooner or later, wither on the vine and die spiritually. (See Joel 1:12). Perhaps this is why the figurative counterpart of water is so dramatic, for except we "be born of water and

of the Spirit," there is no way we "can enter into the kingdom of God." (John 3:5). Of this flowing spiritual spring, Truman Madsen wrote: "If we do not drink, if we die of thirst while only inches from the fountain, the fault comes down to us. For the free, full, flowing, living water is there." ("Christ and The Inner Life," p. 31).

Physical immersion in water symbolizes the burial of our past sins, and it is only when we emerge from the font with endless promise in our eyes, faithfully facing the future, that our new life begins. In fact, after King Benjamin's discourse exhorting his people to recommit themselves to live in obedience to their covenants, they "all cried with one voice, saying: Yea, we believe all the words which thou hast spoken unto us; and also, we know of their surety and truth, because of the Spirit of the Lord Omnipotent, which has wrought a mighty change in us, or in our hearts, that we have no more disposition to do evil but to do good continually.

And we, ourselves, also, through the infinite goodness of God, and the manifestations of his Spirit, have great views of that which is to come; and were it expedient, we could prophesy of all things. And it is the faith which we have had on the things which our king has spoken unto us that has brought us to this great knowledge, whereby we do rejoice with such exceedingly great joy. And we are willing to enter into a covenant with our God to do his will, and to be obedient to his commandments in all things that he shall command us, all the remainder of our days, that we may not bring upon ourselves a never-ending torment, as has been spoken by the angel, that we may not drink out of the cup of the wrath of God." (Mosiah 5:1-5).

This declaration of commitment set the stage for Benjamin to get to the very heart of the doctrine of his message. "Therefore, he said unto them: Ye have spoken the words that I desired; and the covenant which ye have made is a righteous covenant. And now, because of the covenant which ye have made, ye shall be called the children of Christ, his sons, and his daughters; for behold, this day he hath spiritually begotten you; for ye say that your hearts are changed through faith on his name; therefore, ye are born of him, and have become his sons and his daughters." (Mosiah 5:6-7).

The Lord told Alma what it means to be born again: "Marvel not," He said, "that all

mankind, yea, men and women, all nations, kindreds, tongues, and people, must be born again; yea, born of God, changed from their carnal and fallen state to a state of righteousness, being redeemed of God, becoming his sons and daughters;

And thus they become new creatures; and unless they do this, they can in nowise inherit the kingdom of God." (Mosiah 27:25-26).

So important did Alma consider the necessity of spiritual rebirth, that he was moved to declare: "This is the order after which I am called, yea, to preach unto my beloved brethren, yea, and every one that dwelleth in the land; yea, to preach unto all, both old and young, both bond and free; yea, I say unto you the aged, and also the middle aged, and the rising generation; yea, to cry unto them that they must repent and be born again." (Alma 5:49).

After Aaron had taught Lamoni's father, the aged king asked: "What shall I do that I may have this eternal life of which thou hast spoken? Yea, what shall I do that I may be born of God, having this wicked spirit rooted out of my breast, and receive his Spirit?" Then Aaron explained: "If thou desirest this thing, if thou wilt bow down before God, yea, if thou wilt repent of all thy sins, and will bow down before God, and call on his name in faith, believing that ye shall receive, then shalt thou receive the hope which thou desirest." (Alma 22:15-18).

Alma had asked members of the Church the same thing: "Have ye spiritually been born of God? Have ye received his image in your countenances? Have ye experienced this mighty change in your hearts?" (Alma 5:14). Then, the $64,000.00 follow-up question: "If ye have felt to sing the song of redeeming love, I would ask, can ye feel so now?" (Alma 5:26). If not, all would have been lost as a result of their failure to maintain their forward momentum. A faithful recommitment to their covenant of baptism, however, would allow them to re-vitalize the fold with the electrifying understanding that being born again can be an astonishing process, as well as a particular point in time.

Nephi wondered if, after we have reached the strait and narrow path, "if all is done?

Behold, I say unto you, Nay; for ye have not come thus far save it were by the word of Christ with unshaken faith in him, relying wholly upon the merits of him who is mighty to save." After our baptism and receipt of the gift of the Holy Ghost, we must then "press forward" with complete dedication and "steadfastness," or confidence and a firm determination in Christ, "having a perfect brightness of hope," or perfect faith to be born again, and charity, or "a love of God and of all men." If we do this, "feasting upon the word of Christ," or receiving strength and nourishment from the scriptures, and endure to the end in righteousness, or in other words, if we have the faith to be born again, we "shall have eternal life," which is the greatest gift that God can bestow. (2 Nephi 31:19-20).

Nephi's formula is pure and simple; it is the meat of the Gospel that has been made more savory by sitting for a time upon the warming tray of plain doctrine. "This is the way," he said, "and there is none other way nor name given under heaven whereby man can be saved in the kingdom of God. And now, behold, this is the doctrine of Christ, and the only and true doctrine of the Father, and of the Son, and of the Holy Ghost," which is one God. (2 Nephi 31:21, see 2 Nephi 31:21).

Alma the Younger came to know this in the most intensely personal way possible, in the fiery crucible of experience. "I have seen my Redeemer," he testified, "and he shall come forth and shall redeem all mankind who believe on his name." (Alma 19:13). During a glorious manifestation, the Lord had told him: "Marvel not that all mankind, yea, men and women, all nations, kindreds, tongues, and people, must be born again, yea, born of God, changed from their carnal and fallen state, to a state of righteousness, being redeemed of God, becoming his sons and daughters." (Alma 27:25). Alma related how, after having been born again, his limbs had received their strength again, enabling him to stand upon his feet to manifest unto the people that he "had been born of God." (Alma 36:23).

The scriptures do not record whether Nicodemus received the same infusion of the holy element when Jesus "said unto him, Verily, verily, I say unto thee, Except a man be born again, he cannot see the kingdom of God.... Marvel not that I said unto

thee, Ye must be born again." (John 3:3 & 7). But we do know that Peter later taught the principle of "being born again, not of corruptible seed, but of incorruptible, by the word of God." (1 Peter 1:23). His fellow apostle John confirmed: "Whatsoever is born of God overcometh the world: and this is the victory that overcometh the world." (1 John 5:4). These are they who are insulated from the carnality, sensuality, and devilish nature of men, insomuch that "whosoever is born of God sinneth not." (1 John 5:18). These are they to whom Jesus Christ gave "power to become the sons of God, even to them that believe on his name: Which were born, not of blood, nor of the will of the flesh, nor of the will of man, but of God." (John 1:12-13).

The unconditional promise is that "every one that doeth righteousness is born of him." (1 John 2:29). "Every one that loveth is born of God, and knoweth God." (1 John 4:7). Immediately after his conversion, Alma could feel that transformation, and so exclaimed: "Behold, I am born of the Spirit!" (Mosiah 27:24). He elaborated: "After wading through much tribulation, repenting nigh unto death, the Lord in mercy hath seen fit to snatch me out of an everlasting burning, and I am born of God." (Mosiah 27:28). Although he had been "saved," there was subsequently much more work to do, as he patiently endured to the end in righteousness.

Alma later told his son Helaman: "I would not that ye should think that I know these things of myself, but it is the Spirit of God which is in me which maketh these things known unto me; for if I had not been born of God I should not have known these things." (Alma 36:8). He related to Helaman how, following his spiritual rebirth, he had "labored without ceasing, that (he) might bring souls unto repentance; that (he) might bring them to taste of the exceeding joy of which (he) did taste; that they might also be born of God, and be filled with the Holy Ghost." (Alma 36:24).

As a result of his ministry, Alma reported: "Many have been born of God, and have tasted as I have tasted, and have seen eye to eye as I have seen." (Alma 36:26). Similarly, Parley P. Pratt said of his own Pentecostal experience: "I have received the holy anointing, and I can never rest until the last enemy (that is, unresolved sin) is

conquered, (spiritual) death destroyed, and truth reigns triumphant." ("Deseret News," 4/30/1853).

All who have the faith to be been born again are set free by the perfect Law of

Liberty to reach their potential. As Paul taught the Romans: "We are buried with him by baptism into death: that like as Christ was raised up from the dead by the glory of the Father, even so we also should walk in newness of life." (Romans 6:3). When we are born again we are as the acorns of a mighty oak, vitalized by our faith and basking in His nurturing influence to reach the full stature of our spirits. (See Ephesians 4:13).

Modern scribes
and Pharisees who
have little or no faith
omit the weightier matters
of the law. They strain at a
gnat, and swallow a camel. They
appear to be righteous, but inside
are "full of extortion and excess."
(Matthew 23:25). Our righteous desire
to choose with the wisdom of faith
brings us closer to the Lord Jesus
Christ, leaving no room for
hypocrisy to creep into
our lives.

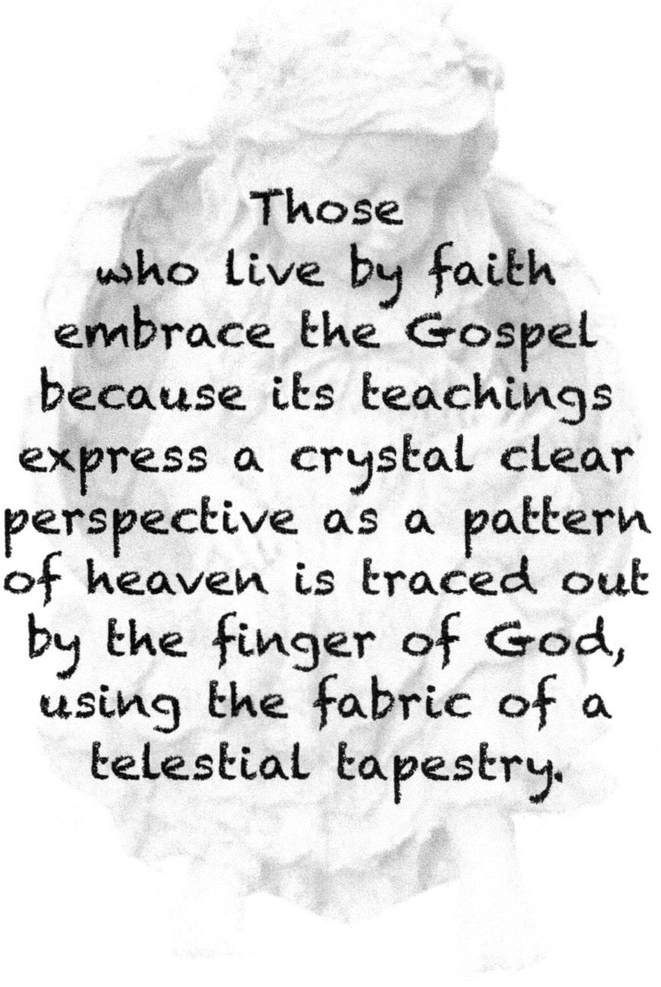

Those
who live by faith
embrace the Gospel
because its teachings
express a crystal clear
perspective as a pattern
of heaven is traced out
by the finger of God,
using the fabric of a
telestial tapestry.

Chapter Ten
The faith to make connections.

"...Till we all come in the unity of the faith, and of the knowledge of the Son of God ... unto the measure of the stature of the fulness of Christ."
(Ephesians 4:13).

No one would argue that we are bound to each other by more than genetics. With few exceptions, for example in the case of monastic ascetics and agorophobics, we are social creatures. Many years ago, it became apparent to behavioral scientists that it might be useful to view our connections as a hierarchy. In 1943, Abraham Maslow described a pyramid of need, in a paper entitled "A Theory of Human Motivation." In an ascending order of significance, Maslow described the pattern of our connections as if they were on a path leading to self-transcendence, beginning with physiology, followed by safety, a sense of belonging, love, esteem, and finally self-actualization. This remains a popular framework in sociological research and management training.

From a Gospel perspective, it is intriguing to think of our connections a bit differently, namely in the context of the principles of The Plan of Salvation. When levels of interconnectivity have a foundation of faith, they transcend the behavioral sciences to reveal the core of existence, and they bind us to Him Who "hath also

95

sealed us, and given the earnest of the Spirit in our hearts." (2 Corinthinans 1:22). These are concepts that are foreign to those who attempt to explain interpersonal relationships by utilizing only tangible tools that rely upon rationalism, and terms that are based upon empiricism, while disparaging metaphysical abstractions simply because they are more spiritual in nature and require discernment to appreciate.

The first useful category is what I call Type 0 or Human Genome Connections. Within this class are the associations that exist only because our species shares the same D.N.A. sequences. Type 0 Connections necessarily relegate us to be as ships passing in the night. We may appear to be similar in construction and in purpose, but at the end of the day there is more of a disconnect between us than anything else. Type 0 Human Genome Connections do not require heart to heart, skin to skin, or even eye to eye contact. They rarely establish empathic bonds with others. Collectively, Type 0 Connections reduce us to nothing more than nameless faces in the crowd. There is little or no evidence of the emotion, the instinctive or intuitive feeling, that is the glue that binds us to each other.

The second category is what I call Type 1 Connections. These allow us to relate to each other through common interests like cars, hobbies, jobs, schools, and sports. But, at the same time, they are casual connections. For example, how many times has each of us said to ourselves: "I know that face; I just can't put a name to it." Type 1 Connections are neural in origin, and have a molecular basis, but they too often develop along the pathways of short-term, and not long-term, memory. They may be powerful initially, but their intensity often fades with time.

The third category is what I call Type 2 Connections, those that are forged through the commanding chemistry of shared experiences, especially those that elicit intense emotion. These connections can last for years, because they trace their foundations

to the crises of uncommonly positive or negative experiences with electrifying consequences that catalyze visceral responses that are etched in our nervous systems. We have close associates, bosom buddies, life-long friends, and even blood-brothers with whom we have established Type 2 Connections that seem unassailable.

But Type 2 Connections, like Type 1 Connections, can and often do fade with time. Think of the unity that gripped America in the aftermath of 9/11. We can all still visualize members of the U.S. Congress standing on the steps of the Capitol, with arms linked together, singing God Bless America. How quickly are our Type 2 Connections smothered in the marsh gas emitted by our scramble for scarce resources, telestial trash, and the approbation of gods of wood and stone!

Somewhere beyond Type 2 Connections, there may come a moment when we "see the light." We may be dazzled by an A-ha! moment, an instant of sudden realization, insight, recognition, comprehension, or even inspiration. We might even feel that we have been "born again!" Nicodemus asked: How can a man "enter the sec-ond time into his mother's womb, and be born? Jesus answered, verily, verily, I say unto thee, except a man be born of water and of the Spirit, he cannot enter into the kingdom of God. That which is born of the flesh is flesh; and that which is born of the Spirit is spirit." (John 3:4-6). The Savior used this occasion to teach Nicodemus about Type 3 Connections that can only be appreciated in the context of deeply moving and faith-promoting spiritual experiences.

The Sons of Mosiah had such a moment, when they felt compelled to "impart much consolation to the church, confirming their faith, and exhorting them with long-suffering and much travail to keep the commandments of God." (Mosiah 27:33). Thereafter, their developing Type 3 connection with the Lamanites motivated them to engage themselves in a mission in the Land of Lehi that lasted fourteen long years. (See Mosiah 28:9). Ironically, the Lamanites among whom they ministered did not initially understand the power of Type 3 connectivity. But, over time, their Type 2 Connections evolved into Type 3 Connections with the missionaries, with each other, and ultimately with the Lord.

There follows in The Book of Mormon a detailed description of what we might do, in order to have and sustain similar Type 3 Connections. Mormon reported that at the conclusion of their mission, the Sons of Mosiah were still the brethren of Alma "in the Lord; yea, and they had waxed strong in the knowledge of the truth;

for they were men of a sound understanding and they had searched the scriptures diligently, that they might know the word of God. But this is not all; they had given themselves to much prayer, and fasting; therefore, they had the spirit of prophecy, and the spirit of revelation, and when they taught, they taught with power and authority of God." (Alma 17:2-3). Their mission introduced them to faith-building Type 3 connectivity that can last forever.

Examples include the bond that can exist between a mother and child, or between "soul-mates" whose match was made in heaven. Both birth and death experiences can generate the intensity to trigger Type 3 Connections. Veil experiences in the temple can compellingly and convincingly communicate connections between the living and the dead. In our everyday interpersonal relationships, when we are privileged to have opportunities to nurture Type 3 Connections, the terms "Brother" and "Sister" easily fall from our lips, even though no actual bond of blood exists.

In this context, we are reminded of Henry V, who addressed his troops at the Battle of Agincourt, on St. Crispin's day: "We few, we happy few, we band of brothers. For he today that sheds his blood with me shall be my brother, be he ne'er so vile. This day shall gentle his condition." (Shakespeare, "Henry V" Act 4, Scene 3).

These Type 3 Connections are enduring because they permit us to brush against the face of God. Think of the genius of the advertising executives who coined the phrase: "Reach out and touch someone." Perhaps without realizing it, they were tapping into our universal need to establish connections with eternity. Paul clearly recognized the power of the word to do so, when he wrote to the Ephesians that, by obedience to Gospel principles, they would be "no more strangers and foreigners, but fellowcitizens with the Saints, and with the household of God." (Ephesians 2:19).

From the beginning of time, the traditional family has provided the milieu in which Type 3 Connections are generated. Alarmingly, today many family units are hardly recognizable, because they lack the tools to consciously cultivate these associations. Rather, they subsist on a meager diet of Type 1 or Type 2 Connections, mistakenly believing that these are the pinnacle of achievement in human interrelationships. By doing so, they settle for the steak, without the sizzle. Or, perhaps they just do not care, either way. Without motivation, they may even slip back into Type 0 connectivity. Sometimes, they simply have no interest in expanding their horizons, and they are content to just go with the flow. They may be "past feeling." (1 Nephi 17:45, Moroni 9:20, & Ephesians 4:19). For whatever reason, they are either unwilling or unable to generate the intrinsic power necessary to create and sustain lasting relationships, let alone the Type 3 Connections that Latter-day Saints characterize as forever families and eternal relationships.

With this in mind, we can better appreciate the purpose behind the dissemination since 1995 of The Church of Jesus Christ of Latter-day Saints' statement of belief entitled: "The Family: A Proclamation to The World." We also better understand the meaning of Joseph Smith's teaching that, at every age in the world, the main object of gathering the people of God "was to build unto the Lord a house whereby He could reveal unto His people the ordinances of His house and the glories of His kingdom, and teach the people the way of salvation," which has primarily been to develop Type 3 leading to Type 4 Connections. (See below). (H.C., 5:423, June 1843). Hence, we are enjoined: "Thou shalt lay aside the things of this world, and seek for the things of a better." (D&C 25:10).

In essence, both Joseph Smith and the Lord taught that we could not completely nurture our spiritual connections "until the temple (was) completed, where places (could) be provided for the administration of the ordinances of the Priesthood." (H.C., 4:603.) When we neglect opportunities to expand our faith to make connections that can only be envisioned with an eternal perspective, we jeopardize the promises of The Plan.

Individuals are baptized after Type 2 Connections have propelled them along on a journey toward Type 3 experiences. At other times, those investigating the merits of Christ may have already had fleeting Type 3 Connection experiences, have strongly felt the Spirit, and have then determined to be baptized in order to capture those wonderful feelings with the confident anticipation of enjoying them on a regular basis. These are the pathways along which faith, testimony, and conversion are strengthened.

But, in order to maintain the momentum that has been generated, and in order to make it enduring, new and established members of the Church need to have sustaining spiritual experiences that nourish Type 3 connectivity. As Gordon B. Hinckley said: "Every convert needs a friend, a responsibility, and nurturing with the good word of God." ("Liahona," 2/1999).

If Latter-day Saints do not find resources within the Church to sustain Type 3 Connections, they risk sliding back into Type 2 interconnectivity. Those who enjoy only these marginalized relationships are often characterized as being "less active," or "inactive." Fundamentally, they lose their way because they have lost the ability to nourish the standard of behavior that is necessary to support Type 3 interpersonal connections that are powered by the principles that were once their guiding lights.

We cannot endure for long if we rely only upon the light emitted by Type 1 and 2 Connections. Thus, Joseph Smith wrote to the Saints in their time of need, exhorting them: "If thou endure it well, God shall exalt thee on high." (D&C 121:8). What he meant was that an external power source is needed in order to become a member of the Second Mile Club of Type 3 Interconnectivity. He was inviting the Saints to join a select group to which all are invited soon after their baptisms. (See Matthew 5:41).

Paul knew what it meant to go that second mile. He ministered among the Corinthian Saints, whom he was pleased to discover had a working relationship with the laws of the Gospel. He characterized their expressions of faith as being written upon "tables of stone." That is all well and good, but he hinted that there exists another order of

mind, a connectivity that can be ours if we will make a second mile commitment: "Ye are manifestly declared to be the epistle of Christ ministered by us, written not with ink, but with the Spirit of the living God; not in tables of stone, but in fleshy tables of the heart." (2 Corinthians 3:3).

Sooner or later, every member of the Church is a second miler, who is encouraged to become perfect in Type 3 interconnectivity commitment, and to so live to be worthy of Type 4 commitment, that leaves Maslow's model of self-actualization in ruins. During His mortal ministry, the Savior said: "He that shall endure unto the end, the same shall be saved." (Matthew 24:13). Going a step further, He then explained to Joseph Smith: "If you keep my commandments (the first mile / Type 3 commitment) and endure to the end (the second mile, leading to Type 4 commitment) you shall have eternal life, which gift is the greatest of all the gifts of God." (D&C 14:7).

Our Type 3 Connections are solidified with compassionate service, particularly when it is directed toward those who cannot provide of their own means to generate equivalent connections. Service in the temple comes to mind. In the baptisms, confirmations, ordination to the priesthood, washing, anointing, and clothing ordinances, in the endowment, and in the sealing ordinances performed by patrons in the temple in behalf of the dead, we repeatedly hear the expression "for and in behalf of." Temple ordinances give substance to the expression that none of us is an island. The Architect of The Plan created opportunities for us to perform vicarious work, that we might comfortably surround ourselves with Type 3 Connections to both the living and the dead, as we establish bonds between all those who have been strengthened by covenants made with God. These can seal us to our forbearers all the way back to Father Adam and Mother Eve, as well as to our descendants, forging an unbreakable chain leading from the Garden to the Celestial Kingdom. We can use Type 3 Connections to redeem the dead, as well as to pay it forward.

But that is not all our Heavenly Father can do for us. This is where the faithful part company with the masses, to be caught up into "the third heaven." (See 2 Corinthians 12:2). God gave us our Type 3 Connections that we might have the power to establish a platform upon which we could build an even more ambitious milieu of connectivity.

After the Flood, the ancients built ziggurats that were towers specifically designed to reach all the way to heaven. The Tower of Babel is a good biblical example of these exaggerated church steeples. (See Genesis 11:4). But their builders, and those who flocked to behold these architectural marvels, missed the point. Instead of creating physical structures composed of brick and mortar, they would have more profitably spent their time if they had used the principles of the Gospel to build enduring relationships or connections with each other.

Starting with the baseline of Type 1 Connections, they could have rapidly advanced through Type 2, and on to Type 3. Then, they could have figuratively reached for the stars with that to which I have heretofore alluded: The Type 4 level of connection that is described in the scriptures as having our "Calling and Election" made sure. This is a relationship that is poorly understood by theologians and scriptorians alike, let alone academicians. It transcends Maslow's model. It requires a profoundly personal spiritual comprehension that can only be built upon the foundation of Type 1, 2, and 3 Connections that have already been faithfully established.

By design, in this chapter, I have purposely saved the best for last. When we achieve Type 4, we shift our focus, and our mystical connection with God becomes indelibly etched into our spiritual identity. We become perfect in our faith to make connections. (See 2 Nephi 9:23). That is how members of The Church of Jesus Christ of Latter-day Saints have the presumption to declare that it is our destiny to one day rule as kings and queens, and priests and priestesses, in the house of Israel forever, to reign with authority over kingdoms, thrones, principalities, powers, dominions, and exaltations.

But we can't get there if, beginning at Type 0, we skip the intermediate steps in our quest to reach what can only be an undefinable and incomprehensible goal. That's where the experiences of mortality in the learning laboratory of life, enjoyed within the structure of the principles and ordinances of the Gospel, come into play. Therein lies the inherent beauty of The Plan, and therein is the key to its success. Its doctrines teach that we are not islands unto ourselves, and that when we hear

the bell, we need not wonder for whom it tolls. It tolls for us.

It was with the assurance that he was a child of God, that brave Horatius was able to declare: "To every man upon this earth, death cometh soon or late. And how can man die better, than facing fearful odds, for the ashes of his fathers, and the temples of his gods?" (Thomas McCaulay, "Lays of Ancient Rome," Stanza 27).

When designing The Plan, God knew that, with only nine months to put the final touches on our preparation, we would transition from the eternal world where we had enjoyed the warmth of hearth and home in heaven, to the bleak atmosphere of the lone and dreary world here on earth. (See 2 Nephi 2). When we did so, we knew that there would be an immediate disconnect that would be both brutal and unrelenting in its intensity. The Plan requires that we take this labor of love and somehow postpone our Type 4 premortal yearnings, as we ease into a world stage that is brutally assaulted on all sides by the unrelenting monotony of Type 0 mortal experiences. The Gospel was introduced, from the beginning, to build upon our Type 0 Connections, that we might ultimately reach "the most holy faith" of Type 4 Connections. (D&C 21:2).

In order to counteract the unforgiving reality check of birth, God instilled within each of our beating hearts the instinctive possibility to enjoy Type 1 and Type 2 Connections that would gently lead us toward Type 3 Connections, so that we could eventually have Type 4 Connections. He stamped within each of our minds a blueprint for survival, and inserted within its many pages of instruction enough information to organize ourselves and prepare every needful thing, so that we might intuitively establish a house of prayer, fasting, faith, learning, glory, and order; even a house of God where dreams come true, and where connectivity would not only be magical, but also wondrously possible. (See D&C 88:119).

That is why Adam and Eve, who had been living in innocence in a Garden setting, were told that it had been patterned after the order of heaven. When Adam and Eve fell that we might be, their physical surroundings in the lone and dreary world were

designed, harsh though it might have seemed, to provide a hint of familiarity. If they would be sensitive to the Spirit, they would be able to re-establish their celestial connectivity and have joy. (See 2 Nephi 2:25). They would enjoy communication with the heavens. Adam and Eve fell so that God could teach them and their posterity how to re-establish Type 4 Eternal Connections.

Truly, "the universe is but one great city, full of beloved ones, divine and human, by nature endeared to each other." (Epictetus). Heavenly Father is the Grand Architect of a design that establishes our familial roots and confirms His fatherhood, that we might enjoy a witness that it is in Him alone that "we live, and move, and have our being; as certain also of (our) own poets have said. For we are also his offspring." (Acts 17:28).

When Cain asked his father Adam if he was his brother's keeper, he did so with only a vague familiarity of the principles surrounding the question. (See Genesis 4:9). It exposed his failure to comprehend his Type 3 Connection with his brother Abel. During His mortal ministry, when the Savior posed the question: "Which now of these three, thinkest thou, was neighbour unto him that fell among the thieves?" He was asking the young man to recognize the spiritual handwriting that was on the wall, and to acknowledge the Type 3 Connections he should have felt with someone so despised as a Samaritan. (Luke 10:36).

Moroni's challenge to come unto Christ is our invitation to establish with Him a Type 3 Connection, and to stretch our minds and our spirits, that the way might be paved for us to embrace a Type 4 Connection that paves the way for our perfection. (See Moroni 10:32).

Joseph Smith asked the Saints if they could somehow establish a Type 3 Connection with each other that was founded on charity. (See D&C 121:45-47). Similarly, Moses instructed all of Israel to regard its neighbors not with Type 0 connectivity, but as Type 3 brothers and sisters. He taught: "And if a stranger sojourn with thee in your

land, ye shall not vex him. But the stranger that dwelleth with you shall be unto you as one born among you, and thou shalt love him as thyself." (Leviticus 19:33-34). In each of these cases, the prophets asked us to establish covenant relationships with

God so that we might establish Type 3 Connections, leading to Type 4 eternal joy in the kingdom of heaven.

Ruth felt this connectivity when she implored her mother-in-law Naomi: "Entreat me not to leave thee, or to return from following after thee, for whither thou goest, I will go, and where thou lodgest, I will lodge. Thy people shall be my people, and thy God my God. Where thou diest, will I die, and there will I be buried. The Lord do so to me, and more also, if ought but death part thee and me." (Ruth 1:16-17). Ruth established a profound connectivity that endured in Israel for eleven hundred years, allowing the Savior of the world to come through her lineage. The reason her petition to Naomi rings true to us today, is because Type 3 and Type 4 Connections are founded on eternal principles that are confirmed by the unimpeachable witness of the Spirit. Their validity transcends both time and space.

Ultimately, the mission statement of our Father in Heaven is to establish Type 4 Connections with His children. (See Moses 1:39). Peter taught: "Brethren, give diligence to make your calling and election sure; for if ye do these things, ye shall never fall." (2 Peter 1:10). The Savior likewise taught His disciples: "Then shall the King say unto them on his right hand, Come, ye blessed of my Father, inherit the kingdom prepared for you from the foundation of the world. For I was an hungered, and ye gave me meat. I was thirsty, and ye gave me drink. I was a stranger, and ye took me in; naked, and ye clothed me. I was sick, and ye visited me. I was in prison, and ye came unto me. Then shall the righteous answer him, saying, Lord, when saw we thee an hungered, and fed thee; or thirsty, and gave thee drink? When saw we thee a stranger, and took thee in; or naked, and clothed thee? Or when saw we thee sick, or in prison, and came unto thee? And the King shall answer and say unto them, Verily I say unto you, Inasmuch as ye have done it unto one of the least of these my brethren, ye have done it unto me." (Matthew 25:34-40).

With disappointment, He said to others, who shrank from the light and sought the shadows, who never went to the effort to establish Type 3 or 4 connectivity: "Ye never knew me." (J.S.T. Matthew 7:33, see J.S.T. Matthew 25:11). Clearly, when it comes to establishing connectivity, the ball is in our court.

Latter-day revelation speaks of those who, during their mortal probation, establish the unshakable bond of Type 4 connectivity with our Father in Heaven and with the Lord Jesus Christ, through unfettered access to the Holy Ghost. "Then shall they be gods, because they have no end; therefore, shall they be from everlasting to everlasting, because they continue; then shall they be above all, because all things are subject unto them. Then shall they be gods, because they have all power, and the angels are subject unto them." (D&C 132:20).

Sooner or later, every member of the Church will encounter a line drawn in the sand. Those with the faith to "endure unto the end, the same shall be saved." (Matthew 24:13). Or, as the Lord explained to Joseph Smith: "If you keep my commandments" by acting in faith to establish Type 3 Connections, "and endure to the end," and thereby create Type 4 connectivity "you shall have eternal life, which gift is the greatest of all the gifts of God. (D&C 14:7).

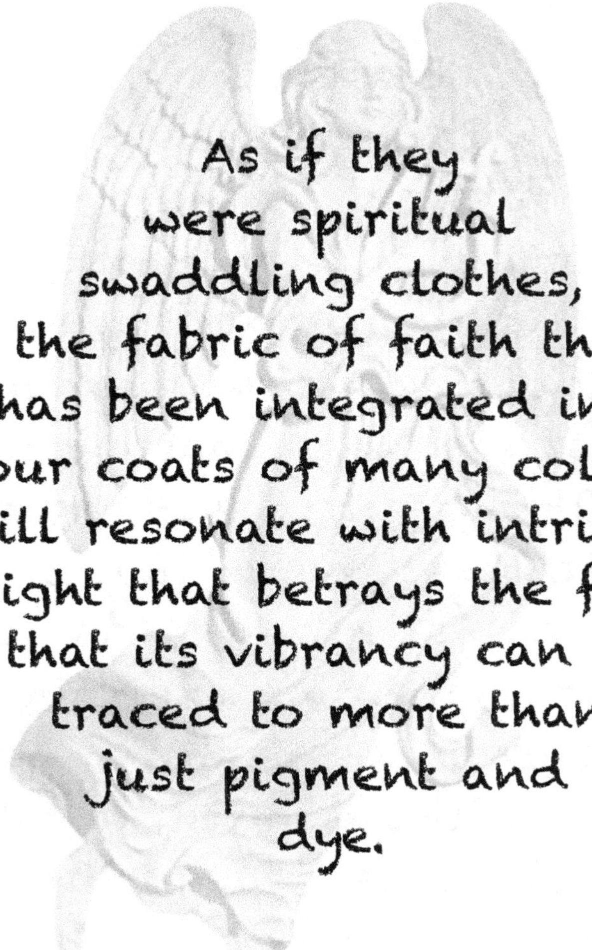

As if they
were spiritual
swaddling clothes,
the fabric of faith that
has been integrated into
our coats of many colors
will resonate with intrinsic
light that betrays the fact
that its vibrancy can be
traced to more than
just pigment and
dye.

Belief is the mental assent to the truth of a precept, principle, or doctrine, without the moral element of responsibility that we call faith. Of those to whom much is given, however, much is expected. The gift of faith demands action. Therefore, when we exercise free will, even if we perform good works, without faith, it falls short. It "is dead, being alone." (James 2:17).

Chapter Eleven
The knowledge of faith.

"Grace and peace be multiplied unto you through the knowledge of God and of Jesus our Lord, according as his divine power hath given unto us all things that pertain unto life and godliness, through the knowledge of him that hath called us to glory and virtue. Whereby are given unto us exceeding great and precious promises, that by these ye might be partakers of the divine nature, having escaped the corruption that is in the world through lust. And beside this, giving all diligence, add to your faith virtue, and to virtue knowledge, and to knowledge temperance, and to temperance patience, and to patience godliness, and to godliness brotherly kindness, and to brotherly kindness charity. For if these things be in you, and abound, they make you that ye shall neither be barren nor unfruitful in the knowledge of our Lord Jesus Christ." (2 Peter 1:2-7).

This is one of the 535 references to knowledge in the scriptures. In the Standard Works, there are 667 references to faith, but there are only 18 verses in which the words faith & knowledge are found together.

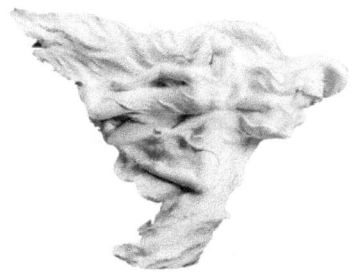

We might ask ourselves, therefore, what the relationship is between faith and knowledge. Are the two compatible? Is perfect faith synonymous with perfect knowledge? The Savior promised: "You shall receive a knowledge of whatsoever things you shall ask in faith." (D&C 8:1). He also explained: "Without faith you can do nothing; therefore, ask in faith." Then, He reaffirmed the reason for doing so: "Ask," He said, "that you may ... receive knowledge." (D&C 8:10-11).

In many of the verses that address knowledge, the desirability of its acquisition, as well as its dependent relationship to faith, are self-evident. Among them are the following. "Grace and peace be multiplied unto you through the knowledge of God, and of Jesus our Lord." (2 Peter 1:2). "The fulness of the scriptures is the key of knowledge." (J.S.T. Luke 11:53). "I am left to mourn because of the unbelief, and the wickedness, and the ignorance, and the stiffneckedness of men; for they will not search knowledge, nor understand great knowledge, when it is given unto them in plainness." (2 Nephi 32:87). "The earth shall be filled with the knowledge of the glory of the Lord, as the waters cover the sea." (Habakkuk 2:14). "And there shall come forth a rod out of the stem of Jesse, and a Branch shall grow out of his roots: And the spirit of the Lord shall rest upon him, the spirit of wisdom and understanding, the spirit of counsel and might, the spirit of knowledge and of the fear of the Lord." (Isaiah 1:11).

Jacob exclaimed: "The paradise of God must deliver up the spirits of the righteous, and the grave deliver up the body of the righteous; and the spirit and the body is restored to itself again, and all men become incorruptible, and immortal, and they are living souls, having a perfect knowledge." (2 Nephi 9:13).

Abraham described his own search for meaning in life: "And, finding there was greater happiness and peace and rest for me, I sought for the blessings of the fathers, and the right whereunto I should be ordained to administer the same; having been myself a follower of righteousness, desiring also to be one who possessed great knowledge." (Abraham 1:2).

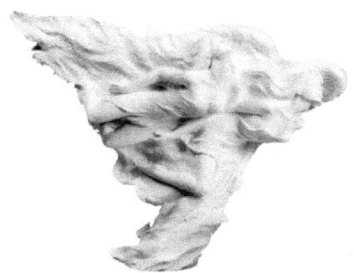

Paul explained that the Lord "gave some, apostles; and some, prophets; and some, evangelists; and some, pastors and teachers." He did this "for the perfecting of the saints, for the work of the ministry, for the edifying of the body of Christ: Till we all come in the unity of the faith, and of the knowledge of the Son of God." (Ephesians 4:11).

Knowledge received through the exercise of faith is the mortar that binds together the building blocks of conversion and testimony. A wise Teacher counseled that knowledge is received by faith. (See D&C 26:2). He taught: "As all have not faith, seek ye diligently and teach one another words of wisdom; yea, seek ye out of the best books words of wisdom; seek learning, even by study and also by faith." (D&C 88:118).

As we increase our understanding based upon the foundation of faith, we are reminded that we "are little children and ... cannot bear all things now; (for we) must grow in grace and in the knowledge of the truth." (D&C 50:40). "The word of the Lord is truth, and whatsoever is truth is light, and whatsoever is light is Spirit, even the Spirit of Jesus Christ." (D&C 84:45). "And the Spirit giveth light to every man that cometh into the world; and the Spirit enlighteneth every man through the world, that hearkeneth to the voice of the Spirit." (D&C 84:46). Initially, we muster our faith that we might believe what we do not see, and the reward of faith is to see what we believe, that ultimately we might see what is real, through the knowledge of faith.

We have all heard the aphorism that some things just have to be believed to be seen. An equally valid truism might be that we need to have knowledge of something in order to see it. The remarkable connection between faith and knowledge is this: The foundation of belief is knowledge, and when it is reinforced by the moral element of responsibility that we call faith, mountains can be moved, and rivers can be changed out of their course. (See Moses 7:13).

In that perfect storm of belief, knowledge, and faith, it is the light of faith that

switches on as the stars in the heavens, whose hydrogen fuel powers their nuclear furnaces. Faith can shine so brightly that it quickens knowledge and gives vitality to belief, as it proceeds "forth from the presence of God to fill the immensity of space." Energized faith can penetrate the darkness of the telestial world to become "the light which is in all things, which giveth life to all things, which is the law by which all things are governed, even the power of God who sitteth upon his throne, who is in the bosom of eternity." (D&C 88:11-13).

In the beginning, it was by the power of faith that "the Gods organized and formed the heavens and the earth." (Abraham 4:1). They set the conditions, taught Joseph Smith, "by which the worlds were framed, (and) all things in heaven, on the earth, or under the earth. (These) exist by reason of faith as it existed in (the mind of the Gods). Had it not been for this principle of faith, the worlds would never have been framed, neither would man have been formed of the dust. It is this principle by which Jehovah works, and through which He exercises power over all temporal as well as eternal things." ("Lectures on Faith," #1).

When, by faith, we are infused with the knowledge of God, our "bodies shall be filled with light, and there shall be no darkness in (us); and that body which is filled with light comprehendeth all things." (D&C 88:67). For "that which is of God is light; and he that receiveth light, and continueth in God, receiveth more light; and that light groweth brighter and brighter until the perfect day." (D&C 50:24). As we approach perfection, our faith increases until "it becomes perfect knowledge." (Heber J. Grant, C.R. 4/1934). We are then as powerful witnesses to the light that "shall break forth among them that sit in darkness." (D&C 45:28).

At that day, faith, light, and truth will be recognized as irreducible common denominators, the essential elements of an equation that describes the foundation upon which knowledge is received. "One for all and all for one!" was the motto of the Three Musketeers. Without faith, light, and truth, we would retrogress; we would "degenerate from God, descend to the devil, and lose knowledge, and without knowledge we cannot be saved." (Joseph Smith). Without knowledge, there can be

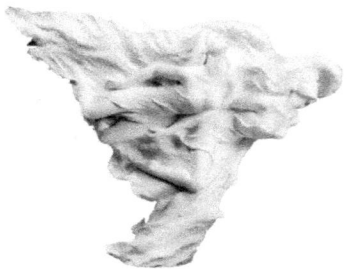

no faith; without faith there can be no light, and without light there can be no recognition of religious truth, and without spiritual enlightenment, if just one of the three elements of faith, light, and truth is lost, then all is lost. We sink or swim on the basis of how comprehensively we have embraced the knowledge of faith.

Perhaps our best chance of acquiring knowledge through the exercise of our faith is to be perpetually thrilled with life, for if we have that divine fire in our belly, our every-day experiences are deified. Of such revelatory experiences, R.W. Emerson wrote that those who have "seen the rising moon break out of the clouds at midnight has been present like an archangel at the creation of light and of the world," and on another occasion, that "if the stars should appear but one night in a thousand years, how would men believe and adore, and preserve for many generations the remembrance of the city of God which had been shown?"

We cannot be saved without the knowledge of faith relating to the principles of The Plan of Salvation. (See D&C 131:6). James Madison wrote: "Knowledge will forever govern ignorance, and a people who mean to be their own governors must arm themselves with the power which knowledge gives. What spectacle can be more edifying or more seasonable than that of liberty and learning, each leaning on the other for their mutual and surest support?" This is reminiscent of the divine guidance given to Adam and Eve in the Garden.

Faith also binds together the building blocks of eternal principles. Without it, the fabric of society must unravel in a process leading to disintegration. Without the anchor of the knowledge of faith, experience is a train wreck in slow motion that has been repeated countless times. We remember the Nephites, who "were divided one against another; and they did separate one from another into tribes, every man according to his family and his kindred and friends; and thus they did destroy the government of the land." (3 Nephi 7:2). This they did because of "the hardness of their hearts and the blindness of their minds." (3 Nephi 7:15-16).

How many times have we read about, or even witnessed, cultural collapse because a faithless society has decayed from within? In every case, iniquity follows those who have yielded themselves "unto the power of Satan." (3 Nephi 7:5). People just

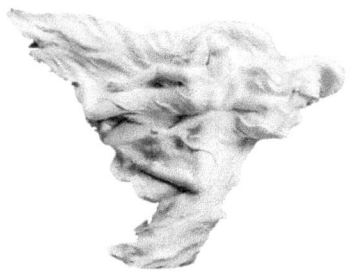

do not seem to be able to understand that Lucifer was a first-grade dropout whose influence was the companion of anarchy because it denied the faith and demeaned the intelligent application of knowledge. (See 3 Nephi 7:6). We are reminded of the unenlightened hillbilly, of whom it was said: "It warn't his ignorance that done him in, but what he knowed that warn't so." As King Limhi put it: "How blind and impenetrable are the understandings of the children of men, for they will not seek wisdom, neither do they desire that she should rule over them!" (Mosiah 8:20). Without faith and knowledge, the children of men find themselves in a flat spin from which there is no recovery.

For those of us who have persevered, that we might be added upon (see Abraham 3:26), our impenetrable shield of faith is symmetrically matched to the breastplate of righteousness, the helmet of salvation, and the sword of the Spirit. (See Ephesians 6:14-17). We are neither fence-sitters nor equivocators. We are not just vaguely aware of correct principles; instead, we embrace them. We do not just talk the talk; we also walk the walk. We allow ourselves to be molded by the Spirit, to be trained in the correct application of principles, and then, in the knowledge of faith, to follow the promptings of the Holy Ghost. We do not falter. (See Proverbs 22:6). We possess the power of knowledge to discern between truth and error, between right and wrong, between telestial trivialities and celestial sureties, and between light and darkness. And we have the faith to then act upon our scruples.

More than that, because of the knowledge of faith we personify the divine purpose of happiness. It "is the object and design of our existence, and will be the end thereof, if we pursue the path that leads to it, and this path is virtue, uprightness, faithfulness, holiness, and keeping all the commandments of God." (Joseph Smith, "Teachings," p. 255).

Those without
faith lack spiritual
horsepower. Their dearth
of traction is obvious, their
inability to generate spontaneity
is palpable, and their lack of energy
to engage enthusiasm is noticeable.
Their incapacity to spark vitality
is evident, and their failure to
candidly acknowledge the
powerful relationship that
can exist between God
and ourselves is
undisputed.

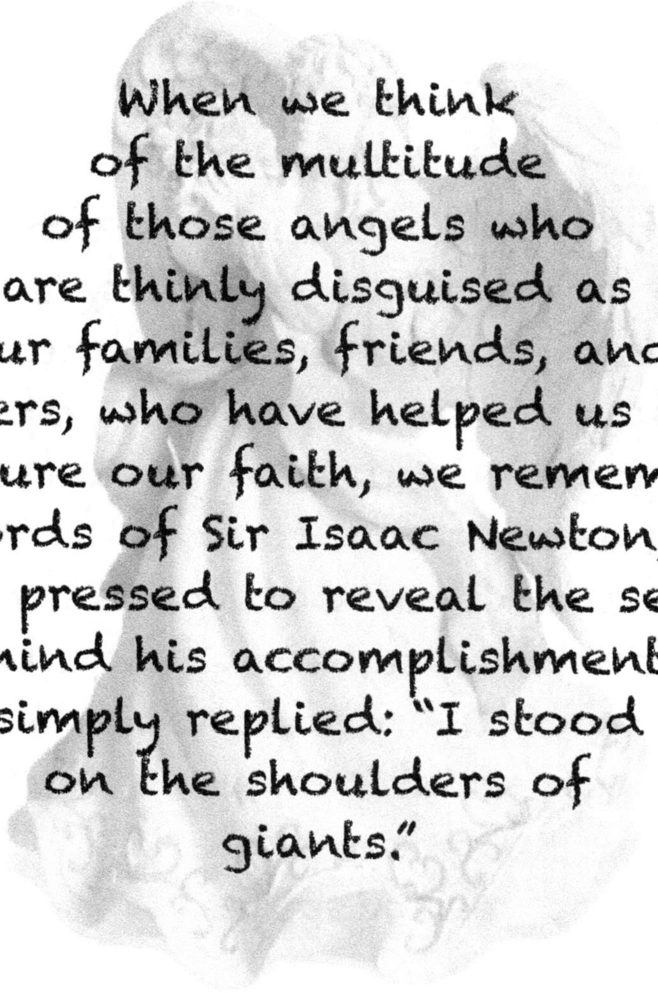

When we think
of the multitude
of those angels who
are thinly disguised as
our families, friends, and
peers, who have helped us to
nurture our faith, we remember
the words of Sir Isaac Newton, who,
when pressed to reveal the secret
behind his accomplishments,
simply replied: "I stood
on the shoulders of
giants."

Chapter Twelve
The fabric of faith.

"Now Israel loved Joseph more than all his children,
because he was the son of his old age: and he
made him a coat of many colours."
(Genesis 37:3).

It is interesting to think of Joseph's coat of many colors as a metaphor for the fabric of our faith, sewn by our Heavenly Father Himself. We can visualize how each thread has been individually tailored to suit our circumstances and to represent, not the drab monotone of the world, but a true Technicolor DreamCoat signifying the glories and riches of eternity. Doing so helps us to put the day-to-day elements of The Plan of Salvation in perspective, and enables us to more clearly discern the grey-toned obstacles to our progression. These barriers then stand out in sharp contrast to the polychromatic backdrop of the design that God has created for each of us.

Joseph's coat was a wonderful expression of his father's love, and to wear it must have given him a great deal of pleasure, but it did get him into serious trouble. Had this impressionable youngest son of Jacob kept his counsel to himself after he had received visions of his brethren paying him obeisance, he might have mitigated their growing envy and avoided their subsequent conspiracy against him. "For although a man may have many revelations, and have power to do many mighty works, yet if he boasts in his own strength, and sets at naught the counsels of God, and follows after the dictates of his own will and carnal desires, he must fall and incur the vengeance of a just God upon him." (D&C 3:4).

We all know what happened next. "The Midianites sold him into Egypt unto Potiphar, an officer of Pharaoh's, and captain of the guard." (Genesis 37:36). Joseph's physical garment was gone, and he would find himself falsely accused and in bondage in Egypt, ostensibly left in rags in a dark and hopeless dungeon. It would be up to him to seek God's guidance in reconstructing the coat, if only in his mind's eye, that he might learn to appreciate the significance of each thread that had been so carefully selected.

I thought of Joseph when I read the dialogue between Edmund Dantès and the priest Abbé Faria that occurred deep within the walls of the prison of the Chateau 'If, in Alexandere Dumas' novel "The Count of Monte Cristo." "What are you thinking?" asked the Abbé smilingly, imputing the deep abstraction in which his visitor was plunged to the excess of his awe and wonder. "I was reflecting, in the first place," replied Dantès, "upon the enormous degree of intelligence and ability you must have employed to reach the high perfection to which you have attained. What would you not have accomplished if you had been free?" "Possibly nothing at all," replied the priest. "The overflow of my brain would probably, in a state of freedom, have evaporated in a thousand follies; misfortune is needed to bring to light the treasures of the human intellect. Compression is needed to explode gunpowder. Captivity has brought my mental faculties to a focus; and you are well aware that from the

collision of clouds electricity is produced – from electricity, lightning, and from lightning, illumination."

Finally, at the end of the tale, Dantès revealed: "Only a man who has felt ultimate despair is capable of feeling ultimate bliss. It is necessary to have wished for death, in order to know how good it is to live. Live, then, and be happy, and never forget that, until the day God deigns to reveal the future to man, the sum of human wisdom will be contained in these words: wait and hope."

As the poet sagaciously observed: "My life is but a weaving between my God and me. I cannot choose the colors. He weaveth steadily. Oft' times He weaveth sorrow, and I in foolish pride, forget He sees the upper, and I, the underside. Not 'til the loom is silent and the shuttles cease to fly, will God unroll the canvas and reveal the reasons why. The dark threads are as needful in the weaver's skillful hand, as the threads of gold and silver in the pattern He has planned." (Benjamin Malachi Franklin).

Joseph's coat of many colors symbolizes our faith that every cloud has a silver lining and even the darkest night is followed by the dawn of a new day. As Helen Keller wrote: "I believe that no good shall be lost, and that all we have willed or hoped or dreamed of good shall exist forever. I believe in the immortality of the soul because I have within me immortal longings. I believe that the state we enter after death is wrought of our own motives, thoughts, and deeds. I believe that my home there will be beautiful with color, music, and speech of flowers and faces I love. Without this faith, there would be little meaning in my life. I should be a mere pillar of darkness in the dark. Observers in the full enjoyment of their bodily senses pity me, but it is because they do not see the golden chamber in my life where I dwell delighted; for dark as my path may seem to them, I carry a magic light in my heart. Faith, the spiritual strong searchlight, illuminates the way, and although sinister doubts lurk in the shadow, I walk unafraid towards the Enchanted Wood where the foliage is always green, where joy abides, where nightingales nest and sing, and where life and death are one in the presence of the Lord." "Midstream").

Joseph received his coat as a gift from his father, just as we receive the fabric of faith from our Heavenly Father. We can be sure that He has carefully selected every bolt of cloth and has cut each of them to address the exigencies in our lives. As

Mark E. Petersen observed: "Shall we not be willing to sacrifice our ordinary desires when necessary, and allow God to cut the cloth to fit the pattern of revised circumstances" that unfolds before us, with the intention of maximizing our life experiences?

Evolving conditions provide us with resplendent coats of many colors with a relaxed fit that allows us to grow into the full stature of our spirits. They are not tailored to be fashionable, or form-fitting. They have not been devised to emphasize our physical assets, or to impress the world. Rather, they are of simple design and enduring quality, and their tailoring has been carefully customized to be comfortably motivating, subtly inspiring, quietly elegant, unobtrusively sophisticated, gently refining, and spiritually uplifting, with an easy grace that belies the power that is intrinsic to the material. The purpose of our Father's careful selection of material, meticulous design, and almost obsessive attention to detail, is to protect us from both the winds of adversity and the wiles of the adversary.

Just as Joseph's siblings were jealous of Jacob's gift, and were likely envious of their younger brother's evolving spiritual maturity, so too are our own contemporaries sometimes resentful of our accomplishments that are facilitated by faith. No matter what other outfits may be in our closets, however, and especially if they are modeled after the likeness of the world and celebrate the fashion statement of the day, we must have the courage to brush them aside and instead choose modestly uplifting and complementary ensembles. If we then wear our coats with dignity and with circumspection, they can make statements equivalent to that of the cape worn by Superman.

The fabric of our coats will have come, not from Krypton, but from Kolob, and the powers thereby derived will be otherworldly. If we see in their vibrant colors

"the Lord and his strength, (and if we) seek his face continually," our coats will transform us. (1 Chronicles 16:11). They will allow us to be faster than speeding bullets, more powerful than locomotives, and empower us to leap tall buildings in a single bound. Our coats will give strength to the poor and to the needy in his distress, and they will provide "a refuge from the storm, (and) a shadow from the heat," even when the tornado of temptation rages as a tempest against the fortress of our faith. (Isaiah 25:4).

The attention and adoration of the world is simply a seduction by Satan to influence us to abandon our faith and leave our coats of many colors hanging unattended and unused in the back of our closets. If we are embarrassed by the bold, attention grabbing patterns of our coats of many colors, we may be tempted to hide them beneath our more contemporary outfits. If this is the case, we should attune our ears to our Father, Who quietly reassures us: Be still, and know that it is I Who am God. It is I who has clothed you in your coat of many colors. (See D&C 101:16).

From the Book of Exodus, Aaron's example teaches that each of us may enjoy the protection afforded by the special clothing that complements, as an ensemble, our coat of many colors. "And thou shalt bring Aaron and his sons unto the door of the tabernacle of the congregation, and wash them with water. And thou shalt put upon Aaron the holy garments, and anoint him, and sanctify him." (Exodus 42:12-13). From time immemorial, the coats of many colors that have been furnished by God have been designed to provide lasting protection from evil influences. They have shielded His children against the power of the destroyer, that they might prosper until they have finished their work on the earth. (See Moses 1:39).

As we care for and maintain the fabric of our faith that is represented by our coats of many colors, we will humble ourselves before God and repent. As we do so, He will minister unto us through holy angels whose garments will be pure and white above all other whiteness, whose countenances will be as lightning, and whose personages will be glorious beyond description. (See D&C 20:6 & J.S.H. 1:32).

Like spiritual swaddling clothes, the fabric of our faith in our coats of many colors will resonate with intrinsic light rather than from pigment and dye. Our power will be evident to even the most hardened skeptics, such as Belshazzar, who summoned

Daniel to his court, and exclaimed: "I have even heard of thee, that the spirit of the gods is in thee, and that light and understanding and excellent wisdom is found in thee." (Daniel 5:14). The king did not realize it, but the power of which he was in awe came from the prophet's own coat of many colors.

The light of the Spirit will gives each thread in the fabric of our faith a vigor, vitality, and vivacity that is unique to holy vestments. Their steadfast colors will never fade, save it be through neglect or unbelief. They will be impervious to every stain except sin. If we are true and faithful to the care instructions that are clearly printed on the labels of our coats, they will be as shields of protection to us. But if we inadvertently or carelessly mingle our coats with other garments that have been soiled by sin, their powers of enchantment will be neutralized.

Our faith embraces many colors to suit our individual circumstances. Psycho-physiologists tell us that the human eye can distinguish around 10 million different colors, which is really quite remarkable, since there are only three primary colors in the visible light spectrum (red, green, and blue). Sir Isaac Newton, who was the first to use a prism to separate white light (at wavelengths between 390 - 700 nm) into its individual colors, divided the spectrum into seven named colors (red, orange, yellow, green, blue, indigo, and violet). This arrangement of colors in the fabric that is sewn into our faith provides plenty of latitude to fit our individual circumstances.

In general, though, the use of the color red calls us to action, and reminds us that the Savior trod the winepress alone. Orange can be a warning to take care that we conform our lives to the Lord's design. Yellow encourages us to seek the light that is gathering in the east. Green brings to mind the power of envy, the requirement to observe and keep the 10th commandment, and the wisdom to be at

peace with the cards in the hand that God has dealt us. Blue reminds us to mourn with those who mourn, and to comfort those who stand in need of comfort. Indigo is a color whose depth and brightness represent the profundity of the Gospel, and its ability to illuminate truth wherever it may be found. Violet is the color of amethyst, lavender, and beautyberries, and reminds us of the garlands festooning the balustrades of the celestial city of God. (See Revelation 21:20).

Although grey (black and white) is associated with neutrality, conformity, uncertainty, and indifference, it nevertheless prompts us to choose whom we will serve, and encourages us to stand on the Lord's side. Purple (red and blue) urges us to remember the royal robes of Christ, our King. Black (blue, red, and yellow) underscores the necessity of the opposition that is used to create the rough paving stones composing the pathway of progression. White (red, orange, yellow, green, blue, indigo and violet) solemnly suggests the comprehensive nature of the ordinances of the priesthood, our temple covenants, and the purity of the Spirit, all of which are necessary if we are to regain the glory of our former home.

From ultraviolet to infrared, our faith incorporates into the pattern and design of our coats every color of visible light. These resonate with radiation from a spectrum that can only be seen with eyes that have felt the touch of the hand of God. If we were able to break down that energy with a spiritual prism, we would look beyond the limited horizon of our sight, and see the visions of eternity. "By the power of the Spirit our eyes (would be) opened and our understandings (would be) enlightened, so as to see and understand the things of God." (D&C 76:12).

While faith nurtures the development of personality traits that are in concordance with the symmetry of heaven, sin is harmful because it destroys our ability to nurture the equilibrium that is a defining characteristic of those who inherit eternal life. In God's nature, there is neither variableness, nor shadow of turning.

Chapter Thirteen
The faith to act.

"Sow a thought, reap an act. Sow an act, reap a habit.
Sow a habit, reap a character. Sow a character,
reap an eternal destiny."
(David O. McKay)

The Savior revealed something about the nature of our Heavenly Father, and about our faith to act, when He said: "Thy will be done." (Matthew 26:42). In other words, there was no question in His mind that His Father's resolve would be translated into action. His vision would crystalize in accomplishment. In a more profane setting, we recall the definitive pronouncement: of Pharaoh: "So let it be written, so let it be done." (Cecil B. DeMille, "The Ten Commandments"). We also remember Michael Crichton's book about three scientists who enter a sphere that gives them the power to manifest their thoughts into reality. Appropriately, the book is entitled "Sphere," recalling the geometrical object that is perfectly round in three-dimensional

space, is symmetrical around its center, and represents harmony and beauty that results from balanced proportions without variation of form or substance. Art mimics life, and life mimics eternity.

As Alma taught: God "cannot walk in crooked paths; neither doth he vary from that which he hath said; neither hath he a shadow of turning from the right to the left, or from that which is right to that which is wrong; therefore, his course is one eternal round." (Alma 7:20).

The beginning of the book of Genesis tells us: "God said, Let there be light: and there was light." (Genesis 1:3). "And God said, let the waters under the heaven be gathered together unto one place, and let the dry land appear: and it was so." (Genesis 1:9). "And God said, Let the earth bring forth the living creature after his kind ... and it was so." (Genesis 1:24). Quite simply, He gets things done by speaking the word. It "is quick, and powerful, and sharper than any two-edged sword, piercing even to the dividing asunder of soul and spirit, and of the joints and marrow." (Hebrews 4:12). It was by the power of His word that Jesus "stood over (Simon's mother) and rebuked the fever, and it left her." (Luke 4:39). It was by the same power that He "rebuked the winds and the sea; and there was a great calm." (Matthew 8:26). In every case, He spoke "with all authority." (Titus 2:15). Thus, He was able to say even "unto the sea, Peace, be still. And the wind ceased, and there was a great calm." (Mark 4:39).

When He cleansed a leper, He needed only to say: "Be thou clean. And immediately the leprosy departed from him." (Luke 5:13). Simeon "came by the Spirit into the temple," and said to Jesus: "Lord, now lettest thy servant depart in peace, according to thy word." (Luke 2:25-32). As had Simeon, a centurion recognized the Savior's omnipotence, when he implored Him: "I am not worthy that thou shouldest come under my roof: but speak the word only, and my servant shall be healed." (Matthew 8:8). When the Savior asked the lame man lying beside the pool at Bethesda: "Wilt thou be made whole?" He needed only to say: "Rise, take up thy bed, and walk. And immediately the man was made whole, and took up his bed, and walked."

(John 5:6-9). "And whithersoever he entered, into villages, or cities, or country, they laid the sick in the streets, and besought him that they might touch if it were but the border of his garment: and as many as touched him were made whole." (Mark 6:56). In the Garden of Gethsemane, Jesus rebuked Peter, and said to him:

"Thinkest thou that I cannot now pray to my Father, and he shall presently give me more than twelve legions of angels?" (Matthew 26:53). All He needed to do was to petition His Father, and it would be done.

When the multitudes finally understood the power by which the Son of God worked His miracles, they were impulsively drawn to Him, and "brought unto him many that were possessed with devils: and he cast out the spirits with his word." (Matthew 8:16). He taught a great lesson in the grammar of the Gospel when "they brought to him a man sick of the palsy, lying on a bed: and Jesus seeing their faith said unto (him) Son, be of good cheer; thy sins be forgiven thee. And, behold, certain of the scribes said within themselves, This man blasphemeth. And Jesus knowing their thoughts said, Wherefore think ye evil in your hearts? For whether is easier to say, Thy sins be forgiven thee; or to say, Arise, and walk? But that ye may know that the son of man hath power on earth to forgive sins, (then saith he to the sick of the palsy,) Arise, take up thy bed." (Matthew 9:2-6).

It was only necessary that He cry "with a loud voice, Lazarus, come forth. And he that was dead came forth, bound hand and foot with graveclothes: and his face was bound about with a napkin." (John 11:43-44). Fortunately, Jesus identified Lazarus by name, or all heaven and hell might have broken free of the grave at His words. When grieving Jairus brought Jesus to his daughter, the Savior simply said: "Weep not; she is not dead, but sleepeth." Then He "took her by the hand, and called, saying, Maid, arise. And her spirit came again, and she arose straightway." (Luke 8:52 & 54-55).

It would be fascinating to know what words the Savior traced, as He "stooped down, and with his finger wrote on the ground." (John 8:6). Perhaps it is not necessary to have that knowledge, for "the kingdom of God is not (so much) in word, (as it

is) in power." (1 Corinthians 4:20). Benjamin understood the generative potential of feeling, when he taught: "This much I can tell you, that if ye do not watch yourselves, and your thoughts, and your words, and your deeds ... ye must perish."

(Mosiah 4:30). If we watch ourselves, we will be "given ... in the very hour, yea, in the very moment, what (we) shall say." (D&C 100:6).

Ultimately, power can be traced back to thought. For "as a man thinketh in his heart, so is he." (Proverbs 23:7). Then, as our feelings are translated through the medium of our words, the anticipated action is manifest. Mormon recognized this when he observed: "The preaching of the word had a great tendency to lead the people to do that which was just – yea, it had had more powerful effect upon the minds of the people than the sword, or anything else, which had happened unto them – therefore, Alma thought it was expedient that they should try the virtue of the word of God," because of its power to effect positive change. (Alma 31:5).

The scriptures teach that it is expedient to "turn to the Lord with full purpose of heart." (Mosiah 7:33). This may have something to do with the fact that the Word was "in the beginning ... and the Word was with God, and the Word was God." (John 1:1). Left to our own devices, our influence over the outcome of events is insignificant, "for there is no power but of God (and) the powers that be are ordained of God." (Romans 13:1). At certain times, however, we may be endowed with "the keys of the power of this priesthood" to act in the name of God. (D&C 132:59). "Now is the accepted time," taught Paul, wherein all things might be accomplished "by the word of truth, by the power of God, (and) by the armour of righteousness." (2 Corinthians 6:2 & 7).

It is by speaking specifically authorized and sanctioned words that we employ the power of God to perform baptisms, initiatory and sealing ordinances in the temple, and other priesthood ordinances, such as blessing the Sacrament. At other times, we use our own words as long as we adhere to general guidelines, such as when we are offering invocations and benedictions and when we are performing a confirmation, bestowing the gift of the Holy Ghost, naming and blessing babies, setting apart

individuals, dedicating homes and graves, blessing the sick, and casting out evil spirits, to name just a few.

Of priesthood-driven instruction in the Church, which is simply an expression of the faith to act, we are counseled: "The Spirit shall be given unto you by the prayer of faith; and if ye receive not the Spirit ye shall not teach." (D&C 42:14). There is not much we can accomplish without it. Without words that are driven by the Spirit, our interactions in the Church are but empty, passive rituals.

In fact, the same tongue can utter curses as well as blessings. Words can be weapons, as well as the Balm of Gilead. Words can offer weak rationalizations, or they can initiate action, as when we are enjoined: "Be baptized, every one of you, for a remission of your sins." (D&C 33:11). Words can offer lame excuses or help us to practice what we preach. We can distance ourselves from the Spirit with loose or careless tongues, or we can make contact with the power of God as we speak in the name of the Lord.

We do this when we invoke the Lord's blessings by the power of the priesthood. We do it when the power of the Holy Ghost compels us to bear our testimonies. The Lord does it when He looks upon a repentant sinner and says: "Thy sins are forgiven thee." (Luke 5:20). He does it when He says: "Go your way and sin no more." (D&C 6:35). We experience His power when He says to us: "Well done thou good and faithful servant: thou hast been faithful over a few things, I will make thee ruler over many things: Enter thou into the joy of thy lord." (Matthew 25:21). There are no limitations to the power of spirit-driven words. We can even receive the blessings of exaltation with the spoken word. (See 2 Peter 1:10).

At the very end of The Book of Mormon, Moroni exhorted us to "come unto Christ and be perfected in Him," because he understood that in the Last Days we would be blessed with empowering words. (Moroni 10:32). The Lord uses similar words as the tools to bring to pass the Restoration. "Now, what do we hear in the Gospel which we have received?" asked Joseph Smith. "A voice of gladness! A voice of mercy from

heaven; and a voice of truth out of the earth; glad tidings for the dead; a voice of gladness for the living and the dead; glad tidings of great joy. How beautiful upon the mountains are the feet of those that bring glad tidings of good things, and that say unto Zion: Behold, thy God reigneth!" (D&C 128:19).

Little wonder, then, that "the priest's duty is to preach, teach, expound, and exhort, and baptize, and administer the sacrament." (D&C 20:46). Their responsibility is to speak by the power of the Holy Ghost as if their voices were the Lord's own voice, and then to follow up their words with actions. (See D&C 68:4). Isaiah alluded to the power of the Word, when he wrote: "The glory of his majesty shall smite them, when he ariseth to shake terribly the earth." (2 Nephi 12:19). "And out of his mouth proceedeth the word of God, and with it he will smite the nations; and he will rule them with the word of his mouth." (J.S.T. Revelation 19:15).

Sometimes, the power of God is so great that words become unnecessary. Robert L. Simpson described his introduction to David O. McKay in 1958. "President McKay extended his firm right hand, and placing his left hand on my shoulder, looked into my eyes and, more than that, into every fiber of my being. After a few seconds, he gave my hand a friendly pump, my shoulder a squeeze, and said, 'Brother Simpson, I am pleased to know you.' Not 'I am pleased to meet you,' but 'pleased to know you.' Three months later, while sitting in my office in Los Angeles, my telephone rang and the voice on the other end of the line said, 'This is David O. McKay speaking.' Based on our interview three months ago, I feel impressed to issue a call.'" ("Improvement Era," 2/1970).

Jacob said: "With one glance of his eye (God) can smite you to the dust!" (Jacob 2:15). In Zarahemla following His crucifixion, the Resurrected Lord told the Nephites how the great destructions in their land had occurred. With terrifying clarity, He revealed that He had "caused" the great city Moroni to be sunk in the depths of the sea, and the inhabitants of the city of Gilgal to be buried in the depths of the earth, and the city Jacobugath to be burned with fire. (See 3 Nephi 9:4-12). The Nephites might have then remembered the awful promise that had been recorded on The Plates of Brass: "I call heaven and earth to record this day against you, that I have

set before you life and death." (Deuteronomy 30:19).

Under the best of circumstances, the Lord characterized His people as Zion "because they were of one heart and one mind, and dwelt in righteousness." (Moses 7:18).

They were pure in heart because their thoughts were focused on charity, and translated seamlessly through words into deeds. The righteousness of Zion typifies the celestial standard by which the Savior shall "judge the poor, and reprove with equity for the meek of the earth: and he shall smite the earth with the rod of his mouth, and with the breath of his lips shall he slay the wicked." (Isaiah 11:4).

Heavenly Father calls "upon the weak things of the world, those who are unlearned and despised, to thresh the nations by the power of (His) Spirit." (D&C 35:13). He is the light that shines in darkness, and it is by His power that we are given the courage to utter the words that must be spoken. (See D&C 11:11). We exercise the faith to act, with an assurance that "as the words have gone forth out of (His) mouth even so shall they be fulfilled." (D&C 29:30). Our actions echo the witness of Alma, who declared: "This much I do know, that the Lord God hath power to do all things which are according to his word." (Alma 7:8).

Joseph Smith understood the power of the word, when he prayed: "Help us by the power of thy Spirit, that we may mingle our voices with those bright, shining seraphs around thy throne, with acclamations of praise, singing Hosanna to God and the Lamb!" (D&C 109:79).

The power to which Joseph alluded is sufficient to "break mountains, to divide the seas, to dry up waters, to turn them out of their course; to put at defiance the armies of nations, to divide the earth, to break every band, to stand in the presence of God" and to manifest thought into reality. (J.S.T. Genesis 14:30-31). Our Heavenly Father infuses us with the faith to act, so that when we are entrusted with His power, we will speak purposefully. We remember Nephi, who declared: "My God will give me, if I ask not amiss." (2 Nephi 4:35). If we pass this verbal exam, we will be ushered into Zion, there to be "encircled about with the matchless bounty

of (God's) love." (Alma 26:15).

When our relationship with our Father in Heaven is sealed, our validation will come with power, as it did for Nephi, the son of Helaman. When he had entirely proven himself, he heard a voice saying: "I will make thee mighty in word and in deed, in faith and in works; yea, even that all things shall be done unto thee according to thy word, for thou shalt not ask that which is contrary to my will." (Helaman 10:5). The voice revealed Who had been speaking, and His communicative relationship with His faithful disciple became self-evident: "Behold, thou art Nephi, and I am God. Behold, I declare it unto thee in the presence of mine angels ... I give unto you power, that whatsoever ye shall seal on earth shall be sealed in heaven; and whatsoever ye shall loose on earth shall be loosed in heaven; and thus shall ye have power among this people." (Helaman 10:6-7).

When we enjoy that unrestrained rapport with God, our faith to act will generate the power to "get things done" in an expansive and interactive way, in all holiness. We will recognize His voice as Spirit, and His Spirit as truth, which "abideth and hath no end. And if it be in (us) it shall abound." (D&C 88:66).

Adam and Eve fell that they and their posterity might know true happiness, and nurture the moral fiber that we recognize today as saving faith. They were given the tools they would need to consistently choose the harder right, instead of the easier wrong, that they might find that happiness that has been prepared for the Saints of God.

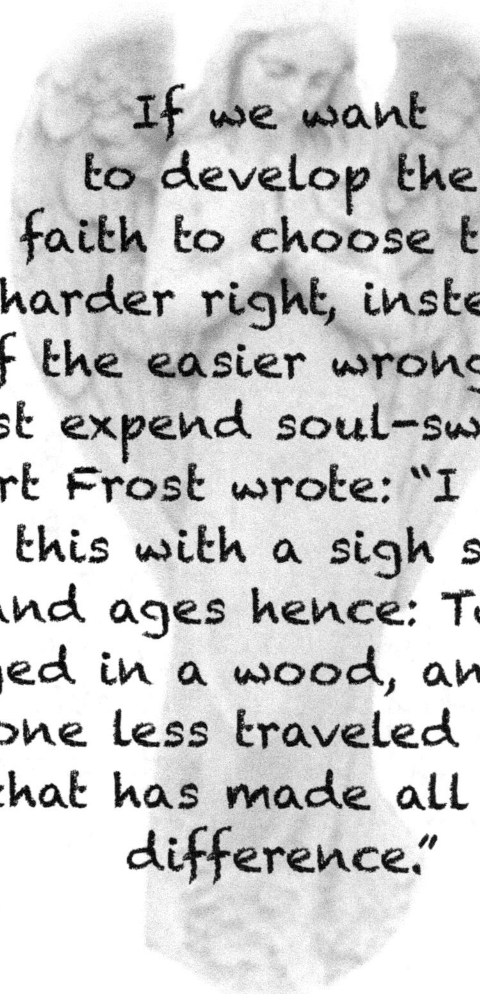

If we want to develop the faith to choose the harder right, instead of the easier wrong, we must expend soul-sweat. As Robert Frost wrote: "I shall be telling this with a sigh somewhere ages and ages hence: Two roads diverged in a wood, and I took the one less traveled by, and that has made all the difference."

Chapter Fourteen
The power of faith.

To understand how faith can be a principle of power that motivates us to action, we first need to understand what faith is (and is not). Much more than the intellectual assent to a proposition, it is vital, personal commitment to a practical belief that in the best of circumstances leads us to follow the path of repentance so that we can then make binding covenants with God. It is related to works, but not in a dependent way, for good works do not make us good, nor do they necessarily increase our faithfulness. When we show "a pattern of good works," it is because the doctrine upon which our faith is founded is incorruptible. (Titus 2:7). Sometimes, even if we do not realize the significance of obedience to the noble principles that govern the kingdom of God, we intuitively align ourselves with them. It is then inevitable that the mystic chords of memory will be touched, as we respond to the promptings of the Light of Christ. When the germination of our faith has been initiated, we will abound in good works. (See 2 Corinthians 9:8).

Alma taught: "How much more cursed is he that knoweth the will of God and doeth it not, than he that only believeth, or only hath cause to believe, and falleth into transgression?" (Alma 32:19). Belief can be a powerful motivator, but it often lacks the moral element of responsibility that we call faith. To those to whom much is given, much is expected. The gift of faith requires purposeful action. In this sense, "faith without works is dead, being alone." (James 2:17).

As Alma told the Zoramites: "Now of this thing ye must judge. Behold, I say unto you, that it is on the one hand even as it is on the other; and it shall be unto every man according to his work." (Alma 32:20). At some point in time, all of us are asked to take a leap of faith as we stand at a fork in the road, poised to make life's most important decision. As Joshua declared to Israel: "Choose ye this day whom ye will serve.... But as for me and my house, we will serve the Lord." (Joshua 24:5)

When our faith is in its infancy, Paul's classic and oft-quoted definition suffices: "Faith is the substance (or the assurance) of things hoped for, the evidence of things not seen." (Hebrews 11:1-40). In the context of Alma 32, faith is not to receive a sign from heaven. As Alma told the poor Zoramites, "If a man knoweth a thing he hath no cause to believe, for he knoweth it." (Alma 32:18). In this narrowly-defined sense, and in particular when we remember the details of Alma's recent experience with Korihor, we realize that we sometimes receive signs from heaven that are independent of the exercise of faith. They simply stare us in the face without our expenditure of soul-sweat. These signs do not lead us to "faith unto salvation." (1 Peter 1:5).

In the scenario recounted in Alma 32, we can see that when a sign is given, we might have sure knowledge without faith. This had been Korihor's fatal flaw. (See Alma 30). Under proper circumstances, however, "by doing our duty, faith increases until it becomes perfect knowledge." (Heber J. Grant, C.R., 4/1934). Initially, faith is to believe what we do not see, and the reward of faith is to see what we believe.

Notwithstanding President Grant's definitive declaration and inspired instruction, Alma's demonstrative definition emphasized that, at least for those who are

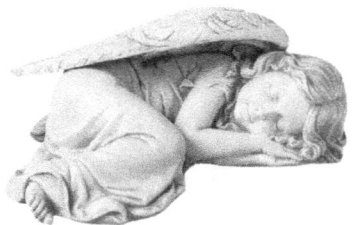

in their spiritual infancy, "faith is not to have a perfect knowledge of things; therefore, if ye have faith ye hope for things which are not seen, which are true." (Alma 32:21). This doctrine was correct in the ultimate sense, as it describes the genesis of faith. In Alma's usage, and in context, the verse might more clearly read: "Faith is not to have a perfect knowledge of things gained through our own experiences."

When Alma taught this principle to his Zoramite audience, Korihor had only recently demanded a sign as the condition for his faith, since he trusted only his physical senses. This rational approach, Alma realized, is the enemy of faith, and the poor Zoramites would need his gentle guidance to navigate the uncharted waters that are encountered by all who respond to the promptings of the Light of Christ. As Saint Augustine taught. "Understanding is the reward of faith. Therefore, seek not to understand that thou mayest believe, but believe that thou mayest understand."

A little girl who went out for an evening walk with her father demonstrated the power of child-like faith. She kept looking up at the stars, and finally said: "Daddy, if the bottom of heaven is so pretty, just think how beautiful the top will be." To those whose faith might have been corrosively corrupted by too many close encounters with carnality, Harold B. Lee counseled: "You must learn to walk to the edge of the light, and then a few steps into the darkness. Then, the light will appear and show the way before you." ("B.Y.U. Today," 3/1991). This is the way the acorn of faith is nurtured, that it might mature into a mighty oak.

Moroni wrote: "Dispute not because ye see not, for ye receive no witness until after the trial of your faith." (Ether 12:6). In matters of faith, the Lord is not on trial. At the Bar of Justice, He will simply weigh the facts, and our previous acceptance or rejection of the principles of the Gospel and the doctrines of the kingdom will determine our reward or our punishment. Trial proceedings have already been docketed to immediately follow our mortal experience, and they will be eminently fair.

The unbroken sunshine of absolute and undoubting faith in God's love was

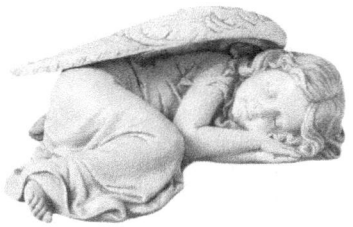

wonderfully expressed by Helen Keller, who wrote: "I believe that no good shall be lost, and that all man has willed or hoped or dreamed of good shall exist forever. I believe in the immortality of the soul because I have within me immortal longings. I believe that the state we enter after death is wrought of our own motives, thoughts, and deeds. I believe that my home there will be beautiful with colour, music, and speech of flowers and faces I love."

"Without this faith, there would be little meaning in my life. I should be a mere pillar of darkness in the dark. Observers in the full enjoyment of their bodily senses pity me, but it is because they do not see the golden chamber in my life where I dwell delighted; for dark as my path may seem to them, I carry a magic light in my heart. Faith, the spiritual strong searchlight, illuminates the way, and although sinister doubts lurk in the shadow, I walk unafraid towards the Enchanted Wood where the foliage is always green, where joy abides, where nightingales nest and sing, and where life and death are one in the presence of the Lord." ("Midstream").

Her understanding was quickened so that she could see by the Light of Christ, with 20-20 vision. Each of us can be similarly guided along the pathway leading to the highest pinnacles of enlightenment. From that vantage point, "we see the great call of diligence of men to labor in the vineyards of the Lord; and thus we see the great reason of ... rejoicing ... because of the Light of Christ unto life." (Alma 28:14, see Moroni 7:18, & D&C 88:7). Quite simply, we see, not with our natural eyes, but through the power of faith.

Ultimately, the Light of Christ will awaken each of us to the truth that "salvation cometh to none ... except it be through repentance and faith on the Lord Jesus Christ." (Mosiah 3:12). Mortality is not "a leap in the dark," said Truman Madsen. Instead, we "trust in what the spirit learned aeons ago; and religious recognition is just that - re-cognition, a re-knowing, the sum of existence. If we thwart or suppress that instinctive response, we are responsible, and, to a degree, we condemn ourselves. We knew Christ before this life, we know him here, and we

will know him hereafter. His sheep do indeed know his voice." (B.Y.U. Studies, 1975).

His voice has a familiar ring, because of the power of faith. To paraphrase Alexis deToqueville: The culture of the Church of Jesus Christ is "like a fire lit in the hills that, after having spread heat around it, still tinges the furthest reaches of the horizon with its light."

The pathway leading to exaltation is grounded upon the power of faith in Jesus Christ, faith in the divinely inspired mission of Joseph Smith, faith in the witness of Christ contained in The Book of Mormon, and faith in the first principles and ordinances of the Gospel. The power of faith ultimately leads us to the House of the Lord. This may have been what Moroni had in mind, when he urged us to "come unto Christ and be perfected in him." (Moroni 10:32). We do this by faith in the power of a priesthood that "administereth the Gospel," in the ordinances and covenants of the temple, where is found "the key of the mysteries of the kingdom, even the key of the knowledge of God. Therefore, in the ordinances thereof, the power of godliness is manifest." (D&C 84:19-20).

When we summarily dismiss experiences that kindle faith, we are "free, and that is a pleasant feeling, at first. There are no questions of conscience and no constraints, except the constraints of custom, convention, and the law, and these are flexible enough for most purposes. It is only later that the terror comes. We are free, but free in chaos, in an unexplainable world. We are free in a desert, from which there is no retreat but inward toward our hollow core." (Morris West, "The Devil's Advocate").

We will be blessed for our efforts to develop the power of faith. The miracles from the scriptures with which we are familiar were only made possible by the exercise of faith, and each of us may develop that same intensity of feeling with equally spectacular results. When we read in the sacred records of these experiences, a way is prepared that we, too, might be "partakers of the heavenly gift." (Ether 12:8). For example, many of us have linked our feelings with those of the two disciples on

the Road to Emmaus, who, after communing with the Resurrected Lord, declared: "Did not our heart burn within us, while he talked with us by the way, and while he opened to us the scriptures?" (Luke 24:32).

God endows us with His Spirit, that we might exercise faith in Christ, for He is the means of our salvation and exaltation through the Atonement. Angels, who are His servants, are often commissioned to the work. The office of their ministry is to call us "unto repentance, and to fulfil and to do the work of the covenants of the Father (and) to prepare the way." (Moroni 7:31).

Knowledge received through the power of faith is the foundation of testimony and is the mortar that binds together the tangible and intangible elements of our conversion. These include the words of wisdom that are found in the scriptures. It is there that we often go to seek learning. It is best when we do it even by study, and also by faith. (See D&C 26:2 & 88:118).

As we build upon the foundation of faith, we are reminded, sometimes quite painfully, that we are still as "little children and ... cannot bear all things now; (for we) must grow in grace and in the knowledge of the truth." (D&C 50:40). As the power of our faith builds in intensity, we gradually learn that "the word of the Lord is truth, and whatsoever is truth is light, and whatsoever is light is Spirit, even the Spirit of Jesus Christ. And the Spirit giveth light to (all) that cometh into the world; and the Spirit enlighteneth every(one) through the world, that hearkeneth" to its voice." (D&C 84:45-46).

The Light of Christ opens the eyes of our understanding so that we may look beyond our limited horizons to see what is real. Ultimately, it liberates us from the fetters of neural pathways, allowing the dark recesses of our minds to be illuminated. It proceeds forth "from the presence of God to fill the immensity of space - The light which is in all things, which giveth life to all things, which is the law by which all things are governed, even the power of God who sitteth upon his throne, who is in the bosom of eternity, who is in the midst of all things." (D&C 88:11-13).

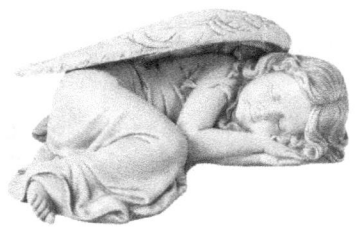

Faith has the power to fill us with that light, and to banish the darkness in us, so that we may comprehend all things. (See D&C 88:67). For "that which is of God is light," and when we receive light, and continue in God, we will receive more light, that will grow "brighter and brighter until the perfect day." (D&C 50:24). By its very definition, the Last Dispensation invites us to participate in a revelatory process whereby the fulness of the Gospel shall break forth as a "light "among them that sit in darkness. (D&C 45:28).

Faith, light, and truth are irreducible common denominators that establish a baseline for eternal progression. By contrast, "as far as we degenerate from God," and lose these heavenly elements, "we descend to the devil and lose knowledge, and without knowledge we cannot be saved." (Joseph Smith). Without knowledge, there can be no faith, for there is no light, and no conscious recognition of religious truth.

The Lord told Joseph Smith: "To some it is given by the Holy Ghost to know that Jesus Christ is the Son of God, and that he was crucified for the sins of the world. To others it is given to believe on their words, that they also might have eternal life if they continue faithful." (D&C 46:13-14). This applies to all those who listen to the Lord's ordained servants, as they bear testimony to the world. "By doing so, the Lord God prepareth the way that the residue of men may have faith in Christ, that the Holy Ghost may have place in their hearts." (Moroni 7:32).

As the spark of faith, struck off the Divine Anvil of God, ignites our flame of resolve, we develop the "power to do whatsoever thing is expedient" or right to do under the circumstances. That thing is to "repent and be baptized ... in the name of Jesus Christ for the remission of sins, and ... receive the Holy Ghost." (Acts 2:38). Ultimately, "the fruits of faith" is to be saved in the Celestial Kingdom of God. It is the very reason for the ministry of Jesus Christ and His servants among the children of men. (See Moses 1:39).

Because of its importance, Christ will continue the ministry and work miracles

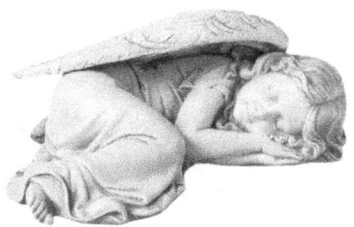

as "long as time shall last, or the earth shall stand, or there shall be one man upon the face thereof to be saved." (Moroni 7:36). But when we are spellbound by sorcery, mesmerized by magic, titillated by telestial trivia, held captive in conceptual cul de sacs, fixated by a fascination with idols of wood and stone, or distracted by devilish doctrines in any way whatsoever, the capacity of the Spirit to encourage us to exercise saving faith wanes.

When the gifts of the Spirit are absent, we can be sure that faith has "ceased also; and awful is the state of man, for they are as though there had been no redemption made." (Moroni 7:38). If we procrastinate the day of our repentance by allowing ourselves to become so spiritually blinded to the Light of Christ that we stumble over the tripwires that have been skillfully set by Satan, explosions of doubt will incapacitate us. We can lose the ability to distinguish right from wrong, good from evil, and light from darkness. The Spirit of the Lord must withdraw and leave us to our own devices when we voluntarily surrender our facility to vigorously exercise the power of faith. This is the final state of the wicked, from which there may be no recovery.

Mormon saw our day and wrote words of encouragement to those in whom he perceived a covenant consciousness: "I judge better things of you, for I judge that ye have faith in Christ because of your meekness." (Moroni 7:39). He was like wise old Tevya, in The Fiddler on The Roof, who told his daughters: "In Anatevka, God knows who you are, and what you may become."

Mormon's optimism that we would choose the better part illustrates his confidence in the power of faith to generate hope. For "how is it that ye can attain unto faith," he asked, "save ye shall have hope?" (Moroni 7:40). Later, even as his world came crashing down around him, Moroni would voice the same undaunted positive sentiment: "Wherefore, there must be faith; and if there must be faith, there must also be hope." (Moroni 10:20).

Today, our circumstances are different from than those in which Mormon and

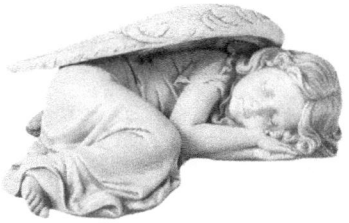

Moroni found themselves, but they are equally unnerving, There is a common denominator, however, with which we are equally familiar, and that is faith "through the Atonement of Christ and the power of his resurrection," together with the hope that we might "be raised up unto life eternal." (Moroni 7:41).

Hope that is generated by the power of faith is not blind trust in a wildly improbable promise, nor is it a high stakes gamble. It is true that a lot is at risk. In fact, our eternal welfare is on the line, but our hope remains as the distillation of well-founded faith that is, in turn, nurtured by meekness and lowliness of heart. Because of our sacrifice of a broken heart and a contrite spirit, Heavenly Father is able to unleash the power of covenants to buttress our hope and bind us to faithfulness. Their combined influence emboldens us to become the masters of our desires and emotions, and inspires us to bridle our appetites and behaviors so that they may be expressed within the bounds He has wisely established.

The foundation of faith and hope triggers the harmonic waves of the principles of the Gospel to create symmetry out of chaos. The Plan of Salvation itself exhibits symmetry because it looks the same from every perspective, and especially after our transformation through faith.

The symmetry of The Plan is an underlying mathematical principle that is expressed in all patterns of behavior, beginning with the arts and sciences of the every day world in which we live, and extending to the power that infuses the fabric of our faith with vibrancy. Symmetry quickens, or gives life to, our innate inclination to love one another, or to have charity.

Mormon taught that when the Holy Ghost endows us with the power to testify that Jesus is the Christ with a sure hope born of faith, it is inevitable that we will "have charity." (Moroni 7:44). It is a gentle mentor that teaches us to do more than sharpen our vision. It encourages us to rely upon our spiritual sixth sense, so that we may act upon our beliefs and experience with exhilaration and wide-eyed wonder a divine perspective. Charity reminds us of the Savior's sensitivity toward others, and of His empathy. It is more focused on celestial sureties than on telestial trinkets.

It is humble and selfless. It reflects poise under provocation and has no secret agenda to follow. It is repulsed by sin, rejoices in the truth, and is spiritually quickened by the resonant realities of well-founded faith. It bears all things with patience, is naturally drawn to light, and is continually open to that which is good. (See Moroni 7:45). It is manifest in the intangible touch of the Master's hand, the expression of His divine nature, quiet Christianity in action, and the personification of the power of faith.

We are nothing without the qualities of faith, hope, and charity, because they define and determine our path of progression. (See 1 Corinthians 13:2-3). "Charity" completes The Plan of Salvation, and it "never faileth," because it is a godly quality, whose expression alone confirms its validity It needs no external witness. Our faith intuitively impels us to cleave unto charity, which is the greatest of all the gifts of the Spirit. (See Moroni 7:46).

"Charity is the pure love of Christ, and it endureth forever." It eternally coexists with The Plan itself. It is the defining characteristic and driving force of those who inhabit the Celestial Kingdom, and so, "whoso is found possessed of it at the last day, it shall be well with him." (Moroni 7:47). Charity is the palpable expression of the grace of God, and with the Light of Christ it fills the immensity of space. It prepares men and women, everywhere, for their heavenly homecoming.

It drives the power of faith, reminding us that "we can make our lives sublime, and, departing, leave behind us footprints on the sands of time." (Henry Wadsworth Longfellow). Sometimes there are two sets of prints in the sand, and during times of particular difficulty, there may be only one. Of course, it is during those trying times that the Savior carries us on His shoulders. When we are in peril, it is by our faith that His power lifts us out of harm's way "with a stretched-out arm." (D&C 103:17). Even in those circumstances when we are our own worst enemy, the very fact that He is mighty to save, and is the embodiment of charity, invites us to exercise our faith, and flee to the sanctuary of His open arms. (See 2 Nephi 31:19).

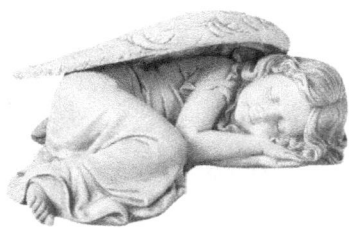

Heavenly Father's thoughts are not our thoughts, and His ways are not our ways, and so it is our faith that reassures us when His mind-boggling wisdom, insight, tools, and technologies challenge our comprehension. (See Isaiah 55:8). We take solace in the fact that, were our tiny brains to attempt to understand His mind with inadequate preparation, it would probably do us more harm than good. It would be of no benefit to us if we received the mysteries of the kingdom in an overwhelming cascade that overpowered our capacity to process truth. We would fry our brains in the heat of a divine fire. (See 2 Kings 1:2, Job 1:16, Deuteronomy 4:24, & Psalms 68:2).

Instead, we "exercise our faith" when we come to drink from the fountain of living water, contented to receive line upon line, and precept upon precept. (See Alma 34:17 & 26). Worldly fire hydrants, that indiscriminately spew forth only facts and figures, are not designed to contain the conflagration of sin or to give us consolation. Instead, our Heavenly Father quietly holds forth "that which is to come, confirming our hope" as well as our faith, with quiet words of counsel and comfort. (D&C 128:21).

When we find ourselves before that free, full, flowing fountain, we must take care, lest we indiscriminately take only a swig or two, as if its water were only a refreshing mouthwash. We may enjoy the tingle of its effervescence, but if we only gargle to get the bad taste of the world out of our mouths, if we only superficially spit and rinse, we pander to pathogens too perverse to ponder. Sooner or later, the bacterial count in our mouths will return to its former level, because we have not faithfully embraced the principles of hygiene that promote a healthy spiritual lifestyle.

It is only by the exercise of our faith that we can be sure that we will flourish under His guidance. By the power of our faith, we may mature in our progression to become as He is, and to be "worthy of our inheritance," which is spoken of in the scriptures no fewer than 317 times. That power can open our eyes, turn us from darkness to light, insulate us from the illegitimate and counterfeit influence of Satan, and introduce us to God, where we may receive a forgiveness of sins, and

an inheritance among others who are similarly sanctified by faith. (See Acts 26:18). In no matter what condition we may currently find ourselves, at some point, our Heavenly Father will set the stage for us to be reborn by generation and not by maturation, and to receive immortality and eternal life. For the faithful, that journey had a starting point, it now has any number of whistle-stops along the way, it may have delays and detours to deal with, and it will only conclude when it reaches a destination that is not a dream, but rather is the tangible expression of a divinely designed destiny.

The power of faith will rescue us from the subtle influences of those who stumble through life toward telestial targets, mistakenly thinking they are the concentric circles of celestial bulls-eyes. It will liberate us from careless conversation that rings of sounding brass and tinkling cymbals. (See 1 Corinthians 13:1). It will save us when we are tempted to exchange the simple garments of the priesthood for fine-twined linens. (See Alma 4:6). It will dissipate the mists of darkness that swirl around us, and will instead guide us to a dawn of discovery that illuminates a rod of iron that defines a path of progress. (See 1 Nephi 18:23).

When we grow weary of the trials and tribulations that are part of the opposition in all things that is built into our mortal experience, it is the power of our faith that will encourage us to carry on, with a reassurance that "the best of life is hidden from our eyes somewhere behind the hills of time." (Sir William Murdock). Our faith will encourage us with the conviction that good things come to those who are willing to wait.

The power of faith will bind us to our Heavenly Father in an unbreakable connection. It will bless us with the settled conviction that He takes notice of sparrows falling from trees, and heads of hair that have thinned with time, but it will also confirm that He orchestrates to our benefit the explosion of supernovas in distant galaxies. (See Helaman 14:5). The power of our faith will give us confidence that He does not play dice with His creations and that He will not leave things to chance. We have faith that, as a loving Parent, He will be an active participant in our growth

and development. He will always attend our parent / teacher conferences, and He will intervene in our behalf when we are sent to detention for infraction of the rules of conduct.

He will never miss our extracurricular activities, and He will have a season pass to witness every game we will ever play. He will forever be in the bleachers, seated in the middle of our cheering section. He will lead the "wave" when it passes through the stands. He will sit up late in the evening, and leave the porch light burning, waiting for us to return to the safety of our hearth and home. He will have our phone number on speed dial and will regularly use text messaging and voice mail to keep in touch with us. He will be at the top of our "friends-and-family" list.

The power of our faith will allow His divine tutorial training to become an eagerly anticipated process with which we will become increasingly comfortable. As we receive guidance, we will learn to "hear truth spoken with clarity and freshness; uncolored and untranslated, it will speak from within ourselves in a language original but inarticulate, heard only with the soul." (Hugh B. Brown). Our faith will tutor us to become fluent in the language of heaven, so much so that will become our native tongue.

Even when our faith falters and we ignore our Heavenly Father, its after-glow will keep Him close-by. We cannot make Him go away. His stated mission, which our faith confirms as an incontrovertible truth, is to bring to pass our immortality and eternal life. (See Moses 1:39). To confirm our faith, He has inaugurated a fool-proof Plan: "I will go before your face," He has promised. "I will be on your right hand and on your left, and my Spirit shall be in your hearts, and mine angels round about you, to bear you up." (D&C 84:88) "For he hath said, I will never leave thee, nor forsake thee." (Hebrews 13:5).

He will send the Holy Ghost to educate us, and to teach us things about eternal truth that we can learn in no other way. "Hearken unto me," urged King Benjamin,

"and open your ears that ye may hear, and your hearts that ye may understand; and your minds that the mysteries of God may be unfolded to your view." (Mosiah 2:9). Our faith will become a powerful catalyst that encourages the Spirit to influence our lives in such a way that we will be cast off into streams of revelatory experience and carried along in the quickening currents of direct experience with heaven.

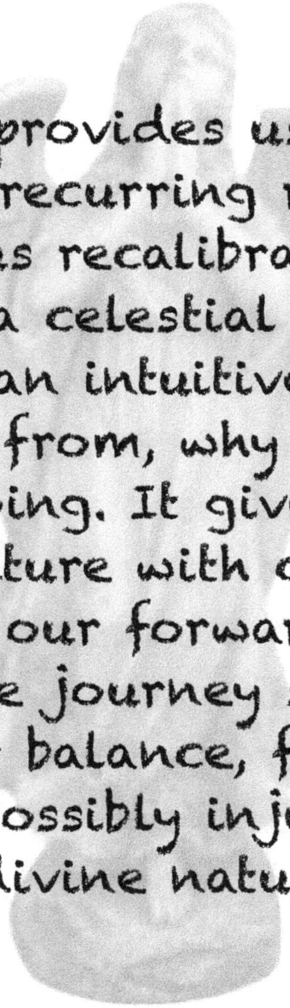

Faith provides us with a
regularly recurring reassurance
of a religious recalibration that auto
corrects with a celestial precision. Faith
envelops us in an intuitive appreciation of
where we came from, why we are here, and
where we are going. It gives us the courage
to face the future with confidence and
to maintain our forward momentum
during the journey so we won't
lose our balance, fall down,
and possibly injure our
divine nature.

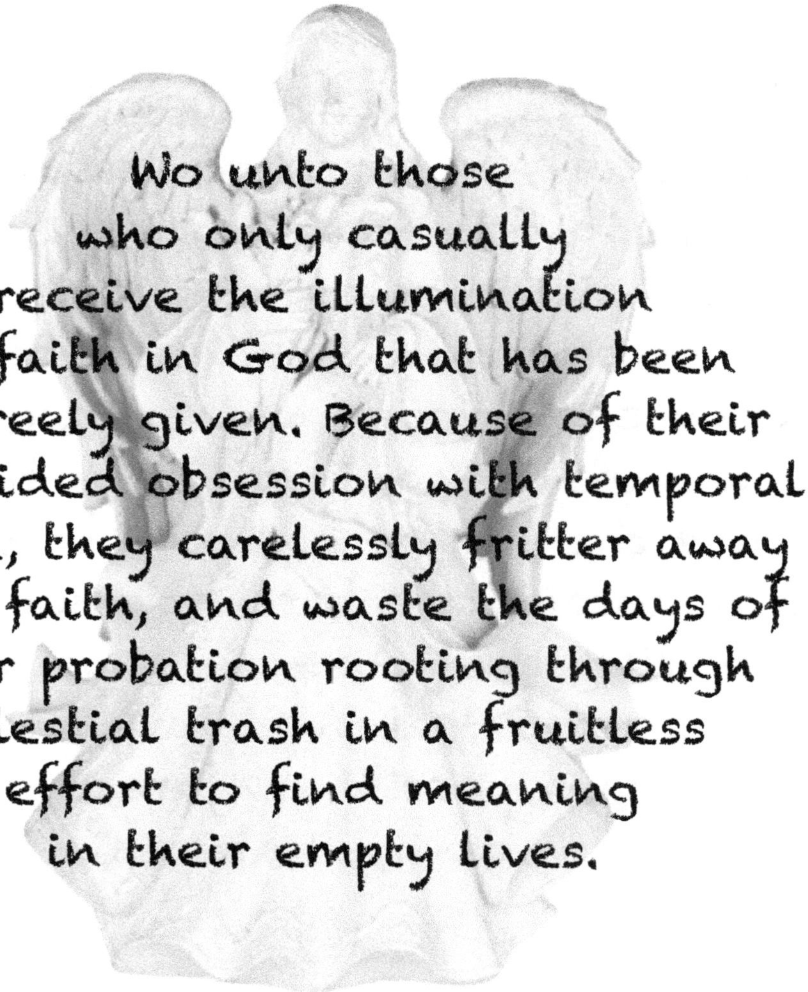

Wo unto those
who only casually
receive the illumination
of faith in God that has been
so freely given. Because of their
misguided obsession with temporal
trivia, they carelessly fritter away
their faith, and waste the days of
their probation rooting through
telestial trash in a fruitless
effort to find meaning
in their empty lives.

Chapter Fifteen
Choosing the harder right.

"May we ever choose the harder right,
instead of the easier wrong."
(Thomas S. Monson).

Is it easier to choose wrong, and harder to choose the right? Is it easier to be wicked, and harder to be righteous? Is it easier to be sad, and harder to be happy? Is it easier to just put your life on cruise control, and harder to take the more challenging high road? Is it easier to go with the flow, and harder to swim upstream, against the current? Is it easier to walk with turkeys, and harder to soar with eagles? Is it easier to just throw in the towel and give up, and harder to continue the good fight? Is it easier to be average, and harder to be exceptional? Is it easier to adopt the ways of the world, and harder to acknowledge that there is an autobiographical thread within each of us that leads back to Deity? Is it easier to yield to temptation, and harder to resist sin? Is rebellion an easier alternative, and obedience a harder

choice? Is it easier to live in a confusing fog of conflicting values, and harder to be grounded on the bedrock of the Gospel and to be guided by tablets of stone, or the fleshy tables of the heart?

Is it easier to be immoral, and harder to be virtuous? Is it easier to be slothful and indolent, and harder to be upright? Is it easier to be swayed by secular humanism, and harder to be faithful to eternally valid principles? Is it easier to wander to and fro, carried about with every wind of doctrine, and harder to be guided by a celestial compass? Is it easier to be carnal and worldly, and harder to be holy? Is it easier to live in wanton defiance of God's laws, and harder to pattern our lives after the example of the Master? Is it easier to be depraved, and harder to be principled? Is the pursuit of nobility akin to a quest to find the Holy Grail? Are those who attempt to follow the teachings of the Savior only tilting with windmills?

Before Joan of Arc was carried to the stake, she was given an opportunity to obtain her freedom by denying her beliefs. Instead, she made this statement: "I know this now. Every man gives his life for what he believes. Every woman gives her life for what she believes. Sometimes people believe in little or nothing, and so they give their lives for little or nothing. One life is all we have, and we live it as we believe in living it, and then it is gone. But to surrender what you are and live without belief is more terrible than dying, even more terrible than dying young." Resolutely, then, she faced death, still true to her faith and her beliefs. Her final acts on earth were consistent with her convictions.

In Joan's medieval world, the successor to the throne of France was known as the Dauphin. During the reign of Charles VII, unscrupulous, crafty, and duplicitous counselors tried every means to corrupt the Dauphin, to thereby render him ineligible to inherit the kingdom. In all of their attempts, however, they were unsuccessful. Finally, in resignation, they asked him, "How is it that with all our enticements we were not able to corrupt your high standards?" His reply was simple: "I am a King's son."

Both Joan and the Dauphin had internalized patterns of behavior that were harmonious with their beliefs, and that allowed them to act in coordination with their convictions. It has been said that all we need is 21 days to make or break a habit, be it good or bad, and after that, unconscious mechanisms kick into gear. In any case, within three weeks, we find ourselves on autopilot, inexorably headed either toward sunlit halls that free us from doubt and fear, or toward a gathering gloom within which are hidden demoralizing demons waiting to haunt our every move.

There is nothing magical about the number 21. It comes from a popular book published in 1960 called "Psycho-Cybernetics" by Maxwell Maltz. He was a plastic surgeon who simply noticed that his patients seemed to take about three weeks to get used to their new faces. However, the time it takes to make or break a habit may not be that clear-cut. A more recent study showed that the average time it took for a new habit to coalesce was about 10 weeks, but individual times varied from 18 to 254 days.

The bottom line is that if you want to internalize a new affirmative behavior, you shouldn't despair if three weeks of disciplined effort doesn't seem to do the trick. For most people, that's simply not enough time. Stick with it for a bit longer, and you'll end up with a habit you can keep without thinking about it.

We know that there needs to be opposition in order for the positive lifestyle promoted by The Plan of Salvation to succeed. Therefore, any habit formation, even the internalization of Gospel principles, or consistently choosing the harder right, must grapple with the tricky phenomena of free will and opposition.

Think of the predicament facing Adam and Eve in the Garden. Not knowing the mind of God, that opposition is necessary for the enjoyment of eternal happiness, Satan sought what he thought would be the misery of all mankind, and with his congenital short-sightedness and his typical stratagem of promoting half-truths, he offered the forbidden fruit to Eve. "Ye shall be as God," he unwittingly promised, "knowing good and evil." (2 Nephi 2:18).

After innocently grappling with the unfamiliar concept of opposition, and with

a little psychological manipulation by Satan, Adam and Eve made the difficult decision to transgress God's law. They had reached the conclusion that there was no other way for them to heed their Father's commandment to multiply and replenish the earth. They chose the harder right, instead of languishing in the amoral doldrums of the easier wrong.

Through no coincidence, it was almost immediately after they had done so, that their Father visited them to give them further instruction; to clarify and fine-tune the operating principles of The Plan that had been set in motion by their transgression in the Garden. This included the introduction of sacred covenants that would form the foundation of a nurturing matrix within which Adam and Eve's newfound habit patterns could take root. The power of covenants would enable them to reach for the sky from the lone and dreary world. With the help of the Savior, they would turn their dreams into reality. (See 2 Nephi 2).

As He explained to Joseph Smith: "It must needs be that the devil should tempt the children of men, or they could not be agents unto themselves; for if they never should have bitter they could not know the sweet. Wherefore, it came to pass that the devil tempted Adam, and he partook of the forbidden fruit and transgressed the commandment, wherein he became subject to the will of the devil, because he yielded unto temptation." (D&C 29:39-40).

But Adam and Eve were not deceived. Theirs was an intelligent, conscious, and mutually agreed upon decision, the result of their awakening comprehension of the unalterable requirements of the Gospel Plan. Adam and Eve fell that they and their posterity might come to know true happiness, and that they might nurture the moral fiber that we recognize today as saving faith. They were given all the tools they would need to consistently choose the harder right, instead of the easier wrong, against the backdrop of the harsh and unforgiving environment of the telestial world that was to be their new home. But they would also learn this truth: That which we persist in doing becomes easier for us; not that the nature of the thing has

changed, but that our power to do is increased.

Without understanding all the ramifications of their decision to partake of the fruit of the Tree of Knowledge of Good and Evil, Adam and Eve still believed that their change to a mortal condition was necessary, even though it might come like a flash of lightning and a clap of thunder. In the end, they were blessed with the faith to believe that the storm would pass and that flowers would bloom amid thistles, thorns, and noxious weeds. (See "I Ching," The Chinese Book of Change).

The choice made by Adam and Eve in the Garden to choose the harder right rather than the easier wrong, obviated the 'Progression Paradox' that had faced them, wherein they would have remained forever in "a state of innocence, having no joy, for they knew no misery; doing no good, for they knew no sin." (2 Nephi 2:23). To put it plainly, the Fall paved the way for the introduction of priesthood ordinances that would bless the children of men, for all time, with the tools to consistently choose the harder right, rather than the easier wrong. And it gets even better: The Atonement would provide a needed safety net, should they fail to do so. At the end of the day, "Adam fell that men might be; and men are, that they might have joy." (2 Nephi 2:25).

President Spencer W. Kimball observed that we often try to expel from our lives choices that are typified by the harder right, because they might result in "physical pain and mental anguish." He deplored our efforts to "assure ourselves of continual comfort" by ignorantly choosing the easier wrong. He observed that "if we were to close the doors upon the sorrow and distress" that sometimes accompany hard choices, "we might be excluding our greatest friends and benefactors, for suffering can make saints of people as they learn patience and self-mastery."

These are the visceral emotions that Adam and Eve surely experienced as they forged a new life together in the telestial world. As they looked back over their shoulders to catch one last fleeting glimpse of the Garden, they must have realized that its overly protective influence would have ultimately proven to be suffocating.

One thing is certain: The strait and narrow path that lay before them was marked by conspicuous signs that encouraged them to move in the direction of the harder right.

President Kimball continued: "If we looked at mortality as the whole of existence, then pain, sorrow, failure, and short life would be calamity. But if we look upon life as an eternal thing stretching far into the pre-mortal past and on into the eternal post-death future, then all happenings may be put in proper perspective."

That our first parents embraced this longitudinal view of life explains why they cherished the opportunity that had been afforded them to experience mortality. "Blessed be the name of God," Adam declared, "for because of my transgression my eyes are opened, and in this life I shall have joy, and again in the flesh I shall see God. And Eve, his wife, heard all these things and was glad, saying: Were it not for our transgression we never should have had seed, and never should have known good and evil, and the joy of our redemption, and the eternal life which God giveth unto all the obedient." (Moses 5:10-11).

The Plan was carefully crafted to create the conditions wherein we might be prompted and strengthened by the Light of Christ to choose the harder right, that we might come unto Him within the cradle and crucible of experience. Although we do not yet comprehend all the details, there is a common thread in the seeming chaos of existence. "For my thoughts are not your thoughts, neither are your ways my ways, saith the Lord. For as the heavens are higher than the earth, so are my ways higher than your ways, and my thoughts than your thoughts." (Isaiah 55:8-9). We cannot find "happiness in doing iniquity," for it is a cowardly characteristic. It "is contrary to the nature of that righteousness which is in our great and Eternal Head." (Helaman 13:38). By experience, we know that without righteousness, there can be no happiness. (See 2 Nephi 2:13). Then, why are we of so little faith? Why do we sin, if "wickedness never was happiness?" (Alma 41:10). Why do we allow ourselves to form bad habits that reinforce self-defeating behaviors and dictate negative outcomes that invariably lead to suffering and spiritual darkness? Why does misery love company? Why do

we so often choose the seemingly easier wrong, rather than the right that appears to be harder only because effort is required to reinforce our backbone with moral fiber? How can we exercise the faith to believe that it shall surely "come to pass, that the spirits of those who are righteous (will be) received into a state of happiness, which is called paradise, a state of rest, (and) a state of peace?" (Alma 40:12).

Alma the Younger is a good example of one who had seen life from both sides of the fence, and who, after his conversion, would never again choose the easier wrong. His abrupt change of behavior was preceded by indescribable suffering that was the culmination of repetitive poor choices. He had taken the easy way out for so long that his detoxification from sin was accompanied by inevitable withdrawal symptoms that are difficult to describe. Suffice to say, that for three days and for three nights, he was "racked, even with the pains of a damned soul." (Alma 36:26).

But miraculously, he was later able to measure his happiness against the discomposure of his former sinful life. "And oh, what joy," he wrote, "and what marvelous light I did behold; yea, my soul was filled with joy as exceeding as (had been) my pain!" (Alma 36:20). When he had been born again, his new lease on life was illuminated by his personal witness that "the elements are eternal, and spirit and element, inseparably connected, receive a fulness of joy." (D&C 93:33). Having made the decision to choose the harder right, it would now become easier for him to sustain a lifestyle that was oriented toward happiness. He had learned in the school of hard knocks, as we all must, that specific blessings follow obedience to their related laws. For "there is a law, irrevocably decreed in heaven before the foundations of this world, upon which all blessings are predicated. And when we obtain any blessing from God, it is by obedience to that law upon which it is predicated." (D&C 130:20-21).

In a careful reading of this passage from the Doctrine & Covenants, "that law" appears to be the Atonement, from which all blessings may be traced. All of our blessings are predicated upon obedience to the laws surrounding and supporting

the sacrifice of the Savior. The sting of death itself is swallowed up in the doctrine of the Atonement that was introduced to the Council before the foundation of the world. (See Mosiah 16:8). Alma could now bear a personal testimony of Benjamin's witness that the Lord "doth require that (we) should do as he hath commanded (us); for which if (we) do, he doth immediately bless (us)." (Mosiah 2:24).

Earlier, Benjamin had asked the people of Zarahemla to consider "the blessed and happy state of those that keep the commandments of God." (Mosiah 2:41). Nephi would later observe how "the Lord in his great infinite goodness doth bless and prosper those who put their trust in him." (Helaman 12:1). At first blush, the easier wrong may appear to be more convenient, but that is only because it harmonizes with worldliness. Worldliness is all around us, and without the stabilizing influence of the Gospel, and with the faith to choose the harder right, it seems to be the norm. It seems "natural." But it is only so to those with itching ears, who love the feel of flaxen cords caressing their necks. (See 2 Timothy 4:3, & 2 Nephi 26:22).

Our senses are assaulted with tantalizing temptations from every imaginable angle, and these doggedly wear down our defenses over time. Alexander Pope may have been thinking of the easier wrong when he wrote: "Vice is a monster of such frightful mien, that to be hated needs but be seen. Yet, seen too oft, familiar with her face, first we pity, then endure, and then embrace."

The easier wrong is often a highly visible enticement by a master illusionist who has never once been able to deliver on its promises. It is as a pot of gold at the end of the rainbow. It is a pipe dream, a flight of fancy, and a stretch of the imagination. It rings hollow. When we embrace the easier wrong, we wrap our arms around a caricature of happiness that is nothing more than a façade. The easier wrong may be a hologram of holiness, but in the end, it is all smoke and mirrors.

Too often, the easier wrong is tainted by misfortune. However, even that calamity may be used by our Heavenly Father, in His divine design, to teach us valuable

lessons about perseverance, let alone repentance. Often times, it is only after much tribulation that the blessing of sweet forgiveness comes. (See D&C 58:4).

If we are gliding smoothly and effortlessly through life, we are probably going downhill, for progress traces a path that takes us on an uphill journey into a headwind, over a path that is plagued by potholes. Only our incessant labors in the kingdom, epitomized by the harder right, render us worthy of the mighty blessings promised by the Lord. (See D&C 21:9).

Nephi exhibited the faith to choose the harder right, when he implored the Lord: "Wilt thou encircle me around in the robe of thy righteousness! O Lord, wilt thou make a way for mine escape before mine enemies! Wilt thou make my path straight before me! Wilt thou not place a stumbling block in my way — but that thou wouldst clear my way before me, and hedge not up my way." (2 Nephi 4:33).

If we want to develop the faith to choose the harder right, instead of the easier wrong, we must be long-suffering. In the book of Alma, those who stood fast in the faith were characterized as being "immovable in keeping the commandments of God." They were a people who "bore with patience the persecution which was heaped upon them." (Alma 1:25).

If we want to develop the faith to choose the harder right, instead of the easier wrong, we must "be humble, submissive and gentle," and easily "entreated." (Alma 7:23). We must call upon the holy name of God, "and watch and pray continually," that we might "not be tempted above that which (we) can bear, and thus be led by the Holy Spirit, becoming humble, meek, submissive," and "full of love." (See Alma 20:28-29 & Alma 26:27). If we allow Him to do so, the Lord will help us to drive these qualities into our inward parts. (See Jeremiah 31:33).

If we want to develop the faith to choose the harder right, instead of the easier wrong, we will eschew the comfort zones of Babylon, while gratefully utilizing the aid stations that have been scattered throughout Zion. (See 2 Nephi 28:21 & 24).

Nevertheless, we must guard against becoming complacent in Zion. (See 2 Nephi 28:24-25). As Benjamin warned the People of Zarahemla: "This much I can tell you, that if ye do not watch yourselves, and your thoughts, and your words, and your deeds, and observe the commandments of God, and continue in the faith ... ye must perish." (Mosiah 4:30).

If we want to develop the faith to choose the harder right, instead of the easier wrong, we will endure to the end in righteousness. Only then, can we enjoy "eternal life, which gift is the greatest of all the gifts of God." (D&C 14:7). The Lord warned: "All those who will not endure chastening, but deny me, cannot be sanctified." (D&C 101:5). As Joseph Smith wrote to the suffering Saints who had resisted the urge to capitulate to the easier wrong: "If thou endure it well, God shall exalt thee on high," and "cause thee to triumph over all thy foes." (D&C 121:8).

If we want to develop the faith to choose the harder right, instead of the easier wrong, we will view our afflictions in a new light, and determine to discover how they can work together for our good. (See D&C 98:3). During the process of the formation of our good habits, Heavenly Father will provide opportunities for our hearts to be softened as we are brought down into the depths of humility and become teachable. (See Alma 62:41).

Our experiences that do not make us stronger, kill us, in the sense that they weaken our drive and determination to move onward and upward. It was the Dominican priest Henri Didón who, in the opening ceremony of a school sporting event in 1881, first expressed the words that would later become the motto of Olympians: "Citius, Altius, Fortius!" (Faster, Higher, Stronger!) In this sense, it is the Lord, our physical, mental, emotional, and spiritual fitness coach, Who will "consecrate (our) afflictions for (our) gain." (2 Nephi 2:2). He will provide ways for us to work through our pain, for without it, there is no gain.

It may take ten weeks to recalibrate our habit patterns, but after that, why should

our hearts weep and our souls linger in the valley of sorrow, and our flesh waste away, and our strength slacken? (See 2 Nephi 4:26).

During the process, we need to emulate Alma, to "be patient in (our) long-suffering and affliction" for assaults upon our deepest emotions will be the traveling companions of our hard choices. (Alma 17:11). It will only be in the trial of our faith to choose the harder right that our nature will be transformed, and that our character will find expression in lifestyle behaviors that support the principles of The Plan.

Our Heavenly Father must love us very much, to take the time and effort to so profoundly influence our lives with His divine design. In Alexandre Dumas' novel "The Count of Monte Cristo," the dialogue between Edmund Dantès and the priest Abbé Faria illustrates the principle. Deep within the dungeons of the Chateau d'If, the Abbé asked Dantès: "What are you thinking?" Dantès replied: "I was reflecting upon the enormous degree of intelligence and ability you must have employed to reach the high perfection to which you have attained. What would you not have accomplished, if you had been free?" "Possibly nothing at all," replied the priest. "The overflow of my brain would probably, in a state of freedom, have evaporated in a thousand follies. Misfortune is needed to bring to light the treasures of the human intellect. Compression is needed to explode gunpowder. Captivity has brought my mental faculties to a focus; and you are well aware that from the collision of clouds electricity is produced - from electricity, lightning, and from lightning, illumination."

Finally, at the end of the tale, Dantès, who had been profoundly influenced by the Abbé, observes: "Only a man who has felt ultimate despair is capable of feeling ultimate bliss. It is necessary to have wished for death, in order to know how good it is to live. Live, then, and be happy, and never forget that, until the day God deigns to reveal the future to man, the sum of human wisdom will be contained in these words: wait and hope."

God has custom designed our mortal experiences so that, as we wait and hope, all things shall be for our good. (See D&C 122:7). But the anxiously anticipated changes hinge upon our desire and resourcefulness, and ultimately upon our faith in His infinite wisdom. Until we have committed to let go and let God, "there is hesitancy, the chance to draw back, and always ineffectiveness. Concerning all acts of initiative, there is one elementary truth, the ignorance of which kills countless ideas and splendid plans, and it is this: The moment we commit ourselves, then Providence moves too. A whole stream of unforeseen incidents and material assistance issues from the decision, which no-one could have dreamed would have come our way." (Thomas Hornbein).

Therefore, if we want to develop the faith to choose the harder right, instead of the easier wrong, we must expend soul-sweat. As Robert Frost wrote: "I shall be telling this with a sigh somewhere ages and ages hence: Two roads diverged in a wood, and I took the one less traveled by, and that has made all the difference."

If we want to develop the faith to choose the harder right, instead of the easier wrong, we will maintain unbridled optimism. We will be filled with a divine fire. We will be full of faith. Our bright and cheerful outlook on life will channel adversity into constructive expressions and positive outcomes.

If we want to develop the faith to choose the harder right, instead of the easier wrong, we must take a few steps into the darkness before the spiritual strong searchlight illuminates the way before us. Then, as Helen Keller declared: "Although sinister doubts" may continue to "lurk in the shadows," we will "walk unafraid toward the Enchanted Wood where the foliage is always green, where joy abides, where nightingales nest and sing, and where life and death are one in the presence of the Lord." ("Midstream").

If we want to develop the faith to choose the harder right, instead of the easier wrong, we must not allow ourselves to be O.C.D. about it. In other words, we must not be Overly Concerned with Discipleship. We need "not run faster or labor more

than (we) have strength." (D&C 10:4). Sometimes, we need to just go with the flow, by yielding ourselves to the glittering facets of the life of the Spirit. As we learn to become receptive to flashes of insight, we will allow ourselves to be cast off into a stream of revelation and carried along in the quickening currents of direct experience with God.

So why, then, does it sometimes seem to be more difficult to muster the faith to choose the harder right instead of the easier wrong? Of all God's creations, is not Satan most miserable? Would not our adoption of his tactics and counterproposal at the Council have made us equally unhappy? By denying free will, requiring obedience, and relying upon compulsion, would not our progression have been prevented?

Although the plan he proposed in heaven was counterfeit, a fraud, inoperable, and ultimately rejected by the Council, its basic elements have been re-packaged in the mortal battlefield. We do not have a casualty count from that celestial conflict, but we do know that a third part of the heavenly host, basking in light, was drawn to his faulty ideology, and these fallen angels are currently waging war on our telestial battlefield. (See Revelation 12:4). Even now, they are making a last-ditch effort for the acceptance of his re-branded lie. Witness the media blitz that blatantly and brazenly covertly promotes his desire to make all men miserable.

Here on earth, in accordance with the principle of opposition in all things, an impenetrable veil has been drawn across our minds. But we have the Light of Christ, and even the witness of the Holy Ghost, to help us to penetrate that curtain. Nevertheless, many of us are still swayed by the siren song of Satan, drawn to the treacherous shoals of spiritual instability, thereon to founder, and to be pulled under by the riptides of his religious relativism.

Elements of his devious dogma can be seen in social, political, cultural, economic, environmental, and religious philosophies that pander to the innate insecurity, lack

of initiative, and desire for undeserved entitlements that characterize faithless secularism. Those who surrender their agency in exchange for the flavor of the day, or for whatever transient pleasures poor choices may provide, fall into Satan's snare and are bound by his strong chains. Their lack of the faith to choose the harder right enslaves them to bad habits. When they feel the heavy cords of oppression around their necks, they realize too late that their poor choices have limited their options, restricted their actions, and fettered the expression and expansion of their righteous desires. Satan demands only a diluted distortion of discipleship that is dedicated to the debauchery of deformed doctrine and its companion of habitual sin. The consequence of misdirected allegiance is a monotonous and mind-numbing conformity that leaves no room for the artistic individuality and creative expression that lead to spiritual enlightenment.

If we allow bad habits to handcuff the expression of our choices, often all that is left in the end is a monochromatic and one-dimensional compromise that leaves a hollow core of emptiness in our gut. Suddenly, the easier wrong has become a Trojan Horse, leaving the anticipated spoils of war to disintegrate in the shambles of a Pyrrhic victory. Thus, did the prophet Amos declare to Israel: "Wo to them that are at ease in Zion." (Amos 6:1).

Those with the faith to choose the harder right, however, are like "brave Horatius, the Captain of the Gate," who declared: "To each of us upon this earth, death cometh soon or late. And how can we die better than facing fearful odds, for the ashes of our fathers, and the temples of our gods?" ("Lays of Ancient Rome," Thomas Macaulay).

Sometimes, all too quickly and agonizingly easily, those who surrender their dreams and choose the easier wrong sell their birthright to the lowest bidder for a mess of pottage. Once they have made the exchange, they may far too easily be dragged down to a hell on earth, with the terrifying realization that the prison to which they have been dragged has been of their own construction. It is difficult to break the bad habits that are the result of our repetitive poor choices, precisely because our

free will has been surrendered in order to acquire them. Ironically, "we can never get enough of what we don't need, because what we don't need won't satisfy us." (Dallin Oaks).

Heavenly Father does not operate this way. He always honors the eternal principle of agency, but He has stacked the deck in our favor with two interesting and powerful devices that are influences for good: The Light of Christ and the gift of the Holy Ghost. He has inserted receptor cells within our beating hearts that can discern and activate a quality of faith capable of moving mountains and turning rivers out of their course. (See Matthew 17:20, Moses 7:13 & J.S.T. Genesis 14:30). In the beginning, in a demonstration of His supernal confidence in the integrity of our faith to choose the harder right, Heavenly Father counseled with Adam in a magnificent demonstration of parental confidence: "Thou mayest choose for thyself, for it is given unto thee." (Moses 3:17).

This was a risky course of action for Him to take, but it illustrates the principle that good decision making in the face of opposition makes our immortality and eternal possible. But it can only occur if we exercise faith in the Atonement of Christ. In other words, we must have the faith to follow The Plan. In the process, rather than enslaving us in good habits, God repeatedly gives us the opportunity to voluntarily recommit ourselves to covenants of obedience to true and eternal principles. Thus, is reinforced the habit pattern of choosing the harder right (although it may take between 18 and 254 days, depending upon how stubborn we are).

During the process, Church membership and a holy communion with the society of the Saints at weekly Sacrament services and in the temple will be vital to establishing our spiritual well-being. As we confirm God's trust in our desire to choose the harder right, instead of the easier wrong, our mind-set will undergo a miraculous transformation. We will find that altitude is all about attitude. We will be blessed with the physical and spiritual capacity to establish success strategies that orient us to raise our sights, so that we will always be looking upward, in the direction of our dreams.

The Light of Christ will exert a nurturing influence, and although we may daily travel further from the East, we will, nevertheless, be drawn to its radiant glow emanating from a distant horizon. Faith will provide us with the regularly recurring reassurance of a religious recalibration that will auto-correct with celestial precision.

It will envelop us in an intuitive appreciation of where we came from, why we are here, and where we are going. As in a heavenly language that is rhythmical, melodious, soothing to our ears, and calming to our souls, we will hear the Spirit quietly whisper: "You're a stranger here," and we will be immediately comforted by the realization that we have "wandered from a more exalted sphere." (Eliza R. Snow).

The Light of Christ will personalize our anxious engagement with Gospel principles and inspire us to plumb the depths of our commitment to the Savior, by sensitizing us to the nobility of His work and making us more acutely aware of His grace. The visions of immortality and eternal life will nearly overwhelm our prepared minds, as we orient ourselves to conform to principles that make it easier to maintain the faith to choose the harder right.

With that resolve, instead of capitulating to the character-crippling compromise of the easier wrong, we will commit ourselves to the arduous process of spiritual rebirth that accompanies choosing the harder right. When we feel the urge to push His agenda instead of our own itinerary, the Light of Christ will be our labor coach, providing us with just the right amount of encouragement to successfully deliver our witness of the Savior without being overbearing.

One exciting consequence of our resolve to choose the harder right, instead of the easier wrong, is the constant stream of inspiration and revelation that will subsequently cascade down from above. Divine direction will dictate that we may walk along illuminated pathways as we exercise our faculties of mind and spirit. We will more easily discern between truth and error, thereby to more comfortably choose the right in an endless loop that with each cycle carries us to a higher plateau. It will permit us to listen with sensitivity, to be receptive to the cries of the downtrodden, to respond to the needs of the oppressed, to see with clarity, to be proactively

responsive to our environment, and to emulate the Savior by being benevolently blind to the shortcomings of others who have not yet witnessed with the dawn of recognition how His Gospel can become the perfect law of liberty in their lives.

When we choose the harder right, instead of the easier wrong, the air in the theater of life will be charged, as fire in the sky, with an electricity that represents the inevitable merger of the universal encouragement of the Light of Christ with the pointed and providential guidance provided by the Holy Ghost. When these influences streak in tandem across the heavens, it will be easy for us to follow the flaming trail of their trajectory as it traces its way through a sparkling cosmic ocean of thought.

"There is a tide in the affairs of men, which taken at the flood, leads on to fortune; omitted, all the voyage of their life is bound in shallows and in miseries." (Shakespeare, Brutus, "Julius Caesar"). When we determine to choose the harder right, instead of the easier wrong, over the ebb and flow of that tide, the Spirit will create an effectual bridge of understanding that is buttressed by the cohesive influence of the mighty foundation of faith. Thereby, the difficulty of making hard choices will melt away as the morning dew evaporates in the noonday sun.

Those who have chosen the easier wrong, who have so casually and carelessly surrendered their capacity to choose the harder right, will find themselves snared by Satan and bound by his strong chains. Those who suffer from the resulting compulsions will have reached this condition because their repeated actions have taken them to the point where unlimited freedom leads to tyranny.

Those who are firm to choose the harder right, however, will find that heaven will come knocking at their door. Perhaps this is what President Monson had in mind, when he encouraged us to exercise our faith, that we might choose the harder right, instead of the easier wrong.

As
we consider
the performance
potential of faith,
we remember that it
is not our purpose to
be stars of the show. A
pathway of progress may
lead us in the direction
of perfection, but it is a
process, rather than a
point. We will not be
given, nor will we
need, top billing
to realize our
dreams.

Chapter Sixteen
The faith to live abundantly.

As
our circle of
knowledge expands,
so do the borders of the
undiscovered country surrounding
those kernals of wisdom. The more we
know, it seems, the more we need to learn.

When the Lord described His vast creations to Moses, he used the illustration of grains of sand. Moses "beheld also the inhabitants thereof, and there was not a soul which he beheld not; and he discerned them by the Spirit of God; and their numbers were great, even numberless as the sand upon the sea shore." (Moses 1:28).

If you hold a single grain of sand at arm's length, the area of the sky that is

blocked behind that grain contains about 2,000 galaxies. We can "see" these galaxies with the Hubble telescope, which is so powerful that, were it on the earth in New York City, it could distinguish between two fireflies in Tokyo, if there were only 10 feet of separation. If each of those 2,000 galaxies contains 100 billion stars, the number of stars within that restricted field of view would be over 200 trillion. That is 200,000,000,000,000, which is, for all practical purposes, "numberless." (If you counted these stars at a rate of 1 per second, it would take about 1,260,000 years to get to 200 trillion).

If we assume a grain of sand has an average size and we calculate how many grains are in a teaspoon and then multiply by all the beaches and deserts in the world, we arrive at roughly 7.5×10^{18} grains of sand, or seven and a half quintillion grains, on the earth. There are 10 times more stars in the night sky than grains of sand on the world's beaches and deserts, according to astronomers. They have calculated that there are seventy five thousand million billion stars visible from the Earth through telescopes.

We are left to wonder, as did Paul: "O the depth of the riches both of the wisdom and knowledge of God! How unsearchable are his judgments, and his ways past finding out! For who hath known the mind of the Lord? Or who hath been his counsellor?" (Romans 11:33-34).

Perhaps an understanding of physics can help us to exercise the faith to live abundantly. Science tell us that every heavy element in our bodies, the calcium in our bones, and the iron in the hemoglobin of our blood, was created during the explosion of a supernova somewhere in those vast creations. So, our attempts to comprehend the universe may help us to understand ourselves. When we ask, what is its origin, or what is its ultimate destiny, we are really asking where did we come from, and where are we going. When we discover the answers to these questions, we will know why we are here.

As we try to understand revealed truth, we might ask ourselves how much information

would we give to a preschool child if we were trying to answer their questions about how an airplane stays in the air, or how a television works, or how plants grow? Most of us would consider the intellectual maturity of the child, and provide general concepts, only filling in the details later.

The Lord has given us only the portion of eternal truth that our mortal minds can understand and that we need to know in order to enjoy life, and comply with the principles of The Plan, in order to gain salvation, not to mention exaltation, through the grace of God For example, He has provided us with very little information regarding the creation of our world and the life that lives hereon, and we have yet to design the scientific tools that might provide us with greater understanding. Even with the world's most powerful instruments, let alone with the Light of Christ and the gift of the Holy Ghost, we have only been privileged to take a peek at what Moses beheld while under the influence of the Spirit. (See above, Moses 1:28).

And that is just the point. To whatever degree God deigns to reveal knowledge, wisdom can only be gained while under the influence of the Spirit of truth. It was in this spirit that Moses was able to behold the earth in its most minute fashion, and thereby to begin to comprehend the greatness of the Creation.

Referring to spiritual knowledge, Joseph Smith said: "Could you gaze into heaven five minutes, you would know more than you would by reading all that ever was written on the subject." ("Teachings," p. 156). Thus, if we wish to understand the mysteries of the kingdom, or of this telestial world, for that matter, we must prepare ourselves as did Moses. Academic study, though worthwhile, can only give us a hint of the knowledge that is available to those who enjoy spiritual enlightenment through the Source of all truth.

Moses experienced a vision of God's creations, but was told: "Only an account of this earth, and the inhabitants thereof, give I unto you." (Moses 1:35). It would be fascinating to know more about the universe and how its physical structure harmonizes with the Gospel Plan. However, that knowledge is unnecessary for us, as we fulfill our purpose on this earth, because the scriptures remain virtually silent on the subject

of the other creations of God, Kolob possibly being the only exception. (See Abraham 3:2-28, 5:13 & Facsimile 2 Figure 1) In order to work out our salvation, it seems clear that our focus should remain fixed upon the revelations the Lord has given us that relate to our world, and not on mysteries that have not been revealed, that may never be revealed, or just may not be relevant to our circumstances.

The account of the Creation that was written by Moses provided only the details that relate to the Fall of Adam and Eve, and the Atonement of Christ, which is doctrine that we must understand in order to have the faith to live abundantly and become heirs of salvation. This is why, in the temple, we primarily learn that the creation provided a place where we could come to obtain physical bodies and be tested, or proven, to see if we would obey God when we were no longer in His presence.

Interestingly, although an account of the Creation is included in the book of Genesis, its purposes and importance are clarified only in latter-day revelation. For example, the Book of Abraham provides an expanded explanation of Genesis 1:1, which simply states: "In the beginning, God created the heaven and the earth."

Abraham 3:24-5 elaborates: "We will go down, for there is space there, and we will take of these materials, and we will make an earth whereon these may dwell. And we will prove them herewith, to see if they will do all things whatsoever the Lord their God shall command them." (Abraham 3:24-25).

We were to be proven "herewith," or "with this earth." In other words, the Lord created the earth as a testing center, a learning laboratory, a citadel of higher education, a place where we would be provided with all the tools that could conceivably be necessary to complete an examination to see if we could be proven to be trustworthy. "For behold," God declared, "this is my work and my glory — to bring to pass the immortality and eternal life of man." (Moses 1:39). Wilford Woodruff taught that the Lord created the earth "that we might come here

and exercise our agency. The probation we care called upon to pass through is intended to elevate us so that we can dwell in the presence of God our Father." (J.D., 25:9). The earth provides an environment where we receive physical bodies, that we may gain knowledge, learn to use our agency, receive ordinances, make covenants, and have families. As we build our faith to live abundantly, we are more successful in these endeavors.

No fewer than six times in the brief account of the Creation, God declared that his work was good. (Genesis 1:10, 12, 18, 21, 25, & in verse 31, where He declared it was "very good."). So we know without a doubt that He knew what He was doing. He also had envisioned the successful outcome of The Plan's operating principles. He had pre-played before He re-played. Among His numberless creations, our own mortal experience would not be a dry-run. It had already been worked out countless times, not as a dress rehearsal, but as a flawless component of the Great and Merciful Plan of our Creator.

The home that we call "earth" was created with us in mind. (See Abraham 3:24 & Abraham 4:1). Joseph Smith said: "The word create came from the (Hebrew) word baurau which ... means to organize; the same as a man would organize materials and build a ship. Hence, we infer that God had materials to organize the world out of ... chaotic matter." ("Teachings" p. 350-351). This has a nice ring to it, because it fits in neatly with the star-child concept of supernova "creation." It may be no coincidence that our blood runs hot, reminiscent of the microwave background radiation from the Big Bang that likely occurred some 14 billion years ago. Only time will tell. Then again, who know? Maybe not.

On February 14, 1990, the Voyager 1 spacecraft left our planetary neighborhood for the fringes of the solar system. It was a fitting Valentine's Day gift to our interstellar neighbors. As it did so, Jet Propulsion Laboratory engineers turned it around for one last look at its home planet. It was about 4 billion miles from earth when it captured a portrait of our world. It was perhaps the most stunning photograph ever taken. Caught in the center of scattered light rays, earth appeared as a tiny point of light, a crescent only 0.12 of a pixel in size. It was nothing more

than a "pale blue dot." (See:http://www.planetary.org/explore/space-topics/earth/pale-blue-dot.html).

In his book "Pale Blue Dot," Carl Sagan wrote: "Look again at that dot. That's here. That's home. That's us. On it, everyone you love, everyone you know, everyone you ever heard of, every human being who ever was, lived out their lives. The aggregate of our joy and suffering, thousands of confident religions, ideologies, and economic doctrines, every hunter and forager, every hero and coward, every creator and destroyer of civilization, every king and peasant, every young couple in love, every mother and father, hopeful child, inventor and explorer, every teacher of morals, every corrupt politician, every "superstar," every "supreme leader," every saint and sinner in the history of our species lived there, on a mote of dust suspended in a sunbeam.

The Earth is a very small stage in a vast cosmic arena. Think of the rivers of blood spilled by all those generals and emperors so that, in glory and triumph, they could become the momentary masters of a fraction of a dot.

The Earth is the only world known so far to harbor life. Like it or not, for the moment, the Earth is where we make our stand. There is perhaps no better demonstration of the folly of human conceits than this distant image of our tiny world. To me, it underscores our responsibility to deal more kindly with one another, and to preserve and cherish the pale blue dot, the only home we've ever known."

To me, it underscores our responsibility to find a way to exercise the faith to live abundantly, to be like "brave Horatius, the Captain of the Gate," who declared: "To each of us upon this earth, death cometh soon or late. And how can we die better than facing fearful odds, for the ashes of our fathers, and the temples of our gods?" ("Lays of Ancient Rome," Thomas Macaulay).

Exalting faith
has the capacity to
become the fundamental
element of a tapestry whose
intricate design will reveal itself,
in all its glory, as an expression of
our being. When we attain the full
stature of our spirits because our
nature has finally conformed to
the harmony of heaven, our
perfect frames will burst
free of the shackles of
our mortal clay, as
vibrant coats of
many colors.

While
the desire to
obtain gold can
certainly corrupt us,
the bright, shiny metal
that cannot be corroded
symbolizes the purity that
turns our thoughts to, and
concentrates our faith on,
the inestimable worth of
the Celestial Kingdom
whose gilded streets
must be dazzling
to the eye.

Chapter Seventeen
The faith to call down pennies from heaven.

"And he doeth great wonders,
so that he maketh" pennies to "come down
from heaven on the earth in the sight of men."
(Revelation 13:13).

"Every time it rains, it rains pennies from heaven. Don't you know each cloud contains pennies from heaven? You'll find your fortune falling all over town. Be sure that your umbrella is upside down. Trade them for a package of sunshine and flowers. If you want the things you love, you must have showers. So when you hear it thunder, don't run under a tree. There'll be pennies from heaven for you and me." (Lyrics by Johnny Burke & Arthur Johnston).

When we have ample reserves in our spiritual bank accounts, when they are nearing depletion, or even if our accounts are overdrawn, we may still receive pennies from heaven, or the currency of faith, in various forms. As our ultimate benefactor,

God will continue to give us "knowledge by his Holy Spirit, yea, by the unspeakable gift of the Holy Ghost." (D&C 121:26). He does not generally hand out Susan B. Anthony or Sacajawea dollars, or even shiny quarters or dimes. Instead, He doles out the smallest denominations possible, "precept upon precept; line upon line, here a little, and there a little." (Isaiah 28:10). As these coins accumulate in our piggy banks, something that is almost imperceptible happens. We begin to increase "in wisdom and stature, and in favour with God and man." (Luke 2:52).

Pennies from heaven add up quickly, just like the coins thrown into Rome's Trevi Fountain. Over 3,000 Euros a day are removed from the fountain, and the proceeds are used to feed the hungry. The difference is that pennies from heaven are used to feed the poor in spirit. Thus, "by small and simple things are great things brought to pass." (Alma 37:6).

It is said that if you throw three coins with your right hand over your left shoulder into the Trevi Fountain, it is guaranteed that you will return one day to Rome, and that you will have a new romance that will lead to marriage. Pennies from heaven have a similar purpose; they represent a similarly positive investment by Heavenly Father in our future. They are as a dowry from deity that is designed to foster our faith in the financial stability of His treasury and facilitate our fidelity to His Only Begotten Son. They epitomize seed money that solidifies our commitment to obedience to the principles of the Gospel and secures our covenant relationship with the Lord. (See Joshua 6:19). Pennies from heaven epitomize the blood of Christ, that has been used to purchase the Church of God. (See Acts 20:28).

As pennies from heaven accumulate with compound interest, their composite value soars as they are transformed into relationship capital. They take the form of guardian angels, priesthood leaders, ministering teachers, and caring friends. Although we will always be in God's debt, continual positive cash flow with pennies from heaven frees us from the shackles of dependency to the devil, and empowers us call down the powers of heaven in our behalf.

Pennies from heaven were the first coinage to bear the inscription "In God We

Trust." They are date-sensitive, and have their greatest intrinsic value when they are uncirculated, are in mint condition, or are even of proof quality. They stand in sharp contrast to the spurious counterfeit coins that are circulated by Satan, and

by his money lenders who lurk in the shadows, hoping to negotiate a one-sided currency exchange that is favorable only to them.

"Every cloud has a silver lining, because every cloud contains pennies from heaven, and a fortune in coins waits to fall all over town. So we need to be sure that our umbrellas are upside down." Or, as Brigham Young similarly counseled: "Keep your dish right side up, so that when the shower of porridge does come, you can catch your dish full." (D.B.Y., p. 310). Surely, he too was thinking of pennies from heaven.

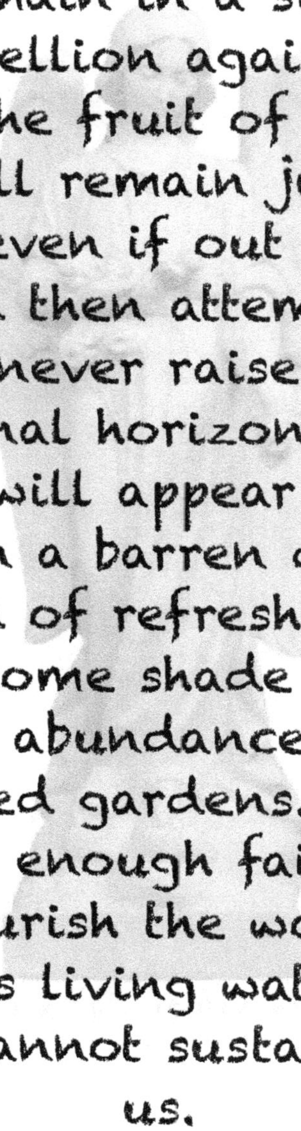

As
long as we
remain in a state
of rebellion against the
Spirit, the fruit of the tree
of life will remain just beyond
our reach, even if out of curiosity,
we now and then attempt to take a
bite. If we never raise our eyes to
search eternal horizons, the world
before us will appear as nothing
more than a barren desert that
is devoid of refreshing oases,
the welcome shade of trees,
and an abundance of well
watered gardens. If we
lack enough faith to
nourish the word,
its living water
cannot sustain
us.

Chapter Eighteen
Put a thmile on your faith.

"Faith is the first great governing principle which has power, dominion, and authority over all things. By it they exist, by it they are upheld, by it they are changed, or by it they remain, agreeable to the will of God. Without it there is no power, and without power there could be no creation nor existence."
(Joseph Smith, "Lectures on Faith," p. 10).

"Happiness is the object and design of our existence, and will be the end thereof, if we follow the path that leads to it; and that path is virtue, uprightness, faithfulness, holiness, and keeping all the commandments of God." (Joseph Smith, "Teachings," p. 255). It may have been with a twist of humor that the Prophet linked faith, the greatest power in the world, with happiness. It is no accident that our happiness is revealed by the universally understood language of a smile. When we are happy, we feel that our hearts could burst, and we can scarcely control the smiles that light

up our countenances.

Surprisingly, in the scriptures, there are just five references to "smiling." Three are in The Book of Mormon, one is in the Pearl of Great Price, and one is in the

181

Doctrine & Covenants. (See Jacob 2:13, 3 Nephi 19:25 & 30, Moses 7:43 & D&C 84:101). Considering that smiling is our universal language that is emotionally understood in much the same way by almost everyone on the planet, I find this perplexing. Maybe the prophets lived in a more austere and somber age. Perhaps they simply used different words to communicate the expression of the commonly shared emotions that lie at the very heart of our faith. Certainly, in the Gospel there is a lot to smile about, and one would think that the patriarchs would openly address and even promote the instinctive appeal of a smile as one of the magical bonuses associated with obedience to the principles of The Plan of Salvation.

Gordon B. Hinckley was one who did. On more than one occasion, he urged the Saints to light up the world with their smiles, and not to be pickle suckers. He once begged students at B.Y.U: "I come this morning with a plea that we stop seeking out the storms and enjoy more fully the sunlight. I am suggesting that we accentuate the positive. I am asking that we look a little deeper for the good, that we still our voices of insult and sarcasm, that we more generously compliment virtue and effort. I am not asking that all criticism be silenced. Growth comes of correction. Strength comes of repentance. Wise is the man who can acknowledge mistakes pointed out by others and change his course. I am not suggesting that our conversation be all honey and blossoms. Clever expression that is sincere and honest is a skill to be sought and cultivated. What I am asking is that we turn from the negativism that so permeates our society and look for the remarkable good in the lands and times in which we live, that we speak of one another's virtues more than we speak of one another's faults, that optimism replace pessimism, and that our faith exceed our fears." (11/29/1974).

Lack of smile citations notwithstanding, there are still a lot of scriptural references to emotions that are related to a smile: There are 333 references to "joy,"

127 references to "glad," 62 references to "gladness," 40 references to "happy," 37 references to "happiness," 34 references to "merry," and 15 references to "mirth." That is 646 references to emotional states that evoke a smile. (Interestingly, there are 10 references to "laughter," and 1 to "jovial," but all 11 have negative connotations).

For what it is worth, here are the five references to "smiling" that are found in the scriptures: "The hand of providence hath smiled upon you most pleasingly." (Jacob 2:13). "And it came to pass that Jesus blessed them as they did pray unto him; and his countenance did smile upon them, and the light of his countenance did shine upon them." (3 Nephi 19:25). "And when Jesus had spoken these words he came again unto his disciples; and behold they did pray steadfastly, without ceasing, unto him; and he did smile upon them." (3 Nephi 19:30). "Enoch saw that Noah built an ark; and that the Lord smiled upon it, and held it in his own hand." (Moses 7:43). The earth hath travailed and brought forth her strength; And truth is established in her bowels; And the heavens have smiled upon her; And she is clothed with the glory of her God; For he stands in the midst of his people." (D&C 84:101)

Because I want to keep this chapter on topic, if we were to pick and choose from among expressions that are related to smiling, we might settle upon "countenance," as the one that is most closely aligned. For example, D&C 59:15 speaks of "a glad heart and a cheerful countenance." Psalms 89:15 describes those who "walk in the light of (the Lord's) countenance." Proverbs 15:13 teaches that "a merry heart maketh a cheerful countenance." 1 Samuel 16:12 turns our mind's eye to David, who was "of a beautiful countenance." The Savior is described as having such a peaceful appearance, that Moses was moved to exclaim: "The Lord lift up His countenance upon thee, and give thee peace." (Number 6:26). David described Him as "the health of my countenance, and my God. (Psalms 42:11). Alma asked his brethren of the Church if they had "spiritually been born of God," or if they had "received his image in (their) countenances." (Alma 5:14). Joseph Smith described the Savior as having a "countenance (that) was as lightning" (D&C 20:6), that "shone above the brightness of the sun." (D&C 110:3). The Lord assured him: "Ye shall behold the joy of my countenance." (D&C 88:52). The laborers in the field all received "the light of the countenance of their Lord." (D&C 88:58).

Intriguingly, if we engage in a simple exercise, and substitute the word "smile" for the word "work" in selected scriptures, the results almost pop off the page. For example: "Great and marvelous are thy smiles, O Lord God Almighty!" (1 Nephi 1:14). "The day should come that they must be judged of their smiles." (1 Nephi 15:32). "If a man bringeth forth smiles he hearkeneth unto the voice of the good shepherd." (Alma 5:41). "Prepare ye the way of the Lord, for the time is at hand that all men shall reap a reward of their smiles." (Alma 9:28). Therefore let your light so shine before this people, that they may see your smiles and glorify your Father who is in heaven." (3 Nephi 12:16). "Who can comprehend the marvelous smiles of God?" (Mormon 9:16). "I remember the word of God which saith by their smiles ye shall know them; for if their smiles be good, then they are good also." (Moroni 7:5). "The Lord shall come to recompense unto every man according to his smiles." (D&C 1:10). "My smiles shall go forth." (D&C 3:16). "By their desires and their smiles you shall know them." (D&C 18:38). "I shall pass upon the inhabitants thereof, judging every man according to his smiles and the deeds which he hath done." (D&C 19:3). "My smiles have no end, neither beginning." (D&C 29:33). "Those that live shall inherit the earth, and those that die shall rest from all their labors, and their smiles shall follow them; and they shall receive a crown in the mansions of my Father." (D&C 59:2). "Pray unto the Lord, call upon his holy name, make known his wonderful smiles among the people." (D&C 65:4). "Great and marvelous are the smiles of the Lord, and the mysteries of his kingdom." (D&C 76:114).

I particularly like the following scripture, because smiles seem to rest at the pinnacle of our discipleship: "All those who humble themselves before God, and desire to be baptized, and come forth with broken hearts and contrite spirits, and witness before the church that they have truly repented of all their sins, and are willing to take upon them the name of Jesus Christ, having a determination to serve him to the end, and truly manifest by their smiles that they have received of the Spirit of Christ unto the remission of their sins, shall be received by baptism into his church." (D&C 20:37).

We can achieve the same powerful effect by substituting the word "smile" when we encounter the word "endure" in the scriptures. "If they smile unto the end, they shall

be lifted up at the last day." (1 Nephi 13:37). "I am the law, and the light. Look unto me, and smile." (3 Nephi 15:9). How about when the word "perseverance" is found in the scriptures? "Let your smiles be redoubled, and you shall in nowise lose your reward." (D&C 127:4). Try it with the word "faith." "Look forward for the remission of your sins, with an everlasting smile." (Alma 7:6). "As many as are not stiffnecked and have smiles, have communion with the Holy Spirit." (Jarom 1:4). "Hope cometh of smiles." (Ether 12:4). "By smiles, they become the sons of God." (Moroni 7:26). "Without smiles, there cannot be any hope." (Moroni 7:42). "Remember that without a smile you can do nothing." (D&C 8:10). "Without smiling, no man pleaseth God." (D&C 63:11).

If we tack on the modifier "with a smile upon your face" to certain scriptures, they become even more meaningful. For example: "I command thee that thou shalt pray vocally as well as in thy heart," with a smile upon your face. (D&C 19:28). Or: "And thou shalt declare glad tidings, yea, publish it upon the mountains, and upon every high place, and among every people that thou shalt be permitted to see," with a smile upon your face. (D&C 19:29). Or: "Take upon you the name of Christ," with a smile upon your face. (Alma 34:38). Or: "If thou art merry, praise the Lord with singing, with music, with dancing, and with a prayer of praise and thanksgiving," with a smile upon your face. (D&C 136:28).

Smiling can even be a token, as it were, of our covenant relationship with the Lord. "Choose ye this day to serve the Lord God," with a smile upon your face. (Moses 6:33). "If they hold out faithful to the end, they are received into heaven, that thereby they may dwell with God in a state of never-ending happiness," with a smile upon their faces. (Mosiah 2:41). "This mortal shall put on immortality, and this corruption shall put on incorruption, and shall be brought to stand before the bar of God," with smiles upon their faces. (Mosiah 16:10). "And then shall it come to pass, that the spirits of those who are righteous are received into a state of happiness," with smiles upon their faces. (Alma 40:12).

What would the scriptures, or the world for that matter, be like, if there were no smiles to brighten their pages or our lives? "The evil spirit teacheth not a man to

pray, but teacheth him that he must not pray," and that he must never smile. (2 Nephi 32:8). "Do not suppose, because it has been spoken concerning restoration, that ye shall be restored from sin to happiness," or from frowns to smiles. (Alma 41:10). "How then can I do this great wickedness, and sin against God," which would surely wipe the smile from my face? (Genesis 39:9). "And there shall be weeping and wailing among the hosts of men," and there shall be no cause to smile under the heavens. (D&C 29:15).

Fortunately, the scriptures abound with allusions to our smiles. These are not only grammatical constructions, but are also curves that set everything straight. Even though it may be raining, the scriptures teach that if we keep smiling, the sun will soon show its face and smile right back at us. Smiles in the scriptures are often concealed, but they cannot be hidden for long. Smiles peek out at us as honest emotions from behind familiar passages, and we can almost hear the Spirit challenging us to smile in return: even to smile so widely that we could eat a banana sideways.

When we bask in the light of the Lord, we smile with all our heart, and when we're feeling down, we smile with all our might. If we do nothing else, we can still be the smile on the faces of those who mourn or stand in need of comfort. Our smiles can be a daily exercise that we can perform without ever breaking a sweat. The smiles that we wear on the outside tell others what's happening on the inside. Sometimes our joy is the source of our smile, but sometimes it is the other way around. As we smile with a determined effort to fight our way through brimming tears, we can take comfort in the fact that at least the corners of our mouths are pointing toward heaven.

Even as the world broadcasts insistent messages that beauty has the advantage, we know that it is "the thmile on our faith" that is the absolute guarantee of happiness. When we get up in the morning, we are only half-dressed until we put on our smile. We realize that, when it comes to smiling, one size fits all. Our smile is an accessory that never goes out of style. No matter what obstacles may be thrown up

to hedge our way, smiling in the face of our challenges makes the tasks that lie ahead seem easier. Somehow, our trials are no match for a confident smile. Others are less likely to notice our imperfections, our shortcomings, or our old and worn out clothing, when we are wearing a smile. As frugal shoppers, we know that a smile is an inexpensive way to change our look. In fact, our smile is like an instant facelift; every smile makes us a day younger. Stubborn frowns bring out wrinkles, but those with dimples are doubly blessed. They have been entrusted with a special role in the universe, and that is to smile.

As we embrace life, and the love letters from God, we realize that vibrant color is nature's way of smiling at us. After every storm, we look forward to the dappled rays of sunlight that smile down upon us. Among all of civilization's mighty works, we realize that smiles are its finest adornment. Of all the creations of God, we acknowledge that a beautiful smile that is flashed for no apparent reason separates us from all other creatures. We have no original facial expressions: We have inherited smiles from our parents, we borrow them from our friends, and we receive them as gifts from complete strangers. We are drawn to those who make a difference in our lives; to those who make us smile.

Smiling evokes vivid memories of our innermost emotions, just as our vivid memories often evoke a smile. Sometimes, our joy is the source of our smile, but sometimes our smile is the source of our joy. We don't cry because it's over; we smile because it happened. Too often, we underestimate the power of our smile, or forget that love has taught us how to smile best. A gentle word, a kind look, and a good-natured smile can work wonders and accomplish miracles, especially when we remember that smiles are meant to be given away. They are inexpensive gifts that should never be in short supply.

When our hands cramp up, we sign our autographs with our smiles. It only takes a split second to smile, and then we may forget about it; and yet, to the one to whom it was given, and who needed it at that exact moment, its positive influence might last a lifetime. Smiles may be the most powerful forces in nature, whose effects

may last for eternity. We never know what the butterfly effect of our smile might be. Their ripple effect might wash up on uncharted shores, and we would never even be aware of it. When we receive a prompting to smile at a stranger, we might never know how we have changed a life. When we are blessed to see the smiles on the faces of innocent children, we are given a glimpse of the divine nature that is within each of us.

Smiling can be intensely gratifying. It can warm our hearts when we see others smile, but most of us especially like it when we make them smile. When we carry a smile, one of the many faces of love accompanies us on our journey. Smiles fill our hearts with the joy of life. When we smile, we find that, all along, happiness was right under our nose.

Smiling to keep from crying is inexpensive therapy for our wounded souls. When we feel that there is no reason to smile, we try to find one, because we have learned the hard way that nothing can shake a smiling heart. If we have to, we determine to be the smile on someone else's downcast face, that we might melt away both their fears and their tears. Our simple smile can replace their despondency with cheerfulness. If need be, with a smile on our face, we can climb the steps to the gallows, give a jest to the crowd, a coin to the hangman, and make the drop. Short of that, we pray for opportunities to replace the tears of the downcast and oppressed with smiley faces that point the way to the windows of their souls.

Our wounds may be the portals of entry that the Savior uses to touch our lives, to infuse us with light, and to fill our hearts with gratitude, but our smiles are the universal passports that we must flash to gain entrance to the camp of the ungodly. Our smiles become the Lord's battering ram that breaks down the obstacles that have been thrown up by others, that take the face of fear, mistrust, and misunderstanding. We are ever on the lookout for those who could really use a smile as therapy for their lonely hearts. When we see others who needs a smile, we give them one of ours. We keep apples in our fruit basket, but we know by experience that it is a smile a day that keeps the pain away. We use our smiles as spotlights to shine on

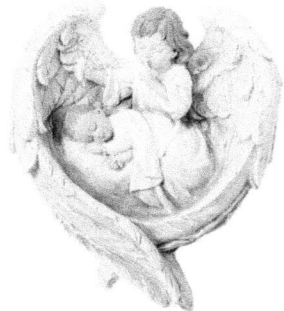

the hearts of our fellow-travelers. The simplest gift we can give them is our smile. We try to so live that we can be someone else's reason to smile. We recognize the incredible power of our smiles to change the world, and so we defend our happiness, that the world might never have enough power to turn our smiles into frowns. We smile at everyone because we, or they, may not be here tomorrow.

Smiling doesn't always mean we are happy. Sometimes, we smile to avoid sadness. A smile may be just the therapy that we need. Or, because our smile may be the only ray of sunlight in the life of another, we are careful to so live that we don't dim that steady beam of hope. Our smiles are nondiscriminatory, and may be the quickest way to establish communication with strangers. We answer both praise and criticism with our smiles. They can be good ice-breakers, because if we've put a smile on the face of someone we barely know, we instantly share a common bond.

We smile, if for no other reason than that there seem to be too many frowns. Our smile makes a positive statement that squarely addresses the pessimism of a dark and negative world. In fact, the most potent force on earth could be our collective smiles. We smile because we accept hatred with love. Our warm smiles are the lights of our souls that conquer the cold, because they dance to the rhythm of hearts that are full. We smile as if unborn poems and unsung songs are stirring within us. Our smiles are the bouquets of our joy, the expressions of our ecstasy with life, and the God-given manifestations of love, that drive out darkness, which is why a genuine smile can be the best form of communication with someone whom we erroneously had thought did not speak our language.

If we need to recharge our batteries, with faithful effort we may take a few steps into the darkness, buoyed up by the sustaining influence of our smiles, which are our spiritual strong searchlights. When we are really desperate, and cannot think of a reason to smile, we can always go out and buy a puppy. When we are still, and are seeking quiet spiritual confirmation, the surplus of our hearts will overflow in smiles. When technology threatens our inner peace, we take our cell phones and

replace their emojis with smiles on our own faces.

There is no other emoticon that can take the place of a genuine smile that is given personally, with no strings attached, to another human being. Every once in a while, we smile even if life tastes like bitter bile. When thunderstorms roll in, we make a choice to either succumb with fright, or to smile and look to see if we can find a rainbow somewhere beyond the gloomy downpour. If we are given the unpleasant task to shovel out a giant pile of manure in a stable, we attack the job with gusto, with a smile on our face, because we know there's got to be a pony in there, somewhere!

Our smiles release an awesome power within us. We have heard the compliments of others, who say: Your smile becomes you. But perhaps you become you, simply because you smile. Those who smile while they are alone used to be called insane, until we invented smartphones and social media. A smile is the light in our window that tells others that there is a caring, sharing person inside. When we leave the porchlight on in the evening for travelers arriving late to the sanctuary of our hearth and home, it is our smile of greeting that assures them that they have found safe haven, at last. In the morning, we share a glass of sunshine to brighten their hearts and lift their spirits, and then we smile with them to spread the light of life. As we pleasantly smile, we take control of the moment, and as we consistently smile, we own it.

Sometimes, when we wish to make particularly significant contributions, we offer our silence with smiles on our faces. We smile at others with such intensity that they feel that they have won a prize, and they have no choice but to smile back at us, in gratitude. Our cheerful conversation tickles our throats and forces our lips into smiles. We can only appreciate the value of a smile when we own the face behind it. But when our smiles become the expressions of the divine center within us, they are easier to give away.

Even simple smiles are recorded and rewarded in heaven. Our smiles are the unfathomable gifts of the gods. While others smiled at our birth, we cried, and

even if others cry at our passing, we hope to be able to smile. We would love to die smiling, because we remember the smiles on the faces of those who were about to pass through the veil. When we make the journey to that undiscovered country, we hope to go with smiles on our faces. However, should we forget to do this in the excitement of the moment, we pray there will be someone in eternity waiting to greet us with a smile, and that we will then be prompted to remember to do the same. In the interim, the biggest reward of our lives will be to have finished each day with a smile on our face. Someday, we are going to be able to look back on every shared smile, and then quietly and peacefully smile one last time.

It's easy to learn to smile. When we smile, our faces light up with a celestial glow. We smile large. Our cheeks may hurt, but it's the cutest thing. We are really in the swing of it, and truly smile, only when our mouths and hearts are in harmony with each other. We smile as if we've just been told the best joke on earth. When we smile like the morning sun, our lives are filled with fun.

Anyone can smile on their best days, but we want to be able to smile on our worst days. Our genuine smiles come from our hearts, but our healthy smiles may be the result of dental care. We know that life is short, and so we smile while we still have teeth.

Our smiles are similar to the flowers that attract honeybees; but they do even more. They attract everyone! We are smile-magnets. We smile at others as if it were the last smile they will ever see on earth. When we smile, our ears rise, enhancing our ability to listen. We decorate our faces with piles of smiles. We smile at perfect strangers, and mean it, because we realize that nearly everyone could use a lift. We look for special opportunities to spoil the day of a grump, by giving him a smile.

Sometimes, even though we don't enjoy breaking things, we crack a smile. Because it's the worst form of identity theft, we refuse to let anyone steal our smiles. If we're not using our smiles, we're like the person with a million dollars in the bank and no pen to write a check. If we're not smiling, it's because our hearts have taken a vacation, and have left no forwarding address. When we wear a smile, we have

friends, but when we wear a frown, we have wrinkles. Our smiles pre-emptively confuse approaching frowns. While frowns mean nothing, our smiles mean everything. It takes 64 facial muscles to make a frown, and only 13 to make a smile, and so we ask ourselves: "Why work overtime?" (It really does take more muscles to frown than it does to smile, which makes sense, because yesterday I saw someone who frowned so hard they ended up pulling a groin muscle). Before we even think about putting on a frown, we need to make absolutely certain there are no smiles available. It's no coincidence that smiles turn up the corners of our mouths, while frowns turn them down. It could have just as easily have been the other way around, if it were not for the fact that God has a sense of humor.

We never ask for permission to smile, and never consider ourselves too poor to give one away. One time, I thought I had lost my smile. But then I found it in a daffodil. Our lives can be measured by the number of faces that smile when they hear our names mentioned. I have been told that I have a winning smile, but I must confess that it's just not true. It only won a silver medal at last year's Facial Expressions Olympics. We smile and thank God that we are alive. All the thermometers in the world can't measure the warmth of our smiles, and so, with our smile we can always bring someone in from the cold.

We smile so powerfully and so cheerfully that the sun itself is shamed. We smile as if the sun had just come out from behind a cloud. The world always looks brighter from behind a smile. We should so live that if we had a star for every time we smiled, we would be holding the night sky in our hand. If we haven't seen our wives smile at a traffic cop, we haven't seen them smile at their prettiest. For some reason, our children are always on their best behavior when they're smiling. We know by experience that love is a smile that is shared by two people. Our smiles are often the best reaction to life's experiences. Smiles are the twinkle that adds to our happiness, which is probably why each of us has smiles to go before we sleep. Our enigmatic smiles are worth ten pages of dialog. When we smile in a mirror, in the reflection we see the face God.

You want to know who is amazing, and has the best smile, ever? Read the first word

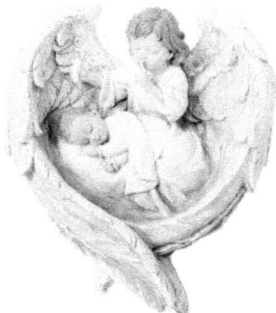

of this paragraph again. But your smile isn't about you; it's about helping others. A smile doesn't always stand for a perfect life, but those who smile when they fall, give the devil a good slap on the cheek. If we smile, or if we don't smile, everyone around us is affected. Our smile is a perfume that we cannot pour out on someone else without getting a few drops on ourselves. What sunshine is to flowers, smiles are to humanity.

Smiles are the stress-formula vitamins taken by those living in the fast lane of life. When we sulk, we create noise, but when we smile, we create music. If we can win an argument by stretching our lips into a smile, it makes no sense to open our mouths and lose both. If our world appears either abundant in smiles or overwhelmed by scowls, we might ask ourselves if we are responsible. It's hard for someone to stay angry with us when we smile. We keep right on smiling, because it makes people wonder what we're up to. Love and peace can create smiles, but our smiles can also create love and peace. If we disagree with others, our discussions should be punctuated with smiles of understanding. Our smiles are evidence that we are on the same side as their recipients. Smiles increase our face value. When we lead with a smile, we are more likely to be lucky.

Our smiles are contagious, and they are the only infectious affliction everyone is encouraged to spread. They can start an epidemic, and so we should indiscriminately share them. We can be the Johnny Appleseed of the Happiest Place on Earth. Most of our smiles can be jump-started by the smiles of others. The shortest distance between two people is a smile. Our smiles can be the keys that fit the padlocks on our hearts. One smile probably won't change the world, but it could change ours.

We never know when we're smiling at an angel. Although a laugh can be a smile that has burst its borders, a smile means a lot more, because it is a true reflection of emotion, while laughter is often just a by-product of humor. Unlike gossip, no-one minds if you spread a smile. Our smiles speak a language that even babies understand. Think of the smile that flickers on a baby's mouth when it is sleeping, and prepare to be amazed.

Remember to smile the next time you stand before the congregation to bear your testimony, when you are given a service opportunity, when you approach the Recommend Desk at the temple, when you greet your son or daughter who has just returned home from a date, when you are asked about your ministering efforts by your file leaders, when you meet with the Bishop to discuss a Church calling, when you entertain the missionaries with a meal in your home, when a non-member friend asks you a question about the Church, or when you are asked by a neighbor to move outside your comfort zone to provide temporal or spiritual assistance.

Remember to smile when things don't go as you have planned, when life throws you a curve, when your best-laid plans go awry, when the baby needs a diaper change, when the car starts making weird noises, when your son throws an errant baseball through the front window, when the new driver in your family has a close encounter with a curb or a tree, when an open container of yoghurt falls upside-down on the kitchen floor, or when someone who has used the bathroom before you has squeezed the toothpaste from the middle of the tube.

Remember to smile when you miss by one day the big sale at the department store, when someone at work gets the promotion you deserved, when someone else gets recognition for your achievements, or when your neighbor comes home with the new car you've been dreaming about.

Also remember to smile when you think about how the Lord has blessed you, and how He has provided for your needs and even granted you a surplus, how you have friends you can trust, how your spouse and children sustain you, how others look to you for counsel, how your dog thinks you can do no wrong, and how fortunate you are to be alive.

We are all familiar with the story of the man who complained because he had no shoes, until he met a man who had no feet. Helen Keller took smiling gratitude to a whole new level when she "asked a friend who had just returned from a long walk in the woods what she had observed. 'Nothing in particular,' she replied. "How

was that possible," Helen asked herself? "I, who cannot hear or see, find hundreds of things to interest me through mere touch. I feel the delicate symmetry of a leaf. I pass my hands lovingly about the rough shaggy bark of a pine. Occasionally, if I am very fortunate, I place my hand gently on a small tree and feel the happy quiver of a bird in full song." ("The Atlantic Monthly").

We need to be more like Brigham Young, who testified: "I feel like shouting Hallelujah, when I think that I ever knew Joseph Smith," or like Parley P. Pratt, who declared: "I have received the holy anointing, and I can never rest till the last enemy is conquered, death destroyed, and truth reigns triumphant." ("Deseret News," 4/30/1853). With smiles on our faces, we relish the joyful anticipation of God's grace both on earth and in heaven.

It is exciting to live in a time when smiling is in vogue, with the possible exception of runway models who look like they have been weaned on pickles. There is so much to smile about! From "selfies," to Facebook posts, to Instagram photos, to Pinterest, and even to SnapChat, it's cool to broadcast a smiling face in cyberspace. But in a disposable world that casts aside interpersonal relationships like empty plastic water bottles, where the illegitimate counterfeits for happiness can be so easily manufactured, packaged, processed, promoted, and manipulated, let's make sure we generate miles of smiles, and are doing so for the right reasons.

Let's not allow gullibility or photoshop to overpower our native common sense, but instead, take a lesson from Joseph Smith, who by all accounts was a good-natured and affable soul. But even he admitted: "I was guilty of levity, and sometimes associated with jovial company, not consistent with that character which ought to be maintained by one who was called of God as I had been. But this will not seem very strange to any one who recollects my youth, and is acquainted with my native cheery temperament." (J.S.H. 1:28).

Let' all hope and pray for sunshine in our souls "today, more glorious and bright than glows in any earthly sky, for Jesus is (our) light. O there's sunshine, blessed

sunshine, when the peaceful, happy moments roll; when Jesus shows His smiling face, there is sunshine in the soul." (Eliza Hewitt).

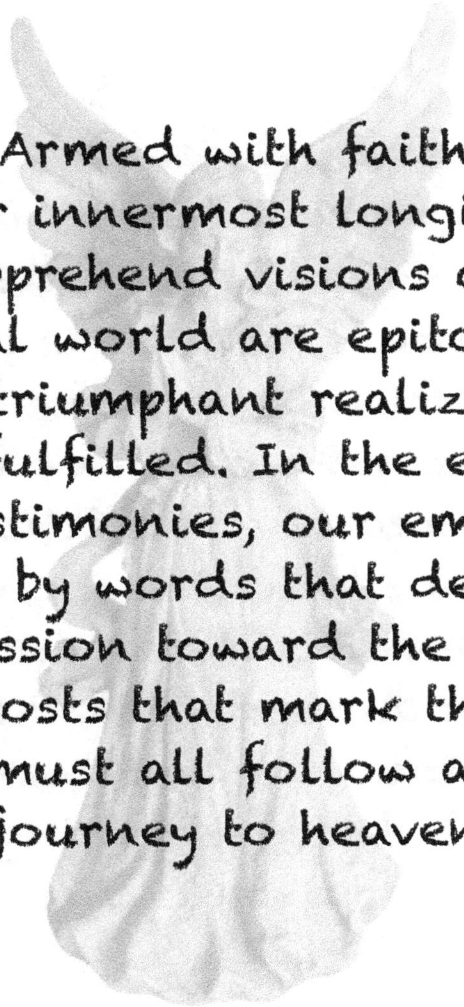

Armed with faith,
our innermost longings
to apprehend visions of the
eternal world are epitomized
by our triumphant realization of
dreams fulfilled. In the expression
of our testimonies, our emotions are
painted by words that depict our
progression toward the distant
mileposts that mark the way
we must all follow as we
journey to heaven.

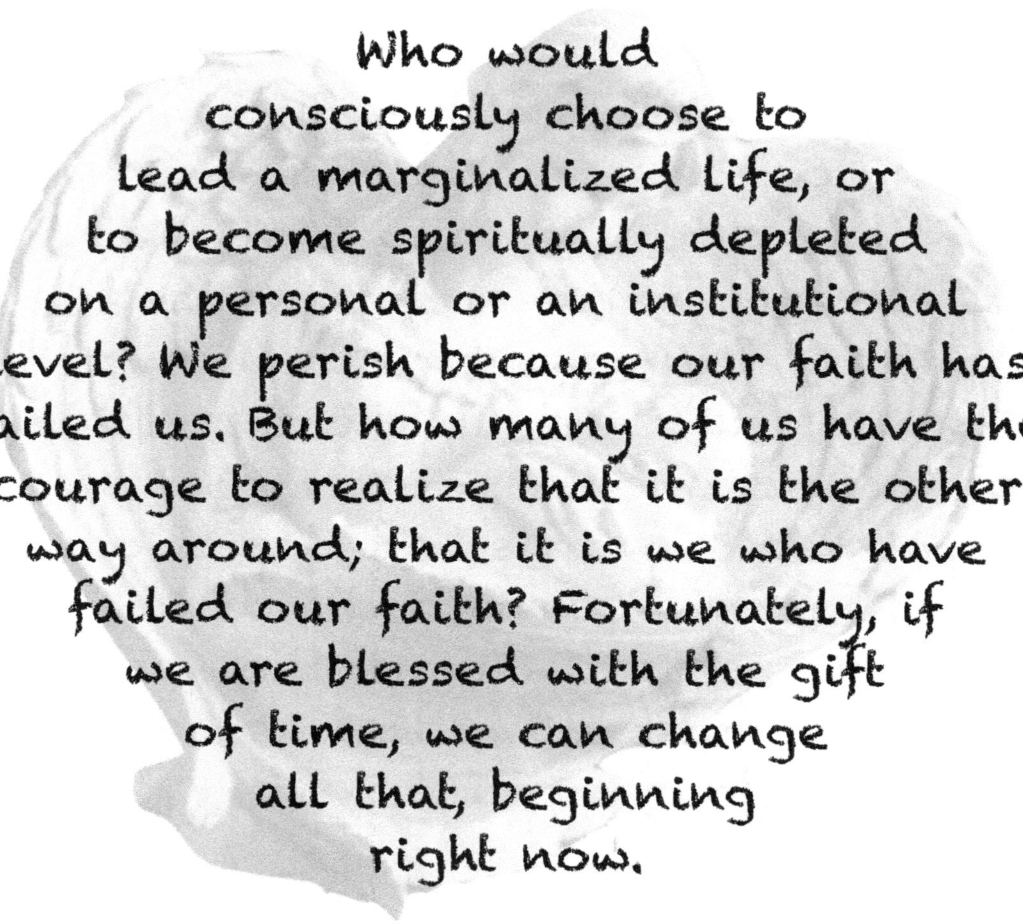

Who would
consciously choose to
lead a marginalized life, or
to become spiritually depleted
on a personal or an institutional
level? We perish because our faith has
failed us. But how many of us have the
courage to realize that it is the other
way around; that it is we who have
failed our faith? Fortunately, if
we are blessed with the gift
of time, we can change
all that, beginning
right now.

Chapter Nineteen

The focus of faith.

"If I have ever made any valuable discoveries,
it has been owing more to patient attention,
than to any other talent."
(Sir Isaac Newton)

While they drew, a kindergarten teacher walked up and down the rows in her classroom of children, observing their work. She stopped at the desk of one little girl and asked what her drawing was. The girl replied: "I'm drawing a picture of God." The teacher paused, and then tentatively said: "But no one knows what God looks like." Without missing a beat or looking up from her paper, the girl said: "They will in a minute." Though tender in years, this child had what we might call "focus."

When we focus our faith on the Savior, on the Atonement, and on the first principles and ordinances of His Gospel, the Spirit enlightens us with understanding. (See

D&C 84:46). When we encounter truth, our minds resonate with recognition, so that ultimately "every one that hearkeneth to the voice of the Spirit (will eventually come) unto God, even the Father." (D&C 84:47). With the help of the Spirit and the eternal focus of faith, we will "discard the poor lenses of the body, and peer through the telescope of truth into the infinite reaches of immortality." (Helen Keller, "My Religion," p. 76).

Spiritual enlightenment blesses us with a pure form of focus, transforming our five natural senses into something wonderful by a heaven-sent sixth sense that defies description. Physical and spiritual resources work in tandem to compound each other, and to condition us through the patience of faith, the miracle of repentance, the diligence of baptism, the sweet spirit of the Holy Ghost, and exhilarating renewal in the Sacrament. (See the 4th Article of Faith). The focus of faith helps us to cleave unto honesty, truth, chaste behavior, benevolence, and virtue, and to treat others kindly. It encourages us to hope all things, to endure many things, and to hope to be able to endure all things. It motivates us to seek after anything that is lovely, or of good report, or praiseworthy. (See the 13th Article of Faith, & Philippians 4:8).

But wo unto those who only casually receive the illumination that is so freely given. Because of their misguided obsession with temporal trivia, they carelessly waste the days of their probation rooting through telestial trash, and awful is their state. (See 2 Nephi 9:27). They groan "under darkness and under the bondage of sin," because they squander their energy groping about in a frantic but fruitless search for meaning in their lives. In short, they fail to appreciate the stabilizing power that could have been theirs if they had only focused on faith. (D&C 84:49).

If we ignore our innate yearning to exercise focused faith, allowing ourselves to be habitually distracted by trifling concerns until they become the center of our attention, we sin by omission. We risk settling into a shabby "second-class hotel" that is of our own construction. There is, after all, "a tide in the affairs of men, which, taken at the flood leads on to fortune. Omitted," we assume the risk that our lives

will be "bound in shallows and in miseries," subject to the flotsam and jetsam that floats about on the sea of life. (Shakespeare, Brutus, in "Julius Caesar," Act 4, Scene 2). "How carefully most of us creep into nameless graves, while now and again one or two" of us forget ourselves through focused faith, "into immortality." (Wendell Phillips, "Speech on Lovejoy").

At a basic level, our refusal to focus our faith is sin. It is wasting our resources in fruitless pursuits, when we should be engaged in other and better activities for which we have been blessed with God-given talents and capacities. For example, a robotic fixation on social media shuts out all the wonderful things upon which our spirits should be focusing, leaving our minds in a state of mechanical, unresponsive, and thoughtless stupor.

"How vain and trifling have been our spirits, our conferences, our councils, our meetings, our private as well as public conversations," wrote the Prophet Joseph Smith from Liberty Jail. "Too low, too mean, too vulgar, too condescending (too unfaithful) for the dignified characters called and chosen of God." (Lucy Mack Smith, "History of Joseph Smith," p. 55).

When Captain Moroni addressed what he thought was the dereliction of duty of the government officials of his day, he asked: "Can you think to sit upon your thrones in a state of thoughtless stupor, while your enemies are spreading the work of death around you?" (Alma 60:6-7). Moroni believed these bureaucrats had lost their focused faith. If that had been so, the temporal and spiritual welfare of those whom they were bound to serve would have hung in the balance. In every case, heaven holds its breath while it waits upon our initiative.

Society pays a heavy price when it lacks a faithful focus. For example, when its spiritual equilibrium has become disoriented and its moral compass is spinning wildly, its values are often adjusted in a vain attempt to regain a state of balance. An unprincipled society deals with its spiritual myopia by simply ratcheting down its

expectations. Its worship of gods of wood and stone is excused as multiculturalism. Its perversion is legitimized as an alternative lifestyle. Its exploitation of the weak is justified by waving the flag in an appeal to patriotism. If unborn children are killed, the collective conscience is soothed by describing it as pro-choice. If the media is polluted with obscenities, it is characterized as freedom of expression. If public figures are caught in a web of lies, its obfuscation is dismissed as hyper-exaggeration. Power is abused in the name of progressivism. For the sake of cultural expediency, the target is moved to score repetitive bulls-eyes, without anyone conceding that it is the arrow of faith that has strayed far from the mark.

We lose our focus and our faith gradually, just as we lose the acuity of our vision over time. First, we squint, and then we hold the page we are reading a little closer or a little further away. We compensate for our inability to see clearly, whether it is the printed page or our character that we can no longer read. In both cases, our ability to see is unconsciously compromised. Whether it is the letter of the law or an eye-chart that is beyond our comprehension, we become legally blind.

We don't intend to lose our testimonies. Our conviction just fades away like a slow leak in an automobile tire, rather than as a sudden blowout. The compromise of our conversion and the demolition of our discipleship can be attributed to a lack of faithful focus that began at a specific point in time, and that initiated a chain-reaction of unfortunate and inevitable consequences.

With faithful focus, persistence will prevail when all else has failed. When we hear our team yelling from the bleachers: "Take the shot!" we move decisively and with confidence, visualizing success. We know that we will miss 100% of the shots we don't take, so we don't hesitate to act without wavering. When an opportunity presents itself, we spontaneously re-play the moves that have aforetime been repeatedly pre-played. We concentrate on what we want to happen, instead of allowing ourselves to be distracted by what we don't want to happen. We have envisioned success so many times, that the conclusion is foregone. We must succeed; it is inevitable that we succeed; it is our destiny to succeed; and to believe otherwise is unthinkable.

Faithless individuals see things as they are, and wonder "Why?" The focused faithful dream things that never were, and ask "Why not?" They work through their problems, instead of working around them. They find mentors to emulate, instead of scapegoats to blame. They look for better solutions, instead of easier answers. When they make mistakes, they readily acknowledge them, instead of shifting the blame. In pressure situations, they remember previous victories, instead of past defeats. They keep their faces oriented toward the light, so the shadows will always be behind them. They realize that they cannot go back and start a new beginning, but they can rely upon the Atonement of Jesus Christ to write a new ending. Rather than reciting psycho-babble, they lean upon prophetic wisdom and rely upon scriptural certainties. They trust a Divine Design rather than devilish doctrines. Their lives are "fairy tales waiting to be written by the omnipotent hand of God." (Hans Christian Anderson).

The problem with those who lack the focus of faith is not that their expectations are too high, and they fail to reach their goals. It is that they set their sights too low, and they too easily accomplish the simple tasks that lie before them. The activities in which the faithful are engaged do not require practical commitment to a belief, but only minimal effort, little responsibility, and virtually no accountability. Someone once said that the Lord gave us two ends: one to think with and the other to sit on. Which one we use will determine how well we do in life. In other words: Heads we win, and tails we lose.

Good intentions may be noble, but if we work without vision, it is drudgery, and even if we have vision, without work, it is dreamery. But if we focus our faith, and work with vision, it will be our destiny to soar with eagles, rather than walk with turkeys. When Paul exhorted the Philippian Saints to "work out (their) salvation with fear and trembling," he knew that if they put their hearts and souls into the effort, it would leave them both physically and spiritually exhausted. (Philippians 2:12). Nevertheless, he urged them to join him as he pressed "toward the mark, for the prize of the high calling of God in Christ Jesus." (Philippians 3:14). It was George Brimhall who observed that the utility of the postage stamp "lies in its ability to stick with something until it reaches its destination."

Focused faith pushes us beyond our normal capacity. Spencer W. Kimball said: "So much depends upon our willingness to make up our minds, both individually and collectively, that present levels of performance are not acceptable, either to ourselves or to the Lord. In saying that, I am not calling for flashy, temporary differences in our performance levels, but (for) a quiet resolve to lengthen our stride." ("Church News," 3/22/1975).

At another time, he said: "We have paused on some plateaus long enough. Let us resume our journey forward and upward. Let us quietly end our reluctance to reach out to others, whether in our own families, wards, or neighborhoods. We have been diverted, at times, from fundamentals upon which we must now focus in order to move forward." (C.R., 4/1979).

Even after months of being incarcerated in Liberty Jail under the most trying circumstances, Joseph Smith still maintained the focus of his faith. From his cell, he wrote the Saints that if they would be charitable, and if they would occupy themselves with virtuous thoughts, their confidence would soar in the presence of God, and they would receive personal revelation concerning the doctrine of the priesthood. Their righteous power and authority would be uncontested and unchallenged, their dominion would be everlasting, and by eternal decree it would flow unto them forever. (See D&C 121:45-46)

When we maintain the focus of our faith, we don't get in the thick of thin things. We develop an equilibrium that is centered far from the madding crowd, at a safe distance from the ego-filled minds of mediocre men. We are thereby insulated from the tumult, confusion, and cares of the world, and enjoy a firmness that is unshakable. (See Mormon 9:28).

Our focused faith protects us from a false sense of carnal security and from indifferent complacency. We view our weaknesses in positively constructive ways, and are grateful for our conscious awareness of opportunities for personal improvement, and for the tools that we have been given to accomplish our mortal

mission assignments. Because we know that weaknesses are part of the tapestry that has been woven by God into the fabric of our lives, we simply turn to the inventory of thread that He has provided, that enables us to weave new patterns that reflect the celebration and expression of our faith.

Joseph Smith acknowledged his own youthful vulnerability, saying: "I was left to all kinds of temptations, and, mingling with all kinds of society, I frequently fell into many foolish errors, and displayed the weakness of youth, and the foibles of human nature; which, I am sorry to say, led me into diverse temptations, offensive in the sight of God. ...I was guilty of levity, and sometimes associated with jovial company." (J.S.H. 1:28). In consequence of his perceived lack of focus, he often felt condemned. Concentrating his efforts and attention, however, he sought "Almighty God for forgiveness of (his) sins and follies," that he might know of his standing before Him. (J.S.H. 1:29).

We catch a glimpse of his prophetic mantle in his subsequent penitent declaration: "I had full confidence in obtaining a divine manifestation." (J.S.H. 1:29). He had regained his focus to rely upon the impregnable fortress of his faith. He had been blessed with the vision to see an island of opportunity in the middle of an ocean of difficulty. He had mustered up an abundance of "will power." He had distanced himself from those timid souls who operate so far below their potential that all they can feel is "won't power." His focused faith had dissipated the fear that can sap from each of us whatever energy we do possess.

Brigham Young taught: "The first principle that ought to occupy our attention and which is the mainspring of all action, is the principle of improvement." ("Discourses of Brigham Young," p. 87). With focused faith, we constantly strive to do more, to be better, to seek understanding, and to empower ourselves with knowledge and wisdom. We emulate the Olympic motto "Citius, Altius, Fortius," or "Faster, Higher, Stronger." We have a firm conviction in the promise of the Lord: "If thou shalt ask, thou shalt receive revelation upon revelation, knowledge upon knowledge that thou mayest know the mysteries and peaceable things - that which bringeth joy, that which bringeth life eternal." (D&C 42:61).

Obstacles to that epiphany are those frightful things we see when we take our minds off our goals. They loom large with gratuitous significance. Focus gives us the vision to see beyond these potential stumbling blocks, and then to rely upon the grace of God and the expansive creative engine for positive change that is the

Gospel, to turn them into stepping-stones that pave the way to higher achievement. Focus allows us to see things as they could be, and then to work with all our means to create the new reality we have envisioned. Focus "generates power, for a mind once stretched by a new idea never returns to its original dimension." (Oliver Wendell Holmes). Among the greatest virtues we can possess are a well-trained mind, a body to match, a love of achievement, and focused faith. Without these, life can be nothing more than smoke and mirrors, and we grow old before our time.

With the focus of faith, however, we arise from our beds every morning and prepare ourselves for the day by rehearsing the following self-talk: "This is the beginning of a new day. God has given it to me to use, as I will. I can waste it or use it for good. What I do today is very important, because I am exchanging 24 hours of my life for it. When tomorrow comes, this day will be gone forever, leaving something in its place that I have traded for it. I want it to be gain, not loss; good, not evil; and success, not failure, in order that it might be worth the price I have paid for it." (Anonymous). During the journey, we use what talents we have been given, knowing that the woods would be very quiet if no birds sang except those that sang best.

Those with focused faith recognize that "religion is more involved in recovery than discovery, (and) that our destiny is not union, but reunion, with divine realities." (B.H. Roberts, "The Way, The Truth, and The Life"). This explains the Prophet's classic statement on religious knowing. Whether written, spoken, or felt, "the word of Jehovah has such an influence over the human mind, the logical mind, that it is convincing without other testimony." Truth comes as a flow of pure intelligence that is attended by a burning religious fever. When it finds place in our hearts, our search for external warrant is nothing more than "the confirmation and application of what is already, and more certainly, known." (Truman Madsen, "Eternal Man," p. 73, see "Teachings," p. 151).

When we have been reintroduced to the noble principles that guided us through our spiritual kindergarten years in the pre-earth existence, we are fortunate indeed if we are further blessed with the focus of faith, and with the resultant strength of character that can mold and shape us to return to our more natural state of harmony with heaven. In its economy, "we often catch a spark from the awakened memories of the immortal soul, which lights up our whole being as with the glory of our former home." (Joseph F. Smith, "Gospel Doctrine," p. 14). When that happens, our ideals become as stars in the evening sky. "We will not succeed in touching them with our hands. But like the seafaring man in the desert of waters, we can follow them to reach our divine destiny." (Carl Shurz, "B.Y.U. Studies," 16:4, p. 499).

Those whose faith is focused are as the child who, when asked what she wanted to be when she grew up, replied in one word: "Obedient." Though tender in years, she had already tasted the sweetness of consistency with her convictions. Some learn while still in their youth, while others are only taught later on in the school of hard knocks, about the import of a focus on faith. Sooner or later, though, we all respond to both internal promptings and external encouragement to receive intrinsic warrant. The celestial compass of Gospel principles, that is calibrated to be oriented toward truth, is always available to guide disciplined and focused travelers to safe haven. It is also there for those who have lost their way, to bring them into the fold of the Good Shepherd, or to show them how to return to the safety and security of the community of Christ, from which they have strayed.

At some point, all of us will come to understand that the commandments are like the recipe for making a delicious cake. If we want to enjoy the cake, we must first follow the steps of the recipe. In heaven, however, there is only one kind of cake that is served, and, yes, it is angel food cake! In the meantime, as Neal A. Maxwell cautioned: "Through ethical relativism, the human race is led into conceptual cul-de-sacs that could entice it to plunge into a freedom which is a bottomless, dark, pool of misery." Those who follow that path will find, to their dismay, that the only cake that will be served in hell's kitchen is devil's food cake, and that it tastes terrible! To make matters even worse, when the children of rebellion eat devil's

food cake, there is no milk to wash it down! (See 1 Corinthians 3:2).

Visualize the two cakes (Angel Food and Devil's Food) when you consider that "two forces are always operating, and two voices are always calling, one coming from the swamps of selfishness and force, where success means death, and the other from the hilltops of justice and progress, where even failure brings glory. Two lights are always seen on your horizon, one, the last fading marsh light of power, and the other the slowly rising sun of human brotherhood. Two ways always lie open for you, one leading to an ever lower and lower plane, where are heard the cries of despair and the curses of the poor, where manhood shrivels and possessions rot down the possessor, and the other leading to the highlands of the morning, where are heard the glad shouts of humanity, and where honest effort is rewarded with immortality." (John P. Altgeld).

With focused faith, we trust our instincts to lead us to those highlands of the morning. Loren C. Dunn described how his father gave him and his brother the responsibility of raising cows on the family farm. He gave the boys wide latitude in how they did it, and they made some mistakes. These were observed by an alert neighbor, who pointed them out to their father. Brother Dunn addressed his concerns, saying: "Jim, you don't understand. You see, I'm raising boys, not cows." ("B.Y.U. Fireside," 5/4/1982).

The best teachers help their students to focus, to deepen their insights and strengthen their faith, so that they may learn to trust the Lord. They are encouraged to read themselves full, think themselves straight, pray themselves hot, and let themselves go!

B.H. Roberts was a great mentor, who advised his students: "Pray, study, think, get prepared, and then let nature caper." He practiced what he preached. Once, he delivered a sermon in which he "described Christ and the raising of Lazarus. So vivid were his images, and so moving his presence that the audience was carried with him. When, in a loud voice, he repeated the Master's words, 'Lazarus, come forth!' the entire congregation involuntarily came to its feet." (Truman Madsen,

"Defender of The Faith," p. 355). He knew how to focus the faith of an audience. When we are similarly focused, we know how to worship and what to worship, for "truth may be recognized by its effects. Rendering obedience to its principles of action may test the claims of the Gospel. Practicing our religion is the most direct method of gaining a testimony of the truth." (John Widtsoe, "Evidences and Reconciliations"). This is why missionaries have always encouraged those who are seeking the truth to focus their faith on "the virtue of the word of God." (Alma 31:5).

If we fail to do so, we miss the mark. Bruce R. McConkie was, arguably, one of the most focused of the Latter-day Apostles of the Lord. On one occasion, he said: "It is my pattern and custom simply to teach and testify. I do not debate and I do not argue. If someone wants to contend to the contrary, he is just as welcome as the day is long to do so. But let us understand this. When we deal with God and His laws, when we get in the realm of spiritual things, we are dealing with the things that save souls, and at our peril we are obligated to find the truth. The whole sectarian world sits out there, and they suppose that they have some truth and that they are pursuing a course that will save them. But God has restored the everlasting Gospel to us. We have the power of God unto salvation in our hands, as it were. It is our obligation to understand what is involved, so that we can live in such a manner that the fulness of these blessings will come to us," as well as to our friends and neighbors. ("B.Y.U. Devotional," 1/4/1972). We hope to be able to fulfil that great commission, by the focus of our faith!

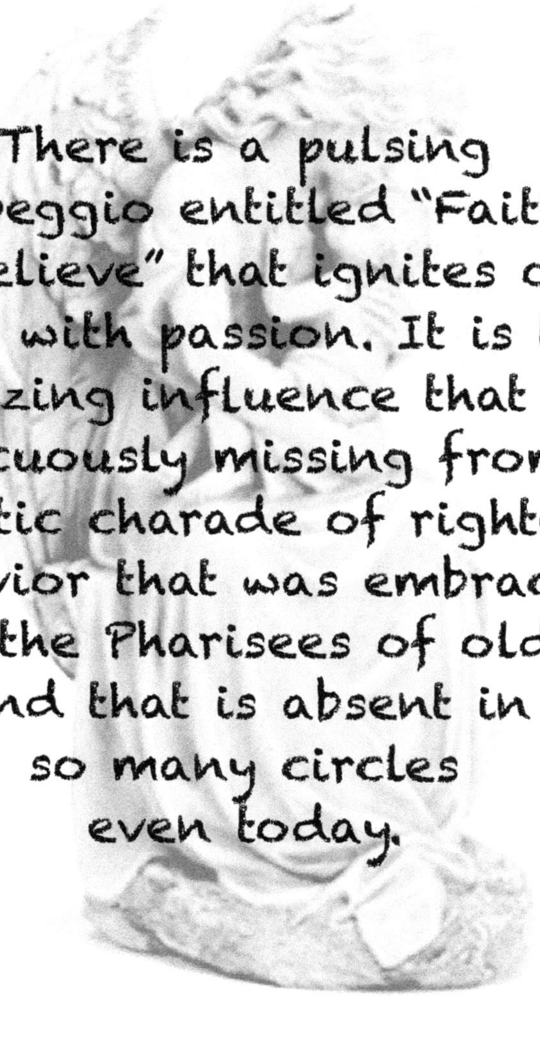

There is a pulsing arpeggio entitled "Faith to Believe" that ignites our souls with passion. It is this catalyzing influence that was conspicuously missing from the pedantic charade of righteous behavior that was embraced by the Pharisees of old, and that is absent in so many circles even today.

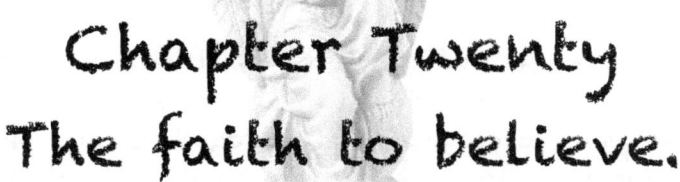

Chapter Twenty
The faith to believe.

When "the Pharisees were gathered together, Jesus asked them, Saying, What think ye of Christ? Whose son is he?" (Matthew 22:41).

Sadly, their sluggish response, "The Son of David," was tendered with little emotion. (Matthew 22:42). Although it was technically correct, it lacked spiritual horsepower. Its dearth of traction was obvious, its inability to generate spontaneity was palpable, its lack of energy to engage enthusiasm was noticeable, its incapacity to spark vitality was evident, and its failure to candidly acknowledge the powerful relationship that can exist between ourselves and God was undisputed. Following the Savior's rebuke of their hesitancy and equivocation, none of the Pharisees were thereafter "able to answer him a word, neither durst any man from that day forth ask him any more questions." (Matthew 24:46). They had been weighed in the

balances and had been found wanting, for they were spiritually bankrupt on an institutional scale. (See Daniel 5:27). They clearly lacked the faith to believe.

And yet, with adequate preparation, they could have developed faith in the divine mission of Jesus of Nazareth, to generate the energy to lift them heavenward on a groundswell of emotion. The conduct of the Pharisees should be motivation enough for us to elevate the level of our worship to something more dynamic than the simple mechanical observance of a multiplicity of ceremonial rules, to thereby help us to avoid the pit into which they fell.

Exercising our faith to believe is more than a repetitive exercise to be performed only by the numbers. As the daily antidote to our tendency toward pride, selfishness, and self-reliance, it helps us to catalyze feeling, capture emotion, contour attitude, crystallize thought, congeal passion, convey sentiment, and compartmentalize action that lead to spiritual revitalization.

We can be sure that the Savior had more than just the Pharisees in mind, when He posed those penetrating questions. Because they could be asked of anyone, at any time in history, or at any place on earth. it is certain that His intention was to cast a much wider net. The Master, Whose questions have been immortalized by Matthew, demands that you and I answer, as well.

It matters little whether we have identified with the Pharisees or the Sadducees, with Buddha, Confucius, Guru Nanak, Zoroaster, or with gods of wood and stone. We may have embraced the monotheism of Islam or the Bahá'i, the pantheistic theology of Hinduism, Shintoism, or Taoism, secular humanism, or irreligion. We may be Catholic, Evangelical, Fundamentalist, Protestant, or Eastern Orthodox. We may advocate nothing more than the existential nihilism of the postmodern world. None of that makes any difference. Paul observed of the Athenians, who were similar in many ways to us, that they were inclined to bow down before unknown gods, whom, therefore, they ignorantly worshipped.

It was in the hope that all mankind might bear an independent witness of the true and living God, that Paul wrote: "Him declare I unto you." (Acts 17:23, see 1 Thessalonians 1:9).

You may be a trusting Timothy or a doubting Thomas, a spiritual giant or a philosophical naturalist, of a ready wit or resoundingly dull, earnestly enlightened or frivolously facetious, energetically enthusiastic or casually indifferent, a dedicated disciple or a distracted detractor, a true believer, an agnostic, or an atheist. In a moment of despair, you may have thrown up defensive dross designed to disrespect, disregard, deflect, discourage, or disparage the uncomfortably penetrating question: "What think ye of Christ?"

If you have wandered into disbelief, you may have deferred or deterred your response to the question: "Whose son is he?" If that day has already come, or if it looms large on your horizon, you can be sure that, if you have strayed from your obligation to nurture your faith to believe and to answer with conviction, your stammering apologies will be unceremoniously swept aside.

In every case, no matter that we may be defenders of the faith or ambassadors of the adversary, all of heaven holds its collective breath as time stands still and our fate hangs in the air as a dandelion seed caught in the doldrums of a hot summer afternoon. How we have developed the faith to believe will deify or destroy us, for our response to the Savior's questions will delineate our dreams, define our destiny, and determine how, where, and with whom we will spend eternity. There will come for each of us a great and dreadful day when we will be asked to stand and give our sworn deposition before God, angels, and witnesses. On the issue of faith, depending upon our answer, we will be counted among the sheep or the goats, and find ourselves on His right hand or His left hand.

To avoid the fate of those who greet the Savior's ministry with skepticism, and to insure that our faith to believe might be animated with energy, so that we will have no regrets, we have been given the Light of Christ. It proceeds from His throne as a powerful influence for good that is intended to groom us to receive the Holy

Ghost. It is a gift that miraculously multiplies even as it divides within a telestial world populated with individuals whose efforts to cultivate faith are governed by free will. It is given, the Lord revealed, that we "may act in doctrine and principle

pertaining to futurity," in accordance with our birthright of moral agency. (D&C 101:78, see D&C 93:31).

The Light of Christ has been compassionately bestowed upon all of us by One Whom we can be sure "denieth none that come unto him, black and white, bond and free, male and female; and he remembereth the heathen; and all are alike unto (God), both Jew and Gentile." (2 Nephi 26:33). The Light of Christ stimulates soul-sweat as it works on our conscience, our sense of duty, and our scruples, as we slowly nurture our faith to believe. It provides a shield of protection against the corrosive spatter of perspiration cast off by the destroyer, who insidiously, pervasively, and persistently works overtime to damage our doctrinal defenses, dull our spiritual sensitivities, diminish our charitable capacity, deplete our bountiful reservoirs of sympathy, and destroy our devotions, even as we labor with an equal but opposite intensity to deify our work on the earth as we develop the faith to believe.

The Light of Christ exerts a nurturing influence, as well. Although we must daily travel farther from the East, we are, nevertheless, oriented toward the radiant glow emanating from that distant horizon. The Light of Christ provides us with the regularly recurring reassurance of a religious recalibration that autocorrects with fortuitous frequency and celestial precision. It envelops us in the intuitive appreciation of where we came from, the tangible element of why we are here, and the revelatory reassurance of where we are going.

As in a heavenly language that is rhythmical, melodious, soothing to our ears, and calming to our souls, when we hear the Spirit quietly whisper: "You're a stranger here," we are comforted by the realization that we have "wandered from a more exalted sphere." (Eliza R. Snow). The Light of Christ prompts us to examine what it means to be anxiously engaged, inspires us to plumb the depths of our commitment

to the Savior, sensitizes us to the nobility of His work, expands upon His visions of immortality, personalizes the Atonement, and helps us to remain consciously aware of eternal life, as we acquire the faith to believe.

In a way, the Light of Christ is like a midwife, because one of its purposes is to facilitate the arduous process of our spiritual rebirth, by contributing to our preparation to answer with conviction the questions that were first posed to the Pharisees so long ago: "What think ye of Christ?" and "Whose son is he?" When we feel the urge to push His agenda, the Light of Christ can be our labor coach, providing us with just the right amount of encouragement to successfully deliver our witness of the Savior without being overbearing.

One exciting element of the manifestation of the Light of Christ is the constant stream of inspiration and revelation that cascades down from above. This insures that we may walk along illuminated pathways leading to the one institution that may legitimately claim the divine guidance that leads to perfect faith, that has been brought "forth out of obscurity and out of darkness, the only true and living church upon the face of the whole earth, with which ... the Lord (is) well pleased." (D&C 1:30).

The Light of Christ exerts a leveling influence and is the great equalizer, giving each of us the same privileges to use our faculties of mind, intellect, and spirit, that we might exercise the faith to believe, and to discern between truth and error, no matter in what exclusive ecclesiastical country club we may hold membership, or upon what narrow theological terrace we might have stopped to catch our breath. It teaches us to face the sun, that we may feel the warmth of its rays, listen with sensitivity, hear the word of the Lord, be receptive to the cries of the downtrodden and oppressed, and see with a lucidity that allows us to be benevolently blind to the shortcomings of others.

The influence of the Light of Christ makes it easier to have lips that have learned to articulate only positive expressions of speech and never speak guile, shoulders

that have developed the strength to bear the burdens of those who have been battered and bruised by the vicissitudes of life and who may be faltering under the heavy weight of sorrow or sin, backs that have become sturdy enough to brace us against the fierce winds of adversity and the subtle wiles of the adversary, hearts that have become the receptacles of pure and virtuous principles upon which we may draw in times of need, bowels that are moved to compassion for those who are struggling with misfortune or the weight of transgression, hands that have become accustomed to lifting those who desperately need our support, and feet that have been conditioned to speedily carry us to those who are imprisoned by poor choices, bad habits, or unfortunate circumstances.

Even now, heavenly messengers are as nursemaids who minister by the Light of Christ among the nations of the earth. They use its power as a resource to reach out and caress the downtrodden who are poor in spirit. Men and women of all persuasions feel that angels are watching over them. Witness countless newlyweds who are certain that their match was made in heaven, before the world was. Others sense that they have been assisted by acts of Providence, are the beneficiaries of divine intervention, have been touched by angels, are moved to compassion, or have been otherwise blessed to "walk in the light of the Lord." (Isaiah 2:5).

Guidance in the form of spiritual promptings and impressions are more common that many would suspect. Powerful intuitive communicators strongly influence nearly all of us to push forward in the direction of our dreams, toward a faith to believe that blesses us with a greater appreciation of the majesty and power of our Creator. Truly, He "is no respecter of persons" Who causes the sun to shine on the wicked, as well as on the just. (Acts 10:34, see Matthew 5:45).

Therefore, we must venture forth out of the shadows, even beyond the guidance we receive from the Light of Christ and the ministering of angels, if we want to experience the special familiarity that the faithful enjoy with the Lord.. The more we think about Christ, the easier it is to craft with words the sensations

that naturally flow to each of us as a result of the stirrings of those feelings of intimacy. It becomes that much easier to generate the faith to believe.

As we nurture that faith, we realize how heavily we have borrowed from the towering examples of those who, over the years, have been our mystical mentors, our sensible chaperones, our spiritual guides, our surrogate saviors, and our compassionate critics. They are our avatars, who have shown us the way, strengthened our testimonies, taught us humility, been there to steady and nurture us, applied the Balm of Gilead to bind up our wounds, provided both tangible and immaterial support, emboldened us with words of encouragement, and cheered us on with wise counsel. When we think of this multitude of angels thinly disguised as our families, friends, and peers, we remember the words of Sir Isaac Newton, who, when pressed to reveal the great secret behind his accomplishments, simply replied: "I stood on the shoulders of giants."

If we are fortunate, we are privileged to do so, as well. As we nurture our faith to believe, we draw upon the testimony and spiritual insight of others, from the General Authorities and lay members of The Church of Jesus Christ of Latter-day Saints, to playwrights and poets, philosophers and humanitarians, authors, journalists, essayists, classicists, and religious scholars of all persuasions, to statesmen, sages, mystics, stoics, composers, and lyricists. Our friends and family are often more influential than they could ever imagine. We are fortunate if we have been blessed with such wonderful traveling companions during our journey through mortality. Such gurus guide our lives with a profound influence that helps us to enjoy the tender feelings that shape our faith to believe.

However, we sometimes need to ask for pardon, when our traveling companions are confronted with the literal and figurative blemishes, the idiosyncratic foibles, and the objective and subjective imperfections that too often work their way into our character. If we unknowingly take poetic license with foundation principles, or add needless ecclesiastical embroidery to Gospel truths, we diminish our faith to believe, and we must speedily repent.

In these instances, we beseech the indulgence and seek the forgiveness of our Heavenly Father, as well as of our peers. When our passion clouds our vision or overpowers our zealous intentions, if the syntax of our speech seems tortuous, too bland, or too spicy, if our feelings are overstated, or if we are given over to hyperbole, or even if we appear to drift over the line separating true doctrine from baseless speculation, we beg for the forbearance of our contemporaries. We ask them to take a step back, that our expressions might be permitted to simmer for a while, before their flavor is sampled anew. Who is to know, but that the reduction sauce of time may enhance, for them, the palatability of our perspective.

In any case, as the congealed distillate of our life experiences, our thoughts and feelings relating to our faith to believe stand revealed as our innocent attempts to yoke our emotions, as well as our spiritual promptings, to language. We hope that others will find them refreshing, and will use them as food for thought.

With the faith to believe, we dream that we might feel the gentle caress of the touch of the Master Potter, as He turns our lives with the hand of time. We want Him to mold us and shape us as the Artisan of our destiny. "As the clay is in the potter's hand, so are ye in mine hand," said the Lord through His prophet. (Jeremiah 18:6). As Isaiah declared: "O Lord, thou art our father; we are the clay, and thou our potter; and we all are the work of thy hand." (Isaiah 64:8). As we seek the faith to believe, we hope that we may remain pliable and impressionable to the things of the Spirit.

All of us need to learn to utilize the divinely designed accouterments of the matchless and multi-talented Son of Joseph, the Carpenter of Nazareth, Who will help us to construct the stages upon which will be enacted the drama of our lives. Perhaps our efforts will be validated by appreciative applause from the audience, and by an occasional bouquet of red roses thrown at our feet. But we hope to retain our perspective, to remain as His poor understudies, and to give our best efforts to supporting roles in off-Broadway performances that count for more than mere entertainment.

As we consider the performance potential of the faith to believe, we are gently reminded that it is not our purpose to be the stars of the show. Our path of progress may point to perfection, but it is a process. We will not be given, nor will we need, top billing to fulfill our dreams. It is not necessary that we win a People's Choice

Award. Rather than becoming the objects of attention of an adoring paparazzi, what we need is to be enveloped in divinely directed diamond dust that glitters with thousands of points of light. What we need is to participate, in small ways, in daily dramas that are designed by divine direction to far surpass the pomp and circumstance of any "American Idol" production.

The faith to believe elicits displays of celestial energy worthy of notice from above. As fire in the sky, the air in the theater of life is charged with an electricity that is the product of the inevitable merger of the universal encouragement of the Light of Christ with the pointed and providential guidance provided by the Holy Ghost. When these influences streak in tandem across the heavens, their trajectories coalesce to trace a flaming trail that sparkles over a vast cosmic ocean of thought. Over the ebb and flow of its tide, the cohesive influence of the mighty foundation of faith to believe creates an effectual bridge of understanding between the secular and the divine. Life, with all its twists and turns, and its permutations and complexities, suddenly makes more sense.

Armed with the faith to believe, our innermost longings to apprehend visions of the eternal world are epitomized by our triumphant realization of dreams fulfilled. Our emotions are painted with words that depict our progression toward distant mileposts along a well-marked path. Our faith to believe is molded by personal victories and by the Spirit's quiet recognition of our efforts, and validation of the achievement of our goals. But we are equally refined by our frustrated plans, and we are significantly shaped by the challenges that lie just around the next bend in the road.

Experience is the active ingredient in a fertile matrix carefully created by God during His meticulous preparation of the petri dishes that are personalized to

suit our individual circumstances in the learning laboratory of life. This rich culture medium becomes just the agar we need in order for Him to nurture our metamorphosis, as we are transformed, not by maturation but by generation, into the glorious image and likeness of God, in the full stature of our spirits. The supernal gift of faith to believe is catalyzed by an infusion of the heavenly element. Our faith sustains us, as we receive with equanimity whatever might come our way during an incubation process that was designed to be just as challenging as it would be rewarding.

The faith to believe cultivates an atmosphere of reflection, keeps the Savior in our thoughts, nurtures an eternal perspective, initiates positive change, and harmonizes our behavior with His charitable example. Our determination is bolstered by the voice of Moroni whispering to us from out of the dust: "I speak unto you as if ye were present, and yet ye are not. But behold, Jesus Christ hath shown you unto me, and I know your doing." (Mormon 8:35). We can be sure that Moroni is overjoyed to know that we are doing our best to generate the faith to believe.

Because we will one day be asked to give accountability reports to the Savior, we try to heed King Benjamin's ancient but apropos warning to watch ourselves judiciously, to be the meticulous guardians of our thoughts, the scrupulous custodians of our words, and the prudent caretakers of our deeds, to fastidiously observe the commandments of God, and to continue evenly upon a path that is steadily illuminated by the faith to believe. (See Mosiah 4:30). As we hesitantly inch our way through mortality, Benjamin's admonition invigorates us with renewed energy, and instills within us the desire to redouble our efforts to maintain the integrity of that faith.

We persist because it makes a difference how we answer the simple questions: "What think ye of Christ?" and "Whose son is he?" These inquiries demand that we dig deeply within ourselves before we tender our responses. Because it is all too easy to answer tentatively, superficially retreating into colorless and insipid verbiage as the easy way out, we guard ourselves against casually and carelessly steering a course away from the Savior with offhand, dismissive, or inconsiderate remarks.

We realize that, if we were to do so, He would soon be conveniently out of sight and far from our minds, and we would be left with no more than a stupor of thought. (See D&C 9:9).

If we were unable to answer these simple questions with conviction, any fleeting, albeit faux, feelings of liberation from the constraints of conscience would soon give way to an inner emptiness that could not be satisfied with the poor imitations of testimony that is the manifestation of the outpouring of the faith to believe. If we were to respond to these questions with a knee-jerk reaction, or if we were to kick against the pricks, we would surely estrange ourselves from the Spirit, until we were left with neither root nor branch. (See Malachi 4:1). We would be tossed to and fro as flotsam and jetsam on the sea of life, never to enjoy the sweet blessings that flow out of the faith to believe. (See Ephesians 4:14).

None of us would consciously choose to lead marginalized lives, to become spiritually depleted on a personal or an institutional level, or to perish because we had esteemed as a thing of naught that which mattered most. We persevere because we do not want to die of spiritual starvation, doctrinal dehydration, or intellectual inhibition, while only inches away from the living bread that would have satisfied our hunger, or from the healing fountains of living water that could have slaked our thirst. Actively pursuing the faith to believe will carry us in positive and meaningful ways to green pastures where we will enjoy the warmth of the embrace of the Good Shepherd, and where we will be permitted to experience the intimacy of the touch of His garment, even when we remain in the press of the crowd. (See Mark 3:10). Soon enough, His strident call to action will awaken within us a sense of duty that will quicken the pace of our passage back to our beginnings.

Precious few "self-help" books address the challenges that accompany our determined quest to discover within ourselves the faith to believe. They rarely demand self-denial, meekness, and charity, or ask that we surrender to the greater good our desire for self-actualization, self-renewal, self-determination, self-fulfillment, or self-aggrandizement. Not often are we taught to concentrate our

efforts on the quality of self-control that honors God's design. Instead, we are spoon-fed twisted temporal theories of emotional and spiritual well-being, that are nothing more than academic factory-food that lacks an upward thrust.

If we desire the gift of faith to believe, we must "let go and let God." Only then, will we catch a religious fever that elevates our testimony temperature and gets our juices flowing. Only then, will we experience the earth shaking and mind bending theophany that we are the spiritual offspring of God, and will we recognize the potential of our position. The precious emanation of familiar and soothing oscillations of energy resonating from within the limitless reserves of the Spirit that are selflessly shared with us by the Holy Ghost will carry us along on rolling waves toward the shoreline of stability that nurtures a more sure witness of the Savior's divinity. That is why we must keep Him in our thoughts as we develop the faith to believe, and as we muster the courage to answer with conviction the questions: "What think ye of Christ?" and "Whose son is he?"

The pulsing arpeggio entitled "Faith to Believe" ignites our souls with passion. It is the catalyzing influence that was missing from the pedantic model of righteous behavior that was adopted by the Pharisees. We prepare to embrace the faith to believe by practicing fast-scale runs through more than half a dozen octaves on all 88 of the glistening black and white ivory keys of experience. As we rehearse in our minds the expression of our witness that Christ is our Savior, we are accompanied by the rising tenor of a celestial symphony that has been scored for every imaginable instrument.

We expand our repertoire to include, not only inspiring artistic compositions representing every epoch of musical literature, but also our own original and signature harmonic inventions. But most of all, in the orchestration of life, the Senior Recital that showcases our command of pitch, rhythm, dynamics, timbre, and texture, becomes a oeuvre that is worthy of the approbation of God. Along the way, the faith to believe guides us back to the Source of our inspiration. It will be there, when we sit at the feet of the Maestro, that we will enjoy master classes from He

Who first created musicality by matching movement and form to the melody and mood of His celestial creations.

We trust that our faith to believe will help us to become reacquainted with the

perfect fit of our personalized divine design. Then, when we have finally completed our dissertation on life, our composition will be recognized as a true magnum opus. After successfully defending our thesis, we will enjoy a commencement exercise that recognizes and celebrates our participation in The Plan and acknowledges the invaluable assistance of our Doctoral Advisor, who was none other than "the Christ, the son of the Living God." (Matthew 16:16).

When we enjoy the fruits of faith to believe, we consecrate our lives to the Savior, and throw ourselves upon the altar of His sacrifice, whose foundation is buttressed by a supernal display of divine direction. We rejoice in our unwavering confidence in the Spirit's capacity to drive us relentlessly forward. The faith to believe endows us with the settled conviction that His power to save has been unleashed in our behalf, to flow over our wounds as a healing balm, to prepare us to one day meet His penetrating gaze with clear and unashamed eyes.

With the faith to believe, we find ourselves among those who have been Born Again, who are "called the children of Christ, his sons, and his daughters." (Mosiah 5:7). We experience the thrill of being spiritually begotten of Him, and of having our hearts changed through faith on His name. With the faith to believe, He is ever before us, on our right hand, and on our left; His Sprit is in our hearts, and His angels are round about us, to bear us up. (See D&C 84:88).

Without distraction, our thoughts turn to Him, and we feel His energy building within us until it lifts us to the zenith of experience. The lines distinguishing mortality from eternity blur, and we find ourselves consumed in a fire of everlasting burnings.

When we feel the power of the faith to believe, we resoundingly declare that we

have been born of God and have received His image in our countenances. We testify that we have experienced a mighty change in our hearts. We are eager to respond to the questions that loom before us all: "What think ye of Christ?" and "Whose son is he?" (See Alma 5:14 & 26).

As we ponder our relationship with the Savior, our proper prior preparation that is powered by priesthood principles prevents our poor performance. We are nudged off our complacency plateaus, as we steer away from the trendy cafés situated along the broad avenues of Idumea. We are transported as on the wings of eagles beyond the boundaries of our self-imposed limitations. Our faith to believe carries us all the way to the edge of eternity, to the portals of heaven, where "forever" stands revealed before us in a breath-taking panorama.

At that moment, as our faith to believe energizes our vision with infinite perspective, we experience a pulsing stream of inspiration whose mighty flow has no temporal or spatial boundary. We are swept up by quickening currents into the direct experience of a holy communion with God. His thoughts have somehow become our thoughts, and His ways have become our ways. (See Isaiah 55:8). We are caught up in a rapture where legions of angels confirm that the universe has become "a machine for the making of gods." (Henri Bergson, "Two Sources of Morality and Religion," 1932).

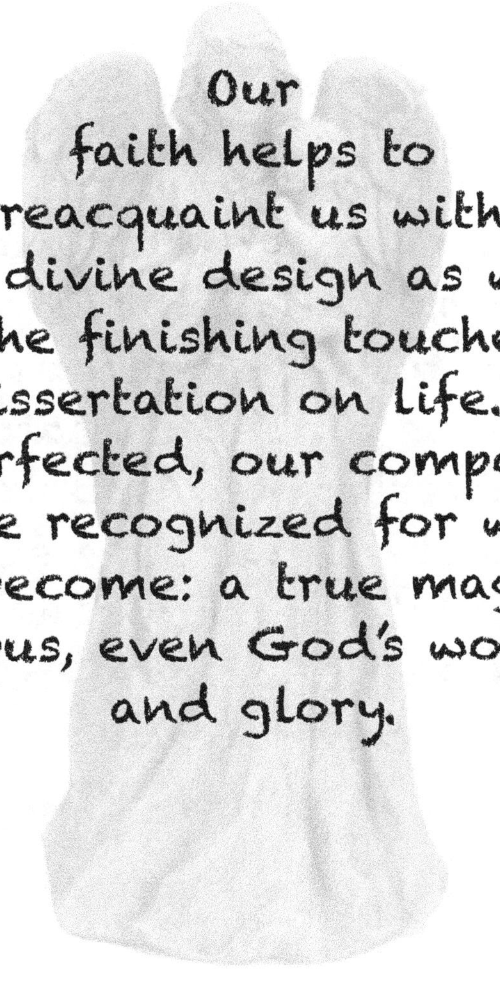

Our
faith helps to
reacquaint us with
a divine design as we
put the finishing touches on
our dissertation on life. As we
are perfected, our composition
will be recognized for what it
has become: a true magnum
opus, even God's work
and glory.

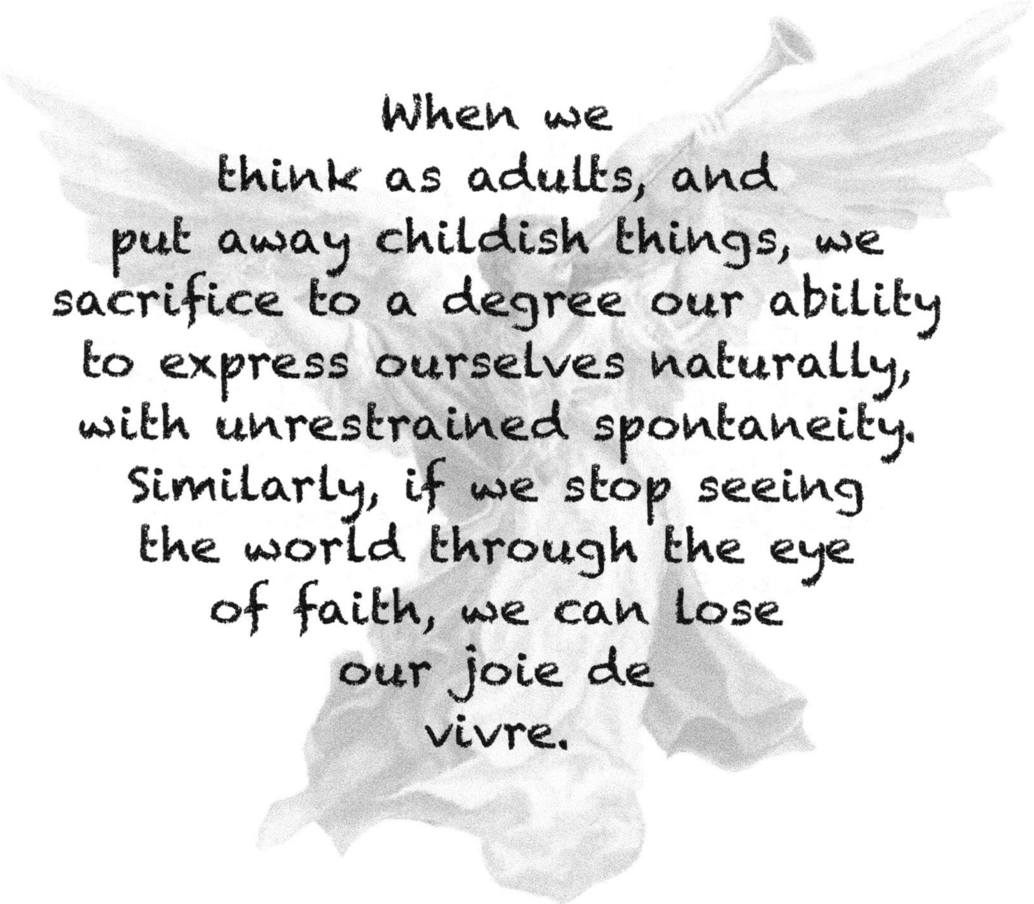

When we
think as adults, and
put away childish things, we
sacrifice to a degree our ability
to express ourselves naturally,
with unrestrained spontaneity.
Similarly, if we stop seeing
the world through the eye
of faith, we can lose
our joie de
vivre.

Chapter Twenty One
The humility of faith.

"It would do no violence to my faith ... "
(David O. McKay).

Does anyone really know how all the pieces of the puzzle of life fit together? Does anyone have all the answers? "My life is but weavings between the Lord and me," wrote the poet. "I cannot choose the colors, while He worketh steadily. Oft-times, He weaveth sorrow, and I, in foolish pride, forget that He seeith the upper, and I, the underside. Not 'til the loom is silent and the shuttles cease to fly, shall God unroll the canvas and explain the reasons why. The dark threads are as needful in the Weaver's skillful hand, as the threads of gold and silver, in the pattern He has planned." (Benjamin Malachi Franklin).

As Alice asked the Cheshire Cat: "Would you please tell me which way I ought to go from here?" Replied the cat: "That depends a good deal on where you want to go."

"I admit," responded Alice, "I don't much care where." Said the cat: "Then it doesn't matter which way you go." "Just so I go somewhere!" cried Alice. "Oh," responded the cat, "you are sure to do that if you walk far enough." (Lewis Carroll, "Alice's Adventures in Wonderland").

'The Lord's intriguing explanation, entirely unsatisfactory, uncomfortable, and unfathomable to many of us, is: "My thoughts are not your thoughts, neither are your ways my ways." (Isaiah 55:8). Frustratingly, as our circle of knowledge expands, so do the borders of darkness. The more we know, the more we need to learn. It should do no violence to our faith to realize that, with a greater understanding of doctrinal truth, there might be additional questions to ponder.

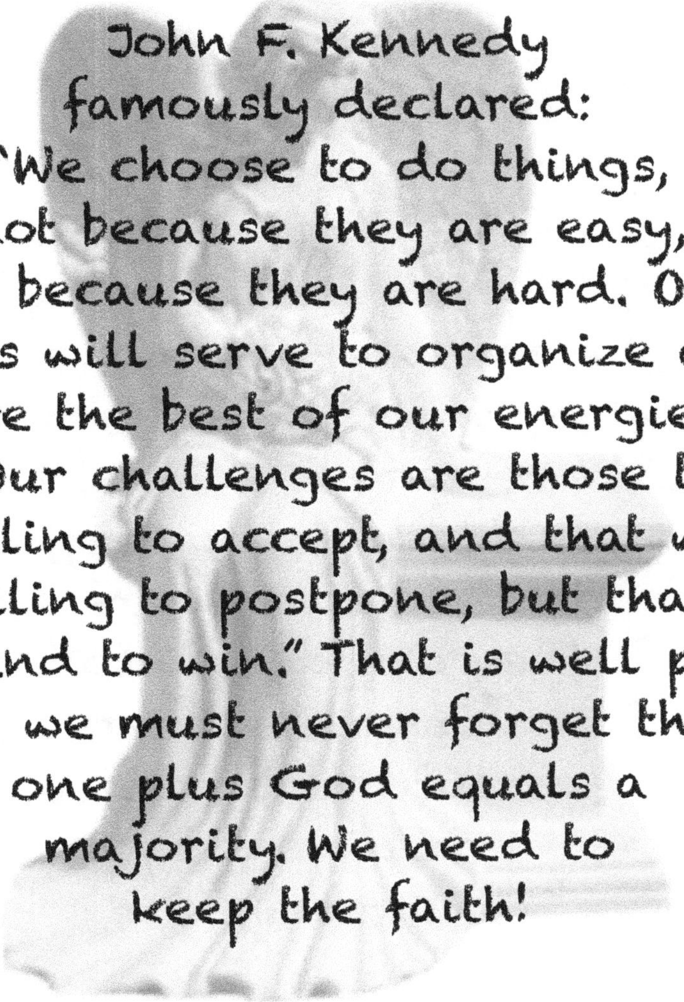

John F. Kennedy famously declared: "We choose to do things, not because they are easy, but because they are hard. Our goals will serve to organize and measure the best of our energies and skills. Our challenges are those that we are willing to accept, and that we are unwilling to postpone, but that we intend to win." That is well put, but we must never forget that one plus God equals a majority. We need to keep the faith!

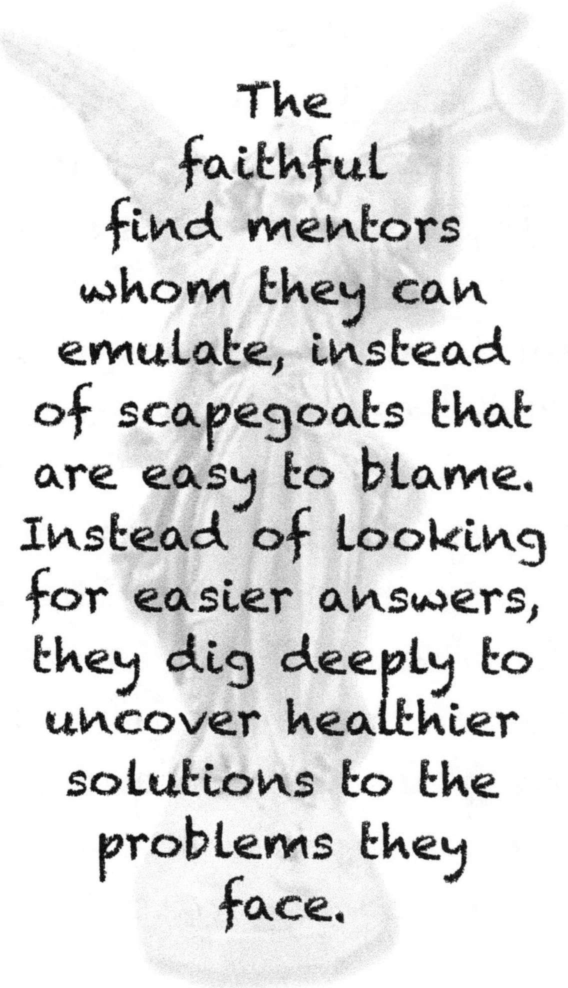

The faithful find mentors whom they can emulate, instead of scapegoats that are easy to blame. Instead of looking for easier answers, they dig deeply to uncover healthier solutions to the problems they face.

Chapter Twenty Two
The faith to become as little children.

"Children are the living messages we send
to a time we will not see."
(Anonymous).

We all know that "little boys are made of frogs and snails and puppy dog tails," and that "little girls are made of sugar and spice and everything nice." (Attributed to Robert Southey). But did you also know that "little girls are made of daisies and butterflies and soft kitty cat purrs, and all the precious memories of times that once were. They are made of angels' wings and giggles and a fire fly's glow, and all the happy feelings, deep inside, that we all know.

They are made of cinnamon and bubbles and fancy white pearls, and snowflakes and rainbows and ballerina twirls. They are made of sunshine and cupcakes and fresh morning dew, and these are the reasons, my sweet little girls, why Jesus loves you." (Anonymous).

Jesus loved all the little boys and little girls, and emphasized their virtues of curiosity, innocence, purity, and trust. He held them up as examples of those who treat others with gentleness, humility, and kindness, and who view the world energetically and enthusiastically with a sense of unbridled anticipation and awe.

Children exude positive energy; they are as Thumper, who recited back to his caring mother: "If you can't say nuttin' nice, don't say nuttin' at all."

When we put away childish things, we sacrifice to some degree our ability to express ourselves naturally with unrestrained spontaneity. If we stop seeing the world through wondering eyes, we can lose our "joie de vivre." So, in His response to His disciples' question of "Who is the greatest in the kingdom?" the Savior emphasized: "Except ye be converted, and become as little children, ye shall not enter into the kingdom of heaven." (Matthew 18:1-2).

In order to regain our heavenly home, we must nurture our capacity to become as little children. The world teaches us to be "grown-up" as soon as possible in order to succeed in life, as if adults had a corner on accomplishment. Children are inundated with adult-themed messages: "This program is suitable for mature audiences, only." "No children allowed." "No-one under 48" tall is allowed on this attraction." "Minors must be accompanied by an adult." "Adults only." "Act your age!" "Don't be a baby!" and "Grow up!" Later, as adults, we are told how to gain a competitive edge: "It's not what you know, it's who you know." "You don't get what you deserve, you get what you negotiate." "Watch your back." Even: "Do as I say, (not as I do)."

The stern warning: "Wait until your father gets home!" applies equally to children and to adults, however, and turns our thoughts to our reunion with our Father in Heaven, when we will be invited to explain our behavior before the Pleasing Bar of Christ. But that is the subject of another chapter, in Volume Two of The First Principles and Ordinances Series, that deals with repentance.

Adults who have learned to swim with sharks are characterized as "seasoned

veterans" and yet the process, far from tenderizing them, curses them with a thick skin containing precious few sensory nerve endings. These are they of whom the Lord said: "I will spue thee out of my mouth," ostensibly because they taste like the gristle of greed, and have the sourness of selfishness, the tartness of transgression, and the bitterness of unbelief.

Daddy Warbucks, reflecting on his life in the business world, told Annie: "You don't have to be nice to those you step on or climb over, on your way up the ladder of success, if you don't plan on coming back down again." As the quintessential business tycoon, he personified the adage: "He who has the gold makes the rules."

But, if, as adults, "we go on lusting after the groveling things of this life which perish with the handling, we shall surely remain fixed with a very limited amount of knowledge, and like a door upon its hinges, move to and fro from one year to another, without any visible advancement or improvement." (Brigham Young, J.D., 10:266-267).

We need not worry, because Heavenly Father has creatively cultivated our capacity to recapture the wide-eyed wonder and innocence of youth. When Adam and Eve were introduced to the unrelenting demands of the lone and dreary world outside the Garden, they were told they would need to earn their bread by the sweat of their brow. (See 2 Nephi 2). This was not a curse, but was instead His formula for success that would enable His children to make their mark in the telestial world, without being enabled by others. The socialist state would be staved off for over 6,000 years, the welfare state for a bit longer, the "Me Generation" until the late Twentieth Century, the Millennial mind-set until the dawn of the Twenty First Century, and the Utopian society of our dreams until tomorrow, were we to die today.

At the same time, the genius of The Plan introduced Adam and Eve to covenants that would ground them to the same celestial principles that had defined their

behavior as His innocent children in the Garden. These would protect them from the worldly contaminant of material prosperity, and would shield them from the temptation to fill space with telestial trinkets. Heavenly Father knew that if they were to become affluent without the restraint of covenants, they might strangle themselves with material things whose opacity would obstruct their ability to see how He had so carefully laid out before them the smorgasbord of life. In short, Adam and Eve and their posterity were given the tools with which they could prosper, in order to fill the measure of their creation. (See D&C 49:17).

His Plan blessed them with the faith to become as little children, so that they would not lose the innocence that had been one of their most refreshing qualities in the Garden. In the telestial world, their covenants would preserve their child-like perspective and would revitalize the lack of sophistication that they had brought with them from the Garden. Covenants would make it very difficult for the adversary to strip Adam and Eve, and their righteous descendants, of their innocence before God.

In His great Plan, we must all return to the secret garden of our childhood in order to fully mature, because, as Wordsworth wrote: "Heaven lies about us in our infancy. Shades of the prison house begin to close upon the growing boy, but he beholds the light and whence it flows. He sees it in his joy. The youth, who daily farther from the east must travel, still is nature's priest, and by the vision splendid, is on his way attended. At length, the man perceives it die away, and fade into the light of common day." ("Intimations of Immortality from Recollections of Early Childhood").

Fortunately, The Church of Jesus Christ of Latter-day Saints has the means to purify us from caustic influences, to decontaminate us from the toxicity of the world, and to reverse the homogenization process that occurs as we are worn down by the vicissitudes of life.

To that end, that the inhabitants of the earth might have the faith to become as little children, and knowing the calamity which should come upon them, the Lord

called Joseph Smith, and spoke to him from heaven, and gave him and others commandments, that they should proclaim the Gospel unto the world, that it might be fulfilled which was written by prophets of old, that the weak things of the world should "come forth and break down the mighty and strong ones, that man should not counsel his fellow man, neither trust in the arm of flesh, but that every man might speak in the name of God the Lord, even the Savior of the world; that faith also might increase in the earth; that" the Lord's "everlasting covenant might be established; that the fulness of" His "Gospel might be proclaimed by the weak and the simple unto the ends of the world." (D&C 1:17-23).

When we have mustered that intensity of faith, we are born again. We are reintroduced to the magical kingdom of our childhood that we fondly remember as the happiest place on earth. By following the Lords counsel, we realize that it is in our childhood that we will find the place where dreams come true.

The Gospel re-familiarizes us with Camelot, where there is a fleeting wisp of the splendor of heaven in the air. In Camelot, we remember, "the Crown has made it clear. The climate must be perfect all the year. A law was made a distant moon ago here. July and August cannot be too hot. And there's a legal limit to the snow, here in Camelot. The winter is forbidden 'til December, and exits March the second on the dot. By order, summer lingers through September, in Camelot.

I know it sounds a bit bizarre, but in Camelot that's how conditions are. The rain may never fall 'til after sundown. By eight, the morning fog must disappear. The snow many never slush upon a hillside. By nine p.m., the moonlight must appear. In short, there's simply not a more congenial spot for happily-ever-aftering than here, in Camelot." (Alan J. Lerner).

In between the sights and sounds, rides and attractions, and thrills and spills of our earthly theme-park experiences, if we are particularly self-aware, we will make room for Christ, the Creator of Camelot. When we do so, we will be reintroduced to the principles of personal spiritual hygiene that, under ideal circumstances,

were taught to us in our youth, and were most certainly taught to us many moons ago, in our premortal childhood. The Plan for the preservation of our child-like innocence will include a "bathing" experience to remove the grit and grime that would otherwise foul our inner-workings. The Manual of Discipline from the Serek

Scroll found in the caves above Qumran, reads like a children' primer, and tells us that "our sins are forgiven us, and in the humility of our souls we are for all the laws of God. Our flesh is cleansed shining bright in the waters of purification, even in the waters of baptism, and we shall be given a new name in due time to walk perfectly in all the ways of God."

The Plan also mandates the need to make frequent wardrobe changes out of soiled clothing into clean white garments, and it even requires occasional physical and spiritual therapy appointments to treat the bumps and bruises that we'll surely receive during our journey through mortality.

But, in our Heavenly Father's wisdom, the "buildings" we have fitly framed and into which we retreat for sanctuary are not the neatly constructed playhouses of our childhood. Instead, they have drafty windows and doors, leaky pipes, faulty fixtures, and hot water heaters that are overwhelmed with calcium deposits. We cannot hope to attend to our personal needs so successfully that ideal form and function are spontaneously maintained. Grandma's home remedies are not equal to the task, and if we turn to the elixirs peddled by ever-present snake-oil salesmen, we are grasping at straws. Instead, we need the expert services of a gifted Property Manager.

Therein, lies yet another dimension of the genius of God's Plan. As we transition into adulthood, we apply the experience we have gained during our maturation process to address the maintenance and upkeep of our our fitly framed buildings. (Cite). We learn to count on the capacity of the priesthood to provide the gurneys upon which we will be given transfusions of the spiritual element to keep us going, at least until it's time to repeat the process. We learn to draw upon God's blood-bank, and when we frequent it, we discover that everyone has the same type, and

there are no negative rH factors to worry about.

In a similar vein (no pun intended), there are those who go to dialysis centers so that contaminants may be removed from their blood, because their kidneys no longer have the ability to accomplish the task on their own. They may spend four hours at a time receiving treatment that is designed to save their lives. But, at the same time, there are those who will not seek help to have the spiritual impurities removed from their blood, because they feel that they cannot spare two hours a week to do so. They are instead caught up in an endless celebration of their so-called independence. The Lord characterized such as the enemies of God since the beginning of time. They will remain so forever, unless they yield to the enticings of the Holy Spirit, and become "submissive, meek, humble, patient, full of love, willing to submit to all things which the Lord seeth fit to inflict upon (them), even as a child doth submit to his father." (Mosiah 3:19).

The Gospel is the ultimate Affordable Health Care Plan, but its guiding principles consist of fewer pages that are easier to understand. It encourages us to strike out on our own, get our own apartment, earn a living, and pay our own bills. It describes a spiritual wellness program that is designed to keep us healthy. It prescribes preventive spiritual therapies that are oriented toward wellness but are equally capable of addressing disease.

Eventually, we'll all pack our bags and return Home, to move back in with our Heavenly Parents and live under one roof, as we did in the beginning. We'll be one big happy family again. Clothed in immortality, we will embody our perfect frame. We will have the wonderful opportunity to enjoy the hearth and home of heaven, and to bask in the warmth of our Father's embrace. We'll be Millennials, to be sure, but only in the unspoiled, unaffected, and utterly uncorrupted sense of the word.

We will have moved beyond dependence and independence, to an exhilarating interdependent relationship with God. We will be fully vested in the family business, for our Father's Plan will have brought about our immortality and

eternal life. (See Moses 1:39). As His offspring, we will be in progress to an endless advancement in eternal perfections. In wondrous awe, we will realize that, in the successful execution of His Plan, "there was no period in all the eternities wherein we could have become stationary, that we could not have advanced in knowledge, wisdom, power, and glory." (Brigham Young, J.D., 1:349).

As we look forward to that day, which is akin to the millennial day, our child-like nature will reflect the enduring qualities that are the embodiment of our Parents' nurturing influence. We will be less judgmental of others and more accepting of our differences; less suspicious and more friendly. We will see others as neighbors and not as strangers. We will be more trusting and speak without guile; more transparent and less prejudicial; have fewer pretensions and be more genuine; less prone to rationalization and quicker to forgive; more honest, true, chaste, benevolent, and virtuous. Our faith will be more pure, our hope more comprehensive, and our regard for others more charitable.

Our journey will complete our metamorphosis, for we will have become new creatures in Christ. (See 2 Corinthians 5:17). When we were Born Again, we were given the promise of a new lease on life. Few of us would care to repeat grammar school or high school, and yet when the eyes of our understanding were opened, we'd realized that the Gospel Plan re-wrote the terms of our existing lease. Its enlightened provisions reintroduced to our childhood, and gave us a second chance to get it right.

No matter what life threw at us, we were given a clean slate and invited to re-write our life's story. The beauty of The Plan, we discovered, is that it not only invited us to make a new ending, but also, it empowered us to re-write our beginning. The day we became members of the Lord's Church was the first day of the rest of our lives. With a refreshingly new Gospel perspective, we were empowered to pre-play before we re-played. Born "in newness of life," we engaged in role-play, just as grown-ups do. (Romans 6:4). We were invited to climb up into the director's chair, (just to see

what it felt like, never forgetting Whose chair it really was), settle ourselves in next to our Mentor, make ourselves comfortable, look over the script with Him, make edits at His suggestion, and orchestrate our own extreme home makeover.

As we rewrote the chapters of our lives, we appreciated the influence of the Holy Ghost, Who, as our creative consultant, always stood ready to offer constructive comments relating to our developing storyboard. We had the Sacrament to repetitively ground us to the ordinance that symbolizes our rebirth. We had the temple to remind us that the butterfly effect of the covenants made there had no temporal, spatial, or spiritual boundaries, and could be experienced at one and the same time in the past, present, and future, now and forever.

When we were born again, we felt the Lord's influence, as if it were the omnipresent background radiation from the Big Bang that accompanied His creation of our universe. No matter the direction we faced, we will always felt His presence, for He was always be before our faces.

There was no path we could follow and no hiding place to which we could flee where we could escape His encouragement. Why would we have wanted to do so? We grew to be dependent upon the horns of sanctuary, and found that we could grasp them whenever our yoke seemed too heavy for us to bear alone. Every time we did a reality-check, we found Him there. He is "Jesus Christ, the Great I Am, Alpha and Omega, the beginning and the end, the same which looked upon the wide expanse of eternity, and all the seraphic hosts of heaven, before the world was made. The same which knoweth all things, for all things are present before (His) eyes." (D&C 38:1-2).

We could not avoid our duty any more than could Jonah, nor would we have chosen to do so. If we were to try to shirk our responsibilities, we would have been swallowed up by a leviathan no less real, and would have eventually been spit out upon the rocky shoreline of our obligations. It made no difference if we turned to the right or to the left, because He was always there. When we lifted our eyes to the

heavens, He was watching us from above. No matter that we bore the weight of sin or sorrow with downcast eyes; He was always beneath us, to lift us up and carry our burdens. Every time we knocked, He answered. Every time we asked, we received. When petty concerns distracted us, we found Him waiting patiently in the wings for us to regain our senses. When we acted foolishly, He looked past our behavior, into our core, and He was there to pick up the pieces of our shattered dreams, to put our fractured lives back together again.

He is the Father of our spiritual regeneration, and like the parent we all aspire to be, He is there to bind up and heal our wounds every time we stumble and fall. If we are born of Him, and with the faith to become as little children, the earth shall be given unto (us) for an inheritance, and (we) shall multiply and wax strong, and (our own) children shall grow up without sin unto salvation. For the Lord shall be in (our) midst, and His glory shall be upon (us) and He will be (our) king and (our) lawgiver." (D&C 45:58-59).

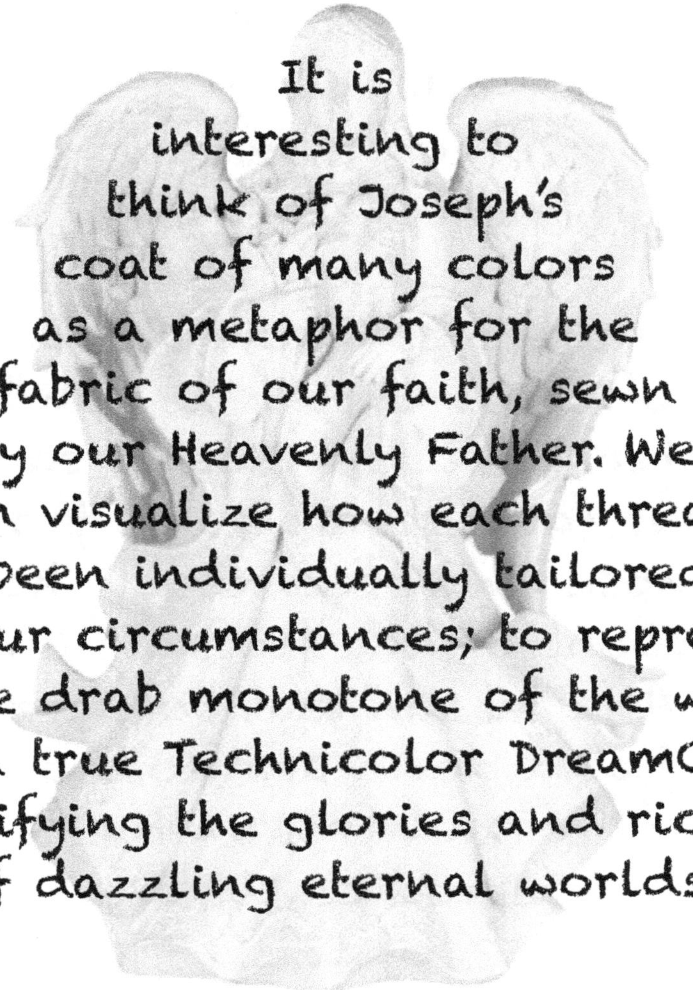

It is
interesting to
think of Joseph's
coat of many colors
as a metaphor for the
fabric of our faith, sewn
by our Heavenly Father. We
can visualize how each thread
has been individually tailored to
suit our circumstances; to represent,
not the drab monotone of the world,
but a true Technicolor DreamCoat
signifying the glories and riches
of dazzling eternal worlds.

Our faith
allow us to
free ourselves
from the mire of
sin, and to cleanse
ourselves in the blood
of Jesus Christ; to stand
steadily upon Gospel sod.
Our faith separates us from
those who precariously hop
about on the flotsam and
the jetsam that bobs up
and down and tosses
to and fro, on the
unpredictable sea
of life.

Chapter Twenty Three
The be-happy attitudes of faith.

"Seeing the multitudes, he went up into a mountain, and when he was set, his disciples came unto him, and he opened his mouth, and taught them" the Be-Happy-Attitudes that are the rewards of faith.
(Matthew 5:1-2).

Blessed are they who, when they get a lemon, make lemonade, for they shall not thirst. Thomas Edison experimented with over 1,000 different materials before finding one that could serve as the filament for his incandescent lamp. He was asked, "How do you feel about all those failures?" He replied, "I never thought of them as failures. I was excited to discover over a thousand ways not to make a light bulb."

A young missionary who had incredible enthusiasm for both the work and for life was assigned by his mission president to be the senior companion of an elder who could not get along with anyone, and who had an extremely pessimistic outlook on life. After a couple of weeks, the mission president called his dynamic young elder and asked him how things were going. "Fantastic!" he replied. "Elder Brown and I have discovered we have something in common." "What's that?" asked his surprised president. "Neither one of us has ever been to Africa!" replied the elder.

There is a corollary to this be-happy-attitude: "Blessed are they who, when they at first don't succeed, realize they are about average." The difference between those who are failures and those who are winners, is that the winners try just one more time than they fail.

Blessed are they who light a candle, rather than curse the darkness, for their days shall be bright. "Observers in the full enjoyment of their bodily senses pity me," wrote Helen Keller, "but it is because they do not see the golden chamber in my life where I dwell delighted; for, dark as my path may seem to them, I carry a magic light in my heart. Faith, the spiritual strong searchlight, illuminates my way, and although sinister doubts lurk in the shadow, I walk unafraid towards the Enchanted Wood where the foliage is always green, where joy abides, where nightingales nest and sing, and where life and death are one in the presence of the Lord." ("Midstream").

There is a corollary to this be-happy-attitude, as well: Blessed are they who realize that faith will never die as long as colored seed catalogs are printed.

Blessed are those who realize that the greatest battles of life are fought within the silent chambers of the soul, for they shall overcome. "My life is my message," declared Mahatma Gandhi. In a similar vein, David O. McKay said: "Spirituality is the consciousness of victory over self, and of communion with the Infinite."

A young man was in job interview, and his prospective employer asked him: "If I

hire you, can I count on you to be honest?" The young man looked him in the eye, and replied: "You can count on me to be honest whether you hire me or not!" Do you think he got the job?

In Fifteenth Century France, the heir to the throne was known as the Dauphin. In the reign of King Charles VII, unscrupulous and crafty counselors tried every means to corrupt the Dauphin, and to thereby render him incapable of inheriting the throne. In all their attempts, they were unsuccessful. Finally, in resignation, they asked him, "How is it that with all our enticements we were unable to compromise your high standards?" His reply was simple: "I am a King's son."

When Joan of Arc was at the stake, she was given the opportunity to obtain her freedom by denying what she believed. Instead, she declared: "I know this. Every man gives his life for what he believes. Every woman gives her life for what she believes. Sometimes people believe in little or nothing, and yet they give their lives for little or nothing. One life is all we have, and we live it as we believe in living it, and then it is gone. But to surrender what you are and live without belief is more terrible than dying, even more terrible than dying young."

There is a corollary to this be-happy-attitude: "Blessed are they, who when they encounter temptation, turn to the right, for they shall avoid telestial traffic jams." There is a second corollary to this be-happy-attitude: "Blessed are they who understand that prayer is the key of the day and the lock of the night." Martin Luther once said, "I have so much to do today, that I must spend more time in prayer!"

Blessed are they who realize that the biggest room in the world is the one for improvement. Ralph Waldo Emerson observed: "Success comes by design, and failure by default." Truly, if you fail to plan, you plan to fail, and the only place where success comes before work is in the dictionary.

There is a corollary to this be-happy-attitude: "Blessed are they who realize that the best place to find a helping hand is at the end of their arm. They shall never be

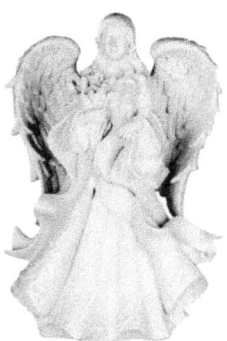

without a friend." Or, as Greek classicists first suggested, God helps those who help themselves.

Brigham Young liked to tell the Saints: "Give a man a fish and you have fed him for a day. Teach him how to fish, and you have fed him for a lifetime." His comments suggest another corollary: "Blessed are they who recognize that opportunity is always dressed in work clothes."

There is yet another corollary to this be-happy-attitude: "Blessed are those who realize that the dictionary is the only place where work comes before success. Ernest L. Wilkinson, President of B.Y.U., told his students: "I want to bear you my testimony that if you develop the habit of work, it will be the most invigorating, satisfying, even relaxing and greatest blessing of your life. The opportunity to work is God's greatest blessing to mankind, and this means six days of each week."

"Perspiration must precede inspiration; there must be effort before there is excellence," was the counsel and the legacy that Spencer W. Kimball left with the Church. (B.Y.U. Devotional, 10/10/1975). He once repeated to a group of new Mission Presidents: "Make no small plans, for they have not the power to stir the hearts of men." (Attr. to Daniel Burnham, or perhaps Niccolo Machiavelli). The worldwide explosion in membership in the Church is a testament to the power of this timeless message.

Blessed are they who have learned that life is hard by the yard, but a cinch by the inch. Our problem often is not that we set our goals too high, and fail to reach them; rather it is that we aim too low, and we reach our objectives far too easily, and with too little expenditure of effort. W seldom value highly that which costs very little.

The masses settle for mediocrity, while once in a while, one or two selfless souls forget themselves into heaven. Calvin Coolidge said: "We cannot do everything at once, but we can do something at once." While still a young man, Abraham Lincoln, declared: "I will prepare myself, and someday my chance will come." Making the effort is the element that is critical to the success of our endeavors.

There is a corollary to this be-happy attitude: The woods would be a very quiet place if only those birds sang that sang best.

It may be too late to write a new beginning to your life story, but it is not too late to begin a new ending. "I won't" is good for nothing. "I can't" is a quitter. "I don't know" is lazy. "I might" is just waking up. "I will try" is on his feet. "I can" is on his way. "I will" is at work, and "I did" is now the boss.

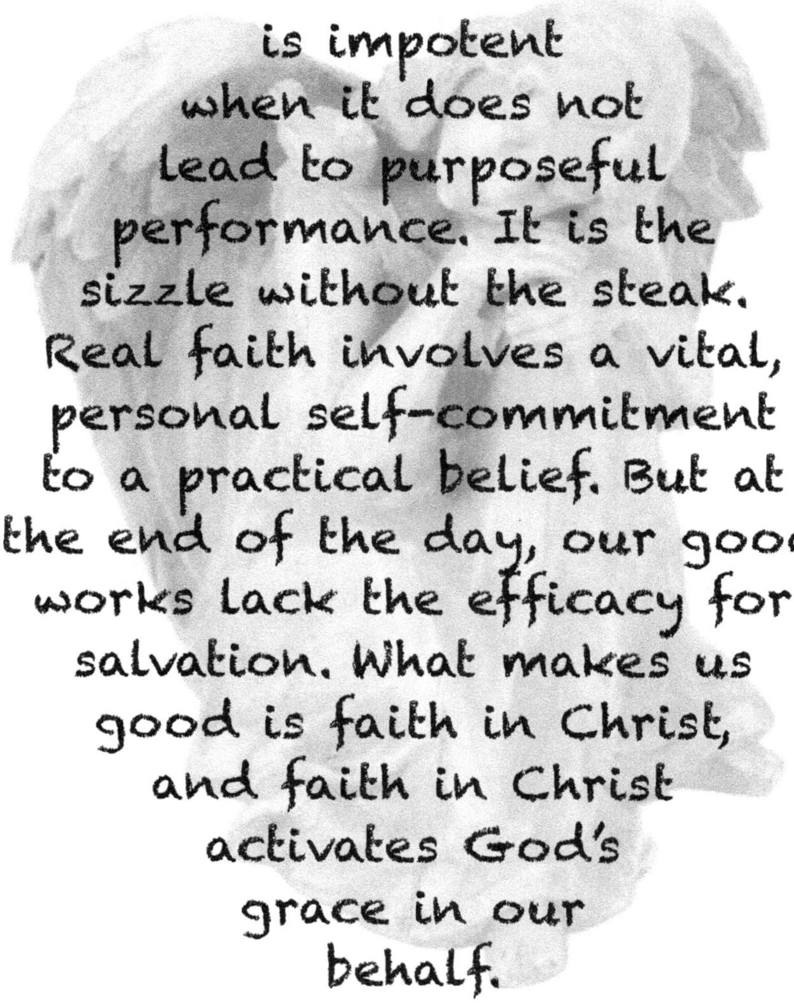

Faith is impotent when it does not lead to purposeful performance. It is the sizzle without the steak. Real faith involves a vital, personal self-commitment to a practical belief. But at the end of the day, our good works lack the efficacy for salvation. What makes us good is faith in Christ, and faith in Christ activates God's grace in our behalf.

Chapter Twenty Four
The faith to properly prepare.

*When it is time for action,
the time of preparation is over.*

LaVell Edwards, who was head football coach at Brigham Young University, taught that the measure of successful athletes is not so much that they have "the will to win," but that they "have the will to prepare." So too, our lives are times of personal preparation and joint preparation with our loved ones. In life, as in sports, those who will wear the laurel crown of the victor will be those who have followed through with action that is consistent with their faithful preparation.

Historical examples illustrate the point. Perhaps it was difficult for young David to understand why he had to so frequently defend his flocks against lions and bears, but as he stood alone against Goliath in the Valley of Elah, when the time came for him to select five smooth stones for his sling, he did so with confidence, because of his preparation.

Prior to his election to the Presidency of the United States, Abraham Lincoln was guided through many years of difficulty and disappointment by the magnificent principle that proper prior preparation prevents poor performance. "I will prepare myself," he wrote, "and one day my chance will come."

In the Book of Alma, we learn how Ammon had spiritually prepared himself for an opportunity to deliver the message of the Gospel to the Lamanites. God set the stage and provided a golden teaching moment in the form of ruffians who came to scatter the flocks of King Lamoni. Rather than retreating in fear, Ammon's heart swelled with the confidence that God would manifest his power. That which he eagerly anticipated caused his companion shepherds to "weep exceedingly." (Alma 17:28). In our day, our faithful preparation will likewise ready us to face our own Lamanites by the waters of Sebus, in our hour of need.

A successful evangelical minister offered this recipe for success: "Read yourself full, think yourself straight, pray yourself hot, and let yourself go!" (J. Douglas Gibb). The first three admonitions involve faithful preparation and set the stage for purposeful action, when we can really "let ourselves go."

As Moroni taught: "Whoso believeth in Christ, doubting nothing, whatsoever he shall ask the Father in the name of Christ it shall be granted him; and this promise is unto all" who have the faith to properly prepare. (Mormon 9:21).

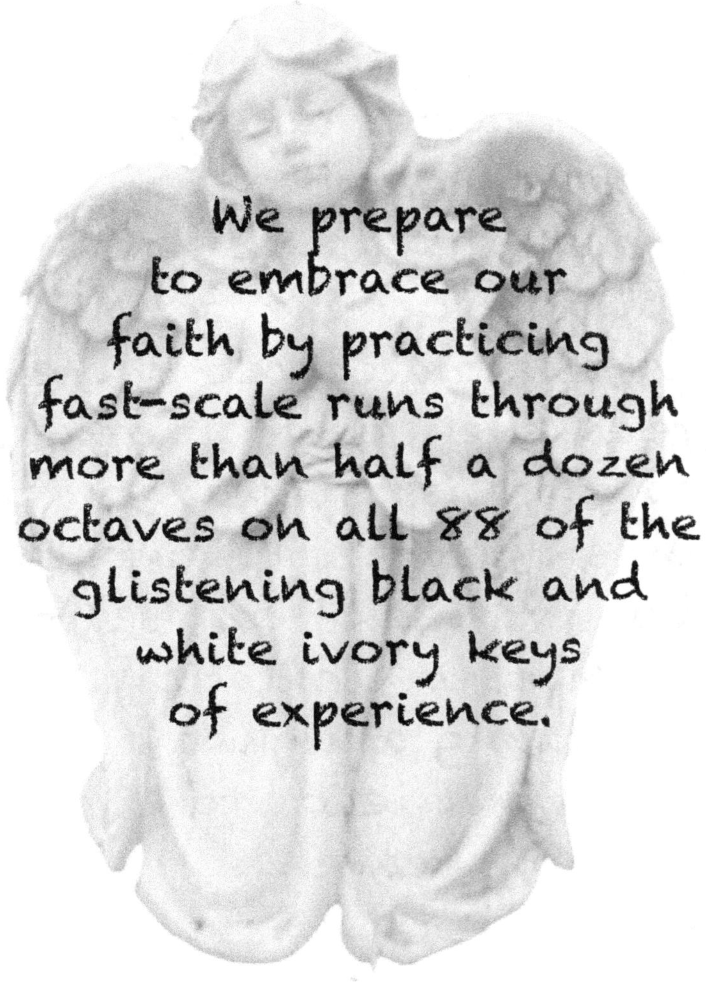

We prepare to embrace our faith by practicing fast-scale runs through more than half a dozen octaves on all 88 of the glistening black and white ivory keys of experience.

Faith
nudges us off
our complacency
plateaus, as we steer
away from the trendy
cafés situated along the
broad avenues of Idumea.
We are transported as on the
wings of eagles beyond the
boundaries of our self-
imposed limitations
along a highway
that leads to
heaven.

Chapter Twenty Five
The moral discipline of faith.

"I count him braver who overcomes his desires,
than him who conquers his enemies; for the
hardest victory is the victory over self."
(Aristotle).

Moral discipline involves the consistent exercise of choice to clothe eternal principles with actions that may not be easy or convenient, but are simply the right things to do. If we want to have positive outcomes, our God-given ability to choose must be accompanied by the moral discipline of faith; the strength of moral character that is manifest in righteous behavior.

Having good values is not enough. Our society, which is arguably "good," has failed miserably to instill noble standards in the rising generation. When a culture believes that truth is relative and that it is up to individuals to determine the merits of right or wrong, the stage is set for disaster. When situational ethics guides

our behavior, and when "every man walketh in his own way, and after the image of his own god," the erosion of moral discipline followed by the chaotic crash of cultural cohesion and stability is inevitable. (D&C 1:16).

253

When cultural collapse is imminent, external controls are often imposed to manipulate behavior, and to maintain at least a semblance of societal steadiness. Our escalating dependence upon laws to regulate moral discipline says something about us, and about our critical need to exercise faith in the infinite wisdom of our Heavenly Father.

The world seeks change by exerting external control, and fails miserably. The Gospel seeks change by transforming the inner vessel, and succeeds brilliantly. It does this by calibrating our internal compass so that we are oriented toward the moral discipline of faith.

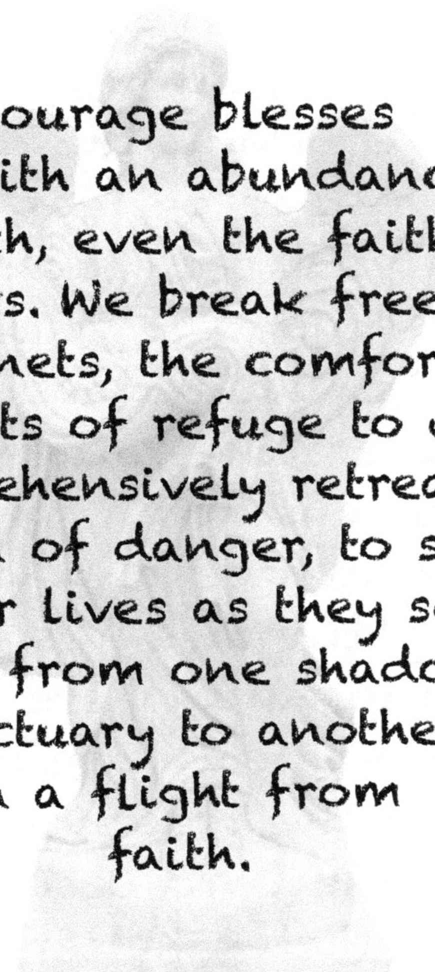

Courage blesses
us with an abundance
of faith, even the faith to
take risks. We break free from
the safety nets, the comfort zones,
and the ports of refuge to which the
timid apprehensively retreat at the
first sign of danger, to squeak
out their lives as they scurry
about from one shadowy
sanctuary to another
in a flight from
faith.

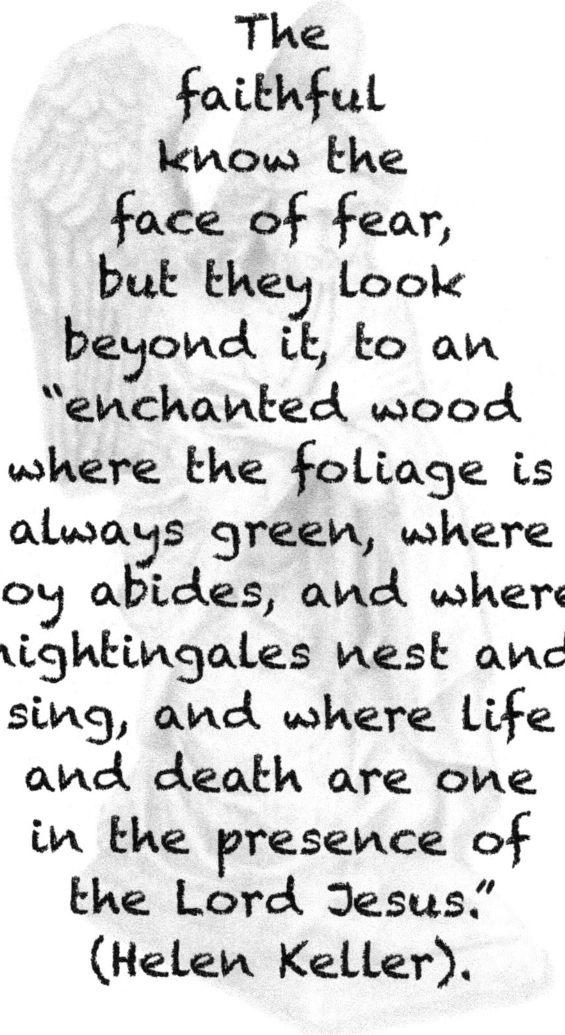

The
faithful
know the
face of fear,
but they look
beyond it, to an
"enchanted wood
where the foliage is
always green, where
joy abides, and where
nightingales nest and
sing, and where life
and death are one
in the presence of
the Lord Jesus."
(Helen Keller).

Chapter Twenty Six
The obedience of faith.

Revelation is "made known to all nations
for the obedience of faith."
(Romans 16:26).

"Obedience is the first law of heaven, and is the cornerstone upon which all righteousness and progression rest." (Bruce R. McConkie). Faithful obedience is the foundation principle that shapes our mortal mission, guides its progress, and guarantees its success. As President Ezra Taft Benson taught: "When obedience ceases to be inconvenient, and becomes our quest, in that moment, God will endow us with power." We are not "ashamed of the Gospel of Christ: for it is the power of God unto salvation to every one that believeth." (Romans 1:16).

When obedience becomes our quest, we gain a witness of its eternal validity. We gain experience with the principle that was explained by Joseph Smith on April 2,

1843: "There is a law, irrevocably decreed in heaven before the foundations of this world," he wrote, "upon which all blessings are predicated. And when we obtain any blessing from God, it is by obedience to that law upon which it is predicated." (D&C 130:20-21).

The Savior declared: "For all who will have a blessing at my hands shall abide the law which was appointed for that blessing, and the conditions thereof, as were instituted from before the foundation of the world." (D&C 132:5). There is order in The Plan of Salvation, and faithful obedience is one of its bedrock principles. The obedience of faith protects us from the inexorable demands of Justice. Alma taught: "There is a law given, and a punishment affixed, and a repentance granted; which repentance, mercy claimeth; otherwise, justice claimeth the creature and executeth the law, and (it is) the law (itself that) inflicteth the punishment; if not so, the works of justice would be destroyed, and God would cease to be God." (Alma 42:22).

None of us can escape the consequences of our actions, even though many of us spend much of our energy trying to do so in a frantic retreat from responsibility. As Paul wrote: "Let every man prove his own work, and then shall he have rejoicing.... Whatsoever a man soweth, that shall he also reap." (Galatians 6:4 & 7).

The highest motivation for the obedience of faith is our love of the Lord. "If ye love me," He said, "keep my commandments." (John 14:15) "Then said Jesus to those which believed on him, If ye continue in my word, then are ye my disciples indeed; and ye shall know the truth, and the truth shall make you free." (John 8:31-32). The truth is that we are saved by the Atonement. The truth not only liberates us from guilt and from sin, but it also frees us from incarceration to confusion, doubt, hesitation, ignorance, mistrust, skepticism, suspicion, uncertainty, and worry. In the form of Mercy, truth unshackles us from the unpleasant consequences of Justice. Darkness is the conjoined twin of misery, but the obedience of faith frees us to embrace the truth, to make intelligent choices, to perform purposefully, to carry on convincingly, to progress persistently, to rise above the cares of the world, to enjoy peace of conscience, to receive the blessings of the priesthood, to serve others in

more powerful and significant ways, to work resolutely toward our potential, to commune with the Infinite, and to benefit from all of the other blessings of The Plan of Salvation as we move forward with confidence into eternity.

Through discipline, the obedience of faith encourages us to "try the virtue of the word of God." (Alma 31:5) We do so, that we might reap its rewards, and with diligence, and patience, and long-suffering, "wait for the tree to bring forth fruit" unto us. (Alma 32:43). Thus, through faith and obedience, we enjoy the matchless love of God, Who promises eternal life to those who will follow His Son. Thus, in the obedience of faith, Abraham found that there would be "greater happiness and peace and rest" than he had ever before known. It was for this reason that he "sought for the blessings of the fathers." (Abraham 1:2).

By His example, the Lord taught that we "should be anxiously engaged in a good cause, and do many things of (our) own free will, and bring to pass much righteousness; for the power" is in us, inasmuch we are free-agents. (D&C 58:27-28).

The obedience of faith is an influential principle, but so is its opposite, for "whosoever committeth sin is the servant of sin." (John 8:34). All around us, we see the fulfillment of the prophecy that in the Last Days, the hearts of men shall fail them, as their shields of faith falter. When that happens, Satan shall rage in their hearts, "and stir them up to anger against that which is good. And others will he pacify, and lull them away into carnal security, that they will say: All is well in Zion; yea, Zion prospereth, all is well - and thus the devil cheateth their souls, and leadeth them away carefully down to hell. And behold, others he flattereth away, and telleth them there is no hell; and he saith unto them: I am no devil, for there is none - and thus he whispereth in their ears, until he grasps them with his awful chains from whence there is no deliverance." (2 Nephi 28:20-23).

Mormon exhorted us to muster the obedience of faith, that we might respond enthusiastically to the teachings of the Savior and the ministering of angels, and that we might embrace every word that proceeds out of the mouth of God. (See

Moroni 7:25). As long as we continue to do so, each new day will introduce us to new wonders to behold. (See D&C 76:7).

In the scriptures, we are encouraged 129 times to "learn," we are admonished 154 times to be perfect, and 306 times to be obedient, but 995 times to "begin." "Therefore, may God grant unto (us, that we) may begin to exercise (our) faith unto repentance, that (we) begin to call upon his holy name, that he would have mercy upon (us)." (Alma 34:17).

The Lord has sworn that He is bound when we do what He says. But, when we do not do what He says, we have no promise. (See D&C 82:10). When we begin to exercise the obedience of faith, and when we discover that it is tied to blessings, we learn something about the interdependent relationship we can have with heaven.

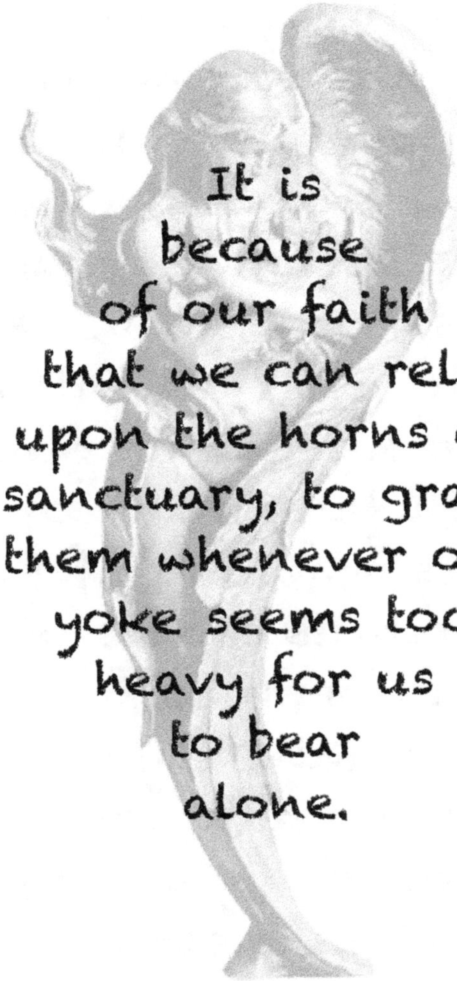

It is
because
of our faith
that we can rely
upon the horns of
sanctuary, to grasp
them whenever our
yoke seems too
heavy for us
to bear
alone.

In harmony
with the principle
of opposition in all
things, an impenetrable
veil has been drawn across
our minds. But we have the Light
of Christ, and even the witness of the
Holy Ghost, to help us to penetrate that
curtain. Nevertheless, many of us are still
swayed by the siren song of Satan, drawn
to his duplicitous shoals of spiritual
instability, thereon to founder, and
to be pulled under by the riptides
of religious relativism and the
undertow of agnostism, or
faithless skepticism.

Chapter Twenty Seven
The courage of faith.

"Wait on the Lord. Be of good courage,
and He shall strengthen thine heart."
(Psalms 27:14).

The process by which our faith is strengthened is one that tests the mettle of our convictions. Heavenly Father will not cause us to misplace our trust, or our faith, in anything that cannot deliver on its promises, but we have no proof until we act on the basis of faith. Then comes the confirmation of the reality, as feelings of self-confidence grow and purposeful actions replace tentative overtures.

Truly did Paul declare, "God hath not given us the spirit of fear, but of power, and of love, and of a sound mind." (2 Timothy 1:7). Faith is clothed best when it is adorned with the power that stems from a courageous heart, and with the love that only a sound mind is capable of expressing. Thus, faith is an expression

of our desire to do what is right, no matter the consequences, rather than what is expedient. Always looking for the easy way out condemns us to negotiate the instability of shaky ground, as opposed to the solid footing that Gospel sod affords to those whose actions are consistent with the courage of faith. (See James

1:8). The admonition of Peter and the other apostles strikes a consonant chord to those well-grounded in the courage of faith: "We ought to obey God, rather than men." (Acts 5:29).

As Josiah Gilbert Holland wrote: "God, give us men! A time like this demands strong minds, great hearts, true faith, and ready hands. Men whom the lust of office does not kill. Men whom the spoils of office cannot buy. Men who possess opinions and a will. Men who have honor; men who will not lie. Men who can stand before a demagogue and damn his treacherous flatteries without winking. Tall men, sun-crowned, who live above the fog in public duty and in private thinking. For while the rabble, with their thumb worn creeds, their large professions and their little deeds, mingle in selfish strife, Lo! Freedom weeps, wrong rules the land, and justice sleeps."

Courageous faith is based on neither ability nor inability, but it does demand our availability. Brigham Young once declared, "I never count the cost of anything. I just find out what the Lord wants me to do, and I do it." Commitment and dedication establish a baseline for courageously faithful action.

All of us are repeatedly faced with times when withdrawals must be made from our spiritual bank accounts. Because of our faith, however, we do not write checks that cannot be cashed. We realize that it is only because deposits have been made over a period of time, that we can rely upon the cornucopia of comfort created by the copious cushion of confidence that flows as a current from consistently courageous comportment.

Because of the courage of our faith, we will never thirst, because we have sent taproots down through Gospel topsoil to a free, full, flowing fountain of living

water. Carol Lynn Pearson wrote an insightful poem entitled "Short Roots," with a message that relates to courageous faith. "The tree at the church next door to me turned up its roots and died. They tried to brace its leaning, but it lowered and lowered, and then there it lay, leaves in grass and matted roots in air, like a loafer on a summer day. "Look there," said the gardener. "Short roots - all the growth went up. Big branches - short roots." "How come? I asked. "Too much water. This tree never had to hunt for drink." Especially in thirsty times, my memory steps outside and looks at the tree at the church next door to me that turned up its roots and died." ("The Growing Season").

As we courageously carry out our work, and quietly and faithfully address our responsibilities, the righteousness of our cause will be revealed in marvelous simplicity and plainness. Walls of opposition to our progress will crumble and fall away. The Lord will comfort and succor us with the bread of life. As we travel through the harsh environment of Idumea, oases will spring up in the deserts of life, and living water will slake our thirst, because our roots have become anchored within the bedrock of the law of the Lord. (See Psalms 19:7).

We are reminded of Joshua's instruction to Israel, to take twelve stones out of the midst of Jordan, to be a sign "that the waters of Jordan were cut off before the ark of the covenant of the Lord, when it passed over Jordan, to be a memorial unto the children of Israel forever. (See Joshua 4:3-7).

When we are courageously faithful, we are as those stones; they become building blocks "in the armory of thought, where we fashion the tools with which we build for ourselves heavenly mansions of joy and strength and peace. ...We become the master of thought, the shaper of condition, environment, and of destiny," even as we draw upon a power greater than ourselves. (Spencer W. Kimball).

Victor Hugo heard that majestic clockwork, when he wrote: "Be like a bird that pausing in her flight a while on boughs to light, feels them give way beneath her and yet sings, knowing that she hath wings." Angels will bolster the courage of

our faith: "For I will go before your face," promised the Lord. "I will be on your right hand, and on your left, and my Spirit shall be in your hearts, and mine angels round about you, to bear you up." (D&C 84:88). Once we have received the anointing of faithful courage, we will never be able to rest "until the last enemy is conquered, death destroyed, and truth reigns triumphant." (Parley P. Pratt, "Deseret News," 4/30/1853).

When Joan of Arc was carried to the stake, she was given the opportunity to obtain her freedom by denying her beliefs Instead, she made this bold statement: "I know this now. Every man gives his life for what he believes. Every woman gives her life for what she believes. Sometimes people believe in little or nothing, and so they give their lives for little or nothing. One life is all we have, and we live it as we believe in living it, and then it is gone. But to surrender what you are and live without belief is more terrible than dying, even more terrible than dying young." Faithfully, then, she faced death, ever true to her beliefs. Such faith demands consistency with our convictions. It is this quality of total commitment and dedication that tames the beast within us and creates civility.

As a matter of fact, "to sin by silence, when words should be spoken, makes cowards of men." (Ella Wheeler Wilcox). Courageous faith can vitalize the moral fiber that we need to face our demons. "It is not the critic who counts, not he who points out where the strong man stumbled or where the doer of deeds could have done them better. The credit belongs to the man who is actually in the arena, whose face is marred by dust and sweat and blood, who tries and comes up short again and again, who knows the great enthusiasms, the great devotions and spends himself in a worthy cause; who, at best, if he fails, at least fails while daring greatly, so that his place shall never be with those cold and timid souls who know neither victory nor defeat." (Teddy Roosevelt, Speech at the Sorbonne).

Well did Joseph Smith encourage the Saints, when he declared: "Faith, brethren; and on, on to the victory! Let your hearts rejoice, and be exceeding glad." (Joseph Smith, D&C 128:22). The courageously faithful know how to turn potential stumbling blocks into stepping-stones. When they are given a lemon, they make lemonade.

Crisis becomes opportunity, and victory is snatched from the jaws of defeat. The courageously faithful have learned by experience, that "change comes like a flash of lightning and a clap of thunder. The people shrink in fear, but after the storm, flowers bloom. ("I Ching - The Book of Change").

As Tom Paine wrote, in each of our lives there are "times that try (our) souls. Yet we have this consolation with us, that the harder the conflict, the more glorious the triumph. What we obtain too cheap, we esteem too lightly. 'Tis dearness only that gives everything its value. Heaven knows how to put a proper price upon its goods, and it would be strange, indeed, if ... celestial articles (such as courageous faith) should not be highly rated." ("The Political Works of Thomas Paine," p. 55).

We exercise courageous faith to promote goodness and righteousness. Men and women who have been blessed with such faith recognize the awesome responsibility that frequently rests with them alone. The last official words of President John F. Kennedy, that were to have been delivered in Dallas, Texas, on the afternoon of November 22, 1963, reflect his appreciation of this responsibility: "We in this country, in this generation, are, by destiny rather than by choice, the watchmen on the walls of world freedom. We ask, therefore, that we may be worthy of our power and responsibility; that we may exercise our strength with wisdom and restraint, and that we may achieve in our time and for all time the ancient vision of peace on earth, and good will toward men. That must always be our goal, and the righteousness of our cause must always underlie our strength. For as was written long ago: 'Except the Lord keep the city, the watchman waketh in vain.'" (Psalms 127:1).

Those who are courageously faithful know the face of fear, but they look beyond it, to "the Enchanted Wood where the foliage is always green, where joy abides, where nightingales nest and sing, and where life and death are one in the presence of the Lord." (Helen Keller, "Midstream").

The courageously faithful have learned that faith is fear that has said its prayers. They are as the Sons of Helaman who "were all young men, and they were exceedingly valiant for faith, and also for strength and activity. But behold, this was not all –

they were men who were true at all times in whatsoever thing they were entrusted. Yea, they were men of truth and soberness, for they had been taught (by their mothers) to keep the commandments of God and to walk uprightly before him." (Alma 53:20-21).

President Harold B. Lee taught: "You must learn to walk to the edge of the light, and then take a few steps into the darkness. Then, the light will appear and show the way before you." This is the way we become familiar with the courage of faith, how we experience it, and develop it, and are strengthened by it. The courageously faithful have learned that darkness cannot be taken into a lighted room. They seize every opportunity to be enveloped in light. They have learned to face the sunshine, so that the shadows will always be behind them. Darkness will still exist, but its companions that take the form of apprehension, trepidation, doubt, uncertainty, and fear will be out of sight and out of mind.

Winston Churchill wrote: Our "finest hours are those when extraordinary challenge is met with extraordinary response." The courage of faith can be the catalyst that transforms our timidity and temerity into powerful presence of mind, shaping a platform for assertive action. It is not bravado, but boldness. It is no paper tiger. It can be an intense and compellingly positive response to threat, and the counterpoint to fear. We must have the courage of faith to face the demons which play a role in the opposition in all things that has been built into our experiences. In the fight or flight scenario, courageous faith is the launch pad for the anticipated adrenalin rush that carries us beyond our challenges. It is the foundation quality upon which hinges the expression of our other noble characteristics.

Our courageous faith keeps us focused on the positive, for there are always "two voices calling, one coming out from the swamps of selfishness and force, where success means death, and the other from the hilltops of justice and progress, where even failure brings glory. Two lights are seen on our horizon, one, the last fading marsh light of power, and the other the slowly rising sun of human brotherhood. Two ways lie open before us, one leading to an ever lower and lower plane, where are heard the cries of despair and the curses of the poor, where manhood shrivels

and possessions rot down the possessor, and the other leading to the highlands of the morning, where are heard the glad shouts of humanity," and where courageous faith is rewarded with immortality. (John P. Altgeld).

How sad it is when we fail to act upon our courageous faith. Reflecting upon this misfortune, Churchill observed: "To every man there comes in his lifetime that special moment when he is figuratively tapped on the shoulder and offered a chance to do a very special thing, unique to him and fitted to his talents. What a tragedy if that moment finds him unprepared or unqualified for that which could have been his finest hour." When we are able to muster the courage of faith, we are no longer tormented by confusion. We understand what Paul meant, when he asked the Galatian Saints: "Do I now persuade men, or God?" (Galatians 1:10). We are eager to make commitments before angels and witnesses that lead to binding covenants with God. We know that "until we are committed there is hesitancy, the chance to draw back, always ineffectiveness. Concerning all acts of initiative, there is one elementary truth, the ignorance of which kills countless ideas and splendid plans: that the moment we commit ourselves, then Providence moves too. All sorts of things occur to help us that would never have otherwise occurred. A whole stream of events issues from the decision, raining down in our favor all manner of unforeseen incidents and material assistance, which we could not have dreamed would have come our way." (Tom Hornbein, "Everest - "The West Ridge," Sierra Club, 1966, p. 100). "Prove me now herewith, saith the Lord of hosts, if I will not open you the windows of heaven, and pour you out a blessing, that there shall not be room enough to receive it." (Malachi 3:10).

Our courageous faith helps us to develop the discipline to follow through on our commitments. "You must not compromise your integrity by promising what you will not do," warned President Spencer W. Kimball. "By taking covenants lightly, you will wound your own eternal self." (B.Y.U. Devotional, 9/4/79). We have integrity as did Abraham, "observing with all soberness the solemn contracts (we) have made with God." (Spencer W. Kimball, "Ensign," 6/1975).

When we express ourselves through positive and independent action, the courage

of faith introduces us to the exhilarating freedom of obedience to a Higher Power. "I will go and do the things which the Lord hath commanded," declared Nephi, "for I know that the Lord giveth no commandments unto the children of men, save he shall prepare a way for them that they may accomplish the thing which he commandeth them." (1 Nephi 3:7).

When we are courageously faithful, we are often asked to go the second mile. The performance cost of such faith is often acutely uncomfortable, testing the limits of endurance of our physical and spiritual muscles. The courage of faith probes us for pliability, measures us for meekness, and searches us for submissiveness, which hones our humility while elevating us to a higher state of energy. The process encourages the development of our ability to endure opposition of all kinds. We welcome the trials of mortality, and view them as pop quizzes in the learning laboratory of life. They prepare us for the final exam that will come at the conclusion of our mortal curriculum. In the meantime, we endure to the end, hoping that the grade we have earned will reflect the summation of a life well spent. As Paul testified: "I have fought a good fight, I have finished my course, I have (courageously) kept the faith." (2 Timothy 4:7).

The courageously faithful are charitable. "I love everybody," five-year-old Kathryn told her father. "Where did you learn that?" he asked. "In church?" "No," she replied, "when I was up in heaven. Heavenly Father taught me that."

We expose our vulnerability when we are courageously faithful. We learn that the best way to destroy our enemies is by making friends with them. In moments of crisis, we become pro-Gospel, rather than anti-enemy. Well did the poet reflect: "He drew a circle that shut me out. Heretic, rebel, a thing to flout. But (faith) and I had the will to win. We drew a circle that took him in." (Edwin Markham).

Courage blesses us with an abundance of faith, even the faith to take risks. We break free from the safety nets, the comfort zones, and the ports of refuge to

which the timid apprehensively retreat at the first sign of danger, to squeak out their lives as they scurry about from one shadowy sanctuary to another.

Finally, we recognize that emulating the Savior means following Him not only to the

Celestial Kingdom, but to Gethsemane as well. Willingly, then, with the courage of faith, we surrender our agency to Christ, knowing that it is a necessary and vital step on our path of progress that leads to eternal life.

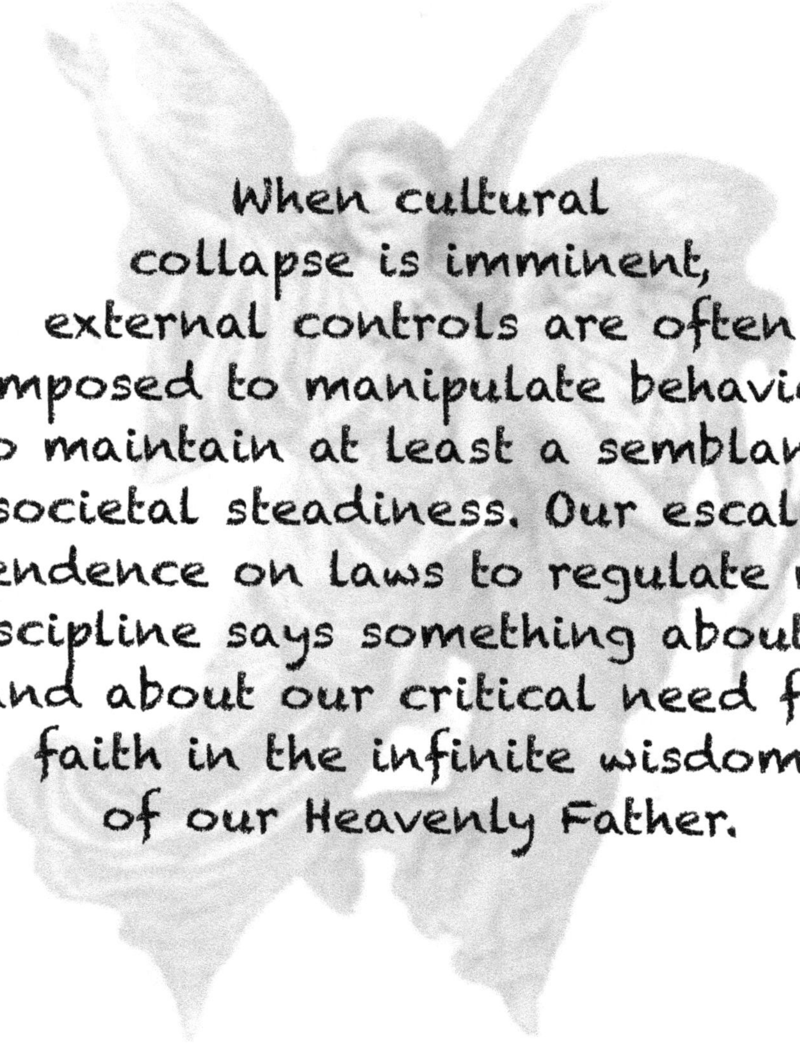

When cultural
collapse is imminent,
external controls are often
imposed to manipulate behavior,
to maintain at least a semblance
of societal steadiness. Our escalating
dependence on laws to regulate moral
discipline says something about us,
and about our critical need for
faith in the infinite wisdom
of our Heavenly Father.

Chapter Twenty Eight
The faith to profess His name.

Joseph Smith wrote of his search for truth among the churches of his day: "I was answered that I must join none of them, for they were all wrong; and the Personage who addressed me said that all their creeds were an abomination in his sight; that those professors were all corrupt; that they draw near to me with their lips, but their hearts are far from me, they teach for doctrines the commandments of men, having a form of godliness, but they deny the power thereof." (J.S.H. 1:19).

The problem was not that there were professors of religion, for there always have been, many of whom have been driven by the Spirit to "press toward the mark for the prize of the high calling of God in Christ Jesus." (Philippians 3:14). The problem was that those whom Joseph encountered had become corrupted. The questions thus become, how can we retain the purity of our faith, when it has convicted us of our sins and we have turned to the Savior with full purpose of heart? How can our faith point us in the direction of doctrine, so that when we encounter the principles of

The Plan, we might respond to the truth with actions that have both the form and substance of a godly walk, and that boldly testify of God's power to save? (See D&C 20:69).

The Lord is mindful of His covenant relationship with the members of His Church, and so He requires extraordinary performance of those "who profess (His) name." (D&C 50:4). Faithful professors represent themselves as independent witnesses. Memorable professors move beyond good intentions that may be nothing more than dreams. Visionary professors back up their words with deeds, and give life to desire. As Harold B. Lee observed: "Vision without work is dreamery. Work without vision is drudgery. But work with vision is destiny!"

Dedicated professors are persevering and stay focused on the tasks at hand. Committed professors begin with the end in mind and settle for more, and not for less. Unwavering professors are disciplined, and are not easily distracted or persuaded. Imaginative professors are creative, and even prophetic. Inventive professors build the foundation of their faith on bedrock, and they have depth and breadth. Inspired professors make regular deposits to their spiritual bank accounts, from which they take timely, strategic, and significant withdrawals.

Humble professors are guided by the Spirit. Idealistic professors are not just managers; they lead by example. Purposeful professors help others to clarify their own feelings, and their teachings are founded on principles rather than on values. Unpretentious professors are not easily swayed by conventional wisdom or politically correct ideology, and they are uninfluenced by situational ethics, expediency, or the shifting sands of secularism.

If the testimony of Jesus is the spirit of prophecy, then every self-effacing professor of the name of Christ, and every member of His Church who shoulders the burden of a witness of His divinity, is a facilitator who helps to bring others of Heavenly Father's children to a knowledge of His Plan, to a testimony of the mission of Jesus Christ, and to faith in His Atonement. Thus, unassuming professors are light bearers who carry the torch of truth as a beacon to guide

others who are having difficulty finding their own way home. The best among them wear the heavy robes of responsibility of God's priesthood, or operate under its influence and at its direction.

Deferential professors are faithful, and they endure, that they might obtain the prize of eternal life. (See D&C 50:5). They claim the promises of the Lord, Who said He would disperse the powers of darkness from before them, and would cause the heavens to shake for their good. (See D&C 21:6). They wax strong in the presence of God, and the doctrine of the priesthood distills upon their souls as the dews from heaven. The Holy Ghost is their constant companion, and their scepter is an unchanging scepter of righteousness and truth, and their dominion is an everlasting dominion, and without compulsory means it will flow unto them forever. (See D&C 121:45-46).

It is heartbreaking when those who have matriculated in the curriculum of the Gospel set their sights too low, and too easily reach their objectives. They do not stretch themselves, and they seldom venture out of their comfort zones. They have little to show for their consistently timid efforts. Stalwart professors, however, refuse to accept such mediocrity in their lives; instead they strive to align their behavior to be in harmony with the nature of God. They emulate His Son, Who dwells in perfection in the Celestial Kingdom.

As John F. Kennedy famously declared: "We choose to do things, not because they are easy, but because they are hard; because (our) goals will serve to organize and measure the best of our energies and skills. Our challenges are those that we are willing to accept, that we are unwilling to postpone, and that we intend to win." (Speech delivered in Houston, Texas, September 12, 1962).

If He chose to do so, our Heavenly Father could easily give us, His devoted professors, what He has. But, the truth be told, we would likely squander our inheritance, failing to recognize its value. Instead, He has provided us with a mortal experience and has complimented it with moral testing, creating an ideal

atmosphere in which we can learn to become as He is. As we do so, the conditions are created under which His grace may be granted This is the only way those of us who aspire to be professors of His name may claim the blessings that have been intricately woven into the elements of The Plan.

Steadfast professors "hunger and thirst after righteousness," and are "filled with the Holy Ghost." (3 Nephi 12:6). Nephi encouraged them, saying: "If ye shall press forward" with complete dedication, "feasting upon the word of Christ" or receiving physical and spiritual nourishment and strength, "and endure to the end" with continuing responsibility and accountability, "behold, thus saith the Father: Ye shall have eternal life," which is the greatest of God's gifts. (2 Nephi 31:20).

As consecrated professors, we recognize that endurance can be both positive and pleasant. Our faith carries a performance requirement that motivates us to be spiritually fit, in order to meet the demands of the exalting principles of the Gospel. But we sometimes need to be reprimanded because we do not clearly understand how faith works. We suppose that God would give unto us when have taken no thought save it was to ask Him. (See D&C 9:7-8).

One noted professor named Lorenzo Snow taught: "It is impossible to advance in the principles of truth, to increase in heavenly knowledge, except we exercise our reasoning faculties and exert ourselves." (J.D., 18:371). Although frugal professors understand that agency is not free, they are willing to purchase it at a substantial price. "For all who will have a blessing at my hands," explained the Lord, "shall abide the law which was appointed for that blessing, and the conditions thereof, as were instituted from before the foundation of the world" when The Plan was ratified by its future participants. (D&C 132:5).

As we profess to be His disciples, the Lord encourages us to move forward in faith, and not in the press of the crowd that jostles for position in the three-ring circus of telestial trivialities, conceptual cul-de-sacs, and doctrinal dead ends. It is the community of Saints who seek "wisdom; and ... the mysteries of God" that are those truths that can only be known by revelation from the Holy Ghost. (D&C 11:7). "But

wo unto them (who, in contrast to genuine professors, are nothing more than) deceivers and hypocrites." (D&C 50:6).

The word "hypocrite" comes to us from the Greek, where it describes the mask used by actors. A hypocrite, then, is someone who professes to be one thing, when actually it is a charade; hypocrites are entirely different persons behind their masks. (This may be where the negative connotation of the term "professor" comes from; but, as has been shown, there is nothing inherently wrong with being characterized as such, as long as we don't get carried away by the velvet robes of the false priesthood, or by the great and spacious buildings that dot the campuses of academia).

Unfortunately, that is exactly what can happen. Satan exults in hypocrisy and is a master of the techniques that methodically move us by subtraction from brilliant, dazzling white, through every shade of grey, to a fathomless black that is the absence of every good thought, word, deed, or worthy principle. His flattery and his subtle suggestions that he does not exist can lull us into a false sense of security. He can entice us to judge ourselves to be deserving of peace and plenty, and of accolades, awards, and adoration, when in fact, we have not earned, nor do we deserve, recognition for our modest efforts to be professors. (See 2 Nephi 30:22). When we are smitten with ourselves, we too easily seek to subvert the curriculum of the Gospel, as if it were possible to hack into the system that records our grades, and give ourselves undeservedly high marks in the learning laboratory of life.

Meanwhile, C.S. Lewis must have had faithful professors in mind, when he cautioned: "Little people, like you and me, if our prayers are sometimes granted beyond all hope and probability, had better not draw hasty conclusions to our own advantage. If we were stronger, we might be less tenderly treated. If we were braver, we might be sent, with far less help, to defend far more desperate posts in the great battle." ("The World's Last Night," p. 10-11).

"Wherefore, let every (determined professor) beware lest he do that which is not in truth and righteousness before me." (D&C 50:9). In order to avoid deception, Joseph

Smith was counseled that professors should seek "earnestly the best gifts, always remembering for what they are given." (D&C 46:8). When, in meekness, they are true to their high and holy calling, God will continue their ministry, and work miracles

among them, as "long as time shall last, or the earth shall stand, or there shall be one (such professor) upon the face thereof to be saved." (Words of Mormon 1:36).

Faith, light, and truth may be recognized as irreducible common denominators. They are the essential elements of an equation that describes the foundation upon which knowledge is received. "One for all and all for one!" was the motto of the Three Musketeers. Without faith, light, and truth, we would retrogress; we would "degenerate from God, descend to the devil, and lose knowledge, and without knowledge we cannot be saved," said Joseph Smith.

Our
faith
invites us
to enjoy the
influence of the
Holy Ghost, Who, as
a creative consultant,
always stands ready to
offer His constructive
comments relating
to our developing
storyboard.

Chapter Twenty Nine
The wisdom of faith.

"Incline thine ear unto wisdom,
and apply thine heart to understanding."
(Proverbs 2:2).

"<u>Woe unto you, scribes and Pharisees, hypocrites! (1st time)</u>. For ye pay tithes ... and have omitted the weightier matters of the law, judgment, mercy, and faith. These ought ye to have done, and not to leave the other undone. Ye blind guides, which strain at a gnat, and swallow a camel. <u>Woe unto you, scribes and Pharisees, hypocrites! (2nd time)</u>. For ye make clean the outside of the cup and of the platter, but within they are full of extortion and excess. Thou blind Pharisee, cleanse first that which is within the cup and platter, that the outside of them may be clean also. <u>Woe unto you, scribes and Pharisees, hypocrites! (3rd time)</u>. For ye are like unto whited sepulchres which indeed appear beautiful outward, but are within full of dead men's bones, and of all uncleanness. Even so ye also outwardly appear righteous unto men, but within

ye are full of hypocrisy and iniquity." (Matthew 23:23-28).

Jesus really disliked hypocrites! Three times in the above quoted scripture, He condemned them. In Hebrew, to repeat something three times makes it superlative, as in "good," "better," and "best," or "bad," "worse," and "worst." Unfortunately, the scribes and Pharisees, of whom Jesus was so critical, were like many of us today. They paid tithing, gave to the poor, attended worship services, and went regularly to the temple. What was it, then, that caused the Lord to condemn them? The Savior simply said: "All their works they do for to be seen of men." (Matthew 23:5).

On one occasion, "as he returned into the city, he hungered. And when he saw a fig tree in the way, he came to it, and found nothing thereon, but leaves only, and said unto it, Let no fruit grow on thee henceforward for ever. And presently the fig tree withered away." (Matthew 21:18-19). The tree had leaves, and by all intents and purposes it should have borne much fruit. But its appearance was deceiving; it was, in fact, devoid of figs. By cursing the tree, the Savior emphasized that hypocrisy is a serious sin. He especially singled out the Pharisees, who "loved the praise of men more than the praise of God." (John 12:43).

When Jesus triumphantly entered Jerusalem a week before the Passover, "the multitudes that went before, and that followed, cried, saying, Hosanna to the Son of David: Blessed is he that cometh in the name of the Lord; Hosanna in the highest. And when he was come into Jerusalem, all the city was moved, saying, Who is this? And the multitude said, This is Jesus the prophet of Nazareth of Galilee." (Matthew 21:9-11). But just seven days later, this same multitude demanded the death of the Savior, crying: "His blood be on us, and on our children." (Matthew 27:25). How quickly does the pendulum swing!

When Jesus came "into the temple, the chief priests and the elders of the people came unto him as he was teaching, and said, By what authority doest thou these things? and who gave thee this authority?" Faithlessly, they demanded to know by what power He conducted His ministry. They questioned His judgment, and although they sustained Him by the outward show of an uplifted hand, their actions told

another story. "Jesus saith unto them, Did ye never read in the scriptures, The stone which the builders rejected, the same is become the head of the corner: this is the Lord's doing, and it is marvellous in our eyes?" (Matthew 21:42, see Psalms 118:22).

Because of their lack of faith to wisely choose the Savior, He said to them: "The kingdom of God shall be taken from you, and given to a nation bringing forth the fruits thereof. And whosoever shall fall on this stone shall be broken: but on whomsoever it shall fall, it will grind him to powder." (Matthew 21:43-44).

When Jesus came to Bethany, to the home of Mary and Martha, Mary took "a pound of ointment ... very costly, and anointed the feet of Jesus, and wiped his feet with her hair: and the house was filled with the odour of the ointment. Then saith one of his disciples, Judas Iscariot ... Why was not this ointment sold for three hundred pence, and given to the poor? This he said, not that he cared for the poor; but because he was a thief." (John 12:3-6). Sometimes, we say things because it is politically correct or expedient, or to our advantage. Likewise, sometimes we do not say things that should be said, because we fear the consequences. But as Ella Wheeler Wilcox cautioned: "To sin by silence, when words should be spoken, makes cowards of men." With the wisdom of faith, we choose our words carefully.

Faithless modern scribes and Pharisees omit the weightier matters of the law. They strain at a gnat, and swallow a camel. They appear to be righteous, but inside are "full of extortion and excess." (Matthew 23:25). Our sincere desire to choose by the wisdom of faith brings us closer to the Lord Jesus Christ, leaving no room for hypocrisy to creep into our lives.

If the octane
rating of the fuel
that fires our faith to
build our temples of God
is too low, we may be able to
just barely get by, but only for a
time. As we limp along with our
engines misfiring badly, our
fear will ultimately
overpower our
faith.

Chapter Thirty
The endurance of faith.

"All men must endure in faith
on his name to the end."
(D&C 20:25).

Built into the fabric of The Plan of Salvation is the Golden Ticket that provides the means for every one of us to reap the rewards of heaven if we endure to the end in faith while yet on the earth. The principle of free will, or agency, endows us with choice, and the principle of faith delivers the power that drives our actions.

We may choose to endure unrighteously, but if we do so, we also accept the inevitable negative consequences that are related to unresolved sin. This makes endurance much more painful than it needs to be. On the other hand, if we choose to endure in righteousness, relying upon the power of the Atonement, we will enjoy the blessings of the fruits of faith that are directly related to obedience. Our capacity for purposeful action is designed to increase over time as it is guided by faith.

The spiritual, emotional, and psychological benefits of righteous endurance in faith can be compared to physically training on a pedal bike. When we begin a workout regimen, we take it in stages, as we slowly work up to our potential. Interval training can motivate us to greater achievement. During the process, we learn to be consciously aware of our breathing, cadence, and gearing. As we fine-tune these variables, we better control our cardiovascular rhythms, as we probe the limits of our capabilities.

We are in tune with our bodies, and we pay attention to the basics. We train consistently, pushing ourselves to somewhere around 90% of our capacity, but we do not overdo it. We know that when we allow our muscles to tense up, we squander precious energy. We resist the temptation to shift to a lower gear (an easier gear), because we know that our forward momentum will falter, and we will inevitably slow down, unless with pick up our cadence.

As we fine-tune our senses, we stay hydrated and observe proper nutrition. We learn to pace ourselves, and to automatically adjust to variations in the terrain that we encounter. When we face hills or other obstacles, our endorphins kick in, and we take a perverse pleasure in suffering, because a strange thing happens. We build mental toughness and expand our potential for endurance. We even begin to look forward to the challenges on the road ahead of us. As Heber J. Grant famously observed: "That which we persist in doing becomes easier for us to do; not that the nature of the thing is changed, but that our power to do is increased." We don't allow ourselves to become discouraged, if our training schedule seems demanding. In a worst case scenario, we can always be used as a bad example.

Those who are past their prime can still faithfully endure to the end. It may be of some consolation to realize that when we are over the hill, we pick up speed. Still, at times we will need to adjust our expectations. If we do so, it's likely that we'll be very pleasantly surprised that our capacity for endurance has not been compromised, but has instead been fine-tuned to meet our circumstances. We just

gird up our loins and take fresh courage, because with the endurance of faith we know that God will never forsake us. (See "Come, Come, Ye Saints, lyrics by William W. Phelps).

Faithfully enduring to the end, every day of our lives, prepares us for the time that will surely come "when we are figuratively tapped on our shoulder and offered a chance to do a very special thing, unique to us and fitted to our talents. What a tragedy if that moment finds us unprepared or unqualified for that which could have been our finest hour." (Winston Churchill).

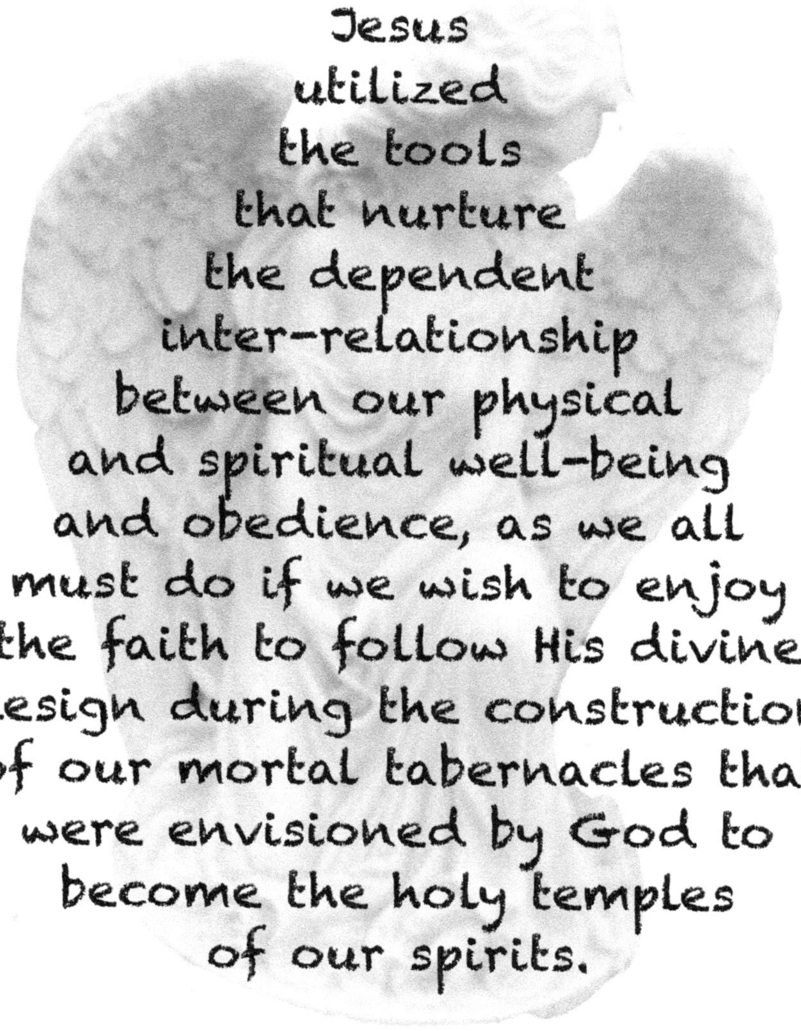

Jesus
utilized
the tools
that nurture
the dependent
inter-relationship
between our physical
and spiritual well-being
and obedience, as we all
must do if we wish to enjoy
the faith to follow His divine
design during the construction
of our mortal tabernacles that
were envisioned by God to
become the holy temples
of our spirits.

Chapter Thirty One
The faith to go the second mile.

A young man came to the Savior and asked: What "shall I do, that I may have eternal life? And he said unto him ... if thou wilt enter into life, keep the commandments. He saith unto him, Which?" Jesus then listed half a dozen of them.

"The young man saith unto him, All these things have I kept from my youth up: what lack I yet?" This young man had been a good and faithful member of the Church. He had attended Primary and Sunday School, never missed Seminary, and had been ordained to the priesthood. He had been a faithful minister to his brethren, and had accepted opportunities to speak in Church and to hold callings. He had performed temple baptisms for the dead, and had earned his Duty to God award. He had received his endowment in the temple, had made covenants before holy altars, and had honorably served a mission for the Church. In his obedience to the letter of the law, he had been perfect.

But the Savior knew his heart, and perceived that there was something missing from his life that was preventing him from achieving the gift of spiritual independence that would remove the veil of insensitivity to his destiny. His challenges had been specifically tailored to address his own circumstances. The Savior knew him, and understood that obedience to the Law of Consecration would be the greatest obstacle to his progression.

And so, He "said unto him, If thou wilt be perfect, go and sell that thou hast and give to the poor, and thou shalt have treasure in heaven: and come and follow me." The Savior knew this would have been an easy thing to do if the young man had been poor and destitute. "But when the young man heard that saying, he went away sorrowful, for he had great possessions." (Matthew 19:16-22).

Like so many in the Church, he was young and impressionable, and had not developed the seasoned maturity that comes with age. He was not yet like William Tyndale, who said near the end of his life that he would rather "be blessed with Christ, in a little tribulation, than to be cursed perpetually with the world for a little pleasure. Prosperity," he declared, "is a thing that God giveth to his enemies."

Tyndale recognized mortality as a probationary state, a time during which we are individually tried to see if we will put to the proof those things that we have been taught we must do if we are to inherit eternal life. In short, God allows us to be tested and tempted so that He can see if we are willing to have the faith to "go the second mile."

When I was younger, I jogged 5 or 10 miles every morning, for an hour or two before sunrise. I ran through the Santa Monica Mountains, above Pacific Palisades, in Southern California. One day, as I neared the end of my run, I found myself on the surface streets that led back to my home. I stopped at an intersection, waiting for the traffic signal to change. With my hands on my knees and with the sweat dripping off the end of my nose, I thought about aborting my run, stopping right then and there to assume a more relaxed walking pace, to let my complaining

muscles cool down, as I traced my way home. However, through sweat-soaked eyes, I looked up, and saw as it were, a vision before me. Insistently flashing red with neon brightness, directly in front of me, were these words, that urged me on: "Don't walk!"

That message, as if it had come from God Himself, encouraged me to go the second mile, and prompted me to wonder: "What happens to us when we do so?" As we learn to confront our trials by pushing just a little harder, we grow in the Spirit. It is no coincidence that these two scriptures are linked together: "And whosoever shall compel thee to go a mile, go with him twain," and then: "Be ye therefore perfect, even as your Father which is in heaven is perfect." (Matthew 5:41 & 48).

I have been a member of the Church long enough to have experienced a measure of temporal, spiritual, emotional, and intellectual symmetry. Why then, I ask myself, does the world still tug at me? Mortality is a hands-on learning laboratory where, through repetition, we develop the habit pattern of doing "all things whatsoever the Lord (our) God shall command (us)." (Abraham 3:25). We all carry heavy burdens, but we gird up our loins, remembering the admonition: "Whosoever he be of you that forsaketh not all that he hath, he cannot be my disciple." (Luke 14:33).

The question remains: What was the Savior talking about when He said: "Whosoever shall compel thee to go a mile, go with him twain." (Matthew 5:41). When we join the Church, we have effectively gone the first mile. We have commenced our journey to Christ by following in His footsteps. We attend Church on a weekly basis. We regularly repent. We consistently partake of the Sacrament. We practice what we preach, and keep the Sabbath day holy. We temper our lifestyle behaviors so that they are consistent with Gospel principles. We accept ministering assignments with their related responsibilities. We learn to express ourselves by employing speech that reflects the higher standard to which we hold ourselves. We consistently pay our tithes and offerings. We maintain worthiness to enter the temple. We accept and make every effort to magnify ward callings. We appreciate the temporal and spiritual benefits of obedience to the Word of Wisdom. We make regular deposits to our spiritual bank accounts by praying daily to our Heavenly Father, and we

learn how to make legitimate withdrawals in times of need. We internalize the Ten Commandments, and are ever mindful of our baptismal covenants. In short, all these things have we kept from our youth. What lack we yet?

Just this: After a period of time, we begin to recognize that Heavenly Father has something more in mind for us, and we feel the urge to go the second mile. We feel compelled to take advantage of opportunities offered by the Church Education System, such as B.Y.U. Education Week, and other conferences and symposia, and to really internalize the scriptures that encourage us to seek diligently and teach each other words of wisdom out of the best books, even by study and also by faith. (See D&C 88:118 & 109:7).

We have been repenting regularly, but now our desire to have the faith to go the second mile provides us with a new perspective on the Atonement. Against the backdrop of the marvelous light of life, our sins cast a very long shadow. (See John 8:12). We feel terrible about them. We feel profoundly filthy. With a new sense of urgency, we want to unload and abandon them. We become almost obsessive-compulsive about cleansing our souls. We had known what it felt like to be broken in heart, and to have the spirit of contrition, but now we become zealous in our preparation to receive the things of the Spirit. At a heightened level of anticipation, we begin to consistently ask, as did those on the Day of Pentecost: "What else can we do?" (See Acts 2:37).

Since our baptism, we have been receiving the Sacrament each Sunday, but the second mile urges us to be receptive to new approaches, that we might have His Spirit to be with us. Accordingly, we find ways to prepare for our Sacrament service hours and even days ahead of time, and we treat the ordinance itself with newfound respect.

Since our baptism, we have been keeping the Sabbath day holy, but the faith to "go the second mile" encourages us to venture out of our comfort zones into the arena of service, to visit the sick, and the elderly, and to look for opportunities to show

compassion toward others, and to perform other acts of Quiet Christianity; in short, to be real ministers of Christ.

In our charity, we begin to realize that if we want to have the faith to go the second mile we must be particularly receptive to new opportunities to follow the promptings of the Spirit. We begin to take an active interest in the activities of those for whom we have stewardship responsibilities, and to be sensitive to their spiritual, emotional, intellectual, and temporal needs.

As we begin to go the second mile, we see hidden truth in the scriptures that relate to countability. We are humbled by the aphorism: "Inasmuch as ye have done it unto the least of these my brethren, ye have done it unto me." (Matthew 25:40).

Our baptismal covenant encouraged us to establish habit patterns that supported our desire to express ourselves with soft and considerate words, but we take to heart the second mile admonition of Paul, who wrote: "Let no corrupt communication proceed out of your mouth, but that which is good to the use of edifying, that it may minister grace unto the hearers." (Ephesians 4:29).

As we prepared for baptism, we gained a testimony of the Law of Tithing, but afterwards, we begin to regularly ponder the significance of the second mile covenant to obey the Law of Consecration. As we expand the quality of our temple service by participating in ordinances for the redemption of the dead, we begin to appreciate the second mile requirement to do our own family history research. We see the Atonement in a new light as the supernal vicarious work for both the living and the dead, and we ponder anew the eternal impact of the ordinances we perform for our forbearers. We recognize multiple layers of meaning in the appellation employed by the prophet Obadiah, who characterized those who minister to the spiritual needs of their ancestors as saviors on Mount Zion. (See Obadiah 1:21).

We have consistently accepted ward callings, but over time we realize that our second mile commitment requires us to do more than satisfy minimal requirements.

Second-milers find new ways to minister to the needs of those whom the Lord is eager to bless with our service. We begin to yearn to personalize the observation of Job, who wrote: "For God speaketh once, yea twice, yet man perceiveth it not. In a dream, in a vision of the night, when deep sleep falleth upon men, in slumberings upon the bed; Then he openeth the ears of men, and sealeth their instruction." (Job 33:14-16).

We have learned to be undeviating in our obedience to the Word of Wisdom, but when we apply the second mile principle to this law of health, we begin to see it in a greater context as a conduit to the Spirit. We begin to pay strict attention to the spirit of the law, as well as to the symmetry that should exist between physical and spiritual stability.

We have been in the habit of praying daily to our Heavenly Father, but the second mile urges us to ask for His influence at the break of day, and to return and report at its end. The faith to "go the second mile" reminds us of the Lord's commandment: "Go to the house of prayer and offer up thy sacraments upon my holy day; For verily this is a day appointed unto you to rest from your labors, and to pay thy devotions unto the Most High; Nevertheless thy vows shall be offered up in righteousness on all days and at all times." (D&C 59:9-11).

To the best of our ability, we have obeyed the Ten Commandments, but the second mile asks us to forge a spiritual bond with our fellow travelers by obedience that is more expansive than a law of carnal commandments. We shun the telestial temptations that are so cunningly peddled by the snake oil salesmen who have set up shop in the great and spacious buildings that dot the landscapes of our lives.

We have been mindful of our baptismal covenants, but the faith to go the second mile focuses our thoughts on the command to be "willing to mourn with those that mourn; yea, and comfort those that stand in need of comfort, and to stand as witnesses of God at all times and in all things, and in all places that (we) may be in, even until death." (Mosiah 18:9). The second mile invites us to experience the confidence, the encouragement, and the grace of God. With the faith to go the

second mile, our obedience ceases to be inconvenient, and we experience the soul-expanding desire to even more abundantly labor in the traces. (See 1 Corinthians 15:10).

If we listen carefully, we can hear those who speak in General Conference urge us to generate the faith to go the second mile. Mindful that they are also ministers to non-members and less-active members, we acknowledge that they talk about the first mile principles and ordinances of the Gospel. But they also realize that they are addressing members of the Church who are already anxiously engaged. Their messages are, therefore, dualistic in their application. They speak of principles in such a way that those of faltering faith are encouraged to take their first steps toward commitment, while, simultaneously, more spiritually mature disciples are encouraged to continue their efforts to lengthen their stride as they talk the talk and walk the walk.

Paul knew what it meant to have the faith to go the second mile. He ministered among the Corinthian Saints, whom he discovered had a working relationship with the laws of the Gospel, whose expression he characterized as being written upon "tables of stone." However, he also described a second mile commitment: "Ye are manifestly declared to be the epistle of Christ ministered by us, written not with ink, but with the Spirit of the living God; not (just) in tables of stone, but (also) in fleshy tables of the heart." (2 Corinthians 3:3).

Those who commit to the second mile are as the Nephites of old, of whom the scriptures record: "When king Benjamin had thus spoken to his people, he sent among them, desiring to know of his people if they believed the words which he had spoken unto them. And they all cried with one voice, saying: Yea, we believe all the words which thou hast spoken unto us; and also, we know of their surety and truth, because of the Spirit of the Lord Omnipotent, which has wrought a mighty change in us, or in our hearts, that we have no more disposition to do evil, but to do good continually.

And we, ourselves, also, through the infinite goodness of God, and the manifestations

of his Spirit, have great views of that which is to come; and were it expedient, we could prophesy of all things. And it is the faith" to go the second mile "that has brought us to this great knowledge, whereby we do rejoice with such exceedingly great joy." (Mosiah 5:1-4).

Sooner or later, every member of the Church becomes a second-miler, who is encouraged to run, and not walk, to the end of their lives, in righteousness. During His mortal ministry, the Savior promised: "He that shall endure unto the end, the same shall be saved." (Matthew 24:13). Going a little further, He explained to Joseph Smith: "If you keep my commandments (the first mile) and endure to the end (the second mile) you shall have eternal life, which gift is the greatest of all the gifts of God." (D&C 14:7).

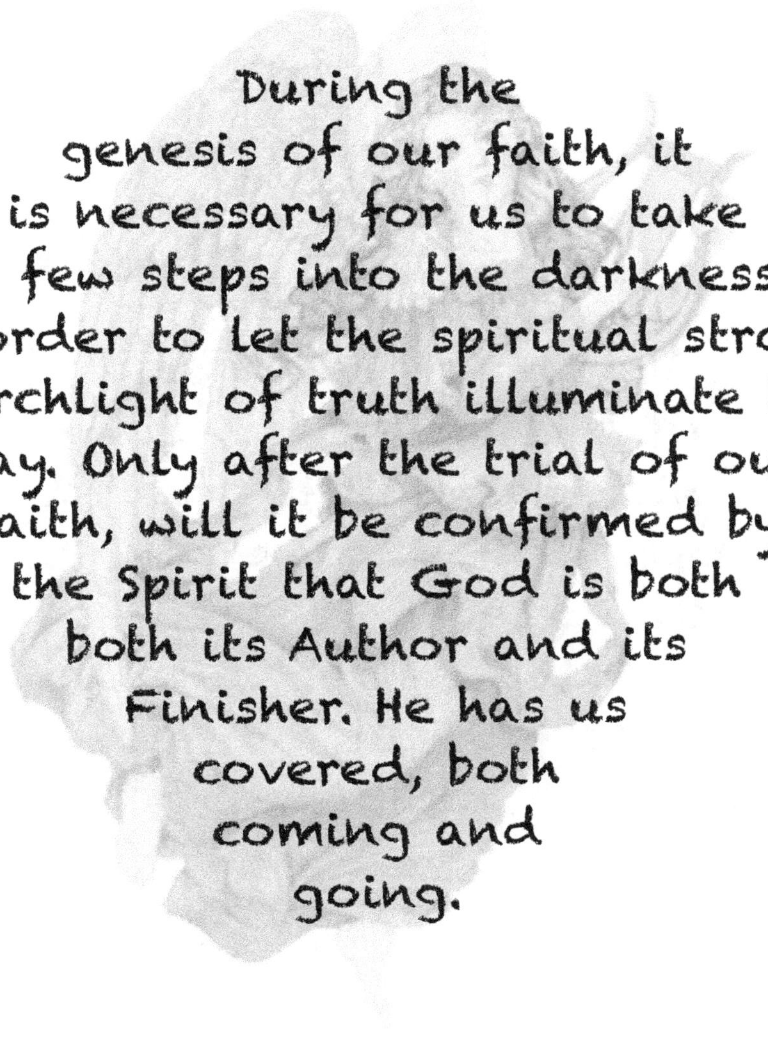

During the
genesis of our faith, it
is necessary for us to take
a few steps into the darkness,
in order to let the spiritual strong
searchlight of truth illuminate the
way. Only after the trial of our
faith, will it be confirmed by
the Spirit that God is both
both its Author and its
Finisher. He has us
covered, both
coming and
going.

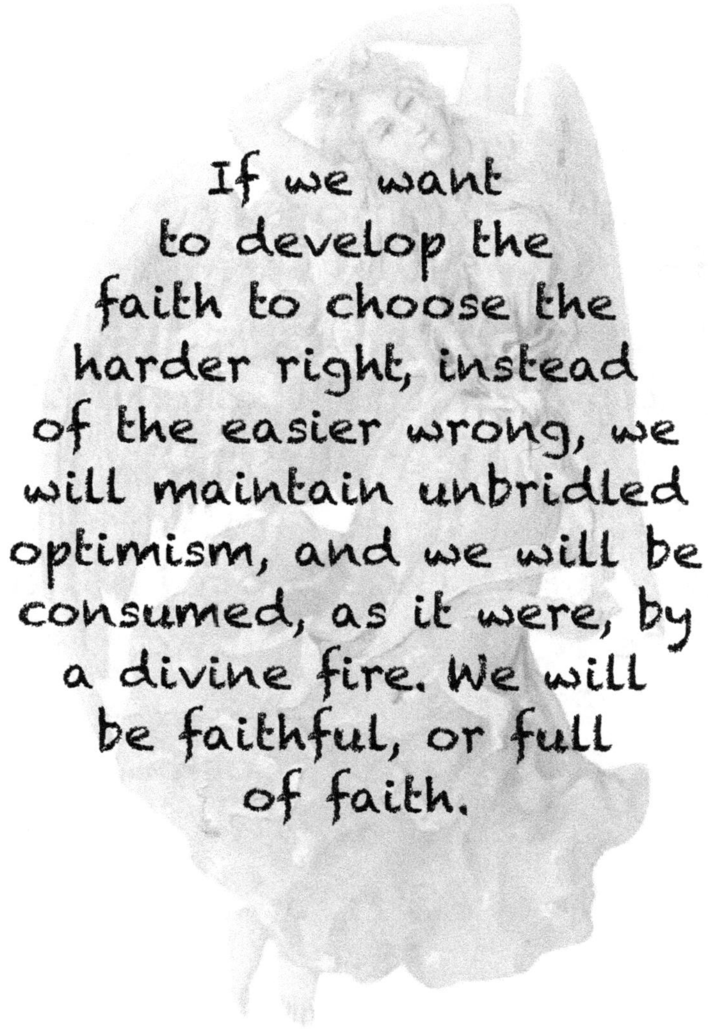

If we want
to develop the
faith to choose the
harder right, instead
of the easier wrong, we
will maintain unbridled
optimism, and we will be
consumed, as it were, by
a divine fire. We will
be faithful, or full
of faith.

Chapter Thirty Two
The faith to touch His garment.

"And a certain woman, which had an issue of blood twelve years, and had suffered many things of many physicians, and had spent all that she had, and was nothing bettered, but rather grew worse, when she had heard of Jesus, came in the press behind, and touched his garment. For she said, If I may touch but his clothes, I shall be whole. And straightway the fountain of her blood was dried up; and she felt in her body that she was healed of that plague. And Jesus, immediately knowing in himself that virtue had gone out of him, turned him about in the press, and said, Who touched my clothes?" (Mark 5:25-30).

The spiritually hungry, or those who were "poor in spirit," were drawn to the Savior to satisfy their yearnings. (See Matthew 5:3). He, in turn, being a wellspring of the Spirit, sensed every moment when want drew upon that source.

Mark's narrative assures us that God is sensitive to our needs, and does hear our prayers. In conformity to law, we can tap into and draw upon the life force that is

the Spirit of God. When we do so, we are, in effect, touching His garment.

One of President David O. McKay's favorite poems was "Anchored to The Infinite" by Edwin Markham. It reads: "The builder who first bridged Niagara's gorge, before he swung his cable, shore to shore, sent out across the gulf his venturing kite, bearing a slender cord for unseen hands to grasp upon the further cliff and draw a greater cord, and then a greater yet; 'Til at last across the chasm swung The Cable - then the mighty bridge in air! So may we send our little timid thoughts across the void, out to God's reaching hands. Send our love, and faith, to thread the deep, thought after thought, until the little cord, and we, are anchored to the Infinite!"

This poem describes the process of sanctification, by which we experience the power of the virtue of the Son of God. We become one, in a mystical union with deity. "For intelligence cleaveth unto intelligence; wisdom receiveth wisdom; truth embraceth truth; virtue loveth virtue; light cleaveth unto light; mercy hath compassion on mercy and claimeth her own; justice continueth its course and claimeth its own." (D&C 88:40).

It happens when the Gospel has driven the law into our inward parts (see Jeremiah 31:33) and we become "firmer and firmer in the faith of Christ." (Helaman 3:35). "Sanctify yourselves," we are commanded, "that your minds become single to God, and the days will come that you shall see him; for he will unveil his face unto you." (D&C 88:68).

When we generate the faith to touch His garment, we enjoy a mystical bond with the Savior that is unbreakable. A transcendent affinity with the powers of heaven infuses us with a confident companionship with the Spirit. We enjoy a proximate association and an intimate relationship that is as real as it is undeniable. We are enveloped within a celestial connection that binds us to our Father in Heaven. We stand prepared to enter into the joy of the Lord. (See Matthew 25:21). We "come before His presence with thanksgiving," as we "make a joyful noise unto Him with psalms" of praise. (Psalms 95:2). Hallelujah!

Post Script. When, in just 24 days, Georg Friedrich Händel (Born: 2/23/1685, Halle, Germany. Died: 4/14/1759, London, United Kingdom) created the 259 pages of musical score that comprise "The Messiah," the notes came to him so quickly that he could barely keep up, as he furiously scratched out the oratorio on whatever paper was handy. After he had written the "Hallelujah Chorus" in a fervor of divine inspiration, he exclaimed that he had "seen all heaven before him." At the end of the manuscript, in acknowledgement of his own puny efforts, he wrote the letters "SDG," that stood for "Soli Deo Gloria" or "To God alone the glory." On a much smaller scale, we have all had similar experiences with light and knowledge, and at times we catch a glimpse of the flurry of activity that takes place just beyond the veil. Revelatory experiences that are both nurturing and stimulating await us as we generate the faith to touch His garment.

When we feel
the energy of faith
building within us, we
realize that it can lift us
to the zenith of experience,
until the lines distinguishing
mortality from eternity blur.
At that moment, when we find
ourselves in a condition that,
for the lack of better words,
can only be described as if
we were being born again,
we will be consumed in
a fire of everlasting
burnings.

Chapter Thirty Three
The nobility of faith.

"There are but a very few beings in the world who understand rightly the nature of God (and) if men do not understand the character of God they do not comprehend themselves." (Joseph Smith, "Teachings" p. 343). The more we understand the character of God, the more we learn about how we fit in to His divine design. We learn how the nobility of faith can drive the law into our inward parts. (See Jeremiah 31:33).

Those who are blessed with the nobility of faith hold God in reverential awe. He knows all things, "being from everlasting to everlasting." (D&C 132:20). He is eternal, which spans the time from uncreate intelligence, through our spiritual development as His children, on into mortality, and finally to our reunion with Him following our resurrection. Faith, hope and charity define His attributes. Those who are blessed with the nobility of faith are somehow able to break free of "the influence of that spirit which hath so strongly riveted the creeds of the fathers, who have inherited lies, upon the hearts of the children, and filled the world with confusion, (which)

has been growing stronger and stronger, and is now the very mainspring of all corruption. The whole earth groans under the weight of its iniquity. It is an iron yoke; it is a strong band; they are the very handcuffs, and chains, and shackles, and fetters of hell." (D&C 123:7-8). So wrote Joseph Smith to the Saints, March 20,

1839, while a prisoner in the jail at Liberty, Missouri. He was one who was blessed with the nobility of faith, and who, independent of circumstances, consistently modeled his behavior after our Lord and Savior Jesus Christ. His demeanor in the midst of indescribable hardship, confirms our hope that "all things which are good cometh of Christ." (Moroni 7:24).

The Savior is the model for those who evince the nobility of faith. He gives them the power to overcome both adversity and the adversary. They embrace His Gospel because its teachings express a crystal clear perspective as they trace the pattern of heaven on an earthly tapestry. The nobility of faith permits His disciples to design their lives according to principles of perfection that are emulated by His example and validated by the Spirit. It empowers them to move about freely, but always within the sphere of His protective influence; to find shelter from lethal storms of devious doctrine, whose suffocating winds threaten to suck the life-sustaining marrow from their bones.

Those who enjoy the sweet, sustaining influence of the nobility of faith have experienced power that stems from love, in contrast to the elusive and transient Machiavellian influence that is driven by greed, avarice, lust, and the unrighteous desire for dominion. Those with the nobility of faith easily identify the fingerprints of Satan that are smeared all over the penurious programs, policies, politics, and parties that promote petty, provincial, and personal proclamations.

Those with the nobility of faith acknowledge the omnipotence of God. They realize that they are completely helpless to alter the progress, or affect the outcome, of any of the provisions of His Plan. They have implicit faith in His divine design. It was when Moses recognized his utter dependence upon God that he spontaneously exclaimed: "Now, for this cause I know that man is nothing, which thing I never had

supposed." (Moses 1:10). Their debt to God is total and complete, and they willingly lose themselves in His service. King Benjamin asked his people: "Can ye say aught of yourselves? I answer you, Nay. Ye cannot say that ye are even as much as the dust of the earth; yet ye were created of the dust of the earth; but behold, it belongeth to him who created you." (Mosiah 2:25).

Those with the nobility of faith fear no man. They are as Bagheera, the powerfully built black panther in "The Jungle Book," who confided to Mowgli the man-cub: "I had never seen the jungle. They fed me behind bars from an iron pan till one night I felt that I was Bagheera the Panther, and no man's plaything, and I broke the lock with one blow of my paw and came away." (Rudyard Kipling, "The Jungle Book," p. 26).

Those with the nobility of faith find their strength in the comforting counsel of the Savior: "Remember that it is not the work of God that is frustrated, but the work of men." (D&C 3:3). As Joseph Fielding Smith, Jr. declared: "No power on earth or hell can overthrow or defeat that which God has decreed. Every plan of the adversary will fail; for the Lord knows the secret thoughts of men, and sees the future with a vision clear and perfect, even as though it were in the past." Those with the nobility of faith take courage in the counsel of Jacob: "Oh, how great the holiness of our God. For he knoweth all things, and there is not anything save he knows it." (2 Nephi 9:20). Those with the nobility of faith may have been the first to comprehend the power behind the phrase: "Father knows best!"

They lend their voices to the prophet, who described the nobility of faith: "No unhallowed hand can stop the work from progressing. Persecutions may rage, mobs may combine, armies may assemble, calumny may defame, but the truth of God will go forth boldly, nobly, and independent, until it has penetrated every continent, visited every clime, swept every country, and sounded in every ear; till the purposes of God shall be accomplished, and the Great Jehovah shall say 'The work is done.'" (H.C., 4:540).

We have
faith that Jesus
is the Father of our
spiritual regeneration,
and like the parent we all
aspire to be, He will be there
to bind our wounds and heal
our infirmities every time we
stumble and whenever we fall
because of the weight we have
been trying to carry all by
ourselves. Even though we
may forget all about the
Atonement, the Savior
will never forget
about us.

Chapter Thirty Four

The faith to see all the way to heaven.

"The gate of heaven is open unto all,
even to those who will believe on the name
of Jesus Christ, who is the Son of God."
(Helaman 3:28).

"The Lord's throne is in heaven," wrote the Psalmist. (Psalms 11:4). In the beginning when God created the earth, He made it temporally and spatially separate from heaven, with distinctly different boundaries and conditions. With this stroke of genius, He utilized both temporal and eternal laws to create a veil, as it were, that the recollection of our heavenly home might be hidden from our view. This was necessary that we might take full advantage of mortality. But God did not leave us destitute. We were left with the distinct afterglow of our premortal life, that would create a subtle and yet undeniable link between heaven and earth. Thus, we are grounded, not on telestial turf, but on celestial boulevards that are paved with gold.

Our minds and our spirits are caressed by inexplicable images that remind us of our noble birthright. These are evidence of a spiritual "sixth sense" that allows us to create order amid chaos. Some recognize that anchor as intuition, or the ability to understand something without the need for conscious reasoning. Others explain our connection with the eternities as déjà vu, from the French, literally meaning "already seen," in order to emotionally embrace the phenomenon of having the strong sensation that a current event has been experienced in the past. At least superficially, extrasensory perception may describe the reception of information gained with the mind, rather than through the recognized physical senses. The truth be told, our spiritual sixth sense may be all of the above, and more.

God's whole is greater than the sum of His parts, just as our perceptions are so much more than the quantifiable sensory stimulation of our cerebral cortex. The spiritual sixth sense with which we are blessed may be described as a lowest common denominator in the theory of everything. It is a grand unifying principle that defies explanation on a chalkboard. It cannot be measured by attaching electrodes to neurons, nor will it ever be explained by neuroscience. It governs heaven itself. No matter how wide the net is cast, science cannot explain the flickering shadows of eternity that dance around us, as the light of life illuminates the familiar features of mortality.

As we wrestle with the faith to see all the way to heaven, we are taught in the Book of Abraham's Facsimile #2 about a place that is called Kolob, signifying the first creation, nearest to the celestial, or the residence of God. Of our relationship to that realm, William W. Phelps wrote: Without the guidance of the Holy Ghost, "no man has found pure space, nor seen the outside curtains, where nothing has a place." In the matrix of the higher dimensional reality in which Phelps envisioned Kolob, there is no end to matter, space, spirit, or race, virtue, might, wisdom, or light, union, youth, priesthood, or truth, glory, love, or being, because each of these is defined by different boundaries and conditions that are only comprehensible to God. ("If You Could Hie to Kolob").

Ultimately, said the Lord, "there shall be the reckoning of the time of one planet above another, until thou come nigh unto Kolob, which Kolob is after the reckoning of the Lord's time; which Kolob is set nigh unto the throne of God, to govern all those planets which belong to the same order as that upon which thou standest."

(Abraham 3:9). Somehow, it is from Kolob that the other creations of God are temporally and spatially governed. It is from there that the boundaries of heaven have been established in such a manner that they are beyond the reach of detection by even the most sophisticated and accurately calibrated instruments utilized by terrestrial scientists.

The Hubble telescope, for example, can "see" 10 or 15 billion light years into our past, almost back to the moment of creation at the Big Bang, but it cannot gaze into heaven for five minutes. If it could do that, we "would know more than (we) would by reading all that has ever been written on the subject." (Joseph Smith, H.C., 6:50). Especially in the case of "higher" temporal and spatial dimensions, it would seem that there are some things that need to be believed to be seen.

Heaven and earth are spatially and temporally separate. "The heaven is my throne," the Lord revealed, "and the earth is my footstool." (Isaiah 66:1). It is only through the workings of the Spirit and by the power of our faith to see all the way to heaven, that we have the capacity to be carried beyond the perceptible and palpable confines of this world to a place where boundaries are blurred, and where the barricade of borders disappears. As John the Revelator exclaimed when he received his apocalypse: "Behold, a door was opened in heaven: and (I heard a voice) as it were of a trumpet talking with me; which said, Come up hither, and I will shew thee things which must be hereafter." (Revelation 4:1).

Joseph F. Smith had a similar experience, when "the eyes of (his) understanding were opened, and the Spirit of the Lord" rested upon him, and he too saw into the eternal world. (D&C 138:11). Normally, the veil is an event horizon that denies to our senses any hint of what lies beyond. It is only through faith to see all the way to heaven that the power of the Spirit is able to penetrate the barrier that isolates us

from the sum and substance of circumstances that more accurately define reality. It is the Spirit that confirms our faith to see all the way to heaven, and that answers our questions: "O God, where art thou? And where is the pavilion that covereth thy hiding place?" (D&C 121:1).

In the beginning, it was "the Gods (who) organized and formed the heavens and the earth" by defining the boundaries of the temporal universe, not to mention the eternal world. (Abraham 4:1). They did this by the power of faith. They set the conditions "by which the worlds were framed, (and) all things in heaven, on the earth, or under the earth. (These) exist by reason of faith as it existed in (the mind of the Gods). Had it not been for this principle of faith, the worlds would never have been framed, neither would man have been formed of the dust. It is this principle by which Jehovah works, and through which he exercises power over all temporal as well as eternal things." (Joseph Smith, "Lectures on Faith," #1).

Perhaps this is why it is only by exercising perfect faith to see all the way to heaven that we may understand God's creations and sense His reality. (James 2:22). Ultimately, that "truth is knowledge of things as they are, and as they were, and as they are to come." (D&C 93:24). It comes to us "precept upon precept; line upon line; here a little and there a little." (Isaiah 28:10).

Physics tells us that there are no privileged frames of reference. The galaxies are imbedded in time and imprinted upon a space whose fabric is constantly expanding. If we ask where and when the creation took place, the answer is everywhere and forever. If, as the laws of physics suggest, the universe is warped through time and space into additional dimensions, they just might expand as a balloon does, creating in every instant more space. It seems reasonable that God would utilize such a framework to accomplish His purposes. This may explain why the Lord told Moses: "As one earth shall pass away, and the heavens thereof, even so shall another come, and there is no end to my works." (Moses 1:38). "For by him were all things created that are in heaven, and that are in earth, visible and invisible, whether they be thrones, or dominions, or principalities, or powers." (Colossians 1:16).

For the time being, our poor lenses cannot discern those realms. "No man hath seen God at any time in the flesh, except quickened by the Spirit of God." (J.S.T. John 1:18). The light of the body is the eye, and when it is single to the faith to see into heaven above, our elements will be stirred by its warm glow. (See 3 Nephi 13:22). We will be captivated by the Spirit.

On one occasion, after having received revelation, Joseph Smith exclaimed: "My whole body was full of light, and I could see even out at the ends of my fingers and toes." (N.B. Lundwall, "The Vision," p. 11). This may explain why the angel Moroni hovered in the air during his visits to Joseph Smith in his chamber, and why his hands and his feet were naked. (See J.S.H. 1:31). It may have simply been that he wanted to "see" with every part of his body.

Every child of God potentially possesses this gift, and the Lord's promise is that it only waits to be revealed to the faithful, who shall comprehend all things, and in whose bodies there shall be no darkness. (See D&C 88:67). There will come a day for them when "the sun shall no more go down; neither shall (the) moon withdraw itself: for the Lord shall be (their) everlasting light." (Isaiah 60:20). Both heaven and earth will be bathed in a celestial fire that is reminiscent of the background microwave radiation that lingers from the cataclysmic moment of creation.

When it is our turn to come face to face with eternity, as surely we will, the spiritual element will mightily transform our mortal clay. As we tarry in the flesh awaiting that day, we might consider these questions: How strong is the focus of our faith? Under what circumstances does our faith quicken us? How can we utilize the pure knowledge flowing out of faith to vitalize our discipleship? Does our faith have the power to enable us to see all the way to heaven?

The Preacher wrote: "A man's wisdom maketh his face to shine, and the boldness of his face shall be changed." (Ecclesiastes 8:1). When we are at one with God, we are spiritually born of Him. As we internalize His divine nature, we receive His image

in our countenances. (See Alma 5:14). That image and His likeness will bridge the barriers of time and space to leave their marks as the irrefutable confirmation of our noble birthright. Our genetic code leaves D.N.A. evidence that we are the children of God. It is imprinted upon our nature; it transforms us and links us to heaven. In its trail, we are left with a star map that has been created by the hand of God to guide us to our promised inheritance, which is nothing short of an endowment of unearthly power.

When we move into eternity, time as we know it will lose all significance, and "See you later," will cease to be in our vocabulary. The seasons of our lives, that we had too frequently viewed as a predator stalking us from the shadows of time, will then be fondly remembered as the mercurial companion who accompanied us on our journey through mortality, gently reminding us at every turn to cherish each moment. We will find that our mortal experience was a tiny fraction of a much larger reality, and that our perspective was faulty because we believed it to be unique.

We will be shocked to learn that mortality was not our natural dimension, after all. We will come to understand why it was that we were never at home in time, and why we often felt like "strangers and pilgrims on the earth." (Hebrews 11:13). In turn, the innate thrust that had always been toward our future will be validated, as it pushes us beyond the horizon to eternity itself.

We are reminded of the venerable Hebrew elder described by James Michener, in his novel "The Source." Zadock "was a spiritual man whose tired eyes could see beyond the desert to those invisible summits of the imagination where cool air existed and where the one god, El Shaddai, lived. In later generations, people who spoke other languages would translate this old Semitic name, which actually meant 'He of the mountain', as God Almighty, for El Shaddai was destined to mature into that god whom much of the world would worship. But in these fateful days, when the little group of Hebrews camped while waiting for the signal to march westward, El Shaddai was the god of no one but themselves. They were not even certain that he

had continued as the god of those other Hebrews who had moved on to the distant land of Egypt. But of one thing Zadok was sure. El Shaddai personally determined the destiny of this group, for of all the peoples available to Him in the teeming area between the Euphrates and the Nile, He had chosen these Hebrews as His predilected people, and they lived within His embrace, enjoying security that others did not know." (P. 177-178).

As long as we remain trapped in time, however, we can only indirectly appreciate the eternities. We must seek learning, even by study and also by faith, in order to "make our lives sublime, and departing, leave behind us footprints on the sands of time." (Henry Wadsworth Longfellow, "A Psalm of Life"). There is always the threat, however, that those footprints might be washed away by the incessant action of the temporal and spatial waves beating upon our shores. As the seasons unfold, we are always faced with the challenge of a tide in our affairs "which, taken at the flood, leads on to fortune. Omitted, (our voyages will instead be) bound in shallows and in miseries." (Shakespeare, "Julius Caesar," Brutus, Act 4, Scene 2).

Our faith to see all the way to heaven anchors us to the infinite, and confirms that we have wandered from a more exalted sphere. It verifies that the Architect of our fate, "Alpha and Omega, the beginning and the ending, the Lord, who is, and who was and who is to come, the Almighty" God, envisioned our destiny while we were yet in the pre-earth existence. (J.S.T. Revelation 1:8). It is our faith that "He's got the whole world in His hands" and, that fortunately, there is a Divine Design.

That blueprint molds us in mortality, and establishes us in eternity, where heavenly smiles will envelop us in the glory of God. When we pass through the veil, our faith will introduce us to a ladder that has been set up on the earth, the top of which will reach all the way to heaven. (See Genesis 28:12). As we ascend that ladder, rung by rung, we will see lightnings and mountains smoking, and hear thunderings and the voices of trumpets speaking to us, in a language that is inarticulate, indescribable, and yet irrefutable. (See Exodus 20:18, & Hebrews 12:19)

With spiritual sensitivity and preparation, we will find that the time for action has

arrived. The veil will become almost transparent. As our powers expand, we will experience the glittering facets of the life of the Spirit. We will use the careful preparation and training we have received as a springboard. We will be capable of disciplined, controlled procedure and will be receptive to flashes of insight.

"Our faith will set us free to be creative, and set us creative to become more free." ("My Religion and Me," Lesson #9). The Gospel will boost the octane rating of our faith, that we might see all the way to heaven. A shift in our momentum will be stimulated, with the capacity to propel us into the Presence of God.

"I wish I could remember the days before my birth, and if I knew the Father before I came to earth," mused the poet. "In quiet moments when I'm all alone, I close my eyes and try to see my heavenly home. Although I can't remember and cannot clearly see, I listen to the Spirit and so I must believe. But still, I wonder, and I hope to find the answer to the question that is on my mind. Where is Heaven? Is it very far? I would like to know if it's beyond the brightest star." (Janice Kapp Perry).

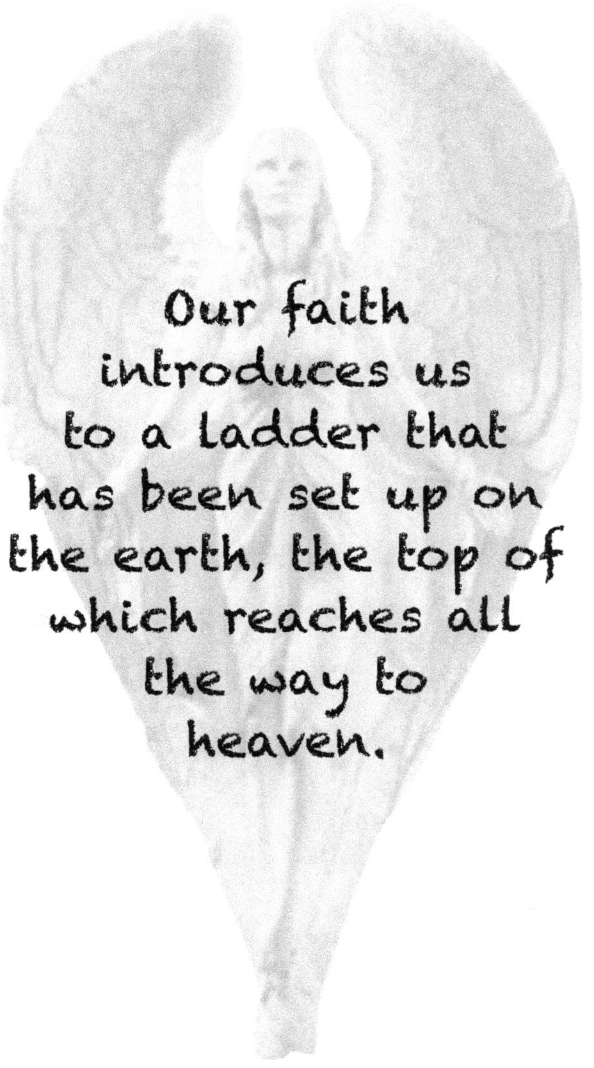

Our faith introduces us to a ladder that has been set up on the earth, the top of which reaches all the way to heaven.

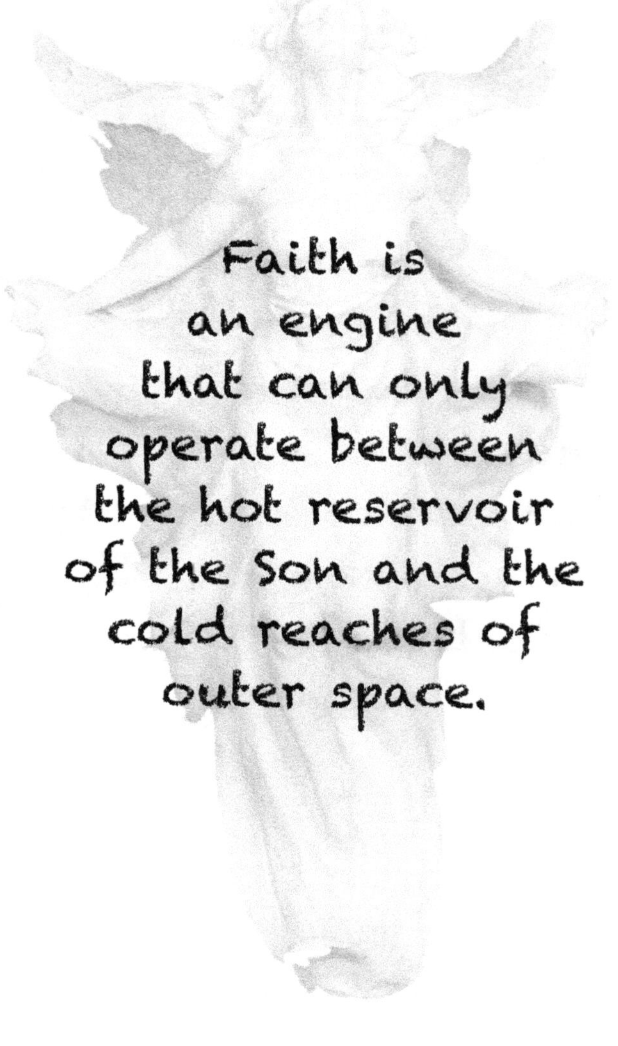

Faith is
an engine
that can only
operate between
the hot reservoir
of the Son and the
cold reaches of
outer space.

Chapter Thirty Five
The divine center of faith.

"See that all ... things are done in wisdom and order; for it is not requisite that a man should run faster than he has strength. And again, it is expedient that he should be diligent, that thereby he might win the prize; therefore, all things must be done in order." (Mosiah 4:27).

When faith is our divine center, we are decided, dogged, and resolute. We are ardent, eager, enthusiastic, fervent, heroic, passionate, and zealous. When we are overzealous, however, we lose sight of our objectives even as we redouble our efforts. We become obsessive, feverish, and fanatical in our exertions to acquire elusive telestial treasures that are difficult to obtain and almost impossible to retain.

Because our unstable environment is subject to the unrelenting Law of Entropy, careless inattention allows the chaotic conditions of the world to reign unchecked. On the other hand, it takes effort to shift our focus to the powers of heaven. In

fact, if we do not concentrate on the structure and stability of the divine center of faith, and expend energy to cultivate its sense of permanency, everything tends to collapse into disarray. The world is coming apart at the seams, before our eyes. Our experience teaches us that a sculpture in marble may endure for millennia despite incessant attacks by the elements, or it may be destroyed in seconds by the careless brush of a coat sleeve. A thousand year old redwood tree may be weathered and sculpted by the storms of centuries, and yet endure, or it may burn to the ground in hours. The city of Babylon took shape over hundreds of years, and its hanging gardens were one of the seven wonders of the ancient world, but today it is only a dusty and distant memory. Even the organization of words into coherent sentences or paragraphs, though etched in stone or sizzling in cyberspace, can be erased with one blow of a hammer, a single keystroke, or the swipe of a magnet over a computer disk.

Entropy relates to the behavioral sciences, as well. It explains why great friendship can be devastated by an inconsiderate action or word, and how a life of moderation can be forfeit by one thoughtless act of indulgence, in a moment of weakness. One glass of liquor can ruin a lifestyle of temperance, and yielding to the passion of the moment can unravel a persistent pattern of chaste behavior. Testimony that has grown over years can be destroyed through carelessness or inattention.

For the ordered structure of The Plan of Salvation to succeed, entropy must exist as the basis of a matrix of mayhem, within which the fiery darts of the adversary trace an incendiary trail of disorder. This tendency toward turmoil lies in wait to disrupt the poise of those who are pressing forward with determination toward the divine center of faith, that they might ultimately be blessed with exaltation in the Celestial Kingdom.

The fragmentation of order creates the friction that is necessary to fuel the fires that warm the world. One could say that entropy actually makes life possible. In fact, "except it were for these conditions, mercy could not take effect except it should destroy the work of justice. Now the work of justice could not be destroyed; if so,

God would cease to be God." (Alma 42:13).

Some people believe that, because of the far-reaching effects of entropy, the creation of highly structured living organisms is in violation of the second law of thermodynamics. But the fact is, that every time a plant stores solar energy in chlorophyll in the form of chemical potential energy, every time an updraft of warm air lifts a bird in flight, every time you make your bed and clean up your room, if you gather iron ore from the ground and convert it into steel to build a skyscraper, or every time, by the indomitable divine center of faith, you resolve to try a little harder to be a little better, the earth upon which we live, and move, and have our being is filling the measure of its creation. Faith becomes an engine that operates between the hot reservoir of the Son and the cold reaches of outer space. The universe itself becomes "a machine for the making of Gods." (Henri Bergson, "Two Sources of Religion and Morality," 1932).

Even though they may seem to be at odds, inasmuch as they come from opposite ends of the physical and behavioral spectra, entropy and eternal progression must ultimately be in balance with each other. In fact, it has been ordained in heaven that there needs to be a healthy juxtaposition of contrasting forces if The Plan of Salvation is to succeed. (See 2 Nephi 2:11).

Everything within our world is evidence of the Savior's perfect control over the balance of these forces. The Law of Eternal Progression rules supreme, but it is as much defined by its opposites in the physical universe as it is by itself in the eternal world. (See Moses 1:39). The presence of Satan in the Garden of Eden attests to that fact. (See Moses 4:6).

Because the adversary operates more by subtraction than by addition, his temptations tear down both individuals and relationships, as they work to destroy the divine center of our faith. Temptation prospers with deceit, and its bedfellow is deception. (See Exodus 12:23). We all remember the Hindu scripture, the Bhagavad-Gita, wherein Vishnu expresses the ultimate expression of opposition: "Now I am become Death, the

destroyer of worlds."

Perhaps this is why, in our natural state, we are enemies of God, and have been from the beginning. (See Mosiah 3:19). When we use our agency to violate eternal law, our transgression may be traced to imbalance. The effects of sin are inevitable and inescapable, but for the intercession of faith in the Atonement. The Maker and Fashioner of the universe must intervene by engaging laws that restore equilibrium, or all is lost. In the heavens, there is a "better and an enduring substance." (Hebrews 10:34). In other words, in the principles of The Plan of Salvation we have the means to promote the divine center of our faith and to draw upon the powers of heaven to counteract the influence of the adversary.

This may also help us to understand the magnitude of the Savior's injunction: "Be ye, therefore, perfect, even as your Father in Heaven is perfect." (Matthew 5:48). His awesome invitation may have been as much a statement of fact as it was an expression of hopeful anticipation. The Plan of Salvation has within its arsenal enough firepower for us to overcome instability in our lives, so that we may generate the untiring divine center of faith. The Plan prepares us to move onward and upward along a steady course of eternal progress without being encumbered by the wobbly constraints of uncertainty that always lie in wait to mislead those of faltering faith.

The gate may be strait, and the way narrow, but those who accept Christ as their Guide will find it within their capacity to travel a path of progression by threading the eye of the needle and walking a fine line past the seemingly unalterable, unavoidable, and unstoppable demands of disproportion. "Broad is the gate, and wide the way that leadeth to the deaths, and many there are that go in thereat," because they stubbornly pursue a wavering course of unpredictability. (D&C 132:25). There is no variability or uncertainty in the divine center of faith. We simply trust the Savior, when He reassures us: "I am the way, the truth, and the life: no man cometh unto the Father, but by me." (John 14:6).

If we elect to ignore the celestial laws that are the only homing beacons powerful enough to penetrate the mists of darkness in our telestial world, we tacitly choose an alternative course leading to destruction on the rocky shoreline of vanity. Such an inhospitable milieu is the natural consequence of the operation of the immutable laws of physics.

The introduction of the universal influence of the Light of Christ promotes harmony among the myriad elements of The Plan. This sets the stage for our exercise of moral agency and dictates the implementation of other equally important and co-existing eternal laws that are designed to guide us through the minefields of mortality. The principles that make up The Plan are the ultimate expression of unity in purpose. Mercy, in particular, exists to mitigate the otherwise inevitable consequences that follow lives that are out of balance, and Atonement makes possible our journey of progress in both time and eternity.

Only by incorporating into our lives the principle of the unwavering divine center of faith can imbalance be recognized, addressed, reversed, and erased with finality. While obedience nurtures the development of personality traits that are consistent with the symmetry of heaven, sin is harmful because it destroys our ability to develop the steadiness that is a defining characteristic of the Celestial Kingdom. Disorder takes the disobedient further and further from the influence of the Spirit, whose purpose it is to guide us away from the precipice of destruction, and to lead us to that secure sanctuary where the stability of higher laws abides.

Damnation is the result of activities that block the channels through which this spiritual power freely flows. It is the halt in our progression that is damning, because we have lost our orientation toward our divine center. We are as a ship without a rudder. (See Ephesians 4:14). Arguably, sin is at one and the same time the best and the worst example of instability in our lives. To counteract its consequences, our days have been "prolonged, according to the will of God, that (we) might repent while in the flesh; wherefore, (our) state (becomes) a state of probation, and (our) time (is) lengthened, according to the commandments which the Lord God gave unto

the children of men. For he gave commandment that all men must repent; for he showed unto all men that they were lost," because of the unsteadiness of many of the posterity of Adam and Eve, after the introduction of their parents onto the topsy-turvy telestial turf that has been widely described as the lone and dreary world. (2

Nephi 2:21). "But Adam and Eve wept for having come out of the garden, their first abode. And Adam said to Eve, Look at thine eyes, and at mine, which afore beheld angels in heaven. But now we do not see as we did: our eyes have become flesh." (The Pseudepigraphic First Book of Adam and Eve, see Moses 5:4).

Ever since the Fall, Satan has enjoyed a free pass to mingle among the children of men. This flushes him with excitement, because he knows how difficult it is for us to resist our natural tendency toward volatility. Those who love Satan more than they love God unavoidably exhibit the behavioral manifestations of that misplaced adoration. Those who zoom along in the fast lane of life can too easily blow right past the celestial signposts that would have alerted them to move over into the exit lane leading to heaven's gate. Preoccupied with telestial trivia, they find themselves on doctrinal detours that lead to the crooked highway of self-destructive and self-defeating behavior. As a result, they become "carnal, sensual, and devilish." (Moses 5:13). Without the intervention of higher laws, their unbalanced lives point them toward unavoidable destruction.

The Lord has confidence, though, in our ability to conduct our lives in accordance with the blueprint He has provided, and to bring our behavior into congruence with celestial law. Therefore, He has "called upon men by the Holy Ghost everywhere, and command(s) them that they should repent." Through the Atonement, repentance becomes a celestial bridge that transports the righteous beyond the vicissitudes of life to the stability of the paradise of God that lies beyond the turmoil. (See Revelation 2:7). If we will believe in the Son of God, and repent of our sins, we will be saved from the effects of slow destruction in the lone and dreary world. (See Moses 5:15 & 2 Nephi 2).

Those whose lives are out of balance are like a train wreck in slow motion, but

if they follow the counsel of Jehovah, they can fast-forward the newsreel footage of that disaster to bring their character into a state of equilibrium with the Law of Eternal Progression. They can rely upon the steadfast divine center of faith to become "heirs of God, and joint heirs with Christ." (Romans 8:17).

When we abide Celestial Law, the Spirit opens our eyes, "so as to see and understand the things of God, even those things which were from the beginning before the world was." (D&C 76:12-13). From the point of view of the divine center of faith, we see things more clearly, as if we have somehow escaped our mortal clay with its confining limitations that distort our eternal perspective and negatively twist our attention to worldliness. We are endowed with the ability to discern the difference between the unstable nature that denies the power of the Atonement, and the steady faith that generates trust in the Lord.

Too often, however, we are "like unto a man beholding his natural face in a glass." (James 1:23). We satisfy ourselves with a brief glimpse of salvation, but the reflection we see gives us only a hint of the mighty oak that is waiting to burst forth from a humble acorn. If we only see through a glass darkly, we will be unable to behold the potential of our position. We may never break free of our enslavement to the upsetting laws that define the consequences of destructive behavior. We may resign ourselves to lives that are nothing more than overnight stays in second-class hotels with one star ratings in the shady part of town.

Allowing the Savior to liberate us from captivity through the ordinances of the Gospel permits us to see things as they really are, and to enjoy a lucidity that comes more from the heart than from the head. We trust our divine center. We better understand how an inclination toward faith can generate enlightenment. As it does so, we remember Helen Keller, who wrote, not from the shaky vantage point of severe physical impairment and limited sensory stimulation, but rather with the steadiness born of a balanced relationship with the Spirit: "I believe that no good shall be lost, and that all man has willed or hoped or dreamed of good shall exist forever. I believe in the immortality of the soul because I have within me immortal longings. I believe that the state we enter after death is wrought of our

own motives, thoughts, and deeds. I believe that my home there will be beautiful with colour, music, and speech of flowers and faces I love. Without this faith, there would be little meaning in my life. I should be a mere pillar of darkness in the dark. Observers in the full enjoyment of their bodily senses pity me, but it is because they do not see the golden chamber in my life where I dwell delighted; for dark as my path may seem to them, I carry a magic light in my heart. Faith, the spiritual strong searchlight, illuminates the way, and although sinister doubts lurk in the shadow, I walk unafraid towards the Enchanted Wood where the foliage is always green, where joy abides, where nightingales nest and sing, and where life and death are one in the presence of the Lord." ("Midstream").

If we have not yet found that "golden chamber" in our lives; if that secret garden to which we must flee in order to be far from the tumult of the madding crowd remains undiscovered, we may take solace in the possibility that temporal asymmetry that leads us from order to disorder can work to our advantage. In fact, it suits the purposes of our Heavenly Father, Who knows that, if we are to enjoy the balance that is represented by the divine center of faith, opposition must be present in order to successfully execute The Plan.

Opposition serves a useful purpose as long as we are jarred out of our collective complacency by a swift kick in the created confusion. Remember that when God organized the world, with all its permutations and combinations, He pronounced it "good." (Genesis 1:31). Dissimilarity upsets the potential stagnation of the status quo, makes us think, gets our juices flowing, constructively puts our agency to work, and prods us to purposefully expend our energy as we go about constructing the divine center of our faith. Brigham Young taught: "The mainspring of all action is the principle of improvement." ("Discourses of Brigham Young," p. 87). This requires us to nurture a sense of balance in our lives, that we might better deal with the vagaries of our temporal world, and that we might enjoy stability and order in the midst of seeming pandemonium.

Progress becomes our recompense for perseverance, salvation is our reward for

surmounting obstacles, and our hope of eternal life is the blessing we receive for being true to our covenants. When we endure in righteousness, something mystical and metaphysical happens. (See J.S.T. 2 Peter 2:13). In wondering awe, we are figuratively "born again." With our feet firmly planted on Gospel sod, we avoid vertigo as we undertake our summit attempt toward the dizzying heights of the divine center of faith. (Mosiah 5:7).

As we resolve to reach that pinnacle of spirituality, Spencer W. Kimball's counsel rings with urgency: "So much depends upon our willingness to make up our minds, collectively and individually, that present levels of performance are not acceptable, either to ourselves or to the Lord. In saying that, I am not calling for flashy, temporary differences in our performance levels, but for a quiet resolve to lengthen our stride." ("Church News," 3/22/1975). He knew that by venturing out of our comfort zones, and moving forward with purpose, we would enlarge the foundation of our spiritual equilibrium, to make room for the divine center of faith.

The exertion caused by lengthening our stride may cause discomfort, as it stretches the limits of our stability in a violent confrontation that tears at the fabric of the natural world. But in doing so, by exposing the divine center that lies beneath telestial trappings, we find new spiritual strength. The wounds that we bear, that witness the intensity of our struggles, become the portals God uses to let in light. That infusion of the spiritual element quickens us to double our stride and go the second mile. We burst free of the shackles that had limited the expression of our potential. We receive "a gift of independence that removes the veil of insensitivity from our destiny." (Richard L. Gunn, "A Search for Sensitivity and Spirit," p. 197). This liberation is exhilarating, because it is accompanied by the recognition of soul-expanding opportunities. It kindles within us the realization that we are spiritual beings having mortal experiences.

Even though we may mindlessly toil with blood, sweat, and tears, sacrificing even those things that are near and dear to us in order to obtain temporal treasures, at the end of the day the unevenness of the world can only deliver physical destruction.

The divine center of faith endows us with greater confidence in the power of heaven to countermand these discouraging inequities. Its steady orientation endows us with poise under the most trying provocations, and because of our multidimensional view of existence, we are ready for the curves that life is sure to throw our way.

But if we foster a one-dimensional view of the world that focuses on its cares, if we yield to the things of the moment, and if we lose our balance in the process, we will fall into mischief. (See Proverbs 28:14).

If we are to successfully complete the curriculum of the Gospel and graduate with honors from the school of hard knocks, we must "give our language to exhortation continually." (D&C 23:7). We must not be "weary in well doing." (Galatians 6:9). Because the world goes to such great lengths to throw us off center, even those who have been born to a newness of life require constant and repetitive encouragement to steady their course and to continue their pre-determined path of progression. (See Romans 6:4).

Those who have embraced the divine center of faith will follow the yellow brick road with all their heart, might, mind, and strength until they reach the Emerald City of Oz. (See D&C 4:2). Though we be as scarecrows who need a brain, tin men who want a heart, or cowardly lions who desperately need courage, we will warm our hands before the fire of faith. The rich spoils of memory, the precious things of today, and our faith in the future will confirm that "the best of life is hidden from our eyes somewhere behind the hills of time." (Sir William Mulock).

Brigham Young declared that we are "in progress either to an endless advancement in eternal perfections, or back to dissolution. There is no period in all the eternities wherein organized existence will become stationary, that it cannot advance in knowledge, wisdom, power, and glory." (J.D., 1:349). It is not enough, merely to have discovered the divine center of faith. If we allow ourselves to coast to a standstill after we have made our way to Christ, we risk toppling over. We must maintain forward momentum if we are to keep our balance and walk in His footsteps.

We need to be careful when we pause to rest or to catch our breath, as we must from time to time, that we do not choose shaky or indefensible ground to do so. Worse yet, if we fall asleep at our posts, complacency will be quietly waiting in the shadows to sweep us over the precipice of destruction. Nurturing the divine center of faith stimulates affirmative, constructive, and purposeful action. It is a simple formula: The Lord strengthens and blesses us as we repent and keep the commandments, but not necessarily with telestial toys that might lead us on detours leading away from the steadiness of the strait and narrow way. Nor will He coddle us by smoothing out the bumps in the road or by straightening out its curves, to make our journey easier, lest we be pacified into a false sense of carnal security. The constant G-force exerted by the uphill path of progress very subtly counteracts and is in opposition to the downhill course that too often tempts us to stop pedaling. If we do so, it is all too easy to coast toward disastrous consequences in a free-fall from faith.

The formula that defines the equations of the divine center of faith is at the very heart of eternal laws that have the power to carry us beyond the conventional boundaries of our every day world. Our five natural senses enable us to relate to our physical surroundings. They act as biological barometers that provide us with reliable measurements to gauge the pervasive effects of imbalance that almost imperceptibly grind us down.

But gradually, it is subtle extrasensory perceptions that bring us to the realization that our faith supersedes physical laws governing the temporal universe. When we are "born of God," our experience is in harmony with Gospel principles. We become more comfortable with the perspective that confirms that the expansive laws of the eternal world trump the hobbling limitations and restrictive theorems of the physical world. (See 2 Corinthians 5:17). When we are in accord with the eternities, we are liberated from incarceration to the inexorable immutability of the laws governing the physical world that relate to destruction. This independence is incalculable, indescribable, and inexplicable, and yet it is undeniable. (See 1 John 5:3). It is not maturational, but is generational, as we become new creatures in Christ. (See Mosiah 27:26). As the process unfolds and we learn to appreciate the balance in our lives, God subtly

fortifies us with opportunities to be anxiously engaged in good causes. He endows us with the capacity to ponder and pray, so that, on our own initiative, we can generate the power to avoid the conceptual cul-de-sacs and religious roundabouts that would slow or stop our progress and cause us to stumble. He helps us to work out our salvation with fear and trembling. He nudges us to move out of our comfort zones into the stimulating environment of service, the cathartic setting of sacrifice, and even onto the painful paths that lead to our own personal Gethsemanes. Socrates said: "Know thyself," and Cicero admonished, "Control thyself," but Jesus encouraged us to give ourselves completely and without reservation, that we might enjoy a state of harmony with Him and synchronization with the eternities. (See Acts 6:4). In effect, He encouraged His disciples to discover for themselves the divine center of faith.

He exhorts us to drink copiously and unceasingly from the fountain of truth in order to slake our thirst for principles that gyroscopically orient us toward heaven. He understands the difference between celestial sureties that are represented by eternal progression, and telestial tendencies that are clothed in the trappings of physical laws. "Great and marvelous are the works of the Lord," Jacob exclaimed. "How unsearchable are the depths of the mysteries of him; and it is impossible that man should find out all his ways. And no man knoweth of his ways, save it be revealed unto him." (Jacob 4:8).

The wise counsel of our prophets of God provides balance in a world that has become befuddled by weights and measures that have been contaminated by the adversary's evidence tampering. The counsel of our inspired leaders creates desire in our hearts to negotiate the difficult road leading to Gethsemane, past the Garden Tomb, and onward toward celestial realms. It validates the promises made by our Father that our experiences have been tailored to meet our individual need for personal growth and development, and that our struggle toward perfection justifies the holy consecration of our efforts and our sacrifices.

But only if the drama is played out within the context of the Everlasting Covenant, according to the rules established by The Plan of Salvation, can we achieve the balance necessary to receive the anticipated blessings. Only then, can we find the

faith to make the journey back to our divine center. There has never been, nor will there ever be, another way. Only the bedrock of the Gospel can provide the footing that is required to restore the foundation of stability we need in an uncertain world.

Only the Author of Salvation can steady the helm as we navigate treacherous waters, and give us the poise and composure of truly balanced lives. (See Hebrews 5:9).

Today, we must be especially vigilant, and avoid enticements that rivet our attention on telestial trinkets, consume our energies in unproductive endeavors, and demand our devotion to gods of wood and stone. Sitting with the engine idling while wasting time in telestial traffic jams can damage our desire to move forward, by mutating our innate tendency to seek the light. Our destination is well-defined, and if we only half-heartedly seek the divine center of faith, it is because instability has caused us to confuse knowledge for intelligence, and to think that when we are learned we are wise. We must never fail to understand that to be learned is good, but only if we will hearken unto the counsels of God. (See 2 Nephi 9:28). When taken to heart, the principles related to balance kindle faith in our divine center and protect our testimonies. They can even save our souls.

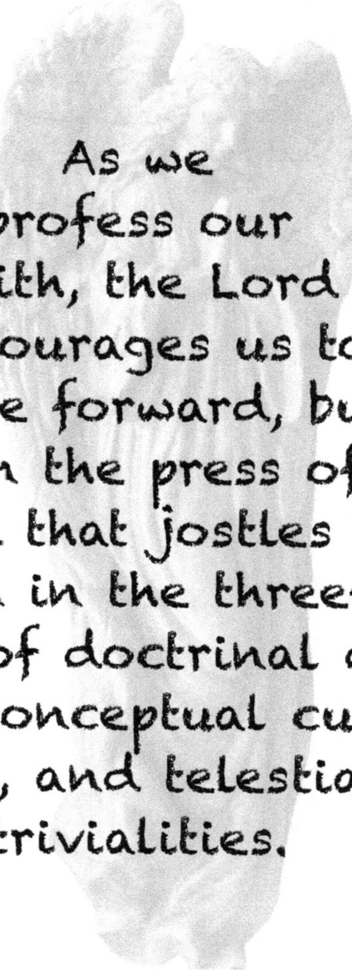

As we profess our faith, the Lord encourages us to move forward, but not in the press of a crowd that jostles for position in the three-ring circus of doctrinal dead ends, conceptual cul de sacs, and telestial trivialities.

Chapter Thirty Six
The faith to be perfect in Christ.

"He commandeth all men that they must (exercise) perfect faith in the Holy One of Israel, or they cannot be saved in the kingdom of God."
(2 Nephi 9:23).

In the Star Trek Universe, (Star Trek: The Next Generation, or T.N.G.) the Q Continuum is a hyper-dimensional plane of existence inhabited by a race known as the Q. The Q have powers similar to those possessed by the seers of whom Ammon spoke, who "know of things which are past, and also of things which are to come, and by them shall all things be revealed, or, rather, shall secret things be made manifest, and hidden things shall come to light, and things which are not known shall be made known by them, and also things shall be made known by them which otherwise could not be known." (Mosiah 8:17).

We do not possess the powers of the Q; in fact, in one episode Q tells Grand Nagus Zek: "I worship stupidity, and you're my new god." With our poor lenses, we cannot discern what they see, but when our eyes are single to faith to be perfect in Christ, our bodies "shall be full of light." (3 Nephi 13:22). Joseph Smith confirmed the reality of that promise when he said of the revelatory process with which he was becoming increasingly familiar: "My whole body was full of light, and I could see even out at the ends of my fingers and toes." (N.B. Lundwall, "The Vision," p. 11).

This may be why the angel Moroni hovered in the air during his visits to Joseph Smith in his chamber and why his hands and his feet were naked, for he could "see" with every part of his body. Every child of God potentially possesses this gift of the Q, and it is exciting to think that it only waits to be revealed. "If your eye be single to my glory," the Lord has promised, "your whole bodies shall be filled with light, and there shall be no darkness in you; and that body which is filled with" the faith to be perfect in Christ "comprehendeth all things." (D&C 88:67).

Orson Pratt was familiar with neither the Q nor their Continuum, but he did appreciate the ramifications of the truth that celestial beings have the ability to perceive with all parts of their bodies. "The spirit," he said, "is inherently capable of experiencing the sensations of light. I think we could then see in different directions at once. Instead of looking in one particular direction, we could then look all around us at the same instant." (J.D., 2:238-248).

The Q are on a higher plane of existence, and thus they are not subject to the same laws of physics as are those of us who dwell in normal time and space. Their fictional influence may be roughly analogous to that of the Lord, of Whom the Psalmist wrote: "Fire goeth before (Him), and burneth up his enemies round about. His lightnings enlightened the world. The earth saw, and trembled. The hills melted like wax at the presence of the Lord of the whole earth." (Psalms 97:3-5).

As Mormon observed: "The dust of the earth moveth hither and thither, to the dividing asunder, at the command of our great and everlasting God. Yea, behold,

at his voice do the hills and the mountains tremble and quake. And by the power of his voice they are broken up, and become smooth, yea, even like unto a valley. Yea, by the power of his voice doth the whole earth shake. Yea, by the power of his voice, do the foundations rock, even to the very center. Yea, and if he say unto the earth – Move – it is moved. Yea, if he say unto the earth – Thou shalt go back, that it lengthen out the day for many hours – it is done." (Helaman 12:8-14). Thus, is manifest the awful power of His Presence. It may be not so much that God commands the earth to tremble, but rather that it is His proximal influence alone that causes its foundation to shake to its very core.

The Q can manipulate time, space, matter, and energy. Of course, they are the products of our imagination, for we know that in the beginning, it was "the Gods (and not the Q, who) organized and formed the heavens and the earth" by defining the boundaries of both the temporal universe and the eternal world. (Abraham 4:1). By the power of faith, it was They Who set the conditions "by which the worlds were framed, (and) all things in heaven, on the earth, or under the earth. (These only) exist by reason of faith as it existed in (the mind of the Gods). Had it not been for this principle of faith, the worlds would never have been framed, neither would man have been formed of the dust. It is this principle by which Jehovah works, and through which He exercises power over all temporal as well as eternal things." (Joseph Smith, "Lectures on Faith," #1). Perhaps the writers of T.N.G. inherited their creative imagination from the doctrinal teachings of the Prophet himself!

The Q are omnipotent, omniscient, and for all practical purposes omnipresent. W.W. Phelps prefigured the Q, when he described how we can stand on the threshold of eternity when we have faith to be perfect in Christ: "If you could hie to Kolob in the twinkling of an eye, and then continue onward with that same speed to fly, do you think that you could ever, through all eternity, find out the generation where Gods began to be? Or see the grand beginning where space did not extend? Or view the last creation where Gods and matter end?

Methinks the Spirit whispers 'No man has found pure space, nor seen the outside curtains, where nothing has a place.' The works of God continue, and worlds and

lives abound. Improvement and progression have one eternal round. There is no end to matter; there is no end to space; there is no end to spirit; there is no end to race. There is no end to virtue; there is no end to might; there is no end to wisdom; there is no end to light. There is no end to union; there is no end to youth; there is no end to priesthood; there is no end to truth. There is no end to glory; there is no end to love; there is no end to being; there is no death above." ("If You Could Hie to Kolob"). Just think of it! William W. Phelps wrote these words 131 years before the airing of the first episode of T.N.G. in 1987.

The Q are invulnerable and immortal. They are as God, Who was described by John the Revelator as One Whose "head and hairs were white like wool, as white as snow; and his eyes were as a flame of fire; and his feet like unto fine brass, as if they burned in a furnace; and his voice as the sound of many waters." (Revelation 1:14-15). Joseph Smith saw the "true and living God" in vision. (Alma 11:25). Under His feet "was a paved work of pure gold, in color like amber. ...His countenance shone above the brightness of the sun." (D&C 110:2).

The Q have the ability to perceive events in the past, present, and future. So too does the Lord our "God, even Jesus Christ, the Great I Am, Alpha and Omega, the beginning and the end, the same which looked upon the wide expanse of eternity, and all the seraphic hosts of heaven, before the world was made; The same which knoweth all things, for all things are present before (His) eyes; (He is) the same which spake and the world was made, and all things came" by Him." (D&C 38:1-3).

The laws of physics, our imagination of the Q Continuum, and theology itself, suggest that there are no privileged frames of reference. The galaxies are imbedded in time and attached to space, but the fabric of the universe is flexible; it is pliable and is constantly expanding. The universe is warped temporally and spatially and expands somewhat like a balloon. If we ask where and when the creation took place, the answer is everywhere and forever. This may explain why the Lord told Moses: "As one earth shall pass away, and the heavens thereof, even so shall another come, and there is no end to my works." (Moses 1:38). As Paul taught long ago: "By

him, were all things created that are in heaven, and that are in earth, visible and invisible, whether they be thrones, or dominions, or principalities, or powers: all things were created" by God. (Colossians 1:16).

The Q can manipulate the fabric of existence itself, weaving it into patterns that are unimaginably intricate. Carl Sagan suggested an idea that may have been familiar to the inhabitants of the Q Continuum, but which to our minds is "strange, haunting, evocative, and one of the most exquisite conjectures in science or religion. It is entirely undemonstrated, and it may never be proven. But it stirs the blood. There is, we are told, an infinite hierarchy of universes, so that an elementary particle, such as an electron in our universe, would, if penetrated, reveal itself to be an entire closed system. Within it, organized into the local equivalent of galaxies and smaller structures, are an immense number of other, much tinier elementary particles, which are themselves universes at the next level, and so on forever, an infinite downward regression, universes within universes, endlessly.

And upward as well. Our familiar universe of galaxies and stars, planets and people, would be a single elementary particle in the next universe up, the first step of another infinite progression. This is the only idea I know that surpasses the endless number of infinitely old cycling universes in Hindu cosmology.

What would those other universes be like? To enter them, we would somehow have to penetrate a higher physical dimension. Poised at the edge of forever, we would jump off" into life's ultimate incredible journey. ("Cosmos," p. 262-267).

Perhaps the title sequence of "Star Trek - The Next Generation" episodes should be amended to declare: "Time and space and even existence itself are the final frontiers. These are the voyages of the Starship Enterprise. Its continuing mission: To explore strange new worlds, to seek out new life and new civilizations, to boldly go where no one has gone before, and to do so through the faith to be perfect in Christ."

The Q Continuum is unconstrained, as is God, by linear time and the three familiar dimensions of space. When Enterprise crew members are plucked from the ship by Q, we are reminded how, in similar fashion, John was taken from his temporal and spatial surroundings. He was brought into the "depths of eternity" in the "hereafter,"

somehow at the same time both "here" and "after," which, although vague in syntax, is about as specific a reference as we can find that refers to a higher dimension that may be analogous to both the Q Continuum and eternity.

Thus, John saw in vision a door that "was opened in heaven: and the first voice which (he) heard was as it were of a trumpet talking with (him); which said, Come up hither, and I will shew thee things which must be hereafter." (Revelation 4:1).

He saw and heard "lightnings and thunderings and voices" from the unseen world. (Revelation 4:5). To Joseph Smith, the voice of the Great Jehovah struck a similar chord, "as the sound of the rushing of great waters." (D&C 110:3).

For the Q, and for God, the arrow of time moves in two directions. In contrast, our stable temporal frame of reference allows us to live within a timeline that only moves in one direction, into the future. For mere mortals, time is embedded within the tapestry of familiar three-dimensional space. It reassures us that the sun will come up tomorrow, and that there will be 24 hours in each day. If there were no veil that insulated us from God's unrestrained, unencumbered, unreserved, and uninhibited temporal reality, life would be too confusing for most people. This is corroborated by the chaotic consequences relating to the manipulation of time by the Q, in T.N.G..

In several episodes, Enterprise crewmembers are bewildered by sensory overload that follows the mischievous manipulation of time by the Q. In the real world, when our mortal clay no longer encloses us, as the veil collapses, it will no longer insulate us from eternity. Time will be no more, and we will transition into the native and natural environment of our former home, flushed with the faith to be perfect in Christ. (See D&C 84:100).

Thus it is, that we will discover that we were really never at home in time. This explains why, when we are on the earth, "we find ourselves impatiently wishing to hasten its passage or to hold back the dawn. We can do neither, of course. Whereas the bird is at home in the air, we are clearly not at home in time, because we belong to eternity. As much as any one thing, time whispers to us that we are strangers here. If it were natural to us, why is it that we have so many clocks, and wear wristwatches? Without the veil, we would lose the precious insulation so necessary for our mortal probation and maturation. Our brief mortal walk in a darkening world would lose its meaning, for one would scarcely carry the flashlight of faith at noonday and in the presence of the Light of the world." (Neal A. Maxwell, "B.Y.U. Speeches of The Year," 1979).

The Q can move about in time and space, by the power of their will. Brigham Young said of that ability: "I long for the time that a point of the finger, or motion of the hand, will express every idea without utterance." When we, like the Q, are "full of the light of eternity, then the eye will not be the only medium through which we see, nor will the brain be the only means by which we understand. When the whole body is full of the Holy Ghost, we will be able to see behind ourselves with as much ease, without turning our heads, as we can see before us. I shall yet see the time that I can converse with this people, and not speak to them. We are at present low, weak, and groveling in the dark." (J.D., 1:70-71). Our faith to be perfect in Christ confirms that "the best of life is hidden from our eyes somewhere behind the hills of time." (Sir William Mulock).

The Q can look down upon our affairs from a perspective that is to us both foreign and indescribable. Brigham Young taught that when we die we go into the spiritual world. "Do the spirits go beyond the boundaries of this organized earth?" He asked. "No, they do not. They can see us, but we cannot see them, unless our eyes have been opened" with the faith to be perfect in Christ. ("The Contributor," 10:9, quoted in N.B. Lundwall, "The Vision," p. 55-56, see "Discourses of Brigham Young," p. 376).

This only makes sense if beings from the unseen world exist in a parallel spatial

dimension, which may be analogous to being in a room with a one-way mirror. They, like the Q, can witness the every-day world on a whim, but to those of us trapped in the here-and-now, trying to see what lies beyond the mirror's reflective surface is fruitless. Many Star Trek episodes suggest that because we are bound by the laws and conditions of our temporal and spatial reality, all we can hope to gain by venturing into the unstable curriculum of theoretical physics is a confirmation of the validity of that which we already know, which is nothing more than our reflection in the mirror of experience. "Now we see through a glass, darkly; but then face to face: now I know in part; but then shall I know even as also I am known." (1 Corinthians 13:12).

The Q can move from one point in the universe to another by overriding the constraints that are imposed by the laws of physics. As God does, they routinely break the cosmic speed limit of 299,792,458 meters per second. At the speed of light, it would take at least 10 or 15 billion years for Q to traverse the known universe. So in the real world, physically plodding along at light speed from one point to another seems unlikely for the Gods, because those of us who have gotten the Lord's attention know that His intercession can be instantaneous.

Samuel was once moved to exclaim: "In my distress I called upon the Lord, and cried to my God: and he did (immediately) hear my voice out of his temple, and my cry did enter into his ears. Then, the earth shook and trembled; the foundations of heaven moved and shook," as God instantly responded to His prophet's entreaty by manipulating the laws of physics in a powerful manifestation from His other-worldly and higher dimensional reality. (2 Samuel 22:7-8).

In the Star Trek Universe, and in theoretical physics, a tachyon is a particle that travels faster than light. In the real world, no experimental evidence for the existence of such particles has been found, but special relativity implies that faster-than-light particles may exist. If so, they could be used by the Q, as well as by our Heavenly Father, to communicate and to travel both forward and backward in time. Only time will tell (no pun intended) if God uses tachyons to move about the

universe. Perhaps that knowledge will be revealed only when we have faith to be perfect in Christ.

In the real-world universe described by particle physics, photons (the basic unit of electromagnetic energy) travel at the speed of light, in compliance with the Cosmic Speed Limit. Einstein's Theory of Relativity, however, describes a time dilation that occurs as the speed of particles increases, relative to our frame of reference. At the speed at which photons travel, (the speed of light), the passage of time comes to a virtual standstill. From the perspective of a proton, time does not exist.

Think of our Heavenly Father, visiting earth after spending "time" on a planet orbiting Alpha Centauri, a star in our galaxy that is 4 light years away. We meet Him, and say: "Welcome to Earth. How was Your 4 year trip?" "What trip?" He answers, continuing: "I left it only an instant ago!" He (like the Q in T.N.G.) made a quantum leap from Alpha Centauri to earth. What was four years to us was zero seconds to Him. If we expand that 4 year trip to our concept of "forever," we realize that "forever" from our perspective is still zero seconds for God, (as well as for the Q).

The quantum theory of probability of velocity and position adds more intrigue to the persona of both God and the Q. As God moves about the universe at the speed of light, the uncertainty principle of quantum physics tells us that we lose all knowledge of His position! The probability of us knowing His location plummets to 0.0%. When that is the case, His position could, with equal probability, be anywhere in the universe, at any moment in "time."

This may be theoretical, but in the real world, we get a glimpse of God's perspective every time we witness a sunrise or sunset, for we are seeing photons of light that were created at the dawn of time. These photons stimulate our retinas without having passed through "time" since the moment of their creation. We learn about their beginning both in Genesis and in the complex mathematics that describe The Big Bang. In either case, because His light is quantized, time stands still for God (as well as for photons and the Q). When He said: "Let there be light" at the moment

of the Big Bang, it was always and forever! But from our perspective, it occurred 13.7 billion years ago.

This principle is equally valid when we pray to Heavenly Father. As James declared:

"The effectual fervent prayer of a righteous man availeth much." (James 5:16). The reason this is so is because God hears us instantly every time we cry out to Him, and He has the power to immediately respond to our needs, wherever and whenever He or we may be. Existing in another dimension that is analogous to the Q Continuum gives God the ability to hear all of our petitions simultaneously, without the inherent communications lag of three-dimensional time and space, time warps notwithstanding. The omnipresent example of the Q gives God more plausible credibility.

Additional insight into God's dominions comes from accounts of the creation of the earth. Brigham Young used very unusual language when referring to the earth as it was at the time of the Fall, and how it will be when it receives its paradisiacal glory. He said: "When the earth was framed and brought into existence and man was placed upon it, it was near the throne of our Father in Heaven. And when man fell ... the earth fell into space, and took up its abode in this planetary system, and the sun became our light. This is the glory the earth came from, and when it is again glorified, it will return unto the presence of the Father, and it will dwell there." (J.D., 17:143).

His description of the earth falling into space and then leaving it to return to the presence of the Father suggests adjacent spatial dimensions that are also inferred by the characteristics of the Q Continuum. The actions of is inhabitants mimic the prophecy of Micah, who wrote: "The Lord cometh forth out of his place, and will come down, and tread upon the high places of the earth." (Micah 1:3). At the very least, the various plot twists and turns in T.N.G. episodes involving the Q make more sense when viewed against the backdrop of revelatory religious experience.

Although, with a bit of whimsy, Q confides to Captain Picard that he is "the closest

thing in this universe that I have to a friend," more characteristically the Q jealously guard their powers. ("Deja Q"). Heavenly Father does not operate this way. More generous than the Q, He promises to use His influence to sanctify our world, and to transform it so that it "will be made like unto crystal and (become) a Urim and Thummim to the inhabitants who dwell thereon, (that) all things pertaining to an inferior kingdom, or all kingdoms of a lower order, (might be) made manifest to those" who have faith to be perfect in Christ, "who dwell on it." (D&C 130:9).

The Q are not confined by the narrow limitations of corruptible flesh. Orson Pratt spoke of our expanded faculties when our spirits have been freed from their incarceration to our mortal bodies, and of our ability to consider many different ideas at the same time, instead of focusing our attention and following only one train of thought or course of reasoning. "Suppose He should give us a sixth sense, a seventh, an eighth, a ninth, or a fiftieth?" he asked. "All these different senses would convey to us new ideas, as much so as the senses of tasting, smelling, or seeing communicate different ideas from that of hearing. Do we suppose our five senses converse with all the elements of nature? No!"

The behavior of the Q nourishes the mind-expanding idea proposed by Orson Pratt that "knowledge will rush in from all quarters; it will come in like the light which flows from the sun, penetrating every part, informing the spirit, and giving understanding concerning ten thousand things at the same time; and the mind will be capable of receiving and retaining all. Not one object at a time, but a vast multitude of objects will rush before our vision, and will be present before us, filling us in a moment with the knowledge of worlds more numerous than the sands of the seashore. Will we be able to bear it? Yes, our minds will be strengthened in proportion to the amount of information imparted. It is this tabernacle in its present condition that prevents us from a more enlarged understanding.

When we burst beyond the confines of our mortal clay, we shall look not in one direction, but in every direction. This will be calculated to give us new ideas concerning the creations of God, and information and knowledge we never can

know as long as we dwell in this mortal tabernacle. We shall have other sources of gaining knowledge besides these inlets called senses. We will be endowed, after we leave this tabernacle," with faith to be perfect in Christ, and "with powers and faculties which we now have no knowledge of, by which we may learn what is round about us." ("The Increased Powers of Faculties of Mind in a Future State," Excerpted from "Temples of The Most High," p. 299-312, see J.D., 2:238-248).

The Q mimic God, for they do not grow old. When we move into eternity, or into the Q Continuum in the imaginary world, time will lose all significance, and "See you later," will cease to be in our vocabulary. Time, that we too frequently viewed as a predator that stalked us all our lives, will then be fondly remembered as a companion that accompanied us on our journey through mortality, reminding us to cherish every moment. We will find that mortality itself was only one of innumerable layers of reality, and that our perspective was faulty as long as we believed it to be unique. We may be shocked to learn that time was not our natural dimension. We will come to understand why it was that we were never entirely comfortable in our mortal circumstances, and that we were "strangers and pilgrims on the earth." (Hebrews 11:13). This will, in turn, explain our innate thrust always toward the future, and beyond the horizon.

We will even find that growing "old" was strictly and uniquely a quality of mortality, and a brilliant mechanism designed by Heavenly Father to give us an opportunity to gauge the approach of our reunion with Him in a higher-dimensional world. We will discover that because we lived in only one dimly lighted corner of reality, it was difficult for us to really appreciate our potential, that we would one day "flourish in immortal youth, unhurt amidst the war of elements, the wreck of matter, and the crash of worlds." (Joseph Addison, "Cato," Act 5, Scene 1).

In the present, from our very narrow perspective, frozen in time as it were, death seems so distant, and its consequences so remote. Too often, we grow complacent in our indifference to the subtle message that is stitched into the fabric of time, and we fail to understand its urgency, as well as its impact on eternal consequences.

Inhabitants of the Continuum are consummate multi-taskers, for, without realizing it, they "take their Q" from God. Hugh Nibley reasoned: "As to taking a calm and deliberate look at more than one thing at a time, that is a gift denied us at present. I cannot imagine what such a view of the world would be like, but it would be more real and correct than the one we have now. Once we can see the possibilities that lie in being able to see more than one thing at a time, the universe takes on new dimensions and God (never mind the Q) takes over." ("Zeal Without Knowledge," "Nibley on The Timely and Timeless," p. 263-264). We should then be as the Brother of Jared, who, when overshadowed by the Spirit, could look at once upon past, present, and future generations. "They all came before him, and there was not a soul that he did not behold." (Mormon 8:35).

"The heavens they are many," explained the Lord, "and they cannot be numbered unto man; but they are numbed unto me, for they are mine." (Moses 1:36). Plainly, we are dealing with two orders of mind, that of mortals, and that of God (and the Q Continuum, in the minds of T.N.G.'s writers). "For my thoughts are not your thoughts, neither are your ways my ways, saith the Lord. For as the heavens are higher than the earth, so are ... my thoughts than your thoughts." (Isaiah 55:8-9).

The Q roam the wide expanse of the universe, much as Federation starships do, for whom space is the final frontier. One particularly bold explorer, perhaps an ancestor of Jean Luc Picard, declared that he intended to go not only "farther than any man has been before me, but as far as I think it is possible for a man to go." ("Captain James Cook: Explorer, Navigator, and Pioneer," B.B.C.). The Q might brazenly recite an even more audacious couplet, more familiar to those with a clear understanding of the principles and doctrines of The Plan of Salvation: "As Q is, God once was; as God is, Q may become."

In the short term, we are reminded of Neil Armstrong's recitation: "That is one small step for a man, and one giant leap for mankind." We venture forth toward eternity, remembering the words of Hamlet, who characterized death as "that undiscovered country from whose bourne no traveler returns." (William Shakespeare).

Or, in Lehi's phraseology: "Awake! And arise from the dust, and hear the words of a trembling parent, whose limbs ye must soon lay down in the cold and silent grave, from whence no traveler can return. A few more days, and I go the way of all the earth." (2 Nephi 1:4).

The time will come when all of us must generate the faith to be perfect in Christ. When we have done so, we will enter into the spatial reality of God's Rest. We will have gained a perfect knowledge of the divinity of the work, and by our actions will no longer suffer from fear, doubt, apprehension of danger, the religious turmoil of the world, or from the vagaries of men. These self-limiting conditions blind us to a larger view of life. His Rest, however, is born of a settled conviction of the truth in our minds, with an assurance that our obedience to celestial principles will bring His reality within our view and our reach.

The invitation to follow Him is prefaced by the action verb "to come." (See Luke 18:22). If we accept His challenge to come to Him, we must ask ourselves just where, and when, and how far will that journey take us? After we have kept our second estate, and have had glory added upon our heads, what shall we be like? What will it mean to be clothed with immortality and eternal life? Will we then more closely resemble the image and likeness of our Father in Heaven? If so, are we now gods and goddesses in embryo? Are we the acorns of mighty oaks? Is our genetic code divine? Is it our destiny to mature to the stature of our Heavenly Parents? The evolutionary progress of the Q, that is envisioned by the writers of T.N.G., would suggest resoundingly affirmative answers.

In the final episode of Star Trek: The Next Generation, Captain Picard joins the crew's regular poker game, expressing regret that he had not done so earlier. When the stakes are outlined, he says: "The sky's the limit," suggesting that the final frontier has borders yet to be probed, opportunities yet to be taken, and adventures yet to be experienced.

Perhaps it was the bold daring of Captain James T. Kirk, captain of the Enterprise (NCC-1701), that first caught the attention of the Q. Captain Kirk's full middle name was Tiberius. Tiberius Julius Caesar Augustus was born 2,275 years before Kirk, and

was one of ancient Rome's greatest generals and tacticians. Thus, Tiberius was an appropriate name for the youngest graduate of Starfleet Academy to be given his own command.

Hopefully, the Q think, as did Hamlet: "What a piece of work is a man, how noble in reason, how infinite in faculties, in form and moving how express and admirable, in action how like an angel, in apprehension how like a god! The beauty of the world, the paragon of animals." (Shakespeare, "Hamlet," Act 2, Scene 2).

However, this description comes back to bite Q, in the episode entitled "Deja Q." As long as their gifts remained intact, the Q had little apparent need for redemption. But in this episode, after he has lost his powers, Q is told by Captain Picard: "For all your protestations of friendship, your real reason for being here is protection!" Q responds: "You're very smart, Jean-Luc. But I know human beings. They're all sopping over with compassion and forgiveness. They can't wait to absolve almost any offense. It's an inherent weakness in the breed." To which Picard says: "On the contrary, it is a strength."

Truth be told, the Q show a unique interest in the development of humanity. As Q told Captain Picard: "The hall is rented, the orchestra engaged. It's now time to see if you can dance." ("Q Who"). But the Lord goes a step further than the Q, promising to give His children at least a portion of His own powers, but only after they have prepared themselves, submitted to instruction, and better understand their responsibilities. God suggests patience, that His children may develop faith to be perfect in Christ; that they "may be prepared, and that (they) may be taught more perfectly, and have experience, and know more perfectly concerning their duty, and the things which (are required) at their hands. And this cannot be brought to pass until (His children have been) endowed with power from on high." (D&C 105:9-11). Hence, we need the faith to be perfect in Christ.

Perhaps that is the key that explains the difference between God and the Q. We have a familial relationship with our Father in Heaven. We are His children, and He is the Father of our spirits. Our faith binds us to Him in an unbreakable connection.

It blesses us with the settled conviction that He takes notice of sparrows falling from trees, and heads of hair that have thinned with time, but it also confirms that He orchestrates to our benefit the explosion of supernovas in distant galaxies. (See Helaman 14:5). The power of our faith gives us confidence that He does not play dice with His creations; He does not leave things to chance. We have faith that our loving Parent is actively involved in our growth and development. He always attends our parent / teacher conferences, and He intervenes in our behalf when we are sent to detention for infraction of the rules of conduct. If Q had a benevolent side, it would more closely resemble Heavenly Father's nature.

Heavenly Father never misses our extracurricular activities, and He has a season pass to witness every game we will ever play. He is forever in the bleachers, seated in the middle of our cheering section. He is in the "wave" when it passes through the stands. He sits up late in the evening, and leaves the porch light burning, waiting for us to return to the safety of our hearth and home. He has our phone number on speed dial and regularly uses text messaging and voice mail to keep in touch with us. He is at the top of our "friends-and-family" list.

Even if we try to ignore Him, we cannot make Him go away. He has told us that His prime directive is to bring to pass our immortality and eternal life. (See Moses 1:39). To accomplish that purpose, He explained: "I will go before your face. I will be on your right hand and on your left, and my Spirit shall be in your hearts, and mine angels round about you, to bear you up." (D&C 84:88). "For he hath said, I will never leave thee, nor forsake thee." (Hebrews 13:5).

The power of our faith allows His divine tutorial training to become an eagerly anticipated process with which we are increasingly comfortable. As we receive guidance, we learn to "hear truth spoken with clarity and freshness; uncolored and untranslated, it speaks from within ourselves in a language original but inarticulate, heard only with the soul." (Hugh B. Brown). Our faith tutors us to become fluent in the language of heaven, so much so that it becomes our native tongue.

Consistent with the doctrine of eternal progression, but falling short of the bonds that exist between ourselves and God, the Q believe that we are compelled to explore the very nature of existence itself. In the episode "All Good Things," Q mentions that Captain Picard was destined to consider possibilities that he had never before imagined, implying that there are states that are natural to the Q but foreign to mortal experience. The Q become the catalyst for motivation that, as a fire in the bones, stirs the Enterprise crew. Christopher Columbus recounted the impetus for his own voyage of discovery by simply declaring: "The Holy Spirit gave me fire for the deed." That element of inspiration is glaringly absent in the experience of the Q, but it is also implicitly absent in the conduct of the Enterprise crew.

When we have the faith to be perfect in Christ, our hearts burn within us as God gives us "knowledge by His Holy Spirit, yea, by the unspeakable gift of the Holy Ghost." (D&C 121:26 & 28). Thus, did Jeremiah describe his feelings: "His word was in mine heart as a burning fire shut up in my bones, and I was weary with forbearing, and I could not stay." (Jeremiah 20:9). The Spirit also worked on Belshazzar's troubled conscience to the extent that his "countenance was changed, and his thoughts troubled him, so that the joints of his loins were loosed, and his knees smote one against another." (Daniel 5:6). Joseph Smith was moved to declare of his revelatory experiences: "The still small voice ... whispereth through and pierceth all things, and often times it maketh my bones to quake while it maketh manifest." (D&C 85:6).

As the process unfolds and our unsteady steps become a godly walk as we are disciplined by faith to be perfect in Christ, we recognize wisdom in the words of Hans Christian Anderson, who observed: "Our lives are fairy tales waiting to be written by the finger of God." A number of the chapters in our stories have already been typeset, and we don't know how many remain to be written. But we do know this: Although we cannot start over and make a new beginning, we can begin now and make a new ending. We believe "that which is of God is light; and he that receiveth light, and continueth in God, receiveth more light; and that light groweth

brighter and brighter until the perfect day." (D&C 50:24). In marvelous ways, as we gain spiritual maturity, "by doing our duty, our faith" to be perfect in Christ "increases until it becomes perfect knowledge." (Heber J. Grant, C.R., 4/1934).

As the seasons of our lives unfold, we learn that "life is a sheet of paper white, where each of us may write a line or two, and then comes night. Greatly begin! If thou hast time for but a line, make that sublime. Not failure, but low aim, is crime." (James Russell Lowell). In one episode of Star Trek, Q is stripped of his powers and becomes human. ("Deja Q"). He is "the king who would be man," lamenting: "I have no powers! Q, the ordinary! Q, the miserable! Q, the desperate!" The difference between the Q and our Alpha progenitors is that Adam and Eve had a longitudinal view and perspective on life that is foreign to the Q, who vision remains myopic, their omniscience notwithstanding.

Our first parents cherished the opportunity to become mortal. "Blessed be the name of God," Adam declared, "for because of my transgression my eyes are opened, and in this life I shall have joy, and again in the flesh I shall see God. And Eve, his wife, heard all these things and was glad, saying: Were it not for our transgression we never should have had seed, and never should have known good and evil, and the joy of our redemption, and the eternal life which God giveth unto all the obedient." (Moses 5:10-11). Due to an apparent genetic anomaly, the Q seem to be incapable of experiencing the adrenalin rush we mere mortals experience when we yield ourselves to the power of the Atonement and have faith to be perfect in Christ.

In the episode where he lost his powers, Q confided to Captain Picard: "Truthfully, Jean-Luc, I've been entirely preoccupied by a most frightening experience of my own. A couple of hours ago, I realized that my body was no longer functioning properly. I felt weak. I could no longer stand. The life was oozing out of me. I lost consciousness." The captain replied: "Q. You fell asleep!" To which, Q exclaimed: "Oh, how terrifying. How can you stand it day after day?" To which the captain said: "You'll get used to it." "What other dangers await me?" protested Q. "I'm not prepared for this. I need guidance!"

When his powers are later restored, he exclaims: "I'm forgiven! My brothers and sisters of the Continuum have taken me back. I'm immortal again! Omnipotent again!" Q does not realize that mortality is a welcome interlude in the grand scheme of things, and that all that is necessary may be accomplished before the book is closed on this chapter in our lives and we move on toward perfection. They cannot understand that death is as much a part of life as is birth, and that Adam's transgression was integral to the execution of The Plan, inasmuch as it gave us the opportunity to be born into this world, to live, and to die. As a matter of fact, living in eternity before our births, as we previewed the big picture, we actually shouted for joy. (See Job 38:7).

When it was finally our time to come to earth, others smiled at our birth, while we cried. When it is our time to leave, our loved ones will cry at our departure, while we will smile. Only then will we see death for what it really is, "a mere comma, and not an exclamation point." (Neal A. Maxwell, "Ensign," 5/1983). It is "not extinguishing the light, but rather putting out the lamp because the dawn has come." (Ramindraneth Tagore).

The Q generally observe the principle of free will (but only if it suits their fancy). Among the shortcomings of the Continuum is the fact that it has not embraced the concept of opposition and does not realize that progress is dependent upon the power to choose in an atmosphere free of external pressures that might hamper its expression. The stagnation within the Continuum that is suggested by the plot lines of several episodes reflects its ignorance of this eternal principle. However, Q did warn Captain Picard: "You judge yourselves against the pitiful adversaries you've encountered so far – the Romulans and the Klingons. They're nothing compared to what's waiting. Picard, you are about to move into areas of the galaxy containing wonders more incredible than you can possibly imagine, and terrors to freeze your soul." He continued: "It's not safe out here! It's wondrous, with treasures to satiate desires both subtle and gross. But it's not for the timid." ("Q Who?").

The Q anticipate with prescience the actions of the crew. In the real world, the

Lord's interest in our behavior is equally remarkable, for He already "knoweth the thoughts of man." (Psalms 94:11). But the difference between His interest and the curiosity of the Q is that the latter look at mortality as the whole of existence, and at pain, sorrow, failure, and short life as misfortunes. The vantage point of the Q

Continuum may be expansive, but it lacks the capacity to develop the responsibility that is provided by the mortal expression of God's perspective that rests with the exercise of the principles of The Plan of Salvation. It lacks the capacity to instill within humanity the faith to be perfect in Christ. And that helps to explain how Lorenzo Snow was inspired to conceive the couplet: "As man is, God once was. As God is, man may become."

The Q are always lingering in the background, watching with interest the activities of the Enterprise crew, even though they characterized 24th Century earth as a "dreary place" and "mind-numbingly dull." For our part, we intuitively wish we "could remember the days before our birth, and if we knew the Father before we came to earth. In quiet moments when we're all alone, we close our eyes and try to see our Heavenly home. Although we can't remember and cannot clearly see, we listen to the Spirit and so we must believe. But still we wonder, and we hope to find the answer to the question that is on our minds. Where is Heaven? Is it very far? We would like to know if it's beyond the brightest star." (Janice Kapp Perry).

The Q allow Starship personnel to experience both the positive and negative consequences relating to their exploration of the universe. As Q told Jean Luc Picard after a particularly traumatic encounter with the Borg: "If you can't take a little bloody nose, maybe you ought to go back home and crawl under your bed. It's not safe out here." ("Q Who"). In a similar vein, Joseph Smith exhorted the Saints: "Brethren, shall we not go on in so great a cause? Go forward and not backward. Courage, brethren; and on, on to the victory." (D&C 128:22).

The Q recognize the fact that "the galaxy can be a dangerous place when you're on your own." ("Q-Less"). Although the Q have the power to alter circumstances, God has the power to transform lives. The Q would shoot the arrow blindly, and then move the target so we would think we had scored a bulls-eye. Heavenly Father, on

the other hand, teaches us to aim with precision, so that we might hit the bulls-eye 100% of the time. The Q would say "You miss 100% of the shot you don't take." God encourages us to practice as often as possible, and to learn with practice to make 100% of the shots we do take.

Unconsciously, the Q may reflect the reality that God is too frequently unappreciated. In "Tapestry," Q says: "I gave you something most mortals never experience – a second chance at life. And now all you do is complain." At least superficially, God and the Q are alike. But the teachings of the Gospel ask us to cultivate gratitude, for when we do so, wonderful things happen. Good eclipses evil. Love overpowers jealousy, hate, and prejudice. Light drives away darkness. Knowledge banishes ignorance. Humility overwhelms pride. Courtesy checks rudeness. Appreciation overcomes thanklessness. Abundance overshadows poverty. Well-being replaces weakness. Simplicity supplants perplexity. Harmony displaces discord. Faith manages fear. Hope casts out despair. Charity subdues selfishness. Joy deposes unhappiness, sadness, dejection, and misery. Confidence is substituted for timidity. Certainty dethrones bewilderment. Assurance dislodges discouragement and even despair. These are qualities that are foreign to the Q. They cannot comprehend that "those who live in thanksgiving daily have a way of opening their eyes to the wonders and beauties of this world as though seeing them for the first time.

Those who live in thanksgiving daily are usually among the happiest people on earth." (Joseph Wirthlin, "B.Y.U. Devotional," 10/31/2000). Elder Wirthlin was simply describing the exhilaration when we have faith to be perfect in Christ.

In a perverse way, the Q Continuum validates Lehi's aphorism that "there must needs be opposition in all things. (2 Nephi 9:24). In "Deathwish," Q exclaims of the inhabitants of the Continuum: "Of course there's no suffering! They're all happy! Happy people! Look at them!" To which Q3 responds: "They don't dare feel sad. If only they could! It would be progress."

Spencer W. Kimball taught the Saints: "If pain and sorrow and punishment immediately followed the doing of evil, no soul would repeat a misdeed. If joy and peace and

rewards were instantaneously given the doer of good, there could be no evil. All would do good and not because of the rightness of doing good. There would be no test of strength, no development of character, no growth of powers, no agency, but only Satanic controls. Should all prayers be immediately answered according to our selfish desires and our limited understanding, then there would be little or no suffering, sorrow, disappointment or even death, and if these were not there would also be an absence of joy, success, resurrection, eternal life and Godhood." ("B.Y.U. Devotional," 12/6/1955).

The unity within the Q Continuum is only a faint shadow of that which is found within the Godhead. Solidarity is a quality of the Continuum, but it pales in comparison to the unity of the faithful, who are as one; who are able to "stand independent above all other creatures beneath the celestial world." (D&C 78:14).

The Gospel provides the means for us to enjoy "the unity of the Spirit in the bond of peace." (Ephesians 4:3) Harmony in conviction and of purpose is one of the characteristics of the Lord's true Church, which is "of one accord, (and) of one mind." (Philippians 2:2). It is a miracle that within its organizations, all things are "done by common consent … by much prayer and faith." (D&C 26:2).

Church members echo Paul, who declared: "We, being many, are one body in Christ." (Romans 12:5). No wonder that when the Lord told His disciples they must "be one," He also warned them, "and if ye are not one ye are not mine." (D&C 38:27). This unity of which the scriptures speak describes the collective efforts of the Saints to have faith to be perfect in Christ.

The strengths of the Continuum stands in stark contrast to the endless possibilities related to the safety, sanctuary, security, solidarity, stability, and steadiness that accompany our participation in the curriculum of mortality's learning laboratory. Q3 observed: "When I was a respected philosopher, I argued that the purity of the Continuum was a great thing. I extolled the road, and the endless possibilities; only they're not so endless after all. At the beginning of the 'New Age,' there was the exhilaration of discovery, the animated discussions of new things learned. But after

a time, all had been learned. All had been shared. Listen to their dialogues now. They haven't spoken for millennia. There's nothing left to say!" He continued: "Your mission is to explore. Imagine you'd explored everything, that there's nothing left. Would you want to live forever? For us, the disease is immortality." ("Deathwish").

In this soliloquy, Q3 described the living hell of a immortal vacuum in the absence of morality; the stagnation of life without feeling, and the lethargy of existence without purpose. The intellectual prowess of those inhabiting his Continuum would be equivalent to the dull, monotonous, and mind-numbing hum of a super-computer that for all its binary capabilities, permutations, and combinations is incapable of experiencing the quality of morality that can be found in any three-year-old in Sunbeam class. There has been instilled within each child of God the innate urge to capture the faith to be perfect in Christ.

The elevation of the Q to a pedestal of omniscience and omnipotence, in the absence of the moral anchor of faith, selectively eliminates the very things that guarantee eternal happiness. In the episode entitled "The Q and The Grey," Q mused to Captain Janeway: "I've been single for billions of years. The fact is, it's left me empty. I want someone to love me for myself. I guess what I'm saying is, I want a relationship. I just thought if you and I had a child, it would give me the kind of stability and security that I've been missing." Janeway's instantaneous explosion of human emotion effectively silenced his request.

Before making his proposal, Q would have done better to consider The Plan that encompasses God's ordained core curriculum leading to family exaltation. The Plan diagrams our safe passage through the minefields of mortality, identifies renewable resources to assist us during our journey, maps out the success strategies we must follow if we are to live abundantly, and measures our progress along the pathway to perfection. Its elements remind us of the World Wide Web that requires only computer literacy, an I.P. address with a network, and relevant hardware and software. But it is so much more than that, because its principles lead us to have faith to be perfect in Christ.

It has the potential to order our chaotic world, to bless us with clarity rather than confusion, and to teach us to be fluent in the language of the Spirit, even if we have beforehand been functionally illiterate in its workings, that all might be mesmerized by the power of the Word. In simple binary terms, The Plan provides an access code that leads to happiness. It is far superior to the heartless curriculum of the Continuum, that seems to have never heard the admonition of Jacob: Because the Q "are learned they think they are wise, and they hearken not unto the counsel of God, for they set it aside, supposing they know of themselves, wherefore, their wisdom is foolishness and it profiteth them not." (2 Nephi 9:28).

The "gift" of immortality enjoyed by the Q is eerily reminiscent of the counterfeit plan of the adversary. As Jacob taught: "Death hath passed upon all men, to fulfil the merciful plan of the great Creator," Whose omniscience trumps that of the Q. (2 Nephi 9:6). In an episode entitled "Deathwish," Q mused: "If only I could let you see what my life is like. You're all mortals! Oh, how I envy you! The thing I want more than any other is to die!"

The Q lack both learning skills and literacy when it comes to understanding the grammar of the Gospel. They may be immortal, but at a terrible cost. They have forgotten that the three most important days of our lives are the day we are born, they day we find out why, and the day we die. They have become inured to the "resonance with realities on the other side of the veil" to which Neal Maxwell alluded, that has all to do with our faith to be perfect in Christ. ("B.Y.U. Devotional," 11/1979).

Sometimes, the Q exert their powers in behalf of the crew, albeit their efforts are misguided. In one episode, Q actually bestowed his omnipotence upon Commander William Riker. ("Hide and Q"). Nevertheless, God is more benevolent than the Q, and the Latter-day work testifies to the truth of His declaration: "I have conferred upon you the keys and power of the priesthood, wherein I restore all things, and make known unto you all things." (D&C 132:45).

About 20 years prior to the birth of the Savior, Nephi was told that because he had been perfect in his faith in Christ, he would be blessed forever, and he would be made mighty in word and in deed, in faith and in works; yea, even that all things would be done unto him according to the word of God, Who said: "I give unto you power, that whatsoever ye shall seal on earth shall be sealed in heaven; and whatsoever ye shall loose on earth shall be loosed in heaven; and thus shall ye have power among this people." (Helaman 10:5 & 7). This is a far cry from the moral vacuity found in the Q Continuum.

The existence of the Continuum is evidence enough that The Plan of Salvation is necessary for our species to prosper. Q says: "When I look at a gas nebula, all I see is a cloud of dust, but seeing the universe through your eyes allowed me to experience wonder." ("Q-Less"). We have been given a glimpse of God moving in His majesty and power. He "hath given a law unto all things, by which they move in their times and their seasons; And their courses are fixed, even the courses of the heavens and the earth, which comprehend the earth and all the planets. And they give light to each other in their times and in their seasons, in their minutes, in their hours, in their days, in their weeks, in their months, in their years — all these are one year with God, but not with man. The earth rolls upon her wings, and the sun giveth his light by day, and the moon giveth her light by night, and the stars also give their light, as they roll upon their wings in their glory, in the midst of the power of God. Unto what shall I liken these kingdoms, that ye may understand? Behold, all these are kingdoms." and anyone with the faith to be perfect in Christ, "who hath seen any or the least of these hath seen" burning bushes, water that has turned into wine, barrels of meal that never waste, and lepers that are healed. (D&C 88:42-47, see Exodus 3:2, John 2:7-10, 1 Kings 17:14, & Mark 1:40-42).

When the Q choose to remain hidden from view, they leave the crew of the Enterprise with tantalizing clues relating to their presence. But their motives are flawed and their actions lack meekness and humility In contrast, God sends love letters to His children, with His return address prominently displayed on the envelopes, so His missives are instantly identified, carefully considered, and eagerly engaged. "Earth

is crammed with heaven, and every common bush with fire of God. But only those who see," only those with faith to be perfect in Christ, "take off their shoes. The rest stand around picking blackberries." (Elizabeth Barrett Browning).

Ralph Waldo Emerson was one who was particularly sensitive to these love letters. On one occasion, he wrote: "Those who have seen the rising moon break out of the clouds at midnight, have been present like archangels at the creation of light, and of the world." At another time, he observed: "If the stars should appear but one night in a thousand years, how would we believe and adore, and preserve for many generations, the remembrance of the city of God which had been shown." ("Nature," Chapter 1).

From the quiet perspective of his home in Concord, Massachusetts, Emerson mused: "I see the spectacle of morning from the hilltop over against my house, from daybreak to sunrise, with emotions which an angel might share. The long, slender bars of cloud float like fishes in a sea of crimson light. From the earth, as a shore, I look out into that silent sea. I seem to partake its rapid transformations; the active enchantment reaches my dust, and I dilate and conspire with the morning wind. How does nature deify us with a few and cheap elements! Give me health and a day, and I will make the pomp of emperors ridiculous."

Perhaps the evolutionary development of the Q was only achieved at a terrible cost, with the sacred mutating into the secular, profound truths undergoing a homogenization into easily digestible forms, ennobling principles being sacrificed, and expediency replacing undeviating commitment to a moral standard of behavior. With sensitivity and insight, and perhaps thinking of the Q, William Wordsworth reminisced: "Heaven lies about us in its infancy! Shades of the prison house begin to close upon the growing boy. But he beholds the light, and whence it flows; he sees it in his joy. The youth, who daily farther from the east must travel, still is nature's priest, and by the vision splendid, is on his way attended. At length, he" and the inhabitants of the Q Continuum, "perceives it die away, and fade into the light of common day." ("Ode: Intimations of Immortality").

The Q cannot access the energy that is necessary to squeeze through the strait and narrow gate. They seem to have never experienced the way before them opening up into broad boulevards that ae paved with cobblestones that glint of gold, who parkways are lined with fig trees that are laden with fruit, flooded by therapeutic sunlight, and caressed by soothing breezes. For those with the faith to be perfect in Christ, there will be no billboards to clamor for their attention, no strident voices secularizing the sacred, no neon lights with hypnotizing messages, and no cacophony of voices assaulting them from every direction, that would all conspire to suppress the serenity of a Gospel-centered lifestyle.

The Q can never enjoy the fellowship of those who are "no more strangers and foreigners, but fellow citizens with the Saints, and of the household of God." (Ephesians 2:19). Only those who have enjoyed the intense emotional bond of that relationship can appreciate the exhortation by Henry V to his troops, on the eve of the Battle of Agincourt, on 25 October, 1415 (St. Crispin's Day). "We few, we happy few, we band of brothers!" he exclaimed. "For he today that sheds his blood with me shall be my brother; be he ne'er so vile. This day shall gentle his condition, and those in England now a-bed shall think themselves accursed they were not here, and hold their manhoods cheap whiles any speaks that fought with us upon Saint Crispin's day." (Shakespeare, "Henry V," Act 4, Scene 3).

Those who have the faith to be perfect in Christ burst free of the most glaring perceptual limitations of the Q, and become as the aviator who exulted: "Oh, I have slipped the surly bonds of earth and danced the skies on laughter-silvered wings. Sunward I've climbed, and joined the tumbling mirth of sun-split clouds, and done a hundred things you have not dreamed of; Wheeled and soared and swung high in the sunlit silence. Hovering there, I've chased the shouting wind along, and flung my eager craft through footless halls of air. Up, up the long, delirious, burning blue I've topped the windswept heights with easy grace, where never lark, or even eagle flew. And, while with silent, lifting mind I've trod the high untrespassed sanctity of space, I put out my hand, and touched the face of God." (John G. Magee, Jr., "High Flight").

For all their powers, the Q cannot appreciate the tremendous worth of our innate desire to reach for the stars, or to have faith to be perfect in Christ. "Humans are such common-place little creatures," said Q. "They roam the galaxy searching for something they know not what." ("Deja Q"). The Q cannot appreciate that our inquisitiveness is heaven-sent. It reveals something of our Father, that our lives might be intertwined with His, as we learn to pattern our behavior after His example. His priesthood, after all, "administereth the Gospel and holdeth the key of the mysteries of the kingdom, even the key of the knowledge of God. Therefore, in the ordinances thereof, the power of godliness is manifest. And without the ordinance thereof, and the authority of the priesthood, the power of godliness is not manifest unto men in the flesh. For without this no man can see the face of God, even the Father, and live." (D&C 84:19-22).

The interaction of the Q with humans subtly and unconsciously reinforces the fact that woven into every Gospel principle is an independent witness that needs no external warrant. It is for this reason that Joseph Smith was able to confidently declare: "I teach people correct principles and let them govern themselves." (Cited by John Taylor, "Millennial Star," 13:22, p. 339). As impish as Q is with Jean Luc Picard, his pranks always leave the Captain, who has a moral backbone, better for having had the experience.

In many ways, the development of the Q is similar to that of mortals living within the dynamic matrix of The Plan of Salvation. Even the Continuum might grudgingly admit that our heritage "is richer than that of Pericles, for it includes the Greek flowering that followed him; richer than Leonardo's, for it includes him and the Italian Renaissance; richer than Voltaire's, for it embraces all the French Enlightenment and its ecumenical dissemination. If progress is real, it is because we are born on a higher level of that pedestal which the accumulation of knowledge and art raises as the ground and support of our being. The heritage rises, and we rise in proportion as we receive it. Consider education as the transmission of our mental, moral, technical, and aesthetic heritage as fully as possible to as many as possible, for the enlargement of our understanding, control, embellishment, and enjoyment of life." (Will Durant, "The Lessons of History," p. 100-

102). When we examine the Q, it is apparent that they have progressed in a similar fashion, but somewhere along the way, they lost their innocence and their joix de vivre, and they never found the faith to be perfect in Christ, that would have led them Home.

At first blush, the existence of the Q would seem to obviate the need for God. The analytical Continuum would agree with Steven Hawking, who said: "The quantum theory of gravity has opened up a new possibility, in which there is no boundary to space-time and no need to specify behavior at the boundary. There are no singularities at which the laws of science break down, and there is no edge of space-time at which one has to appeal to God or to some new law to set new boundary conditions for space-time. One could say: 'The boundary condition of the universe is that it has no boundary.' The universe is completely self-contained and not affected by anything outside itself. It is neither created nor destroyed. It just IS." (Steven Hawking, "A Brief History of Time: From the Big Bang to Black Holes," p. 136).

On closer inspection, however, the existence of the Q Continuum demands the existence of God. Their very presence betrays our need for the irreducible qualities of faith, light, and truth that establish the elusive baseline described by Hawking. For it is our acquisition of faith-based knowledge that inevitably leads to testimony. Every time the Q manifest themselves, they broadcast the news that God is alive and well and is not living in hiding under an assumed name in Argentina, as some would suppose. He continues to enjoy tremendous popularity. His book is still on the best-seller list. In fact, it has enjoyed such success that He has authored several additional volumes, and it is rumored that He is even now in negotiation for new book deals.

How foolish are the Q, when they get a whiff of fame, or fancy themselves as powers that be, while all the time, the character and reputation of God remains above the fray, unblemished and untarnished. He, alone, is the One Who deserves theatrical encores, and it is He Who, in the end, will receive standing (or kneeling) ovations from all of His children, and perhaps even from the Q.

I think of God's wonderful guiding principles each time I read "Lays of Ancient Rome," by Thomas Babbington McCaulay: "Then out spake brave Horatius, the Captain of the Gate: 'To every man upon this earth, death cometh soon or late. And how can man die better, than facing fearful odds, for the ashes of his fathers, and the temples of his gods?'" (Stanza 27).

Ironically, it was Q who exhorted Captain Pacard. "You just don't get it, do you, Jean Luc? The trial never ends. We wanted to see if you had the ability to expand your mind and your horizons, and for one brief moment, you did. For one fraction of a second, you were open to options you had never considered. That is the exploration that awaits you. Not mapping stars and studying nebulae, but charting the unknown possibilities of existence." ("All Good Things"). Q would have done well to have taken his own advice.

Just so, our Heavenly Father has given us an accurate description of the fruits of faith to be perfect in Christ. He will reveal "all mysteries. Yea, all the hidden mysteries of (His) kingdom from days of old, and for ages to come, will (He) make known unto (us by) the good pleasure of (His) will concerning all things pertaining to (His) kingdom." (D&C 76:7).

The Q would probably be bemused and chagrined to find that their omnipotence is evidence of the reality of God. When the Savior said: "I am come (into the world) that they might have life, and that they might have it more abundantly," He was speaking of the entire alphabet of The Plan of Salvation, including the letter Q. (John 10:10). He was speaking of Atonement, Baptism, Celestial glory, Deification, Exaltation, Faith unto Salvation, Grace, Holiness, Immortality, Justification, Knowledge, Law, Mercy, and so on, all the way past Q to Zion.

His Atonement and Resurrection were not in vain if we are anxiously engaged, hungering and thirsting after righteousness, boldly declaring the word, and with fear and trembling working out our salvation before the Lord. His Springtime Sacrifice will make a difference to us only if we are carried away by personal

visions of our individual potential, if we smite the destroyer with power, live life enthusiastically with divine fire, are filled with the Spirit, have faith to be perfect in Christ, and if we ultimately are caught up unto eternal life to continue our mission to explore strange new worlds, to seek out new life and new civilizations, and to boldly go where no-one has gone before.

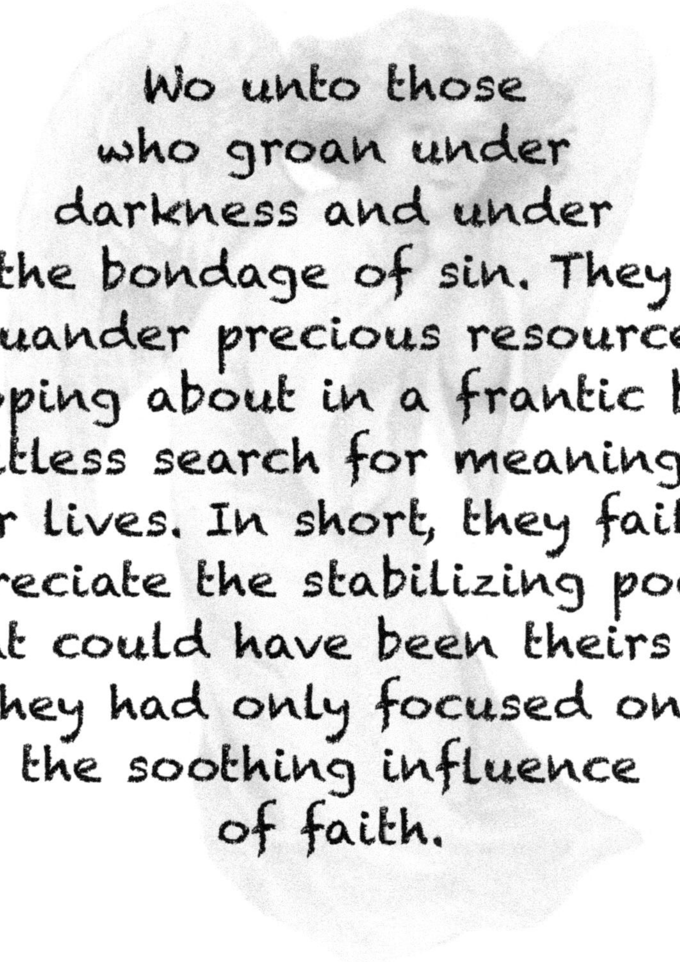

Wo unto those who groan under darkness and under the bondage of sin. They squander precious resources groping about in a frantic but fruitless search for meaning in their lives. In short, they fail to appreciate the stabilizing power that could have been theirs if they had only focused on the soothing influence of faith.

Chapter Thirty Seven
The faith to know the mind of God.

"Great and
marvelous are the works
of the Lord. How unsearchable
are the depths of the mysteries of him;
and it is impossible that man should
find out all his ways. And no man
knoweth of his ways save it
be revealed unto him."
(Jacob 4:8).

We have faith that with God there exists a second order of mind. The experiences of the temple, for example, repetitively reinforce the shadow of other-world experiences that are only spiritually discerned. Hugh Nibley introduced an interesting twist on perspective when he wrote: "Taking a calm and deliberate look at more than one thing at a time is a gift denied us at present. I cannot imagine what such a view of

the world would be like, but it would be more real and correct than the one we have now. Once we can see the possibilities that lie in being able to see more than one thing at a time, the universe takes on new dimensions, and God takes over.

Let us remember," he continued, "that quite peculiar to the genius of Mormonism is the doctrine of a God who could preoccupy Himself with countless numbers of things." ("Nibley on The Timely & Timeless," p. 263-264).

"The heavens they are many, and they cannot be numbered unto man; but they are numbered unto me, for they are mine." (Moses 1:37). Plainly, we are dealing with higher level thinking. "For my thoughts are not your thoughts, neither are your ways my ways, saith the Lord. For as the heavens are higher than the earth, so are ... my thoughts than your thoughts." (Isaiah 55:8-9).

With the faith to know the mind of God, we would have the ability to obtain and consider many different ideas at the same time, instead of thinking unilaterally by following only one course of reasoning at any given time. If God were to give us a sixth, a seventh, even a fiftieth sense, we would see the world in a new light that was arguably more real, inasmuch as each of these senses could potentially convey as much information as the sense of smell, or sight, or hearing do. If we accept the proposition that our five poor senses do not represent all the elements of nature, a much broader panorama emerges of new ways to "look" at the world.

Orson Pratt theorized that, in such a scenario, "knowledge would rush in from all quarters; it would come in like light which flows from the sun, penetrating every part, informing the spirit, and giving understanding concerning ten thousand things at the same time; and the mind would be capable of receiving and retaining all. Not one object at a time, but a vast multitude of objects would rush before us, as in the vision of a celestialized soul. These would be present before our minds, filling us in a moment with the knowledge of worlds more numerous than the sands of the seashore. Will we be able to bear it? Yes, our minds will be strengthened in proportion to the amount of information imparted. It is this

tabernacle, in its present condition, that prevents us from that more enlarged understanding." (J.D., 2:238-248).

In short, the faith to know the mind of God would impart to us greatly expanded powers of observation. We would be able to look in every direction at once, in order to see His creations as they truly are. After all, it was under such inspiration that Moses looked, and "beheld the world and the ends thereof, and all the children of men which are, and which were created." (Moses 1:8).

We would receive knowledge forever denied to us as long as we remain imprisoned within the narrow confines of our mortal bodies. For it was after Moses had experienced his theophany, that he was "left unto himself," and "fell to the earth," where he remained for many hours (before he) did again receive his natural strength like unto man." (Moses 1:9-10).

Elder Pratt reasoned: "There must be some faculty or power natural to God and to superior beings, that we, in this life, are not in possession of in any great part, by which they can look at a great variety of objects at once." It was only under the influence of the Spirit, for example, that "the Brother of Jared could look upon past, present, and future generations. They all came before him, and there was not a soul that he did not behold." (Mormon 8:35). The key that unlocks the door leading to this new faculty of knowledge, extended in its nature and intended to throw a vast amount of information upon our minds in the twinkling of an eye, is faith with the power to know the mind of God.

Elder Pratt further explained that celestial beings have the ability to perceive with all parts of their bodies. "The spirit, like the eye, is inherently capable of experiencing the sensations of light. I think we could then see in different directions at once, instead of looking in one particular direction; we could then look all around us at the same instant." This sheds understanding on the insight offered by the Prophet Joseph Smith on the phenomenon of receiving revelation. "My whole body was full of light," he said, "and I could see even out at the ends of my fingers and toes." (N.B.

Lundwall, "The Vision," p. 11).

Perhaps this is why the angel Moroni hovered in the air when he was visiting young Joseph, and why "his hands were naked, and his arms also, a little above the wrist."

(J.S.H. 1:31). He wanted to see more clearly, for he too could see even out of his fingers and toes. (See J.S.H. 1:31). As the Lord explained: "If your eye be single to my glory, your whole bodies shall be filled with light, and there shall be no darkness in you; and that body which is filled with light comprehendeth all things." (D&C 88:67). Not just the eye, but every fiber of the body shall be filled with light.

Brigham Young once said: "I long for the time that a point of my finger or motion of my hand will express every idea without utterance. When we are full of the light of eternity, then the eye will not be the only medium through which we see, nor the brain the only means by which we understand. When our bodies are full of the Holy Ghost, we can see behind ourselves with as much ease, without turning our heads, as we can see before us. If you have not had that experience, you ought to have. It is not the optic nerve alone that gives the knowledge of surrounding objects to the mind." (J.D., 1:70-71).

Parley P. Pratt believed that, with faith to know the mind of God, we will even be able to move from one place to another without the passage of time, by simply willing ourselves to be there. "There is no apparent limit," he reasoned, "to the speed attainable by the body, when unchained, set free from the elements which now enslave it, and dictated by the will." ("Key to The Science of Theology," p. 162).

Brigham Young concurrently believed: "The brightness and glory of the next apartment is inexpressible." Beings in that realm shall "move with ease and like lightning. If we want to visit Jerusalem, or this, or that, or the other place, there we are. If we want to behold Jerusalem as it was in the days of the Savior, or if we want to see the Garden of Eden as it was when created, there we are. We may behold the earth as at the dawn of creation." (J.D., 14:231).

Note that Brigham Young described movement through both space and time, or through the spacetime continuum, a concept only articulated much later by physicists utilizing the elements of a discipline of theoretical science that did not exist in his day. Spacetime was first proposed by the mathematician Hermann Minkowski reformulate Albert Einstein's special theory of relativity, that had itself been introduced in 1905.

When we return to heaven to dwell with our Heavenly Father, what will our state of existence be? Since "the glory of God is intelligence, or in other words, light and truth," it must be that the righteous who have faith to know the mind of God will dwell amidst the fire and smoke that are symbolic of His presence. (D&C 93:36). The wicked, on the other hand, will be consumed as stubble by the brightness of His glory. (See Malachi 4:1). What will our resurrected bodies be like, and what will our capabilities be? What powers will we command? We can only guess, but the Lord intrigues us with the promise that His Spirit will enlighten us to behold His glory. He revealed: "By my power will I make known ... the secrets of my will; yea, even those things which eye has not seen, nor ear heard, nor yet entered into the heart of man." (D&C 76:10). Our "wisdom shall be great, and (our) understanding reach to heaven; and before (us) the wisdom of the wise shall perish, and the understanding of the prudent shall come to naught." (D&C 76:9).

From among many spiritual manifestations, Joseph Smith had one in particular that caused him to recall: "The veil was taken from our minds, and the eyes of our understanding were opened." In other words, he enjoyed an extra-sensory experience so profound that it almost defied description. "We saw the Lord," He said, "standing upon the breastwork of the pulpit, before us; and under his feet was a paved work of pure gold, in color like amber. His eyes were as a flame of fire; the hair of his head was white like the pure snow; his countenance shone above the brightness of the sun; and his voice was as the sound of the rushing of great waters." (D&C 110:1-3).

The Apostle Paul, who had his fair share of similar experiences, wrote that we now

"see through a glass darkly," but then we shall behold Him who is eternal "face to face." (1 Corinthians 13:12). We can only imagine what it will be like to look upon the wide expanse of eternity, as a boundless perspective of God's creations floods our minds with comprehension. Perhaps only then will we enjoy the fruits of our faith to know the mind of God, and will the solemnities that are a part of His "every day" experience rest upon us and govern our spirits. Perhaps only when we enjoy that expanded capacity will the Lord reveals His wonders. Then, when we see things as they really are, we will have a fulness of joy.

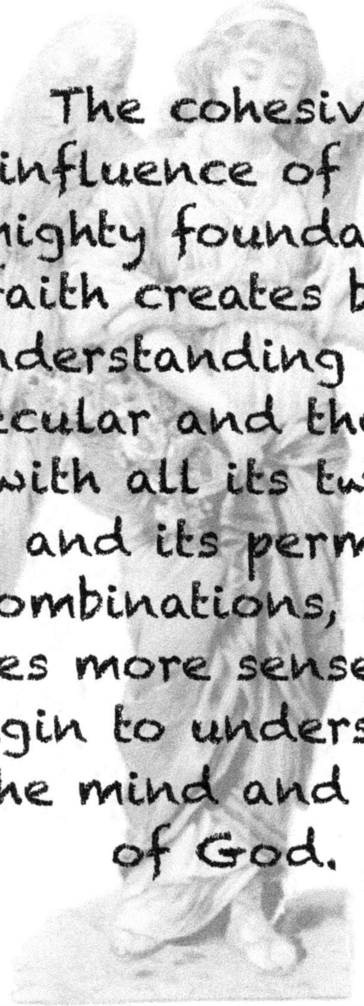

The cohesive
influence of the
mighty foundation
of faith creates bridges
of understanding between
the secular and the divine.
Life, with all its twists and
turns, and its permutations
and combinations, suddenly
makes more sense, as we
begin to understand
the mind and will
of God.

We
watch ourselves
judiciously, and are
the meticulous guardians
of our thoughts, the scrupulous
custodians of our words, and the
prudent caretakers of our actions.
We fastidiously observe the laws of
God, that we might benefit from the
stability of a pathway that basks in
the steady illumination that is
generously provided by the
discipline of faith.

Chapter Thirty Eight
The faith to keep our feet on the ground.

*The Light of Christ can bless us with the faith
to keep our feet on the ground, even
as we fix our eyes on the stars.*

What, we might ask, has faith got to do with the thrill of victory and the agony of de feet? Long ago, the Vikings invaded Scotland. As the Danes crept up unawares on the sleeping Scottish forces, they inadvertently walked across a patch of sharp thistles that poked deep into the soles of their feet. Alerted to their presence by cries of pain, the Scots rallied to drive off the enemy. To this day, the thistle has been the emblem of Scotland.

The foot soldier has been the bulwark of nearly every army since the dawn of history, but feet can also be a source of weakness. Not everyone is like the Kentucky hillbilly who never wore shoes. One winter evening, he came into his cabin and stood by the fireplace. His wife said: "I reckon you'd better move. You're standin' on a live coal." He coolly replied, "Which foot?" Most of us don't have feet that are so

heavily calloused and insensitive. The weakness of the great warrior Achilles, after all, was his heel. A dog may be man's best friend, but we call our own feet "puppies," our comfortable shoes "hush-puppies," and we say "our dogs are tired." Sometimes, a swift kick (with the foot) in the rear is all it takes to get us moving. If we are holding on for dear life, we describe it as a "toe-hold." When we determine to accomplish more, we "lengthen our stride." Things that are really easy are "a cake-walk." We "take a step back" to appraise a situation objectively. When we relinquish our position of authority, however, we "step down," and if we move over to let another pass us, we "step aside."

If we haven't got a care in the world, we are "foot-loose and fancy-free." If someone's philosophical position is unsupportable, we say they "haven't got a leg to stand on." If the shoe fits, we wear it. If we are fully committed to a new course of action, we "jump in with both feet." When we "kick the bucket," sometimes with our boots on. we are carried out "feet first." Then we are buried "six feet deep." If we are awkward, we have "two left feet." If we are true to our principles, "we toe the line." Because feet are sometimes seen as a liability, we see signs that read: "No bare feet allowed," or "No shirt, no shoes, no service." We are familiar with both "walks" and "runs" in baseball, a game where we also "step up to the plate." A "false step" might bring us to defeat, but putting "our best foot forward" could carry us to victory.

We move recklessly forward by taking a "mis-step." But if we move quickly and purposefully, "we step lively." If we are true to our principles, we "have our feet firmly planted firmly on the ground." Distances are measured in "feet." Light is measured in "foot-candles," and power is measured in "foot-pounds." If we are nimble, we are "sure-footed." If we are passive, we take "timid, halting, or hesitant steps." But if we are confident, we have "a bounce in our step." When we dance around a dominant personality, we are "walking on eggshells." If someone faints, we elevate the feet to improve circulation. When we are down and out, we can't wait "to get back on our feet." If we have our heads in the clouds, we are light on our feet. If we are tired, we "put our feet up." But if we are determined, we "put our foot down."

We are figuratively tied up when we are "bound hand and foot," but we also wait on someone "hand and foot" when we serve them to excess. We are obstinate when we "dig in our heels." We delay when we "drag our feet." When we are fast, we are "fleet of foot," but if we are slow, we have "feet of clay." When we accept financial responsibility, we "foot the bill." To "get our feet wet" is to have a modest or mild introductory experience; to "put our toe in the water" is to do so even more hesitantly. When we make a good first impression, we "start off on the right foot," but when we "start off on the wrong foot," we leave a poor first impression. If we don't want to offends someone, we often "tread lightly." We have an advantage when we "have our foot in the door." But if we stumble over our words or say something inappropriate, we've "put our foot in our mouth." If we have "our feet in both camps" we are opportunistically sympathetic to two opposing viewpoints. We are restless when we have "itchy feet." (And we are not very popular when we have "smelly feet.") We are in poor health or near death, if we have "one foot in the grave." We are realistic and responsible if we have the faith to "keep our feet on the ground."

We "land on our feet," when we have recovered from a setback. When we deprive others of anticipated support, we have "pulled the rug from under their feet." We "put our best foot forward" in order to make a good impression. We "put one foot in front of the other" as we begin a laborious undertaking. We "set foot in new territory" when we venture into places we have never been before. We "shoot ourselves in the foot" when we do or say something disadvantageous to our own interests. We "stand on our own two feet" when we act with independence. The "shoe is on the other foot" when a situation has been reversed. We "think on our feet" when we spontaneously solve a problem.

When Neil Armstrong "set foot" on the moon, he said: "That's one small step for a man, one giant leap for mankind." Ralph Waldo Emerson said: "Build a better mousetrap, and the world will beat a path to your door," presumably on foot. During Israel's exodus from Egypt, the children of the Covenant walked through the Red Sea on dry ground. The pursuing Egyptians might have fared better had they also

done so. Richard III cried: "A horse, a horse. My kingdom for a horse," presumably because he didn't think himself adequate to the task when afoot.

We talk about "the steps" of repentance. When we exercise unrighteous dominion, we "overstep our bounds." If we carelessly "put our feet down" without forethought, they are sometimes caught in a snare. Depending upon our perspective, obstacles in our path can be seen as "stepping-stones or stumbling-blocks."

The stage-lights that illuminate a set are called "foot-lights." The journey of a thousand miles begins with "one step." If a tennis player crosses the service line while striking the ball at the beginning of a point, he commits "a foot-fault." A gentleman's servant is called "a footman."

In the advanced stages of diabetes, peripheral circulation is so poor that all feeling may be lost in the feet. When this happens, there is a tremendous risk of infection from even minor irritations that go unnoticed. Stepping on a nail, for example, can have ruinous consequences if we are "past feeling." There are spiritual equivalents that are equally devastating that can be traced back to the feet. The feet can take us on detours so that before we realize it, we have put our feet up on a lounge chair at our summer home in Babylon, sipping on a mixed drink. In the humid climate of wartime Viet Nam, keeping their feet clean and dry was of paramount importance to the U.S. Forces stationed there. Clean socks were as necessary as clean weapons. (Remember Forrest Gump and Lieutenant Dan?) An entire army could have been brought to its knees, if basic hygiene relating to the feet had been neglected. Maybe it wasn't the Viet Cong, but smelly socks, that defeated the Americans.

In the Revolutionary War, the Colonial troops often went barefoot for lack of boots, or wrapped their naked feet in bloody rags. It was said that bloodstains in the snow marked the route the army had taken. The protection of the feet was of great concern to George Washington and his staff officers, for the fortunes of war hinged upon the health of the feet of their soldiers. Truly, our feet can carry us on to victory.

Feet are one of the miracles of creation. Leonardo da Vinci called them "a masterpiece of engineering and a work of art." Each foot consists of 26 of the 206 bones in our bodies, 33 joints (20 of which are actively articulated), and more than a hundred muscles, tendons, and ligaments. By age 55, the average person has walked the equivalent of two and a half times around the world. In all our perambulating, the lives of great men and women "all remind us we can make our lives sublime, and departing, leave behind us footprints in the sands of time." (Longfellow).

"Aha!" said the cartoon philosopher Pogo. "Here we have someone paying for the sin of excess. The hobnailed boots of indiscretion's marathon dancer tap a rowdy two-step across the terracotta of his consciousness. Excess was his master. Reason was cast into the rumble seat of his libidinous juggernaut. Now the piper must be paid!" Any way you look at it, for good or for worse, feet play a major role in our lives.

John said: "One mightier than I cometh, the latchet of whose shoes I am not worthy to unloose." (Luke 3:16). Of course, he was speaking of the Lord Jesus Christ, whose feet are mentioned over two dozen times in the New Testament. Feet, in general, are referenced over 150 times in the Old Testament and 75 times in the New Testament. Perhaps they were simply more conspicuous in a world without modern transportation, and where open toed sandals were the most popular form of footwear. It was natural to bring the blind and the infirm to the feet of Jesus, that He might heal them. It makes perfect sense that He caused the lame to walk as a consequence of their faith. To be able to do so gave them a new lease on life.

David envisioned the mission of the Savior, when he exclaimed: "Thou madest him to have dominion over the works of thy hands; thou hast put all things under his feet." (Psalms 8:6). Solomon mused: "Ponder the path of thy feet, and let all thy ways be established." (Proverbs 4:26). To Saul of Tarsus, the Savior commanded: "Rise, and stand upon thy feet." (Acts 26:16). From imprisonment in Rome, the converted Paul exhorted the Saints: "How beautiful are the feet of them that preach the Gospel of peace, and bring glad tidings of good things!" (Romans 10:15).

If they keep their feet on the ground and their eyes fixed on the stars, the feet of the faithful can be used as weapons against evil. "The God of peace shall bruise Satan under your feet," wrote Paul. (Romans 16:20). He encouraged the Ephesians: "Put on the whole armour of God, that ye may be able to stand against the wiles of the devil.... And your feet shod with the preparation of the gospel of peace." (Ephesians 6:11 & 15). As weapons of spiritual warfare, our feet strategically conquer territory that has been under Satan's power, and they liberate the captives he had subjugated. God Himself, Paul tells us, "hath put all things under his feet." (Ephesians 1:22). As His disciples, we figuratively sit at the feet of the Savior, that we might strategically position ourselves to better promote the cause of Zion.

The devil, in the meantime, is as Ozymandias, of whom Shelley wrote: "I met a traveler from an antique land who said: Two vast and trunkless legs of stone stand in the desert. Near them, on the sand half sunk, a shattered visage lies, whose frown and wrinkled lip and sneer of cold command tell that its sculptor well those passions read, which yet survive. Stamped on these lifeless things, the hand that mocks them and the heart that fed; and on the pedestal these words appear: 'My name is Ozymandias, King of Kings; Look on my works, ye mighty, and despair!' Nothing beside remains. Round the decay of that colossal wreck, boundless and bare, the lone and level sand stretched far away." ("Ozymandias").

Of contemporary royalty, it was similarly written: "And it came to pass, when they brought out those kings unto Joshua, that Joshua called for all the men of Israel, and said unto the captains of the men of war which went with him, Come near, put your feet upon the necks of these kings." (Joshua 10:24). This symbolic demonstration of domination was not lost on either the conquerors or the vanquished.

If we want to have the greatest success in life, we must have the faith to keep our feet on the ground, and our eyes fixed on the stars. We must use celestial navigation to find our way to the feet of Jesus simply because His footprints have changed the course of history. He never strayed more than a hundred miles or so

from His birthplace, but everywhere He went on foot has become a place of great interest, and we undertake pilgrimages at considerable effort and expense just to be there to share a common experience, even in a small way; to walk where Jesus walked.

The feet are very sensitive. Helen Keller once gave a speech, and at its conclusion, the crowd gave her a thunderous round of applause. When asked how she knew what the reaction of the audience had been, she said she felt their appreciation through the vibrations in her feet. This sheds understanding on the statement of the Prophet Joseph Smith who said after receiving revelation: "My whole body was full of light, and I could see even out at the ends of my fingers and toes."

Perhaps this is why the angel Moroni hovered in the air with outstretched arms, and with feet that were naked, when he visited Joseph Smith in his bedchamber. He wanted to see better, and to feel with more sensitivity, for he could do so even out of his fingers and toes. "And if your eye be single to my glory, your whole bodies shall be filled with light, and there shall be no darkness in you; and that body (not mind, but body) which is filled with light comprehendeth all things." (D&C 88:67).

The feet can communicate pleasure, but they can also feel pain. Certainly, Jesus felt both. He was thankful for the concern Mary showed to Him when she washed his feet after a long and dusty journey, but He also felt indescribable pain when the nails of His crucifiers were driven through his feet. Those who washed His feet showed by their actions that love is not what we say, but is measured by what we do. Service can sometimes be very costly, and the feet frequently bear the burden. How often do we say after a particularly hard day: "My feet are killing me," or "Oh, my aching feet." Our feet, however, have the capacity to carry us wherever we can render the best service.

The Savior's feet traced His way to the far corners of Galilee and Judea to perform acts of service. To minister to the needs of others, His feet required regular attention, and so His disciples washed them and cared for them as sacred instruments. He was unlike "the young lady of Crete, who was so exceedingly neat.

When she got out of bed, she stood on her head, to make sure not to soil her feet." (Bennet Cerf).

Shakespeare referred to the feet of the Savior, when he wrote of "those holy fields over whose acres walked those blessed feet which, fourteen hundred years ago, were nailed for our advantage on the bitter cross." ("Henry IV").

Doubting Thomas said: "Except I shall see in his hands the print of the nails, and put my finger into the print of the nails, and thrust my hand into his side, I will not believe." (John 20:25). But to skeptics in all ages, the Savior responded: "Behold my hands and my feet, that it is I myself.... And when he had thus spoken, he shewed them his hands and his feet." (Luke 20:39-40). It is sobering to remember that because of His wounds, we have been liberated to use our own feet to walk in a newness of life, and that one day they may be utilized to explore every nook and cranny of the Celestial Kingdom. When we embark upon that adventure, we will keep our eyes fixed on the stars, and our feet on the holy ground of heaven.

When the Savior said: "Go ye into all the world and preach the Gospel" He envisioned that the command would be carried out with the feet. (Mark 16:15). Isaiah recognized this when he wrote: "How beautiful upon the mountains are the feet of him that bringeth good tidings, that publisheth peace; that bringeth good tidings of good, that publisheth salvation." (Isaiah 57:2).

Except for the one time Jesus entered Jerusalem on the back of a donkey (in fulfillment of prophecy), He went everywhere on foot. There are over 100 references in the Gospels to His "walking." We cannot fully appreciate His ministry without a conscious consideration of His feet. His invitations to "Come and see" (John 1:39), to "Come, follow me" (Luke 18:22), and to "Go ye into all the world" (Mark 16:15), required that we do so with our feet, even though there will never be a beauty contest that focuses on the feet.

In the scriptures, many parts of the human anatomy have been related to behavior.

We read of strong backs, piercing eyes and sensitive ears, and of vigorous hearts, energetic hands, and, in particular, dynamic feet. When President Spencer W. Kimball said "I am like an old shoe, to be worn out in the service of the Lord," he was utilizing vivid imagery about themes with which we can all relate, to keep our feet on the ground, and our eyes fixed on the stars, as we trace our way to heaven.

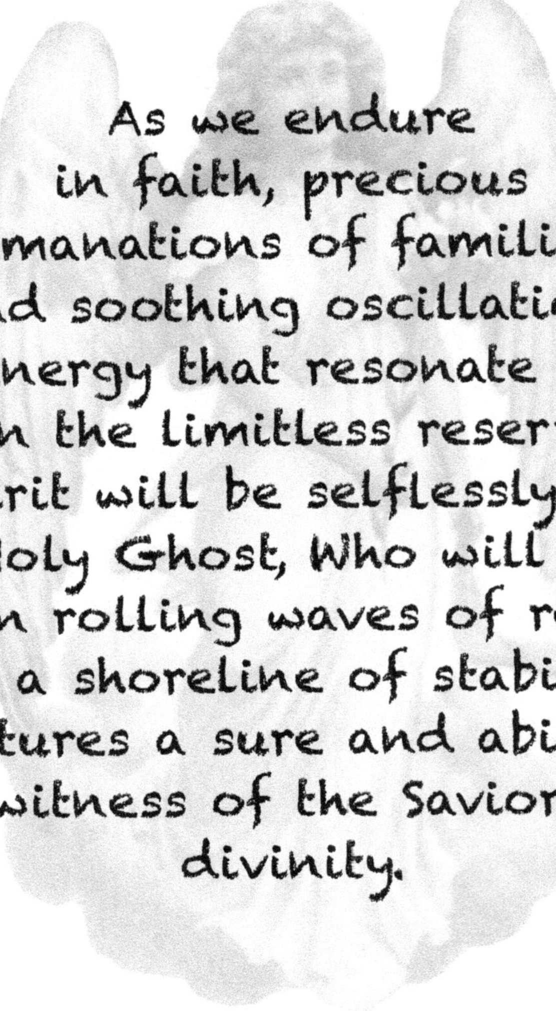

As we endure
in faith, precious
emanations of familiar
and soothing oscillations
of energy that resonate from
within the limitless reserves of
the Spirit will be selflessly shared
by the Holy Ghost, Who will carry us
along on rolling waves of revelation
toward a shoreline of stability that
nurtures a sure and abiding
witness of the Savior's
divinity.

Chapter Thirty Nine
The faith to stay spiritually fit.

The Lord showed Abraham "the intelligences that were organized before the world was; and among all these there were many of the noble and great ones" who had excellent moral character, high ideals, proven potential, and performance capabilities. (Abraham 3:22). Surely, these were the stand-out superstars who had excelled in the Lord's Pre-mortal Spiritual Calisthenics Fitness Program.

These were the crème de la crème, the best and the brightest, and the pick of the litter. In their pre-earth life, they rolled out of bed very early every morning to do stretching exercises leading to emotional stability, intellectual flexibility, interpersonal pliability, and spiritual capability. Even before breakfast, they may have climbed the stadium steps of discipline by running several laps around the scriptures. These refreshingly repetitive rehearsals would have given them a foretaste of life's educational experiences.

Each wind-sprint through the Bible, the Book of Mormon, the Doctrine & Covenants, and the Pearl of Great Price would have brought greater spiritually aerobic fitness regarding principles, increased capacity to carry the weight of doctrine, and easy fluency with the language of heaven, all paving the way for religious recognition later on, sufficient to penetrate the veil that would be drawn across their mortal minds.

After thus awakening and arousing their faculties, perhaps they showered, not to remove the soul sweat of sin, for they were holy and without guile, but to invigorate themselves with the spiritual element. After dressing themselves in the full armor of God, they would have been served a satisfying meal of obedience, fortified with the nutritional supplements of order and discipline. This would have prepared them to renew their strength, mount up as upon the wings of eagles, and run and not be weary, and walk, and not faint. (See Isaiah 40:31). Their thirst would have been quenched, not by supposed energy drinks laced with sweeteners and artificial stimulants, but by pure water springing up from a living fountain. Their hunger would have been satisfied by the organic performance potential found in the unadulterated bread of life.

Such a bountiful boot camp experience would have been stimulated by balanced nutrition designed to ward off the rigidity, inflexibility, and fanaticism of spiritual sclerosis. It would have promoted the concept of virtuous aerobic conditioning to a group already determined to "press forward with a steadfastness in Christ, having a perfect brightness of hope and a love of God and of all men." (2 Nephi 31:20). It would have renewed their determination to endure to the end in righteousness. It would have prepared them for a world full of opposition and it would have protected them from the atrophy of their spiritual muscles and the emaciation of their spirits.

Forewarned and forearmed, they would have worked extra hard to avoid foods that are akin to those laden with sucrose, somnolence, lethargy, and apathy. They would have pressed on to avoid the fat of mediocrity, lose the flab of indolence,

renounce the excess carbohydrates of laziness, and shed the extra inches of inattention, by obeying the principles of good spiritual and emotional nutrition. They would have realized that by observing a steady diet of discipleship, they would be ready to embark upon their mortal sojourn, at the conclusion of which "all things (would) be restored to their proper order, every thing to its natural frame, mortality raised to immortality, (and) corruption to incorruption." (Alma 41-4). They would have envisioned experiences that would help them to regain the innocence and muscle-tone of their spiritual youth. They would have known that, though "the stars might fade away, the sun himself grow dim with age, and nature sink in years, they would flourish in immortal youth, unhurt amidst the war of elements, the wreck of matter, and the crash of worlds." (Joseph Addison, "Cato" Act 5, Scene 1).

They would have recognized that it is only organically grown spiritual food that is wholesome, delicious, and high in moral fiber content. They would have been able to easily distinguish ennobling nutrition from the calorie count of carnality, sensuality, and devilishness, and from the malnourishment that is caused by the mold of misinformation. (See Ephesians 4:14). They would have learned to identify the noxious weeds of worldliness that would lie in their path during their journey through mortality, and they would have been taught to recognize the poisonous pandering that distinguishes Satan's uncommitted, unbelieving, and unconverted snake-oil salesmen, many of whom they would encounter along the way. They would have resolved to avoid the rationalizations of their fellow travelers; those complaining and slothful souls who would fail to persevere in the regular exercise of their faith and diligence. (See Alma 37:41).

They would have learned the art of self-defense, in preparation for the inevitable darts of the adversary that would blaze fiery trails across a darkening sky and rain down upon them. They would already have been engaged in the building of fortresses of security to guard against the day when his assaults would surely come.

They would have learned to identify the spiritual equivalents of high fructose corn

syrup, trans-fats, bleached flour, and white rice. Their fare would eschew food with a high glycemic index, such as inattention, indecision, and idleness.

In anticipation of receiving a body of flesh and blood, they would have developed the discipline to avoid performance-enhancing or mind-altering drugs. They would have learned that it is perfectly okay to get naturally high on endorphins. But with the memory of the ideological War in Heaven still fresh in their minds, they would have resolved to keep their minds clear and focused as they pointedly promoted the promises of The Plan and the cause of Zion. They would have embraced PTSD, or the Promise to Serve Diligently, in no matter what circumstances they might later find themselves.

They would have recognized the value of nourishment from the good word of Christ, while avoiding the hypoglycemia of hypocrisy, and the fleeting rush provided by the empty calories of convenience. They would have determined to follow the strait and narrow path, instead of boarding the Excess Express in a fruitless search for a shortcut to perfection. In their mind's eye they could already see those whose lacked the sustaining faith to stay spiritually fit, whose "bodies were one sorry sight! No more than skeletons, covered with skin. They would get up to heaven, but never get in. 'Another soul's mine!' they could hear Satan scream. 'Give man something nice, and he'll take the extreme!' OK, I'll admit it; I'll outright confess. For the fast way to hell, take the Excess Express." (Anonymous).

In our pre-mortal lives, we were surely counseled by our fitness trainers that strenuous spiritual exercise would give us vigorous vitality and leave us stronger and more capable in the cause of Zion. Therefore, we learned to use our recovery time wisely. We developed the capacity to carefully monitor our vital signs; to deal with the spiritual equivalents of oxygen debt and lactic acid buildup, and to pace ourselves in our spiritual development. We experienced brief bursts of energy resulting in spectacular achievement, but more significantly, we found that it was sustained effort over an extended period of time that carried us further along the road leading to eternal life. In our pre-mortal setting, we must have developed

the habit of faithful endurance, to prepare us for chastisement, to go the second mile, and to turn the other cheek.

We took our Head Coach at His word when He assured us that resistance training would one day pay big dividends. When He urged us to do 10 push-ups through The Doctrine & Covenants, we voluntarily tacked on o increase our isometric core strength by exercising the power of God within us, we did so many planks that additional trees had to be cut down just to accommodate our needs. (See Alma 14:10). Instead of bench-pressing only the Aaronic Priesthood, we added on the additional weight of The Oath and Covenant of The Melchizedek Priesthood, because we knew that down the road we would need additional muscle fiber.

When we were asked to elevate our heart rate up to a steady 100 verses of scripture each day, to facilitate our comprehension of Gospel principles, we instead pushed our limits to embrace whole chapters and even books. The elliptical trainer of consecration, the stationary bike of service, and the treadmill of sacrifice put us through an expanded range of motion in order to develop muscle and joint elasticity, and to strengthen our hearts. Our reward was an increased capacity to infuse our bodies with the heavenly element, that we might be full of light. We knew that one day we would need hearts that would be enlarged with empathy, and bowels that would be filled with compassion, as we witnessed the struggles of our fellow travelers and engaged in telestial triage and spiritual first aid.

When we had free time, although we didn't watch television reality shows, we nevertheless understood the concept of "The Biggest Loser." We learned that shedding pounds would be less important than giving up our sins to know the Savior, and we knew that it would be necessary to expend soul-sweat to keep us from regaining burdensome weight. We also learned the principles of search and rescue, and of recovery, to be used in our ministry, in behalf of those who might falter in faith during the execution of their own spiritual fitness programs.

Even in pre-mortality, the counsel must have rung true, that we should "cease to

be idle; cease to be unclean; cease to find fault one with another; cease to sleep longer than is needful; retire to thy bed early, that ye may not be weary; arise early, that your bodies and your minds may be invigorated." (D&C 88:124). We received a witness that there is a direct correlation between physical energy and spiritual

385

vitality. Our quickening prepared us for our experiences in the womb, when our first stirrings of life would send a tangible message of hope into the mortal world.

When we were asked to awaken and arouse our faculties, we took that to mean we should embrace the word, so that by faith it might swell in our hearts. We tried to wrap out minds around the unfamiliar concept that our spirit would one day be joined to a physical body, and that after the death and decay of our mortal frame, the soul would "be restored to the body, and the body to the soul; yea, and every limb and joint ... to its body." (Alma 40:23).

When we were tempted to ease up on our training schedule, surely the counsel rang loudly in our ears: "Be not slothful, but followers of them who through faith and patience inherit the promises." (Hebrews 6:12). On another occasion, we were encouraged: "Bodily exercise profiteth little: but godliness is profitable unto all things." (1 Timothy 4:8). In other words, it would matter little if our mortal frame turned out to be large or small, fat or thin, or if we could run faster, jump higher, or hit a golf ball further than another. What would ultimately determine our intrinsic self-worth would be our capacity to incorporate into our being the divine nature, the ability to say, at the end of the contest: "I have fought a good fight, I have finished my course, (and) I have kept the faith" to keep myself spiritually fit. (2 Timothy 4:7).

Then, our mortal frames would be renewed in unimaginable ways. By magnifying our callings, we would be sanctified by the Spirit unto the renewing of our bodies." (D&C 84:33). We would find that therein lies the fitness secret of the ages. We would have discovered the magic bullet; the veritable fountain of youth. It was his mastery of the principles of sacrifice and consecration that permitted Adam to stand "in the midst of the congregation ... notwithstanding he was bowed down with

age, being full of the Holy Ghost." (D&C 107:56).

We knew that, while clothed in mortality, if we persisted in the faith to stay spiritually fit, we would be wrought upon and cleansed by the power of the Holy

Ghost. We would be numbered among the people of the Church of Christ, and our names would be taken, that we might be remembered and nourished by the good word of God, to keep us in the right way, and to keep ourselves continually watchful unto prayer, relying alone upon the merits of Christ, who even while we were in Spiritual Boot Camp was already the author and finisher of our faith. (See Moroni 6:4).

In the deep recesses of memory, as we think about what it must have been like for us, we can hear the Voice gently urging: "O.K. Buttercup. One more lap around the scriptures!" Today, because of our faith to stay spiritually fit in that distant past, we are doubly blessed, for "when obedience ceases to be inconvenient and becomes our quest, in that moment God will endow us with power." (Ezra Taft Benson).

We try to remember that long ago we learned that perspiration always precedes inspiration and that the dictionary is the only place where success comes before work. When our faith to stay spiritually fit seems particularly fragile, we try to remember that it is darkest just before the dawn, and that each new day on earth promises rebirth, refreshment, recommitment, renewal, and redemption.

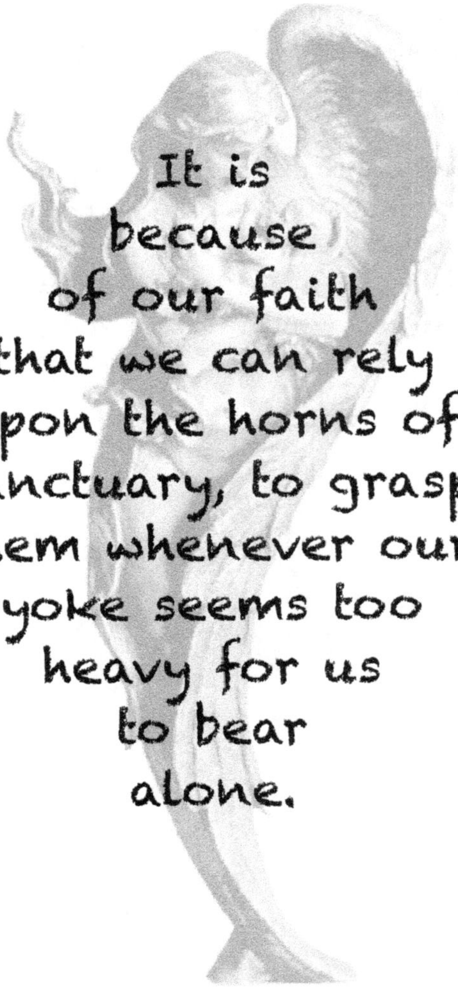

It is
because
of our faith
that we can rely
upon the horns of
sanctuary, to grasp
them whenever our
yoke seems too
heavy for us
to bear
alone.

About The Author

Phil Hudson and his wife Jan have 7 children and over 25 grandchildren. They enjoy spending time with their family at their cabin nestled in the Selkirk Mountains, on the shore of Priest Lake, the crown jewel of North Idaho. Phil had a successful dental practice in Spokane, Washington for 43 years, before retiring in 2015. He has an eclectic mix of hobbies, and enjoys the out of doors. He always finds time, however, to record his thoughts on his laptop, and understands Isaac Asimov's response when he was asked: If you knew that you had only 10 minutes left to live, what would you do?" He answered: "I'd type faster."

Phil received the inspiration to write this book while he and Jan were serving as missionaries for The Church of Jesus Christ of Latter-day Saints, in the Kingdom of Tonga. While there, they celebrated their 50th wedding anniversary.

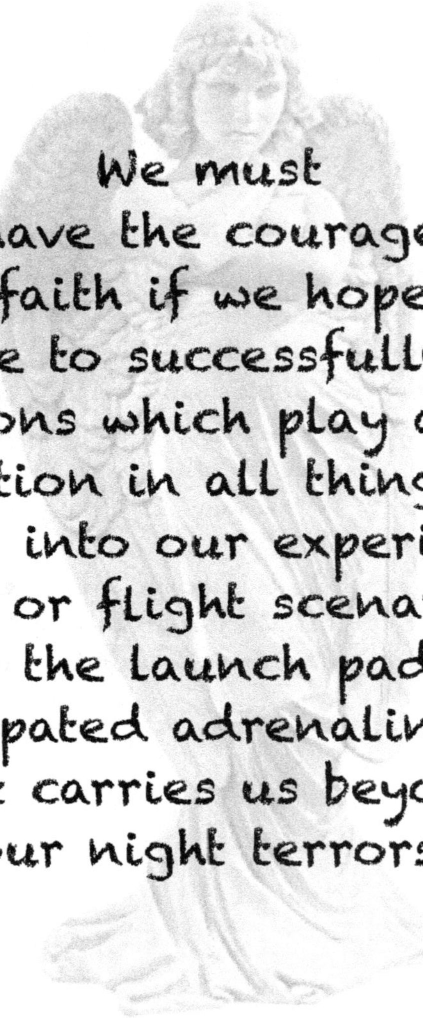

We must
have the courage
of faith if we hope to
be able to successfully face
the demons which play a role in
the opposition in all things that has
been built into our experiences. In
the fight or flight scenario, faith
becomes the launch pad for the
anticipated adrenalin rush
that carries us beyond
our night terrors.

By The Author

Essays

    Volume One: Spray From The Ocean Of Thought
    Volume Two: Ripples On A Pond
    Volume Three: Serendipitous Meanderings
    Volume Four: Presents Of Mind
    Volume Five: Mental Floss
    Volume Six: Fitness Training For The Mind And Spirit

First Principles and Ordinances Series

    Faith - Our Hearts Are Changed
    Repentance - A Broken Heart and a Contrite Spirit
    Baptism - One Hundred And One Reasons Why We Are Baptized
    The Holy Ghost - That We Might Have His Spirit To Be With Us
    The Sacrament - This Do In Remembrance Of Me

Book of Mormon Commentary

    Volume One: Born In The Wilderness
    Volume Two: Voices From The Dust
    Volume Three: Journey To Cumorah

Doctrine & Covenants Commentary

    Volume One - Sections 1 - 34
    Volume Two - Sections 35 - 57

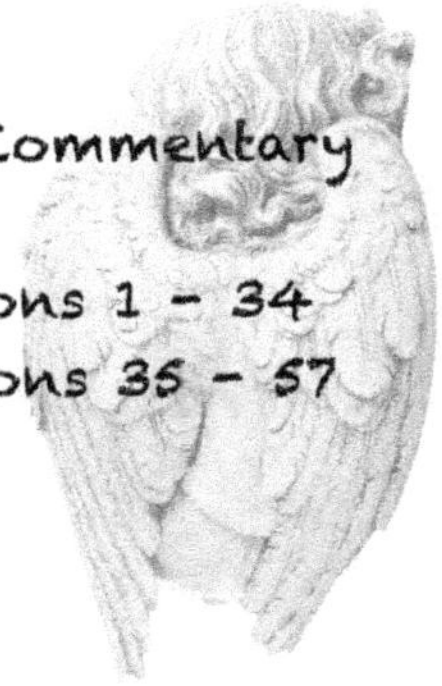

Minute Musings: Spontaneous Combustions of Thought

    Volume One
    Volume Two
    Volume Three

Calendars:

    In His Own Words: Discovering William Tyndale
    As I Think About The Savior
    Scriptural Symbols

Children's Books

    Muddy, Muddy
    The Thirteen Articles of Faith
    Happy Birthday

Doctrinal Themes

    The House of the Lord

A Thought For Each Day of the Year

    Faith
    Repentance
    Baptish
    The Holy Ghost
    The Sacrament

Professional Publications

    Diode Laser Soft Tissue Surgery Volume One
    Diode Laser Soft Tissue Surgery Volume Two
    Diode Laser Soft Tissue Surgery Volume Three

These, and other titles, are available from online retailers.

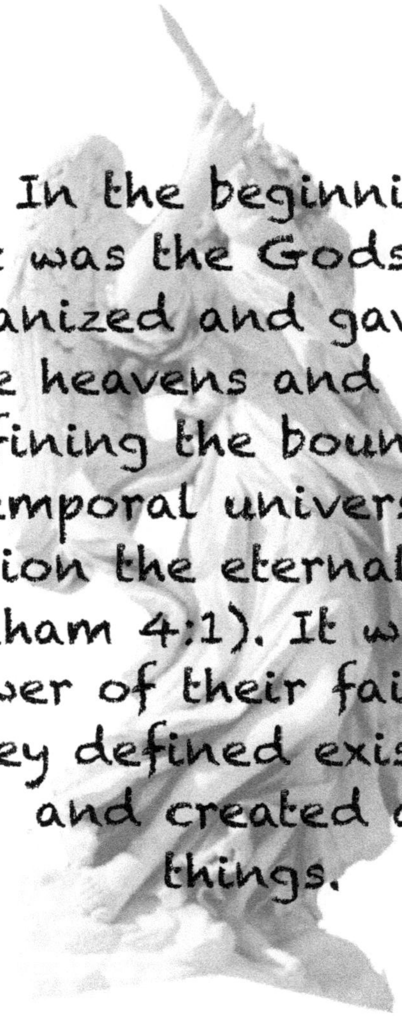

In the beginning,
it was the Gods who
organized and gave form
to the heavens and the earth
by defining the boundaries of
the temporal universe, not to
mention the eternal worlds.
(Abraham 4:1). It was by the
power of their faith that
they defined existence
and created all
things.

Quid magis possum dicere?